THE
100

THE 100

A RANKING OF THE MOST INFLUENTIAL PERSONS IN HISTORY

Michael H. Hart

A Citadel Press Book

Published by Carol Publishing Group

Carol Publishing Group Edition, 1996

A Citadel Press Book
Published by Carol Publishing Group
Citadel Press is a registered trademark of Carol Communications, Inc.

Editorial Offices: 600 Madison Avenue, New York, N.Y. 10022
Sales and Distribution Offices: 120 Enterprise Avenue, Secaucus,
    N.J. 07094
In Canada: Canadian Manda Group, One Atlantic Avenue, Suite 105,
    Toronto, Ontario M6K 3E7

Queries regarding rights and permissions should be addressed to
Carol Publishing Group, 600 Madison Avenue, New York, N.Y. 10022

Carol Publishing Group books are available at special discounts
for bulk purchases, sales promotions, fund-raising, or
educational purposes. Special editions can also be created to
specifications. For details contact: Special Sales Department,
Carol Publishing Group, 120 Enterprise Avenue, Secaucus, N.J. 07094

Manufactured in the United States of America
ISBN 0-8065-1343-8 (cloth)
ISBN 0-8065-1350-0 (pbk)

15 14 13 12 11 10 9 8 7 6 5

Library of Congress Cataloging-in-Publication Data

   The 100: a ranking of the most influential persons in history /
Michael H. Hart.–Rev. ed.
       p. cm.
Originally published: New York : Hart Pub. Co., 1978.
1. Biography. I. Title. II. Title: One-Hundred.
CT105.H32   1992
920.02—dc20   92-35426
                                            CIP

*To the memory of my father, without
whose encouragement and inspiration
this book would never have been written*

ACKNOWLEDGMENTS

I would particularly like to thank Dr. J. Richard Gott, III for the many insights he provided me on the historical significance of various individuals. Discussions with Harrison Roth and with Donald Archer have also proven most helpful.

The encouragement and assistance of my mother and my sister is gratefully acknowledged. Most of all, I wish to thank my wife, Sherry, whose help in both the research and the writing contributed so greatly to this book.

CONTENTS

LIST OF ILLUSTRATIONS

PREFACE TO THE SECOND EDITION

Today, a dozen years after *The 100* was first published, the book is still selling well, and translations into other languages keep appearing. Why then, should there be a revised edition of the book?

One reason for making revisions is that history did not come to a halt in 1978, when the first edition of this book was written. On the contrary, many new events have occurred since then—some of them quite unanticipated—and new historical figures have emerged. Even had my knowledge of the past been perfect twelve years ago, this book would still need revising, because the world has changed since then.

Of course, my knowledge of the past was far from perfect in 1978. In the intervening years, I have (I hope) learned a lot from my own studies, and in addition, the response to my book has been educational. Many of the letters I received from readers mentioned historical facts that I had overlooked; or they pointed out new—and often better—ways of interpreting the facts I already knew. The same is true of many remarks made by callers-in to radio talk shows where I was a guest. A second reason, therefore, for this edition is to correct some of the shortcomings of the first.

One of the most difficult (and interesting) tasks involved in writing *The 100* was evaluating the relative importance of various political leaders. We all tend to overestimate the importance of current heads of state. They seem to us like giants; whereas statesmen who lived a few centuries ago—and who seemed every bit as important to *their* contemporaries—are now nearly forgotten.

It is far easier to evaluate the significance of an ancient leader. We can see the consequences—or at least the aftermath—of his or her actions, and can use that information to estimate the person's importance. To estimate the importance of a current political figure is much harder. No matter how powerful a leader seems today, and no matter how innovative, it is difficult to foretell how long his or her influence will endure.

A case in point is my ranking (#20) of Mao Tse-tung (now spelled *Mao Zedong*) in the first edition. That edition was written shortly after the death of Mao, when the memory of his achievements was still fresh. Of course, I realized at the time that Mao's importance would probably fade as the years went by; but I greatly underestimated the extent and swiftness of that decline. Within a few years of Mao's death, the reforms instituted by his successor (Deng Xiaoping) have drastically altered many of Mao's most cherished policies. Since Deng seems to be undoing a good deal of Mao's program, it has been apparent for some time that the first edition of this book seriously overestimated Mao's long-term importance.

But this edition is not being written merely in order to change the ranking of a single person. Much more has happened in the past decade than just the decline of Mao's influence. When the first edition of this book was being written, it seemed as though the Communist movement—as dreadful as it appeared to me—was so firmly entrenched in so many countries, and so skilled and ruthless in its hold on power, that it might well endure for many decades, perhaps even for centuries; indeed, it might even succeed in triumphing over a West that was more humane, but less determined.

If that was so, then the founders of the Communist system (Marx, Lenin, Stalin) were all extremely influential men. However, the events of the past few years have shown that the Communist system was not nearly as powerful, nor as firmly entrenched, as I had feared. In fact, the decline of Marxism is the most striking historical feature of the past decade.

The entire Soviet empire in Eastern Europe has collapsed, and the liberated countries have all renounced Communism. Various other countries (such as Ethiopia and Mongolia) that had once been client states of the Soviet Union have also abandoned Marxism. The Soviet Union itself has disintegrated and has been replaced by fifteen independent republics, and none of them are retaining the Marxist-Leninist system.

There are still a few Communist governments remaining in the world—Vietnam, North Korea, Cuba, Laos, and the People's Republic of China. But none of those are strong economically, and none seem secure. Although over a billion people still live under Communist tyrannies, and though a resurgence of Marxism is still theoretically possible, it would not be surprising if, ten or twenty years from now, there was not even *one* Communist government left in the whole world!

It follows that the founders of the Communist system were far less important figures than I had originally estimated. And it suggests that various persons whose ideas are particularly antithetical to Communism—men such as Thomas Jefferson and Adam Smith—were probably more influential than I had estimated in the first edition.

It also suggests that a new name should be added to the list of influential persons. Mikhail Gorbachev was the leader of the Soviet Union during its last fateful years (1985–1991). His policies and his actions—and his inactions at critical junctures!—were a major factor in the end of the Cold War, the decline of Communism, and the breakup of the Soviet Union. In view of the enormous importance of these events, Gorbachev has been included in this edition. He has been ranked in position #95, somewhat below Lenin, but far higher that most of the famous political leaders of the past.

Another revision—and one which is likely to be controversial—is my inclusion of Edward de Vere as the real "William Shakespeare," rather than the man from Stratford-on-Avon who is described as the author by most "orthodox" textbooks. This change was only made reluctantly: It represents an admission that I made a serious error in the first edition when, without carefully checking the facts, I simply "followed the crowd" and accepted the Stratford man as the author of the plays. Since then, I have carefully examined the arguments on both sides of the question and have concluded that the weight of the evidence is heavily against the Stratford man, and in favor of de Vere.

I regret that, in a book this size, space does not permit the inclusion of *all* the arguments which show that Edward de Vere, rather than the Stratford man, was the author of the plays. I hope that the facts presented in my article will be sufficient for most readers. For a fuller and more detailed exposition the interested reader might consult the excellent book by Charlton Ogburn, *The Mysterious William Shakespeare*, which is perhaps the definitive book on this interesting topic.

Besides Gorbachev, two other persons—Ernest Rutherford and Henry Ford—have been included in this revised edition who were not in the original book.

Rutherford was one of the most celebrated scientists of the twentieth century. I am not sure how I managed to overlook him when I wrote the first edition, and several scientists expressed surprise at my omission. On reviewing his scientific accomplishments, I have concluded that his contributions to modern atomic theory exceed those of Niels Bohr (who was #100 in the first edition), while his contributions to our knowledge of radioactivity were more important than those of Becquerel (who was #58).

Henry Ford was one of the "honorable mentions" in the first edition. However, many readers wrote in, claiming that I had underestimated his importance, and presenting reasons why he should have been included in the first hundred. On reconsidering the matter, I have concluded that the critics were right, and I have altered this edition accordingly.

One should not infer, though, that the revised edition is simply the result of a poll. It was not the *number* of objecting letters which caused me to change my mind about Ford—indeed, I received more objections on some other points—but the soundness of the reasoning in those letters. The rankings in this book are, for better or worse, my own opinions, not some consensus of readers or experts.

To make room for the three additions to the top hundred (Gorbachev, Rutherford, and Ford), it was necessary to delete three persons who had been included in that group in the first edition. Those three men are: Niels Bohr, Pablo Picasso, and Antoine Henri Becquerel. This, of course, does not in any way imply that I consider them to be *unimportant* figures. On the contrary, those three—like most of those listed as honorable mentions, and like many other men and women whom I have not had the space to mention—were talented and influential persons who have helped create this fascinating world we live in.

Michael H. Hart
January 1992

We see, then, how far the monuments of wit and learning are more durable than the monuments of power or of the hands. For have not the verses of Homer continued twenty-five hundred years or more, without the loss of a syllable or letter; during which time infinite palaces, temples, castles, cities, have been decayed and demolished?

FRANCIS BACON
The Advancement of Learning (1605)

INTRODUCTION

In his book *Letters on the English,* Voltaire relates that during his stay in England, in 1726, he overheard some learned men discussing the question: who was the greatest man—Caesar, Alexander, Tamerlane, or Cromwell? One speaker maintained that Sir Isaac Newton was beyond a doubt the greatest man. Voltaire agreed with this judgment, for: "It is to him who masters our minds by the force of truth, and not to those who enslave them by violence, that we owe our reverence."

Whether Voltaire was truly convinced that Sir Isaac Newton was the greatest man who ever lived or was simply trying to make a philosophical point, the anecdote raises an interesting question: of the billions of human beings who have populated the earth, which persons have most influenced the course of history?

This book presents my own answer to that question, my list of the 100 persons in history whom I believe to have been the most influential. I must emphasize that this is a list of the *most influential* persons in history, not a list of the *greatest.* For example, there is room in my list for an enormously influential, wicked, and heartless man like Stalin, but no place at all for the saintly Mother Cabrini.

This book is solely involved with the question of who were the 100 persons who had the greatest effect on history and on the course of the world. I have ranked these 100 persons in order of importance: that is, according to the total amount of influence that each of them had on human history and on the everyday lives of other human beings. Such a group of exceptional people, whether noble or reprehensible, famous or obscure, flamboyant or modest, cannot fail to be interesting; they are the people who have shaped our lives and formed our world.

Before composing such a catalogue, it is necessary to formulate the ground rules as to who is eligible for inclusion and on what basis. The first rule is that only *real* persons are eligible for consideration. That rule is sometimes difficult to apply; for example, did the Chinese sage Lao Tzu actually exist, or is he merely a legendary figure? How about Homer? How about Aesop, the putative author of the famous *Aesop's Fables?* In cases such as these, where the facts are uncertain, I have been obliged to make a guess—an educated guess, I trust—based on the information available.

Anonymous persons are also disqualified. Obviously the individual who invented the wheel—if indeed the wheel was invented by a single person—was a very influential figure, probably far more important than most of the people listed in this book. However, under the rules that I postulate, that individual, along with the inventor of writing, and all the other anonymous benefactors of the human race, has been excluded from consideration.

In composing this list, I have not simply selected the most famous or prestigious figures in history. Neither fame, nor talent, nor nobility of character is the same thing as influence. Thus, Benjamin Franklin, Martin Luther King, Jr., Babe Ruth, and even Leonardo da Vinci are omitted from this list—although some find a place among the Honorable Mentions that follow the One Hundred. On the other hand, influence is not always exerted benevolently; thus, an evil genius such as Hitler meets the criteria for inclusion.

Since the influence with which we are concerned must be averaged over the world at large, the names of many outstanding political figures whose influence was primarily local are absent. However, a significant impact on one important country is equivalent to a less commanding influence affecting the entire earth; thus, Peter the Great of Russia, whose influence extended primarily to his own country, appears on my list.

I have not confined my list to persons who have affected the *present* situation of mankind. Influence on past generations was taken equally into account.

What about the future? In ranking the men and women in this book, I considered the influence that their accomplishments may have on future generations and events. Since our knowledge of the future is severely limited, it is obvious I could not estimate continued influence with anything approaching certitude. Nevertheless, it seems safe to predict that electricity, for example, will still be important 500 years from now, and the contributions of such scientists as Faraday and Maxwell will therefore continue to affect the daily lives of our remote descendants.

In deciding exactly where to place an individual, I gave much weight to the importance of the historical movement to which he contributed. Generally speaking, major historical developments are never due to the actions of one person alone. Because this book is concerned with *individual, personal influence,* I have tried to divide the credit for a given development in proportion to each participant's contribution. Individuals, therefore, are not ranked in the same order as would be the important events or movements with which they are associated. Sometimes a person who is almost exclusively responsible for a significant event or movement has been ranked higher than one who played a less dominant role in a more important movement.

A striking example of this is my ranking Muhammad higher than Jesus, in large part because of my belief that Muhammad had a much greater personal influence on the formulation of the Moslem religion than Jesus had on the formulation of the Christian religion. This does not imply, of course, that I think Muhammad was a *greater* man than Jesus.

There are some important developments to which a large number of persons contributed, but in which no one individual was of overriding importance. A good illustration is the development of explosives and firearms; another is the women's liberation movement; still another is the rise and evolution of Hinduism. Although each of these developments is of major importance, if credit were apportioned among the many contributors, no one person would qualify for inclusion on this list.

Would it then be advisable to choose a representative individual for each of these developments, and to accord that person all of the credit? I think not. Under such a procedure, the Hindu philosopher Sankara would appear near the top of the list as a representative of Hinduism. But Sankara himself is neither particularly famous—he is virtually unknown outside India—nor outstandingly influential. Similarly, it would strike me as frivolous to rank Richard Gatling, the inventor of an early model of machine gun, higher than Albert Einstein, purely on the grounds that the evolution of firearms was more important than the formulation of the theory of relativity. In all such cases, I have decided *not* to try to choose a "first among equals." Each person included in this book has been selected on the basis of his or her actual influence, rather than as a representative of an important movement.

Where two individuals, in close collaboration, have produced what is essentially a joint accomplishment, a special rule has been adopted. For example, Orville and Wilbur Wright worked so closely together in inventing the airplane that it is nearly impossible to separate their individual contributions. In this case, it seems pointless to attempt to ascertain the proportion of credit due to each man, and then to assign each man a separate place on the list. Instead, the two men have been treated as a joint entry.

Like the Wright brothers, Karl Marx and Friedrich Engels share a chapter, although it is headed only by the name of Marx, whom I consider the more important of the two. A few other joint contributors have been treated in the same fashion. Let me stress that this rule about joint entry does not apply to persons who merely worked in the same general field, but only to close collaborators.

There is one other factor, which it has been suggested, should be considered in determining an individual's place on this list. In retrospect, we can see that if Guglielmo Marconi had not invented the radio, some other person would have done so within a few years. Similarly, it seems likely that Mexico would have been conquered by Spain even had Hernando Cortés never existed, and that the theory of evolution would have been formulated without Charles Darwin. But these accomplishments were *actually* carried out by Marconi, Cortés, and Darwin, respectively. These three men have therefore been ranked on this list in accordance with their achievements, and the argument that "it would have happened anyway" has been disregarded.

On the other hand, a few rare people were responsible for important events that might *never* have occurred without them. In assessing and ranking these people—an oddly-mixed group whose members include Genghis Khan, Beethoven, Muhammad, and William the Conqueror—their particular achievements have been assigned greater weight, because these individuals have been personally influential in the profoundest sense of the term.

Of the tens of billions of individuals who have inhabited the world, fewer than one in a million is listed in a large biographical dictionary. Of the perhaps twenty thousand individuals whose achievements have merited mention in biographical dictionaries, only about one-half of one percent are included on this list. Thus, every person on this list, in my opinion, is one of the truly monumental figures of history.

The influence of women on human affairs, as well as the contributions that females have made to human civilization, is obviously far greater than might be indicated by their numbers in this list. But a galaxy of influential figures will naturally be composed of individuals who had both the talent *and* the opportunity to exert a great influence. Throughout history, women have generally been denied such opportunities, and my inclusion of only two females is simply a reflection of that regrettable truth. I see no point in trying to cover up the disagreeable fact of discrimination by adding a few token women to my list. This book is based on what actually *did* occur in the past; not on what should have occurred, or on what might have occurred had human institutions been more equitable. Similar observations might be made concerning various racial or ethnic groups whose members have been disadvantaged in the past.

I have stressed that influence has been the sole criterion in ranking the individuals in this compendium. It would, of course, be possible to construct lists of "outstanding persons," based on other criteria, such as fame, prestige, talent, versatility, and nobility of character.

You, the reader, are urged to experiment by composing your own list—whether it be of the most influential, or of the most outstanding, or of otherwise superlative personages in any particular field. I have found the creation of this book on the one hundred most influential figures both fascinating and entertaining, and I am confident that you, too, will enjoy the intellectual exercise of assembling your own list or lists. Your list of names will not and need not coincide with mine. You may prefer to ponder, for example, the one hundred most powerful individuals who ever lived, or the one hundred most charismatic characters. But should you choose to nominate the most *influential* figures, I hope the exercise will open up for you, as it did for me, a new perspective on history.

HISTORICAL CHART

Some Important Events and Developments

NOTE: The names of the first twenty people in this book appear in full caps.

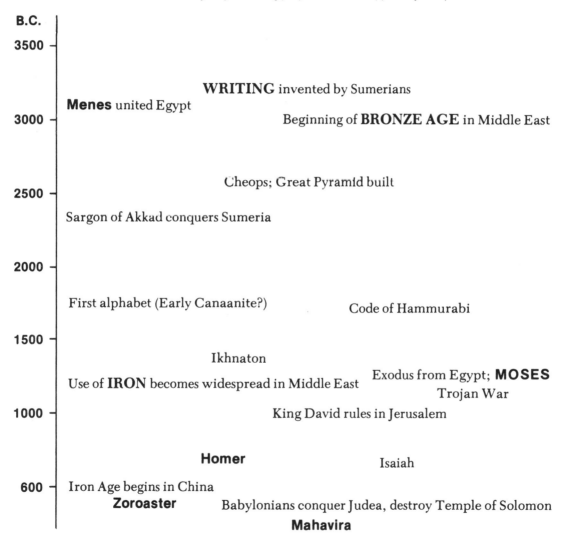

B.C.

3500 —

WRITING invented by Sumerians

Menes united Egypt

3000 —

Beginning of **BRONZE AGE** in Middle East

Cheops; Great Pyramid built

2500 —

Sargon of Akkad conquers Sumeria

2000 —

First alphabet (Early Canaanite?)

Code of Hammurabi

1500 —

Ikhnaton

Exodus from Egypt; **MOSES**

Use of **IRON** becomes widespread in Middle East

Trojan War

1000 —

King David rules in Jerusalem

Homer

Isaiah

600 —

Iron Age begins in China

Zoroaster

Babylonians conquer Judea, destroy Temple of Solomon

Mahavira

BUDDHA   **Cyrus the Great** conquers Babylonia

500 — **CONFUCIUS**

Battle of Marathon; heavily armed infantry prevails

Pericles   Sophocles

Herodotus   Hippocrates   Democritus

400 — Death of Socrates

Plato

ARISTOTLE   **Alexander the Great**

Mencius   **Lao Tzu**

300 —   **EUCLID**

Asoka

Archimedes   Aristarchus of Samos

SHIH HUANG TI unites China

200 — Rome defeats Carthage in Second Punic War   Liu Pang founds Han dynasty

Rome conquers Greece

100 —

Julius Caesar conquers Gaul

AUGUSTUS CAESAR, first Roman emperor

B.C. —
_____

A.D.

Crucifixion of **JESUS**

ST. PAUL preaching and writing

100 — Height of Roman power   **TS'AI LUN** invents paper

Ptolemy

Galen

200 —

End of Han dynasty in China

Mani preaching in Mesopotamia, Persia

300 — **Constantine the Great,** first Christian emperor of Rome

Gothic cavalry (with stirrups, saddles) defeats Roman infantry at Battle of Adrianople

400 – Rome declining **St. Augustine**

Anglo-Saxon conquest of England
End of Western Roman Empire

500 –

Code of **Justinian**

Sui Wen Ti reunites China

600 –

MUHAMMAD founds Islam
'Umar Ibn al-Khattab, second Caliph; Arabs conquer Egypt, Persia, Iraq

Beginning of block printing in China

700 – Moslems conquer Spain

Moslems defeated in France at Battle of Tours   T'ang dynasty in China at peak

800 – **Charlemagne** crowned in Rome   Harun al-Rashid
Height of Caliphate in Baghdad; Mamun the Great

900 – Height of Viking raids in Europe   Beginning of Viking state in Normandy

1000 –   Leif Ericson

William the Conqueror wins Battle of Hastings, conquers England
Pope Urban II; Crusades begin

1100 –

Increasing use of crossbows in warfare

1200 – Height of papal power under Innocent III   Temujin = **Genghis Khan**
Magna Carta
Mongols conquer Russia
Thomas Aquinas   Mongols conquer China; height of Mongol power; Kubilai Khan

1300 – **RENAISSANCE** begins in Italy   Marco Polo

Dante   **CANNONS** coming into use in Europe

English longbowmen rout French   Black Death ravages Europe
knights at Battle of Crécy

1400 –   Tamerlane ravages India, Persia

Henry the Navigator

Joan of Arc

1450 –   Siege artillery makes castles obsolete   Primitive handguns

Turks conquer Constantinople   **GUTENBERG** develops printing with
(= end of Byzantine Empire)   movable type

1475 –

Ferdinand and **Isabella** unite Spain;   Russia gains independence
Spanish Inquisition begins   from Mongols

COLUMBUS discovers America

1500 – **Vasco da Gama** discovers route to India   Leonardo da Vinci

Michelangelo   **Machiavelli**
PROTESTANT REFORMATION begins; **Luther**

Magellan   **Cortés** conquers Mexico

1525 –

Pizarro conquers Peru

Henry VIII   **Calvin**

COPERNICUS

1550 –

Elizabeth I begins reign in England   From here on **FIREARMS**
          dominate warfare

1575 –

Spanish Armada defeated by English navy

1600 – **Edward de Vere** (= "William Shakespeare")

Kepler   Telescope invented

GALILEO

1625 — **Francis Bacon**   Pilgrims land at Plymouth Rock

Harvey discovers circulation of the blood

Germany devastated by Thirty Years' War   **Japan shuts out West**

Descartes   Rembrandt   Taj Mahal built

1650 —   English Civil War; **Oliver Cromwell**

1675 —   **Leeuwenhoek** discovers bacteria

Glorious Revolution in England   **ISAAC NEWTON** writes *Principia*

John Locke

1700 —   **Peter the Great**   Early steam engine

1725 —

Voltaire writes *Letters on the English;* beginning of French Enlightenment

Johann Sebastian Bach

1750 — Montesquieu   **Rousseau**

Leonhard Euler   Benjamin Franklin

INDUSTRIAL REVOLUTION beginning in England

1770 —   **James Watt** invents improved steam engine

Jefferson writes   **Adam Smith** writes
Declaration of Independence   *The Wealth of Nations*

1780 — **George Washington**   Immanuel Kant

U.S. Constitution written   Coulomb discovers electrostatic law

LAVOISIER   **FRENCH REVOLUTION** begins   Mozart

1790 —

Jenner   **Malthus**

1800 –   Volta invents first electric battery

Napoleon Bonaparte

John Dalton   England bans slave trade
1810 –

                              Battle of Waterloo   **Beethoven**
         David Ricardo
1820 –   British dominate India   **Bolívar** wins Battle of Boyaca

1830 –
         Railroads becoming important   **Faraday** discovers electromagnetic induction

         Telegraph invented
1840 –   **Daguerre** invents photography

                                 Morton introduces anesthesia
1850 –

1860 –   Lenoir invents 2-stroke internal   **DARWIN** publishes
         combustion engine   *The Origin of Species*
                              Gatling invents machine gun
                                              American Civil War; Lincoln
         James Clerk Maxwell   **Mendel**
1870 –   Meiji restoration in Japan   **Karl Marx**   **Lister**

                              PASTEUR
         Otto invents 4-stroke internal combustion engine   **Bell** invents telephone
1880 –
                         Edison invents electric light

1890 –   British Empire at peak   Automobiles first sold commercially (Daimler, Benz)

	Motion pictures invented **Röntgen** discovers X-rays
	Marconi invents the radio · Becquerel discovers radioactivity
1900	**Sigmund Freud** · **Max Planck**
	Wright brothers invent airplane
	EINSTEIN formulates special theory of relativity
	Henry Ford introduces Model T
1910	
	Rutherford discovers atomic nucleus
	Russian Revolution; **Lenin** · World War I: trench warfare; gas warfare, tanks
1920	
	Quantum mechanics: de Broglie, **Heisenberg,** Schrödinger
	Fleming discovers penicillin
1930	
	Picasso
	Franklin D. Roosevelt · **Stalin** · Keynes
	Hitler
1940	
	Fermi builds first nuclear reactor · World War II
	ATOMIC BOMBS · first general purpose **COMPUTERS**
	Transistor invented (Shockley, et. al.)
1950	**Mao Zedong** · **TELEVISION** becomes important
	H-bomb invented · Crick & Watson discover stucture of DNA · Masers
	Pincus develops contraceptive pill
1960	Lasers
	John F. Kennedy institutes Apollo project
	first **MOON LANDING** (Apollo 11)
1970	Vietnam war
	Artificial gene implanted in bacteria
1980	
	Gorbachev
1990	Soviet empire in Eastern Europe ends · Cold War ends
	USSR abandons Communism, breaks apart

THE
100

Mecca, the holy city of Islam; the black building at center is the Kaaba, the sanctuary that houses the black stone.

1 MUHAMMAD 570-632

My choice of Muhammad to lead the list of the world's most influential persons may surprise some readers and may be questioned by others, but he was the only man in history who was supremely successful on both the religious and secular levels.

Of humble origins, Muhammad founded and promulgated one of the world's great religions, and became an immensely effective political leader. Today, thirteen centuries after his death, his influence is still powerful and pervasive.

The majority of the persons in this book had the advantage of being born and raised in centers of civilization, highly cultured or politically pivotal nations. Muhammad, however, was born in the year 570, in the city of Mecca, in southern

Arabia, at that time a backward area of the world, far from the centers of trade, art, and learning. Orphaned at age six, he was reared in modest surroundings. Islamic tradition tells us that he was illiterate. His economic position improved when, at age twenty-five, he married a wealthy widow. Nevertheless, as he approached forty, there was little outward indication that he was a remarkable person.

Most Arabs at that time were pagans, and believed in many gods. There were, however, in Mecca, a small number of Jews and Christians; it was from them, most probably, that Muhammad first learned of a single, omnipotent God who ruled the entire universe. When he was forty years old, Muhammad became convinced that this one true God (Allah) was speaking to him (through the Archangel Gabriel) and had chosen him to spread the true faith.

For three years, Muhammad preached only to close friends and associates. Then, about 613, he began preaching in public. As he slowly gained converts, the Meccan authorities came to consider him a dangerous nuisance. In 622, fearing for his safety, Muhammad fled to Medina (a city some 200 miles north of Mecca), where he had been offered a position of considerable political power.

This flight, called the *Hegira*, was the turning point of the Prophet's life. In Mecca, he had had few followers. In Medina, he had many more, and he soon acquired an influence that made him virtually an absolute ruler. During the next few years, while Muhammad's following grew rapidly, a series of battles were fought between Medina and Mecca. This war ended in 630 with Muhammad's triumphant return to Mecca as conqueror. The remaining two and one-half years of his life witnessed the rapid conversion of the Arab tribes to the new religion. When Muhammad died, in 632, he was the effective ruler of all of southern Arabia.

The Bedouin tribesmen of Arabia had a reputation as fierce warriors. But their number was small; and plagued by disunity and internecine warfare, they had been no match for the larger armies of the kingdoms in the settled agricultural areas to the north. However, unified by Muhammad for the first time in history, and inspired by their fervent belief in the one true God, these small Arab armies now embarked upon one of the most astonishing series of conquests in human history. To the northeast of Arabia lay the large Neo-Persian Empire of the Sassanids; to the northwest lay the Byzantine, or Eastern Roman Empire, centered in Constantinople. Numerically, the Arabs were no match for their opponents. On the field of battle, though, it was far different, and the inspired Arabs rapidly conquered all of Mesopotamia, Syria, and Palestine. By 642, Egypt had been wrested from the Byzantine Empire, while the Persian armies had been crushed at the key battles of Qadisiya in 637, and Nehavend in 642.

But even these enormous conquests—which were made under the leadership of Muhammad's close friends and immediate successors, Abu Bakr and 'Umar ibn al-Khattab—did not mark the end of the Arab advance. By 711, the Arab armies had swept completely across North Africa to the Atlantic Ocean. There they turned north and, crossing the Strait of Gibraltar, overwhelmed the Visigothic kingdom in Spain.

For a while, it must have seemed that the Moslems would overwhelm all of Christian Europe. However, in 732, at the famous Battle of Tours, a Moslem army, which had advanced into the center of France, was at last defeated by the Franks. Nevertheless, in a scant century of fighting, these Bedouin tribesmen, inspired by the word of the Prophet, had carved out an empire stretching from the borders of India to the Atlantic Ocean—the largest empire that the world had yet seen. And everywhere that the armies conquered, large-scale conversion to the new faith eventually followed.

Now, not all of these conquests proved permanent. The Persians, though they have remained faithful to the religion of the Prophet, have since regained their independence from the Arabs. And in Spain, more than seven centuries of warfare finally resulted in the Christians reconquering the entire peninsula. However, Mesopotamia and Egypt, the two cradles of ancient civilization, have remained Arab, as has the entire coast of North

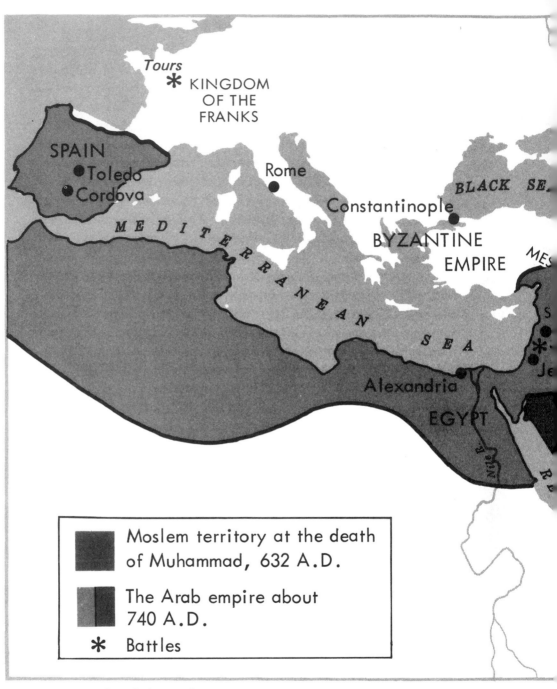

Muhammad and the Arab conquests.

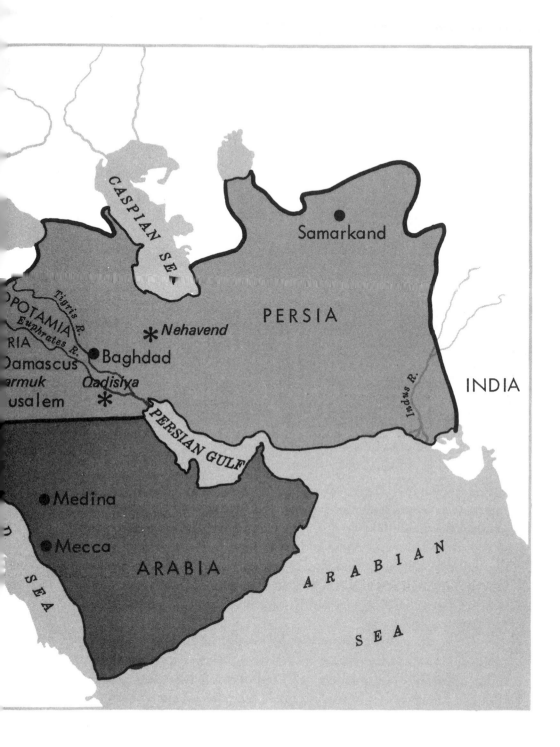

CASPIAN SEA

Samarkand

PERSIA

Tigris R.

POTAMIA

Euphrates R.

RIA

Damascus

*Nehavend

Baghdad

armuk

Qadisiya

*

usalem

Indus R.

INDIA

PERSIAN GULF

Medina

Mecca

ARABIA

ARABIAN

SEA

SEA

7

Moslem crusaders under Muhammad conquer in Allah's name.

Africa. The new religion, of course, continued to spread, in the intervening centuries, far beyond the borders of the original Moslem conquests. Currently, it has tens of millions of adherents in Africa and Central Asia, and even more in Pakistan and northern India, and in Indonesia. In Indonesia, the new faith has been a unifying factor. In the Indian subcontinent, however, the conflict between Moslems and Hindus is still a major obstacle to unity.

How, then, is one to assess the overall impact of Muhammad on human history? Like all religions, Islam exerts an enormous influence upon the lives of its followers. It is for this reason that the founders of the world's great religions all figure prominently in this book. Since there are roughly twice as many Christians as Moslems in the world, it may initially seem strange that

8

Muhammad has been ranked higher than Jesus. There are two principal reasons for that decision. First, Muhammad played a far more important role in the development of Islam than Jesus did in the development of Christianity. Although Jesus was responsible for the main ethical and moral precepts of Christianity (insofar as these differed from Judaism), it was St. Paul who was the main developer of Christian theology, its principal proselytizer, and the author of a large portion of the New Testament.

Muhammad, however, was responsible for both the theology of Islam and its main ethical and moral principles. In addition, he played the key role in proselytizing the new faith, and in establishing the religious practices of Islam. Moreover, he is the author of the Moslem holy scriptures, the Koran, a collection of Muhammad's statements that he believed had been divinely inspired. Most of these utterances were copied more or less faithfully during Muhammad's lifetime and were collected together in authoritative form not long after his death. The Koran, therefore, closely represents Muhammad's ideas and teachings and, to a considerable extent, his exact words. No such detailed compilation of the teachings of Christ has survived. Since the Koran is at least as important to Moslems as the Bible is to Christians, the influence of Muhammad through the medium of the Koran has been enormous. It is probable that the relative influence of Muhammad on Islam has been larger than the combined influence of Jesus Christ and St. Paul on Christianity. On the purely religious level, then, it seems likely that Muhammad has been as influential in human history as Jesus.

Furthermore, Muhammad (unlike Jesus) was a secular as well as a religious leader. In fact, as the driving force behind the Arab conquests, he may well rank as the most influential political leader of all time.

Of many important historical events, one might say that they were inevitable and would have occurred even without the particular political leader who guided them. For example, the South American colonies would probably have won their independence from Spain even if Simón Bolívar had never lived. But this cannot be said of the Arab conquests. Nothing similar had occurred before Muhammad, and there is no reason to believe that the conquests would have been achieved without him. The only comparable conquests in human history are those of the Mongols in the thirteenth century, which were primarily due to the influence of Genghis Khan. These conquests, however, though more extensive than those of the Arabs, did not prove permanent, and today the only areas occupied by the Mongols are those that they held prior to the time of Genghis Khan.

It is far different with the conquests of the Arabs. From Iraq to Morocco, there extends a whole chain of Arab nations united not merely by their faith in Islam, but also by their Arabic language, history, and culture. The centrality of the Koran in the Moslem religion and the fact that it is written in Arabic have probably prevented the Arab language from breaking up into mutually unintelligible dialects, which might otherwise have occurred in the intervening thirteen centuries. Differences and divisions between these Arab states exist, of course, and they are considerable, but the partial disunity should not blind us to the important elements of unity that have continued to exist. For instance, neither Iran nor Indonesia, both oil-producing states and both Islamic in religion, joined in the oil embargo of the winter of 1973-74. It is no coincidence that all of the Arab states, and only the Arab states, participated in the embargo.

We see, then, that the Arab conquests of the seventh century have continued to play an important role in human history, down to the present day. It is this unparalleled combination of secular and religious influence which I feel entitles Muhammad to be considered the most influential single figure in human history.

2

ISAAC

NEWTON

1 6 4 2 - 1 7 2 7

Nature and Nature's laws lay hid in night:
God said, Let Newton be! and all was light.
ALEXANDER POPE

Isaac Newton, the greatest and most influential scientist who ever lived, was born in Woolsthorpe, England, on Christmas Day, 1642, the same year that Galileo died. Like Muhammad, he was born after the death of his father. As a child, he showed considerable mechanical aptitude, and was very clever with his hands. Although a bright child, he was inattentive in school and did not attract much attention. When he was a teenager, his mother took him out of school, hoping that he would become a successful farmer. Fortunately, she was persuaded that his principal talents lay elsewhere, and at eighteen, he entered Cambridge University. There, he rapidly absorbed what was then known of science and mathematics, and soon moved on to his own independent research. Between his twenty-first and twenty-seventh years, he laid the foundations for the scientific theories that subsequently revolutionized the world.

The middle of the seventeenth century was a period of great scientific ferment. The invention of the telescope near the begin-

11

ning of the century had revolutionized the entire study of astronomy. The English philosopher Francis Bacon and the French philosopher René Descartes had both urged scientists throughout Europe to cease relying on the authority of Aristotle and to experiment and observe for themselves. What Bacon and Descartes had preached, the great Galileo had practiced. His astronomical observations, using the newly invented telescope, had revolutionized the study of astronomy, and his mechanical experiments had established what is now known as Newton's first law of motion.

Other great scientists, such as William Harvey, who discovered the circulation of the blood, and Johannes Kepler, who discovered the laws describing the motions of the planets around the sun, were bringing new basic information to the scientific community. Still, pure science was largely a plaything of intellectuals, and as yet there was no proof that when applied to technology, science could revolutionize the whole mode of human life, as Francis Bacon had predicted.

Although Copernicus and Galileo had swept aside some of the misconceptions of ancient science and contributed to a greater understanding of the universe, no set of principles had been formulated that could turn this collection of seemingly unrelated facts into a unified theory with which to make scientific predictions. It was Isaac Newton who supplied that unified theory and set modern science on the course which it has followed ever since.

Newton was always reluctant to publish his results, and although he had formulated the basic ideas behind most of his work by 1669, many of his theories were not made public until much later. The first of his discoveries to be published was his ground-breaking work on the nature of light. In a series of careful experiments, Newton had discovered that ordinary white light is a mixture of all the colors of the rainbow. He had also made a careful analysis of the consequences of the laws of the reflection and refraction of light. Using these laws, he had in 1668 designed and actually built the first reflecting telescope, the type of telescope that is used in most major astronomical observatories today. These discoveries, together with the results of many other optical experiments which he had performed, were presented by Newton before the British Royal Society when he was twenty-nine years old.

Newton's achievements in optics alone would probably entitle him to a place on this list; however, they are considerably less important than his accomplishments in pure mathematics and mechanics. His major mathematical contribution was his invention of integral calculus, which he probably devised when he was twenty-three or twenty-four years old. That invention, the most important achievement of modern mathematics, is not merely the seed out of which much of modern mathematical theory has grown, it is also the essential tool without which most of the subsequent progess in modern science would have been impossible. Had Newton done nothing else, the invention of integral calculus by itself would have entitled him to a fairly high place on this list.

Newton's most important discoveries, however, were in the field of mechanics, the science of how material objects move. Galileo had discovered the first law of motion, which describes the motion of objects if they are not subjected to any exterior forces. In practice, of course, all objects are subjected to exterior forces, and the most important question in mechanics is how objects move under such circumstances. This problem was solved by Newton in his famous second law of motion, which may rightly be considered the most fundamental law of classical physics. The second law (described mathematically by the equation $F = ma$) states that the acceleration of an object (i.e., the rate at which its velocity changes) is equal to the net force on the object divided by the object's mass. To those first two laws, Newton added his famous third law of motion (which states that for each action—i.e., physical force—there is an equal and opposite reaction), and the most famous of his scientific laws, the law of universal gravitation. This set of four laws, taken conjointly, form a unified system by means of which virtually all macroscopic mechanical systems, from the swinging of a pendulum to the motion of the planets in their orbits around the sun, may be investigated, and their behavior predicted. Newton did not merely state these laws of mechanics; he himself, using the mathematical tools of the calculus, showed how these fundamental laws could be applied to the solution of actual problems.

Newton's laws can be and have been applied to an extremely broad range of scientific and engineering problems. During his lifetime, the most dramatic application of his laws was made in the field of astronomy. In this area, too, Newton led the way. In 1687, he published his great work, the *Mathematical Principles of Natural Philosophy* (usually referred to simply as the *Principia*), in which he presented his law of gravitation and laws of motion. Newton showed how these laws could be used to predict precisely the motions of the planets around the sun. The principal problem of dynamical astronomy—that is, the problem of predicting exactly the positions and motions of the stars and planets—was thereby completely solved by Newton in one magnificent sweep. For this reason, Newton is often considered the greatest of all astronomers.

What, then, is our assessment of Newton's scientific importance? If one looks at the index of an encyclopedia of science, one will find more references (perhaps two or three times as many) to Newton and to his laws and discoveries than to any other individual scientist. Furthermore, one should consider what other great scientists have said about Newton. Leibniz, no friend of Sir Isaac's, and a man with whom he engaged in a bitter dispute, wrote: "Taking mathematics from the beginning of the world to the time when Newton lived, what he has done is much the better part." The great French scientist Laplace wrote: "The *Principia* is preeminent above any other production of human genius." Lagrange frequently stated that Newton was the greatest genius who ever lived, while Ernst Mach, writing in 1901, said: "All that has been accomplished in mathematics since his day has been a deductive, formal, and mathematical development of mechanics on the basis of Newton's laws." This, perhaps, is the crux of Newton's great accomplishment: he found

Newton analyzes a ray of light.

science a hodgepodge of isolated facts and laws, capable of describing some phenomena but of predicting only a few; he left us a unified system of laws, which were capable of application to an enormous range of physical phenomena, and which could be used to make exact predictions.

In a brief summary like this, it is not possible to detail all of Newton's discoveries; consequently, many of the lesser ones have been omitted, although they were important achievements in their own right. Newton made significant contributions to thermodynamics (the study of heat) and to acoustics (the study of sound); he enunciated the extremely important physical principles of conservation of momentum and conservation of angular momentum; he discovered the binomial theorem in mathematics; and he gave the first cogent explanation of the origin of the stars.

Now, one might grant that Newton was by far the greatest and most influential scientist who ever lived but still ask why he should be ranked higher than such major political figures as Alexander the Great or George Washington, and ahead of such major religious figures as Jesus Christ and Gautama Buddha. My own view is that even though political changes are of significance, it is fair to say that most people in the world were living the same way 500 years after Alexander's death as their forebears had lived five centuries before his time. Similarly, in most of their daily activities, the majority of human beings were living the same way in 1500 A.D. as human beings had been living in 1500 B.C.. In the last five centuries, however, with the rise of modern science, the everyday life of most human beings has been completely revolutionized. We dress differently, eat different foods, work at different jobs, and spend our leisure time a great deal differently than people did in 1500 A.D. Scientific discoveries have not only revolutionized technology and economics; they have also completely changed politics, religious thinking, art, and philosophy. Few aspects of human activity have remained unchanged by this scientific revolution, and it is for this reason that so many scientists and inventors are to be found on this list. Newton was not only the most brilliant of all scientists; he was also the most influential figure in the development of scientific theory, and therefore well merits a position at or near the top of any list of the world's most influential persons.

Newton died in 1727, and was buried in Westminster Abbey, the first scientist to be accorded that honor.

3

JESUS

CHRIST

c. 6 B.C. - *c.* 3 0 A.D.

The impact of Jesus on human history is so obvious and so enormous that few people would question his placement near the top of this list. Indeed, the more likely question is why Jesus, who is the inspiration for the most influential religion in history, has not been placed first.

There is no question that Christianity, over the course of time, has had far more adherents than any other religion. However, it is not the relative influence of different religions that is being estimated in this book, but rather the relative influence of individual men. Christianity, unlike Islam, was not founded by a single person but by two people—Jesus and St. Paul—and the principal credit for its development must therefore be apportioned between those two figures.

Jesus formulated the basic ethical ideas of Christianity, as well as its basic spiritual outlook and its main ideas concerning human conduct. Christian theology, however, was shaped principally by the work of St. Paul. Jesus presented a spiritual message; Paul added to that the worship of Christ. Furthermore,

St. Paul was the author of a considerable portion of the New Testament, and was the main proselytizing force for Christianity during the first century.

Jesus was still fairly young when he died (unlike Buddha or Muhammad), and he left behind a limited number of disciples. At the time of Jesus' death, his followers simply formed a small Jewish sect. It was due in considerable measure to Paul's writings, and to his tireless proselytizing efforts, that this small sect was transformed into a dynamic and much greater movement, which reached non-Jews as well as Jews, and which eventually grew into one of the great religions of the world.

For these reasons, some people even contend that it is Paul, rather than Jesus, who should really be considered the founder of Christianity. Carried to its logical conclusion, that argument would lead one to place Paul higher on this list than Jesus! However, although it is not clear what Christianity would be like without the influence of St. Paul, it is quite apparent that without Jesus, Christianity would not exist at all.

However, it does not seem reasonable to consider Jesus responsible for all the things which Christian churches or individual Christians later did in his name, particularly since he would obviously disapprove of many of those things. Some of them—for example the religious wars between various Christian sects, and the barbaric massacres and persecutions of the Jews—are in such obvious contradiction to the attitudes and teachings of Jesus that it seems entirely unreasonable to say that Jesus inspired them.

Similarly, even though modern science first arose in the Christian nations of western Europe, it seems inappropriate to think of Jesus as responsible for the rise of science. Certainly, none of the early Christians interpreted the teachings of Jesus as a call for scientific investigation of the physical world. Indeed, the conversion of the Roman world to Christianity was accompanied and followed by a drastic decline in both the general level of technology and the general degree of interest in science.

That science did eventually arise in Europe is indeed an indication that there was something in the European cultural heritage that was favorable to the scientific way of thinking. That something, however, was not the sayings of Jesus, but rather Greek rationalism, as typified by the works of Aristotle and Euclid. It is noteworthy that modern science developed, not during the heyday of church power and of Christian piety, but rather on the heels of the Renaissance, a period during which Europe experienced a renewal of interest in its pre-Christian heritage.

The story of Jesus' life, as it is related in the New Testament, is familiar to most readers and will not be repeated here. However, a few points are worth noting. In the first place, most of the information that we have about Jesus' life is uncertain. We are not even sure what his original name was. Most probably it was the common Jewish name, Yehoshua (Joshua in English). The year of his birth, too, is uncertain, although 6 B.C. is a likely date. Even the year of his death, which must have been well known to his followers, is not definitely known today. Jesus himself left no writings behind, and virtually all our information concerning his life comes from the accounts in the New Testament.

Unfortunately, the Gospels contradict each other on various points. For example, Matthew and Luke give completely different versions of Jesus' last words; both of these versions, incidentally, are direct quotations from the Old Testament.

It was no accident that Jesus was able to quote from the Old Testament; though the progenitor of Christianity, he was himself a devout Jew. It has been frequently pointed out that Jesus was in many ways very similar to the Hebrew prophets of the Old Testament, and was deeply influenced by them. Like the prophets, Jesus had an extraordinarily impressive personality, which made a deep and lasting impression on the people who met him. He was charismatic in the deepest and fullest sense of the word.

However, in sharp contrast to Muhammad, who exercised political as well as religious authority, Jesus had virtually no influence on political developments during his own lifetime, or during the succeeding century. (Both men, of course, have had an enormous indirect influence on long-term political developments.) Jesus made his influence felt entirely as an ethical and spiritual leader.

If it was primarily as an ethical leader that Jesus left his mark, it is surely pertinent to ask to what extent his ethical ideas have influenced the world. One of Jesus' central precepts, certainly, was the Golden Rule. Today, the Golden Rule is accepted by most people, Christians and non-Christians alike, as a reasonable guide to moral conduct. We may not always act in accordance with it, but we usually try to do so. If Jesus had actually originated that almost universally accepted principle, he would surely have been the first man on this list.

In fact, though, the Golden Rule was an accepted precept of Judaism long before Jesus was born. Rabbi Hillel, the leading Jewish rabbi of the first century B.C., explicitly enunciated the Golden Rule and pronounced it the foremost principle of Judaism. Nor was the notion known only to the Western world. The Chinese philosopher Confucius had proposed it in about 500 B.C., and the saying also appears in the *Mahabharata*, an ancient Hindu poem. In fact, the philosophy behind the Golden Rule is accepted by almost every major religious group.

Does this mean that Jesus had no original ethical ideas? Not at all! A highly distinctive viewpoint is presented in Matthew 5:43-44:

> *Ye have heard that it hath been said, Thou shalt love thy neighbor, and hate thine enemy. But I say unto you, Love your enemies, bless them that curse you, do good to them that hate you, and pray for them which despitefully use you, and persecute you.*

And a few lines earlier: "...resist not evil: but whosoever shall smite thee on the right cheek, turn to him the other also."

Now, these ideas—which were not a part of the Judaism of Jesus' day, nor of most other religions—are surely among the most remarkable and original ethical ideas ever presented. If they were widely followed, I would have had no hesitation in placing Jesus first in this book.

But the truth is that they are not widely followed. In fact,

Rembrandt's "Hundred Guilder Print" of Christ preaching.

they are not even generally accepted. Most Christians consider the injunction to "Love your enemy" as—at most—an ideal which might be realized in some perfect world, but one which is *not* a reasonable guide to conduct in the actual world we live in. We do not normally practice it, do not expect others to practice it, and do not teach our children to practice it. Jesus' most distinctive teaching, therefore, remains an intriguing but basically untried suggestion.

4 BUDDHA 563 B.C. - 483 B.C.

Gautama Buddha, whose original name was Prince Siddhartha, was the founder of Buddhism, one of the world's great religions. Siddhartha was the son of a king ruling in Kapilavastu, a city in northeast India, near the borders of Nepal. Siddhartha himself (of the clan of Gautama and the tribe of Sakya) was purportedly born in 563 B.C., in Lumbini, within the present borders of Nepal. He was married at sixteen to a cousin of the same age. Brought up in the luxurious royal palace, Prince Siddhartha did not want for material comforts. Nevertheless, he was profoundly dissatisfied. He observed that most human beings were poor and continually suffered from want. Even those who were wealthy were frequently frustrated and unhappy, and all men were subject to disease and ultimately succumbed to death. Surely, Siddhartha thought, there must be more to life than transitory pleasures, which were all too soon obliterated by suffering and death.

When he was twenty-nine, just after the birth of his first son, Gautama decided that he must abandon the life he was living and devote himself wholeheartedly to the search for truth. He departed from the palace, leaving behind his wife, his infant son, and all his worldly possessions, and became a penniless wanderer. For a while he studied with some of the famed holy men of the day, but after mastering their teachings, he found their solutions to the problems of the human situation unsatisfactory. It was widely believed that extreme asceticism was the pathway to true wisdom. Gautama therefore attempted to become an ascetic, for several years engaging in extreme fasts and self-mortification. Eventually, however, he realized that tormenting his body only clouded his brain, without leading him any closer to true wisdom. He therefore resumed eating normally, and abandoned asceticism.

In solitude, he grappled with the problems of human existence. Finally, one evening, as he sat beneath a giant fig tree, all the pieces of the puzzle seemed to fall into place. Siddhartha spent the whole night in deep reflection, and when the morning came, he was convinced that he had found the solution and that he was now a Buddha, an "enlightened one."

At this time, he was thirty-five years old. For the remaining forty-five years of his life, he traveled throughout northern India, preaching his new philosophy to all who were willing to listen. By the time he died, in 483 B.C., he had made thousands of converts. Though his words had not been written down, his disciples had memorized many of his teachings, and they were passed to succeeding generations by word of mouth.

The principal teachings of the Buddha can be summarized in what Buddhists call the "Four Noble Truths": first, that human life is intrinsically unhappy; second, that the cause of this unhappiness is human selfishness and desire; third, that individual selfishness and desire can be brought to an end—the resulting state, when all desires and cravings have been eliminated, is termed *nirvana* (literally "blowing out" or "extinction"); fourth, that the method of escape from selfishness and desire is what is called the "Eightfold Path": right views, right thought, right speech, right action, right livelihood, right effort, right mindfulness, and right meditation. It might be added that Buddhism is open to all, regardless of race, and that (unlike Hinduism) it recognizes no distinctions of caste.

For some time after Gautama's death the new religion spread slowly. In the third century B.C., the great Indian emperor Asoka became converted to Buddhism. His support brought about the rapid expansion of Buddhist influence and teachings in India and the spread of Buddhism to neighboring countries. Buddhism spread south into Ceylon, and eastward into Burma. From there it spread into all of southeast Asia, and down into Malaya, and into what is now Indonesia. Buddhism also spread north, directly into Tibet, and to the northwest, into Afghanistan and Central Asia. It spread into China, where it won a large following, and from there into Korea and Japan.

Within India itself, the new faith started to decline after about 500, and almost vanished after about 1200. In China and Japan, on the other hand, Buddhism remained a major religion. In Tibet and in southeast Asia, it has been the principal religion for many centuries.

Buddha's teachings were not written down until several centuries after his death, and, understandably, his movement has split into various sects. The two principal divisions of Buddhism are the Theravada branch, dominant in southern Asia, and considered by most Western scholars as the one closer to the Buddha's original teachings, and the Mahayana branch, dominant in Tibet, China, and northern Asia generally.

Buddha, as the founder of one of the world's major religions, clearly deserved a place near the head of this list. Since there are only about 200 million Buddhists in the world, compared with over 500 million Moslems and about one billion Christians, it would seem evident that Buddha has influenced fewer people than either Muhammad or Jesus. However, the dif-

The belfry of a Japanese Buddhist temple.

ference in numbers can be misleading. One reason that Buddhism died out in India is that Hinduism absorbed many of its ideas and principles. In China, too, large numbers of persons who do not call themselves Buddhists have been strongly influenced by Buddhist philosophy.

Buddhism, far more than Christianity or Islam, has a very strong pacifist element. The orientation toward nonviolence has played a significant role in the political history of Buddhist countries.

It has often been said that if Christ were to return to earth, he would be shocked at many of the things which have been done in his name, and horrified at the bloody fights between different sects of persons who call themselves his followers. Buddha, too, would doubtless be amazed at many of the doctrines that have been presented as Buddhist. But while there are many sects of Buddhism, and large differences between those sects, there is nothing in Buddhist history that remotely compares with the bloody religious wars that took place in Christian Europe. In this respect, at least, Buddha's teachings seem to have had far greater influence on his followers than Christ's teachings had on his.

Buddha and Confucius have had an approximately equal influence upon the world. Both lived at about the same time, and the number of their adherents has not been too different. I have chosen to place Buddha before Confucius for two reasons: first, the advent of Communism in China seems to have greatly diminished Confucian influence; and second, the failure of Confucianism to spread widely outside of China indicates how closely the ideas of Confucius were grounded in pre-existing Chinese attitudes. Buddhist teachings, on the other hand, are in no sense a restatement of previous Indian philosophy, and Buddhism has spread far beyond the boundaries of India due to the originality of Gautama Buddha's concept, and the wide appeal of his philosophy.

"Buddha's Return from Heaven,"
by Nanda Lal Bose.

5
CONFUCIUS
5 5 1 B.C. - 4 7 9 B.C.

The great Chinese philosopher Confucius was the first man to develop a system of beliefs synthesizing the basic ideas of the Chinese people. His philosophy, based on personal morality and on the concept of a government that served its people and ruled by moral example, permeated Chinese life and culture for well over two thousand years, and has greatly influenced a substantial portion of the world's population.

Confucius was born about 551 B.C., in the small state of Lu, which is in the present province of Shantung, in northeastern China. His father died when he was quite young, and Confucius and his mother lived in poverty. As a young man, the future philosopher served as a minor government official, but after several years he resigned his post. He spent the next sixteen years teaching, attracting a considerable number of disciples to his philosophy. When he was about fifty years old, he was awarded a high position in the government of Lu; however, after about four years, enemies at court brought about his dismissal, and, indeed, his exile from the state. He spent the next thirteen years as

27

an itinerant teacher, and then returned to his home state for the
last five years of his life. He died in 479 B.C.

Confucius is often credited as the founder of a religion, but
this description is inaccurate. He very rarely referred to the Deity, refused to discuss the afterlife, and avoided all forms of
metaphysical speculation. He was basically a secular
philosopher, interested in personal and political morality and
conduct.

The two most important virtues, according to Confucius,
are *jen* and *li*, and the superior man guides his conduct by them.
Jen has sometimes been translated as "love," but it might better
be defined as "benevolent concern for one's fellow men." *Li*
describes a combination of manners, ritual, custom, etiquette,
and propriety.

Ancestor worship, the basic Chinese religion even before
Confucius, was reinforced by the strong emphasis that he placed
on family loyalty and respect for one's parents. Confucius also
taught that respect and obedience were owed by wives to their
husbands and by subjects to their rulers. But the Chinese sage did
not approve of tyranny. He believed that the state exists for the
benefit of the people, not vice versa, and he repeatedly stressed
that a ruler should govern primarily by moral example rather
than by force. Another of his tenets was a slight variant of the
Golden Rule: "What you do not want done to yourself, do not do
to others."

Confucius's basic outlook was highly conservative. He
believed that the Golden Age was in the past, and he urged both
rulers and people to return to the good old moral standards. In
fact, however, the Confucian ideal of government by moral example had *not* been the prevailing practice in earlier times, and
Confucius was therefore a more innovative reformer than he
claimed to be.

Confucius lived during the Chou dynasty, a period of great
intellectual ferment in China. Contemporary rulers did not accept his program, but after his death his ideas spread widely
throughout his country. However, with the advent of the Ch'in

The legendary meeting of Confucius (left) with Lao Tzu.

dynasty, in 221 B.C., Confucianism fell upon evil days. The first emperor of the Ch'in dynasty, Shih Huang Ti, was determined to eradicate Confucius's influence, and to make a clean break with the past. He ordered the suppression of Confucian teachings and the burning of all Confucian books. This attempt at suppression was unsuccessful, and when the Ch'in dynasty came to a close a few years later, Confucian scholars were again free to teach their doctrine. During the succeeding dynasty, the Han (206 B.C.-220 A.D.), Confucianism became established as the official Chinese state philosophy.

Starting with the Han dynasty, Chinese emperors gradually developed the practice of selecting government officials by means of civil service examinations. In the course of time these examinations came to be based to a large extent on a knowledge of the Confucian classics. Since entry into the government bureaucracy was the main route to financial success and social prestige in the Chinese empire, the civil service examinations were extremely competitive. Consequently, for generations a large number of the most intelligent and ambitious young men in China devoted many years to intensive study of the Confucian classics, and, for many centuries the entire civil administration of China was composed of persons whose basic outlook had been permeated by the Confucian philosophy. This system endured in China (with some interruptions) for roughly two thousand years, from about 100 B.C. to about 1900 A.D.

But Confucianism was not merely the official philosophy of

the Chinese administration. Confucian ideals were accepted by the majority of the Chinese people, and for over two thousand years deeply influenced their life and thought.

There are several reasons for Confucius's enormous appeal to the Chinese. First, his personal sincerity and integrity were beyond question. Second, he was a moderate and practical person, and did not demand of men what they could not achieve. If he asked them to be honorable, he did not expect them to be saintly. In this regard as in others, he reflected the practical temperament of the Chinese people. And this perhaps, was the key to the immense success that his ideas achieved in China. Confucius was not asking the Chinese to change their basic beliefs. Rather, he was restating, in a clear and impressive form, their basic traditional ideals. Perhaps no philosopher in history has been so closely in touch with the fundamental views of his countrymen as Confucius.

Confucianism, which stresses the *obligations* of individuals rather than their rights, may seem rather stodgy and unappealing by current Western standard. As a philosophy of government, though, it proved remarkably effective in practice. Judged on the basis of its ability to maintain internal peace and prosperity, China, for a period of two thousand years, was on the average the best-governed region on earth.

The ideals of Confucius, closely grounded as they are in Chinese culture, have not been widely influential outside East Asia. They have, however, had a major impact in Korea and Japan, both of which have been greatly influenced by Chinese culture.

At the present time, Confucianism is in low estate in China. The Chinese Communists, in an effort to break completely with the past, have vigorously attacked Confucius and his doctrines, and it is possible that the period of his influence upon history has drawn to a close. In the past, however, the ideas of Confucius have proven to be very deeply rooted within China, and we should not be surprised if there is a resurgence of Confucianism in the course of the next century.

6 ST. PAUL c. 4 A.D. - c. 64 A.D.

The apostle Paul, who was a younger contemporary of Jesus, became the foremost proselytizer of the new religion of Christianity. His influence on Christian theology proved to be the most permanent and far-reaching of all Christian writers and thinkers.

Paul, also known as Saul, was born in Tarsus, a city in Cilicia (in present-day Turkey), a few years into the Christian era. Although a Roman citizen, he was of Jewish birth, and in his youth he learned Hebrew and received a thorough Jewish education. He also learned the trade of tentmaking. As a young man, he went to Jerusalem to study under Rabbi Gamaliel, an eminent Jewish teacher. Though Paul was in Jerusalem at the same time as Jesus, it is doubtful whether the two men ever met.

After the death of Jesus, the early Christians were regarded as heretics and suffered persecution. For a while, Paul himself participated in this persecution. However, during a journey to Damascus he had a vision in which Jesus spoke to him, and he was converted to the new faith. It was the turning point of his life. The one-time opponent of Christianity became the most vigorous and influential proponent of the new religion.

Paul spent the rest of his life thinking and writing about Christianity, and winning converts to the new religion. During his missionary activities, he traveled extensively in Asia Minor, Greece, Syria, and Palestine. Paul was not as successful in preaching to the Jews as some of the other early Christians. Indeed, his manner often aroused great antagonism, and on several occasions his life was endangered. In preaching to non-Jews, however, Paul was outstandingly successful, so much so that he is often referred to as the "Apostle to the Gentiles." No other man played so large a role in the propagation of Christianity.

After three long missionary trips within the eastern part of the Roman Empire, Paul returned to Jerusalem. He was arrested there, and was eventually sent to Rome to stand trial. It is unclear how that trial ended, or if he ever left Rome. Eventually, however (most likely about 64 A.D.), he was executed near Rome.

Paul's immense influence on the development of Christianity rests upon three things: (1) his great success as a missionary; (2) his writings, which constitute an important part of the New Testament; and (3) his role in the development of Christian theology.

Of the twenty-seven books of the New Testament, no fewer than fourteen are attributed to Paul. Even though modern scholars believe that four or five of those books were actually written by other people, it is clear that Paul is the most important single author of the New Testament.

Paul's influence on Christian theology has been incalculable. His ideas include the following: Jesus was not merely

Detail of Michelangelo's fresco,
"The Conversion of Saint Paul," in the Vatican.

an inspired human prophet, but was actually divine. Christ died for our sins, and his suffering can redeem us. Man cannot achieve salvation by attempting to conform to biblical injunctions, but only by accepting Christ; conversely, if one accepts Christ, his sins will be forgiven. Paul also enunciated the doctrine of original sin (see Romans 5:12-19).

Since obedience to the law alone cannot provide salvation, Paul insisted that there was no need for converts to Christianity to accept Jewish dietary restrictions, or to conform to the rituals of the Mosaic Code, or even to be circumcised. Several of the other early Christian leaders disagreed strongly with Paul on this point, and if their views had prevailed, it seems doubtful that Christianity would have spread so rapidly throughout the Roman Empire.

Paul never married, and though there seems to be no way of proving it, he apparently never had sexual relations with a woman. His views on sex and on women, because of their incorporation into Holy Scripture, have had a marked influence upon later attitudes. His most famous dictum on the subject (I Corinthians 7:8-9) is: "I say therefore to the unmarried and the widows, it is good for them if they can abide even as I. But if they cannot contain, let them marry: for it is better to marry than to burn."

Paul also had rather strong ideas on the proper status of women: "Let the woman learn in silence with all subjection. But I suffer not a woman to teach, nor usurp authority over the man, but to be in silence. For Adam was first formed then Eve" (I Timothy 2:11-13). Similar ideas are expressed perhaps even more forcefully in I Corinthians 11:7-9. Doubtless, in such passages Paul was expressing a view already held by many of his contemporaries; it is noteworthy, though, that Jesus does not appear to have made similar statements.

Paul, more than any other man, was responsible for the transformation of Christianity from a Jewish sect into a world religion. His central ideas of the divinity of Christ and of justification by faith alone have remained basic to Christian thought throughout all the intervening centuries. All subsequent Christian theologians, including Augustine, Aquinas, Luther, and Calvin, have been profoundly influenced by his writings. Indeed, the influence of Paul's ideas has been so great that some scholars have claimed that he, rather than Jesus, should be regarded as the principal founder of the Christian religion. Such a view seems too extreme. However, even if Paul's influence has not been on a par with Jesus', it has been vastly greater than that of any other Christian thinker.

Christian pilgrims march in a Good Friday procession on the Via Dolorosa in Jerusalem.

7   TS'AI LUN

fl. c. 1 0 5 A.D

Ts'ai Lun, the inventor of paper, is a man whose name is probably unfamiliar to most readers. Considering the importance of his invention, the extent to which he has been ignored in the West is indeed surprising. There are major encyclopedias which do not have even brief articles on Ts'ai Lun, and his name is seldom mentioned in standard history textbooks. In view of the obvious importance of paper, this paucity of references to Ts'ai Lun may arouse suspicion that he is a purely apocryphal figure. Careful research, however, makes it absolutely clear that Ts'ai Lun was a real man, an official at the Chinese imperial court, who, in or about the year 105, presented Emperor Ho Ti with samples of paper. The Chinese account of Ts'ai Lun's invention (which appears in the official history of the Han dynasty) is entirely straightforward and believable, without the least hint of magic or legend about it. The Chinese have always credited Ts'ai Lun with the invention of paper, and his name is well known in China.

Not a great deal is known about Ts'ai Lun's life. Chinese records do mention that he was a eunuch. It is also recorded that the emperor was greatly pleased by Ts'ai Lun's invention, and that as a result Ts'ai Lun was promoted, received an aristocratic title, and became wealthy. Later on, however, he became involved in palace intrigue, and this eventually led to his downfall. The Chinese records relate that upon his being disgraced, Ts'ai Lun took a bath, dressed in his finest robes, and drank poison.

The use of paper became widespread in China during the second century, and within a few centuries the Chinese were exporting paper to other parts of Asia. For a long time, they kept the technique of papermaking a secret. In 751, however, some Chinese papermakers were captured by the Arabs, and not long afterwards paper was being manufactured in both Samarkand and Baghdad. The art of papermaking gradually spread throughout the Arab world, and in the twelfth century the Europeans learned the art from the Arabs. The use of paper gradually spread, and after Gutenberg invented modern printing, paper replaced parchment as the principal writing material in the West.

Today, paper is so common that we take it for granted, and it is hard to envisage what the world was like without it. In China, before Ts'ai Lun, most books were made of bamboo. Obviously, such books were extremely heavy and clumsy. Some books were written on silk, but that was too expensive for general use. In the West, before paper was introduced, most books were written on parchment or vellum, which were made of specially processed sheepskin or calfskin. This material had replaced the papyrus favored by the Greeks, Romans, and Egyptians. Both parchment and papyrus, however, not only were scarce, but were also expensive to prepare.

That books and other written materials can today be produced so cheaply and in such large quantities is due in considerable part to the existence of paper. It is true that paper would not be as important as it is today were it not for the printing press; however, it is equally true that the printing press would not be nearly so important were it not for the existence of a cheap and plentiful material on which to print.

Which man, then, should be ranked higher: Ts'ai Lun or Gutenberg? Although I consider the two of almost equal importance, I have ranked Ts'ai Lun slightly higher for the following reasons: (1) Paper has many other applications besides its use as a writing material. In fact, it is an amazingly versatile material, and a large percentage of the paper currently produced is used for purposes other than printing. (2) Ts'ai Lun preceded Gutenberg, and it is altogether possible that Gutenberg would not have invented printing had paper not already existed. (3) If only one of the two had ever been invented, I suspect that more books would be produced by the combination of block printing (which was known long before Gutenberg) and paper than by the combination of movable type and parchment.

Is it appropriate to include both Gutenberg and Ts'ai Lun among the ten most influential people who ever lived? In order to realize the full importance of the inventions of paper and printing, it is necessary to consider the relative cultural development of China and the West. Prior to the second century A.D., Chinese civilization was consistently less advanced than Western civilization. During the next millenium, China's accomplishments exceeded those of the West, and for a period of seven or eight centuries, Chinese civilization was by most standards the most advanced on earth. After the fifteenth century, however, western Europe outstripped China. Various cultural explanations for these changes have been advanced, but most such theories seem to ignore what I believe is the simplest explanation.

It is true, of course, that agriculture and writing developed earlier in the Middle East than they did in China. That alone, however, would not explain why Chinese civilization so persistently lagged behind that of the West. The crucial factor, I believe, was that prior to Ts'ai Lun there was no convenient writing material available in China. In the Western world, papyrus was available, and although that material had its drawbacks, papyrus rolls were infinitely superior to books made of wood or bamboo. Lack of a suitable writing material was an overpowering obstacle to Chinese cultural progress. A Chinese scholar needed a wagon to carry around what we would consider a quite modest number of books. One can imagine the difficulty of trying to run a government administration on such a basis!

Ts'ai Lun's invention of paper, however, changed the situation entirely. With a suitable writing material available, Chinese civilization advanced rapidly, and within a few centuries, was able to catch up with the West. (Of course, political disunity in the West played a role, but that was far from being the whole story. In the fourth century, China was less united than the West, but nevertheless was developing rapidly in cultural matters.) During the succeeding centuries, while progress in the West was comparatively slow the Chinese brought forth such major inventions as the compass, gunpowder, and block printing. Since paper was cheaper than parchment, and available in larger quantities, the tables were now turned.

After Western nations began using paper, they were able to hold their own vis-à-vis China, and even succeeded in narrowing the cultural gap. The writings of Marco Polo, however, confirm the fact that even in the thirteenth century, China was far more prosperous than Europe.

Why, then, did China eventually fall behind the West? Various complex cultural explanations have been offered, but perhaps a simple technological one will serve. In fifteenth-century Europe, a genius named Johann Gutenberg developed a technique for the mass production of books. Thereafter, European culture advanced rapidly. As China had no Gutenberg, the Chinese stayed with block printing, and their culture progressed relatively slowly.

If one accepts the foregoing analysis, one is forced to the

conclusion that Ts'ai Lun and Johann Gutenberg are two of the central figures in human history. Indeed, Ts'ai Lun stands out well above most other inventors for another reason. Most inventions are a product of their times, and would have come about even if the person who actually invented them had never lived. But such is clearly *not* the case with regard to paper. Europeans did not start to manufacture it until a thousand years after Ts'ai Lun, and then only because they had learned the process from the Arabs. For that matter, even after they had seen paper of Chinese manufacture, other Asian peoples were never able to discover how to manufacture it by themselves. Clearly, the invention of a method of manufacturing true paper was suffi-

ciently difficult that it was not bound to occur in any moderately advanced culture, but rather required the explicit contribution of some very gifted individual. Ts'ai Lun was such an individual, and the method of papermaking that he employed is (aside from mechanization, introduced about 1800 A.D.) basically the same technique that has been used ever since.

These are the reasons I think it appropriate to place both Gutenberg and Ts'ai Lun among the first ten persons in this book, with Ts'ai Lun ahead of Gutenberg.

Cut bamboo is washed and steeped in a water pit to prepare material for making paper.

Digesting the bamboo pulp.

Making a sheet of paper.

Pressing the sheets of paper.

Drying the sheets of paper.

8

JOHANN

GUTENBERG

1 4 0 0 - 1 4 6 8

Johann Gutenberg is often called the inventor of printing. What he actually did was to develop the first method of utilizing movable type and the printing press in such a way that a large variety of written material could be printed with speed and accuracy.

No invention springs full-blown from the mind of a single man, and certainly printing did not. Seals and signet rings, which work on the same principle as block printing, had been used since ancient times. Block printing had been known in China many centuries before Gutenberg, and, in fact, a printed book dating from about 868 has been discovered there. The process was also known in the West before Gutenberg. Block printing makes possible the production of many copies of a given book. However, the process has one major drawback: since a completely new set of woodcuts or plates must be made for each new book, it is impractical for producing a large variety of books.

It is sometimes said that Gutenberg's main contribution was the invention of movable type. However, movable type was invented in China, some time in the middle of the eleventh century, by a man named Pi Sheng. His original type was made of earthenware, which is not very durable; however, other Chinese and Koreans made a series of improvements, and well before Gutenberg, Koreans were using metal type. In fact, the Korean government was supporting a foundry for the production of printing type in the early fifteenth century. Despite all this, it would be a mistake to think of Pi Sheng as a particularly influential person. In the first place, Europe did not learn of movable type from China, but developed it independently. In the second place, printing by means of movable type never came into general use in China itself until comparatively recent times, when modern printing procedures were learned from the West.

There are four essential components of modern printing methods. The first is movable type, along with some procedure for setting it and fixing it in position. The second is the printing press itself. The third is a suitable type of ink, and the last is a suitable material, such as paper, on which to print. Paper had been invented in China many years earlier (by Ts'ai Lun), and its use had spread to the West before Gutenberg's day. That was the only element of the printing process that Gutenberg found ready-made. Although some work had been done before him on each of the other three elements, Gutenberg made a variety of important improvements. For example, he developed a metal alloy suitable for type; a mold for casting blocks of type precisely and accurately; an oil-based printing ink; and a press suitable for printing.

But Gutenberg's overall contribution was far greater than any of his individual inventions or improvements. He is important principally because he combined all the elements of printing into an effective system of production. For printing, unlike all prior inventions, is essentially a process of mass production. A

single rifle is in itself a more effective weapon than a single bow
and arrow. A single printed book, however, is no different in its
effect from a single hand-written book. The advantage of printing therefore is mass production. What Gutenberg developed
was not a single gadget or device, or even a series of improvements, but a complete manufacturing process.

Our biographical information concerning Gutenberg is
scanty. We know that he was born about 1400, in the city of
Mainz, Germany. His contributions to the art of printing were
made in the middle of the century, and his best known work, the

Gutenberg and friends examine the first printed page.

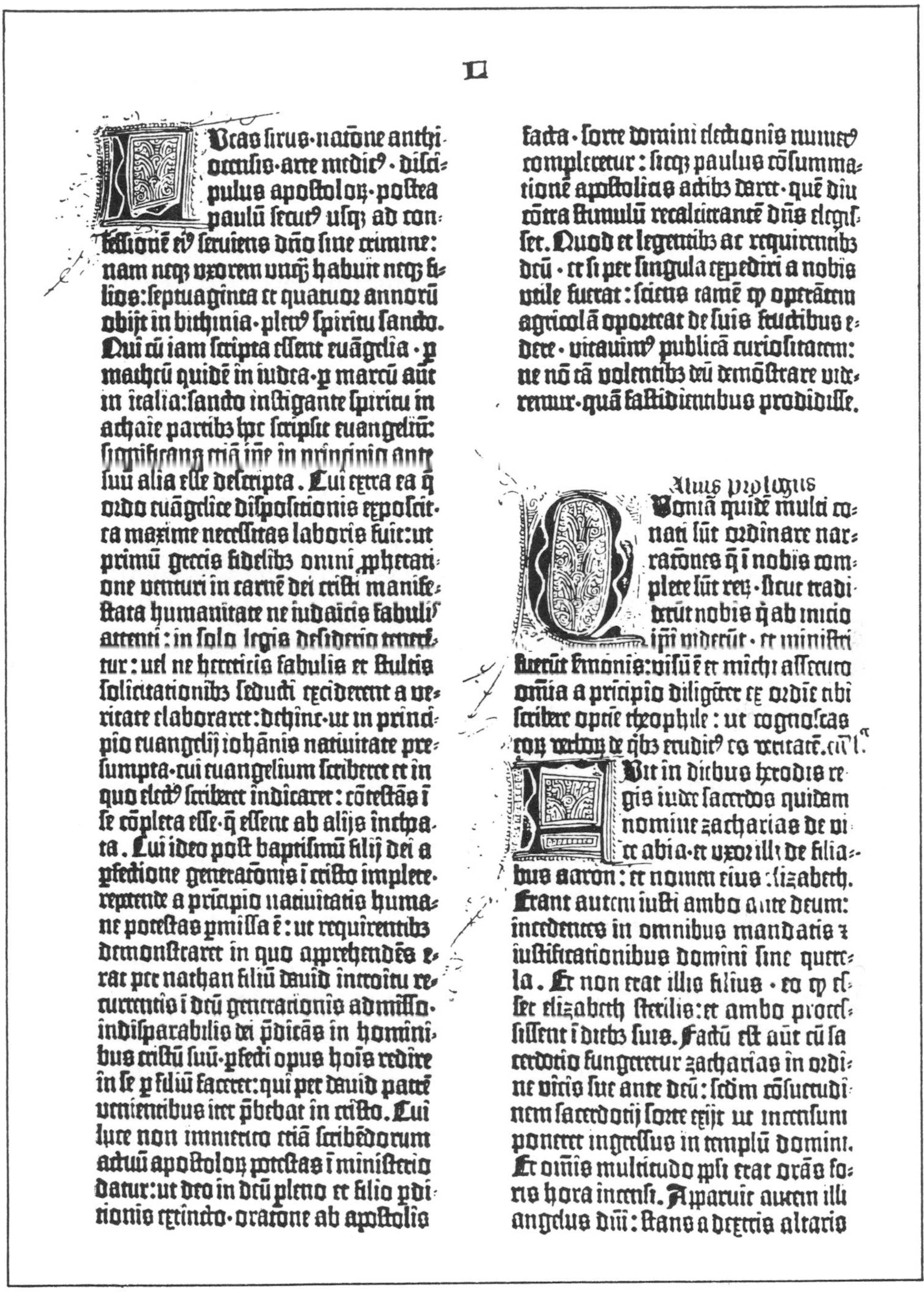

LI

Lucas sirus nacione anthi-
ocensis · arte medic⁹ · disci-
pulus apostoloꝝ · postea
paulū secut⁹ usq; ad con-
fessionē ei⁹ serviens dño sine crimine:
nam neq; uxorem unq̄ habuit neq; fi-
lios: septuaginta et quatuor annorū
obijt in bithinia · plen⁹ spiritu sancto.
Qui cū iam scripta essent euāgelia · p
matheū quidē in iudea · p marcū aūt
in italia: sancto instigante spiritu in
achaie partibꝫ hoc scripsit euangeliū:
significans etiā ipse in principio ante
suū alia esse descripta. Cui extra ea q̄
ordo euāgelice disposicionis exposcit ·
ea maxime necessitas laboris fuit: ut
primū grecis fidelibꝫ omni ꝓphetati-
one venturi in carnē dei cristi manife-
stata humanitate ne iudaicis fabulis
attenti: in solo legis desiderio tenere-
tur: uel ne hereticis fabulis et stultis
solicitationibꝫ seducti exciderent a ve-
ritate elaboraret: dehinc · ut in principio euangelij iohānis natiuitate pre-
sumpta · cui euangelium scriberet et in
quo elect⁹ scriberet indicaret: cōtestās i
se cōpleta esse · q̄ essent ab alijs incho-
ata. Cui ideo post baptismū filij dei a
pfectione generacōnis i cristo implete ·
repetende a principio natiuitatis humane potestas pmissa ē: ut requirentibꝫ
demonstraret in quo apprehendēs e-
rat per nathan filiū dauid introitu re-
currentis i deū generacionis admisso ·
indisparabilis dei p̄dicās in homini-
bus cristū suū · pfecti opus hoīs redire
in se p filiū faceret: qui per dauid patrē
venientibus iter p̄bebat in cristo. Cui
luce non immerito etiā scribēdorum
actuū apostoloꝝ potestas i ministerio
datur: ut deo in deū pleno et filio pdi-
tionis extincto · oracōne ab apostolis
facta · sorte domini electionis numer⁹
compleretur: sicq; paulus cōsumma-
tionē apostolicis actibꝫ daret · quē diu
cōtra stimulū recalcitrantē dñs elegis-
set. Quod et legentibꝫ ac requirentibꝫ
deū · et si per singula expediri a nobis
utile fuerat: sciens tamē q operantem
agricolā oporteat de suis fructibus e-
dere · vitauim⁹ publicā curiositatem:
ne nō tā volentibꝫ deū demōstrare vide-
remur · quā fastidientibus prodidisse.

Alius prologus

Quoniā quidē multi co-
nati sūt ordinare nar-
racōnes q̄ i nobis com-
plete sūt rerū · sicut tradi-
derūt nobis q̄ ab inicio
ipsi viderūt · et ministri
fuerūt sermonis: visū ē et michi assecuto
omnia a principio diligēter ex ordīe tibi
scribere optime theophile: ut cognoscas
eoꝝ verboꝝ de q̄bꝫ erudit⁹ es veritatē.

Fuit in diebus herodis re-
gis iudee sacerdos quidam
nomine zacharias de vi-
ce abia · et uxor illi de filia-
bus aaron: et nomen eius elizabeth.
Erant autem iusti ambo ante deum:
incedentes in omnibus mandatis et
iustificationibus domini sine quere-
la. Et non erat illis filius · eo q el-
set elizabeth sterilis: et ambo proces-
sissent i diebꝫ suis. Factū est aūt cū sa-
cerdocio fungeretur zacharias in ordi-
ne vicis sue ante deū: scdm cōsuetudi-
nem sacerdocij sorte exijt ut incensum
poneret ingressus in templū domini.
Et omnis multitudo pli erat orās fo-
ris hora incensi. Apparuit autem illi
angelus dñi: stans a dextris altaris

A page from an original Gutenberg Bible.

so-called Gutenberg Bible, was printed at Mainz, around 1454. (Curiously, Gutenberg's name does not actually appear on any of his books, not even on the Gutenberg Bible, although it was clearly printed with his equipment.) He does not appear to have been a particularly good businessman; certainly he never managed to make much money on his invention. He was involved in several lawsuits, one of which seems to have resulted in his forfeiting his equipment to his partner, Johann Fust. Gutenberg died in 1468, in Mainz.

Some idea of Gutenberg's impact on world history can be gained by comparing the subsequent development of China and Europe. At the time Gutenberg was born, the two regions were about equally advanced technologically. But after Gutenberg's invention of modern printing, Europe progressed very rapidly, while in China—where the use of block printing was continued until much later—progress was comparatively slow. It is probably an overstatement to say that the development of printing was the only factor causing this divergence; certainly, however, it was an important factor.

It is also worth noting that only three persons on this list lived during the five centuries preceding Gutenberg, whereas sixty-seven lived during the five centuries following his death. This suggests that Gutenberg's invention was a major factor— possibly even the crucial factor—in triggering the revolutionary developments of modern times.

It seems fairly certain that even had Alexander Graham Bell never lived, the telephone would still have been invented, and at about the same point in history. The same can be said of many other inventions. Without Gutenberg, though, the invention of modern printing might have been delayed for generations, and in view of the overwhelming impact of printing on subsequent history, Gutenberg assuredly deserves a high place on our list.

9
CHRISTOPHER COLUMBUS

1451-1506

Columbus, by attempting to find a westward route from Europe to the Orient, inadvertently discovered the Americas, and thereby had a greater influence on world history than he could possibly have anticipated. His discovery, which inaugurated the age of exploration and colonization in the New World, was one of the critical turning points in history. It opened to the people of Europe two new continents for the settlement of their expanding populations, and provided a source of mineral wealth and raw materials that altered the economy of Europe. His discovery led to the destruction of the civilizations of the American Indians. In the long run, it also led to the formation of a new set of nations in the western hemisphere, vastly different from the Indian nations which had once inhabited the region, and greatly affecting the nations of the Old World.

The main outlines of Columbus's story are well known. He was born in Genoa, Italy, in 1451. When he grew up, he became a ship's captain and a skilled navigator. He eventually became convinced that it was possible to find a practical route to East Asia by sailing due west across the Atlantic Ocean, and he pur-

"Columbus before Isabella," by Vacslav Brozik.

sued this idea with great tenacity. Eventually, he persuaded
Queen Isabella I of Castile to finance his voyage of exploration.

His ships left Spain on August 3, 1492. Their first stop was at
the Canary Islands, off the coast of Africa. They left the Canaries
on September 6 and sailed due west. It was a long voyage, and
his sailors became frightened and wished to turn back. Columbus, however, insisted upon continuing, and on October 12,
1492, land was sighted.

Columbus arrived back in Spain the following March, and
the triumphant explorer was received with the highest honors.
He made three subsequent voyages across the Atlantic in the vain
hope of making direct contact with China or Japan. Columbus
clung to the idea that he had found a route to East Asia long after
most other people realized that he had not.

Isabella had promised Columbus that he would become

governor of any lands which he discovered. However, he was so unsuccessful as an administrator that he was eventually relieved of his duties, and sent back to Spain in chains. There, he was promptly set free, but he was never again given an administrative postition. However, the common rumor that he died in poverty is without foundation. At the time of his death, in 1506, he was fairly wealthy.

It is obvious that Columbus's first trip had a revolutionary impact upon European history, and an even greater effect on the Americas. The one date that every schoolchild knows is 1492. Still, there are several possible objections to ranking Columbus so high upon this list.

One objection is that Columbus was not the first European to discover the New World. Leif Ericson, the Viking sailor, had reached America several centuries before him, and it is plausible that several other Europeans crossed the Atlantic in the interval between the Viking and Columbus. Historically, however, Leif Ericson is a relatively unimportant figure. Knowledge of his discoveries never became widespread, nor did they trigger any large changes in either Europe or America. News of Columbus's discoveries, on the other hand, spread very rapidly throughout Europe. Within a few years of his return, and as a direct consequence of his discoveries, many additional expeditions to the New World were made and the conquest and colonization of the new territories began.

Like other figures in this book, Columbus is vulnerable to the argument that what he did would have been accomplished even if he had never lived. Fifteenth-century Europe was already in a ferment: commerce was expanding, and exploration was inevitable. The Portuguese, in fact, had actively been searching for a new route to the Indies for a considerable time before Columbus.

It indeed seems probable that America would sooner or later have been discovered by the Europeans; it is even possible that the delay would not have been very great. But subsequent developments would have been quite different if America had

originally been discovered in 1510, say, by a French or English
expedition, instead of in 1492 by Columbus. In any event, Columbus was the man who actually *did* discover America.

The Nina, *the* Pinta, *and the* Santa Maria *sail to the New World.*

A third possible objection is that even before Columbus's
voyages, many fifteenth-century Europeans already knew that
the world was round. That theory had been suggested by Greek
philosophers many centuries earlier, and the firm endorsement of
the hypothesis by Aristotle was enough to cause its acceptance by
educated Europeans in the 1400s. However, Columbus is not
famous for showing that the earth was round. (As a matter of
fact, he didn't really succeed in doing that.) He is famous for

discovering the New World, and neither fifteenth-century Europeans nor Aristotle had had any knowledge of the existence of the American continents.

Columbus's character was not entirely admirable. He was exceptionally avaricious; in fact, one important reason that Columbus encountered difficulties in persuading Isabella to finance him was that he drove an extremely greedy bargain. Also, though it may not be fair to judge him by today's ethical standards, he treated the Indians with shocking cruelty. This is not, however, a list of the noblest characters in history, but rather of the most influential ones, and by that criterion Columbus deserves a place near the top of the list.

"The Landing of Columbus," by John Vanderlyn.

10 ALBERT EINSTEIN

1879-1955

Albert Einstein, the greatest scientist of the twentieth century and one of the supreme intellects of all time, is best known for his theory of relativity. There are actually two theories involved: the special theory of relativity, formulated in 1905, and the general theory of relativity, formulated in 1915, which might better be called Einstein's law of gravitation. Both theories are highly complicated, and no attempt will be made to explain them here; however, a few comments on special relativity are in order.

A familiar maxim has it that "everything is relative." Einstein's theory, however, is not a repetition of this philosophical platitude, but rather a precise mathematical statement of the way in which scientific measurements are relative. It is obvious that subjective perceptions of time and space depend on the observer. Before Einstein, however, most people had always believed that behind these subjective impressions were real distances and an absolute time, which accurate instruments could measure objectively. Einstein's theory revolutionized scientific thought by denying the existence of any absolute time. The following example may illustrate just how radically his theory revised our ideas of time and space.

Imagine a spaceship, spaceship X, moving away from Earth at a speed of 100,000 kilometers per second. The speed is measured by observers on both the spaceship and on Earth, and their measurements agree. Meanwhile, another spaceship, spaceship Y, is moving in exactly the same direction as spaceship X, but at a much greater speed. If observers on Earth measure the speed of spaceship Y, they find that it is moving away from the Earth at a speed of 180,000 kilometers per second. Observers on spaceship Y will reach the same conclusion.

Now, as both spaceships are moving in the same direction, it would seem that the difference in their speeds is 80,000 kilometers per second, and that the faster ship must be moving away from the slower ship at this rate.

However, Einstein's theory predicts that when observations are taken from the two spaceships, observers on both ships will agree that the distance between them is increasing at the rate of 100,000 kilometers per second, not 80,000 kilometers per second.

Now, on the face of it such a result is ridiculous, and the reader may suspect that some trick of wording is involved, or that some significant details of the problem have not been mentioned. Not at all. The result has nothing to do with the details of construction of the spaceships or with the forces used to propel them. Nor is it due to any errors of observation, nor to any defects in the measuring instruments. No trick is involved. According to Einstein, the foregoing result (which can readily be computed from his formula for the composition of velocities) is a consequence only of the basic nature of time and space.

Now, all of this may seem awfully theoretical, and indeed for years many persons dismissed the theory of relativity as a sort of "ivory tower" hypothesis, which had no practical significance. No one, of course, has made that mistake since 1945, when atomic bombs were dropped on Hiroshima and Nagasaki. One of the conclusions of Einstein's theory of relativity is that matter and energy are in a certain sense equivalent, and the relation between them is given by the formula $E = Mc^2$ in which E represents energy, M equals mass, and c represents the speed of light. Now since c, which is equal to 186,000 miles per second, is a very large number, c^2 (that is, c times c) is a simply enormous number. It follows that even the partial conversion of a small amount of matter will release tremendous quantities of energy.

One cannot, of course, build an atomic bomb or a nuclear power plant simply from the formula $E = Mc^2$. It must be borne in mind, too, that many other persons played important roles in the development of atomic energy; however, the importance of Einstein's contribution is indisputable. Furthermore, it was Einstein's letter to President Roosevelt, in 1939, pointing out the possibility of developing atomic weapons and stressing the importance of the United States developing such weapons before the Germans did, which helped launch the Manhattan Project, and which led to the development of the first atomic bomb.

Special relativity aroused heated controversy, but on one point everyone was agreed; it was the most mind-boggling scientific theory that would ever be invented. But everyone was wrong, for Einstein's general theory of relativity takes as a starting point the premise that gravitational effects are not due to physical forces in the normal sense of the word, but rather result from a curvature of space itself—a truly astonishing idea!

How can one measure a curvature of space itself? What does it even *mean* to say that space is curved? Einstein had not only advanced such a theory, but he had put his theory in a clear mathematical form, from which explicit predictions could be made and his hypothesis tested. Subsequent observations—the most celebrated of which are those made during total eclipses of the sun—have repeatedly confirmed the correctness of Einstein's equations.

The general theory of relativity stands apart in several ways from all other scientific laws. In the first place, Einstein derived his theory not on the basis of careful experiments, but rather on grounds of symmetry and mathematical elegance—on rationalistic grounds, as the Greek philosophers and the medieval scholastics had attempted to do. (In so doing, he ran counter to the basically empirical outlook of modern science.) But whereas the Greeks, in their search for beauty and symmetry, had never managed to find a mechanical theory that could survive the crucial test of experiment, Einstein's theory has so far successfully withstood every test. One result of Einstein's approach is that the general theory of relativity is generally acknowledged to be the most beautiful, elegant, powerful, and intellectually satisfying of all scientific theories.

General relativity stands apart in another way also. Most other scientific laws are only approximately valid. They hold in many circumstances, but not in all. So far as we know, however, there are no exceptions at all to the general theory of relativity. There is no known circumstance, either theoretical or experimental, in which the predictions of general relativity are only approximately valid. Future experiments may mar the theory's perfect record; but so far the general theory of relativity remains the closest approach to ultimate truth that any scientist has yet devised.

Though Einstein is best known for his theories of relativity, his other scientific achievements would have won him renown as a scientist in any case. In fact, Einstein was awarded the Nobel Prize in physics primarily for his paper explaining the photoelectric effect, an important phenomenon that had previously puzzled physicists. In that paper, he postulated the existence of

The atomic bomb explodes at Hiroshima, August 6, 1945.

photons, or particles of light. Since it had been long established through interference experiments that light consisted of electromagnetic waves, and since it was considered "obvious" that waves and particles were antithetical concepts, Einstein's hypothesis represented a radical and paradoxical break with classical theory. Not only did his photoelectric law turn out to have important practical applications, but his hypothesis of the photon had a major influence on the development of quantum theory, and is today an integral part of that theory.

In evaluating Einstein's importance, a comparison with Isaac Newton is revealing. Newton's theories were basically easy to understand, and his genius lay in being the first to develop them. Einstein's theories of relativity, on the other hand, are extremely difficult to understand, even when they are carefully explained. How much more difficult, therefore, to devise them originally! While some of Newton's ideas were in strong contradiction to the prevailing scientific ideas of his time, his theory never appeared to lack self-consistency. The theory of relativity, on the other hand, abounds with paradoxes. It was part of Einstein's genius that at the beginning, when his ideas were still the untested hypothesis of an unknown teenager, he did not let these apparent contradictions cause him to discard his theories. Rather, he carefully thought them through until he could show that these contradictions were apparent only, and that in each case there was a subtle but correct way of resolving the paradox.

Today, we think of Einstein's theory as being basically more "correct" than Newton's. Why, then, is Einstein lower on this list? Primarily because it was Newton's theories that laid the groundwork for modern science and technology. Most of modern technology would be the same today had only Newton's work been done, and not Einstein's.

There is another factor which affects Einstein's place on this list. In most cases, many men have contributed to the development of an important idea, as was obviously the case in the history of socialism, or in the development of the theory of electricity and magnetism. Though Einstein does not deserve 100 percent of the credit for the invention of the theory of relativity, he certainly deserves most of it. It seems fair to say that, to a larger degree than is the case for any other ideas of comparable importance, the theories of relativity are primarily the creation of a single, outstanding genius.

Einstein was born in 1879, in the city of Ulm, Germany. He attended high school in Switzerland, and became a Swiss citizen in the year 1900. He received his Ph.D. in 1905 from the University of Zurich, but was unable to find an academic position at that time. However, that same year, he published his papers on special relativity, on the photoelectric effect, and on the theory of Brownian motion. Within a few years, these papers, particularly the one on relativity, established his reputation as one of the most brilliant and original scientists in the world. His theories were highly controversial; no modern scientist except Darwin has ever engendered as much controversy as Einstein. In spite of this, in 1913 he was appointed a professor at the University of Berlin, at the same time becoming director of the Kaiser Wilheim Institute of Physics and a member of the Prussian Academy of Science. These posts left him free to devote his full time to research, if he so chose.

The German government had little reason to regret offering Einstein this unusually generous package, for just two years later he succeeded in formulating the general theory of relativity, and in 1921 he was awarded the Nobel Prize. For the last half of his life, Einstein was world-famous, in all probability the most famous scientist that ever lived.

Since Einstein was Jewish, his situation in Germany became precarious when Hitler rose to power. In 1933, he moved to Princeton, New Jersey, to work at the Institute for Advanced Study, and in 1940 he became a United States citizen. Einstein's first marriage ended in divorce; his second was apparently happy. He had two children, both boys. He died in 1955, in Princeton.

Einstein was always interested in the human world about him, and frequently expressed his views on political matters. He was a consistent opponent of political tyranny, an ardent pacifist, and a firm supporter of Zionism. In matters of dress and social conventions, he was a marked individualist. He had a fine sense of humor, a becoming modesty, and some talent as a violinist. The inscription on Newton's tomb might be applied even more appropriately to Einstein: "Let mortals rejoice that so great an ornament to the human race has existed!"

Einstein discusses his theories.

11 LOUIS PASTEUR

1822 - 1895

The French chemist and biologist Louis Pasteur is generally acknowledged to be the most important single figure in the history of medicine. Pasteur made many contributions to science, but he is most famous for his advocacy of the germ theory of disease and for his development of the technique of preventive inoculation.

Pasteur was born in 1822, in the town of Dôle, in eastern France. As a college student in Paris, he studied science. His genius was not evident during his student days; in fact, one of his professors recorded him as "mediocre" in chemistry. However, after receiving his doctorate in 1847, Pasteur soon showed that his professor's judgment had been in error. His research on the mirror-image isomers of tartaric acid made Pasteur a renowned chemist when he was only twenty-six years old.

He then turned his attention to the study of fermentation, and showed that that process is due to the action of certain types of microorganisms. He also demonstrated that the presence of certain other species of microorganisms could produce undesirable products in the fermenting beverages. This soon led him to the idea that some species of microorganisms could produce undesirable products and effects in human beings and other animals.

Pasteur was not the first person to suggest the germ theory of disease. Similar hypotheses had been advanced earlier by Girolamo Fracastoro, Friedrich Henle, and others. But it was Pasteur's vigorous championship of the germ theory, substantiated by his numerous experiments and demonstrations, that were the principle factor in convincing the scientific community that the theory was correct.

If diseases were caused by germs, it seemed logical that by preventing harmful germs from entering the human body, diseases might be avoided. Pasteur therefore stressed the importance of antiseptic methods for physicians, and he was a major influence on Joseph Lister who introduced antiseptic methods into surgical practice.

Harmful bacteria can enter the human body through food and beverages. Pasteur developed a technique (called *pasteurization*) for destroying microorganisms in beverages. That technique, where practiced, has all but eradicated contaminated milk as a source of infection.

When he was in his mid-fifties, Pasteur turned his attention to the study of anthrax, a serious infectious disease which attacks cattle and many other animals, including human beings. Pasteur was able to show that a particular species of bacterium was responsible for the disease. Of far greater importance, however, was his development of a technique for producing a weakened strain of the anthrax bacillus. Injected into cattle, this weakened strain produced a mild form of the disease, which was not fatal but which enabled the cattle to develop an immunity to the normal form of the disease. Pasteur's public demonstration of the effectiveness of his technique in immunizing cattle against anthrax aroused great excitement. It was soon realized that his general method might be applied to the prevention of many other communicable diseases.

Pasteur himself, in his most renowned single achievement, developed a technique for inoculating people against the dreaded disease of rabies. Other scientists, applying Pasteur's basic ideas, have since developed vaccines against many other serious diseases, such as epidemic typhus and poliomyelitis.

Pasteur in his laboratory.

Pasteur, who was an unusually hard worker, has a variety of lesser but still useful achievements to his credit. It was his experiments, more than any others, which convincingly demonstrated that microorganisms do not arise through spontaneous generation. Pasteur also discovered the phenomenon of anaerobiosis; i.e., that certain microorganisms can live in the absence of any air or free oxygen. Pasteur's work on diseases of silkworms has been of great commercial value. Among his other achievements was the development of a vaccine for the prevention of chicken cholera, a disease that attacks fowl. Pasteur died in 1895, near Paris.

A comparison is often made between Pasteur and Edward Jenner, the English physician who developed a vaccine against smallpox. Though Jenner's work was done more than eighty years before Pasteur's, I consider Jenner much less important because his method of immunization worked for only one disease, whereas Pasteur's methods could be—and have been—applied to the prevention of a large number of diseases.

Since the mid-nineteenth century, life expectancies in much of the world have roughly doubled. This enormous increase in human life spans has probably had a greater effect on the lives of individual human beings than has any other development in the entire history of the human race. In effect, modern science and medicine have presented each of us now living with virtually a second lifetime. If this increase in longevity could be solely attributed to the work of Pasteur, I would have had no hesitation at all in placing him first in this book. Nevertheless, Pasteur's contributions are so fundamental that there is no question that he deserves the largest share of the credit for the decline in death rates that has occurred in the last century, and that he is therefore assigned a high place on this list.

12

GALILEO
GALILEI

1 5 6 4 - 1 6 4 2

Galileo Galilei, the great Italian scientist who was probably more responsible for the development of the scientific method than any other individual, was born in 1564, in the city of Pisa. As a young man, he studied at the University of Pisa, but dropped out for financial reasons. Nevertheless, he was able, in 1589, to obtain a teaching position at that university. A few years later, he joined the faculty of the University of Padua and remained there until 1610. It was during this period that the bulk of his scientific discoveries were made.

Galileo's first important contributions were made in mechanics. Aristotle had taught that heavy objects fall at a more rapid rate than light objects, and generations of scholars had accepted this assertion on the Greek philosopher's authority. Galileo, however, decided to test it, and through a series of experiments, he soon found that Aristotle had been incorrect. The fact is that heavy and light objects fall at the same velocity except

64

to the extent that they are retarded by the friction of the air. (Incidently, the tradition that Galileo performed these experiments by dropping objects from the Leaning Tower of Pisa seems to be without foundation.)

Having learned this, Galileo took the next step. He carefully measured the distance that objects fall in a given period of time and found that the distance traversed by a falling object is proportional to the square of the number of seconds it has been falling. This discovery (which implies a uniform rate of acceleration) is significant in itself. Even more important, Galileo was able to summarize the results of a series of experiments by a mathematical formula. The extensive use of mathematical formulas and mathematical methods is an important characteristic of modern science.

Another of Galileo's major contributions was his discovery of the law of inertia. Previously, people had believed that a moving object would naturally tend to slow down and stop unless some force were exerted to keep it moving. But Galileo's experiments indicated that the common belief was erroneous. If retarding forces, such as friction, could be eliminated, a moving object would naturally tend to continue moving indefinitely. This important principle, which Newton restated clearly and incorporated into his own system as the first law of motion, is one of the vital principles of physics.

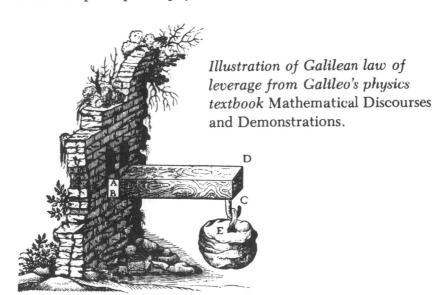

Illustration of Galilean law of leverage from Galileo's physics textbook Mathematical Discourses and Demonstrations.

Galileo's telescope.

Galileo's most celebrated discoveries were in the field of astronomy. Astronomical theory in the early 1600s was in a state of great ferment, with an important dispute going on between the followers of the heliocentric theory of Copernicus and the adherents of the earlier geocentric theory. As early as 1604, Galileo had announced his belief that Copernicus was correct, but at that time he had no method of proving it. In 1609, however, Galileo heard of the invention of the telescope in Holland. Although he had only the barest description of the device, Galileo's genius was such that he was soon able to construct a vastly superior telescope himself. With this new tool, he turned his observational talents to the heavens, and in a single year made a whole series of major discoveries.

He looked at the moon and saw that it was not a smooth sphere, but had numerous craters and high mountains on it. Celestial objects, he concluded, were not smooth and perfect after all, but had the same sort of irregularities that one observed on earth. He looked at the Milky Way and saw that it was not a milky, nebulous body after all, but was composed of an enormous number of individual stars, which were so far away that the naked eye tended to blur them together. He looked at the planets and saw that four moons revolved around Jupiter. Here was clear evidence that an astronomical body could revolve about a planet other than Earth. He looked at the sun and observed sunspots. (Actually, other persons had observed sunspots before him, but Galileo publicized his observations more effectively and brought sunspots to the attention of the scientific world.) He observed that the planet Venus had phases quite similar to the phases of the moon. This became a significant piece of evidence corroborating the Copernican theory that the earth and all the other planets revolve around the sun.

The invention of the telescope and the series of discoveries that resulted from it made Galileo famous. However, by supporting the theory of Copernicus he aroused opposition in important Church circles, and in 1616 he was ordered to refrain from teaching the Copernican hypothesis. Galileo chafed under this restriction for several years. When the Pope died, in 1623, he was succeeded by a man who had been an admirer of Galileo. The following year the new Pope, Urban VIII, hinted (though somewhat ambiguously) that the prohibition would no longer be in force.

Galileo spent the next six years composing his most famous work, the *Dialogue Concerning the Two Chief World Systems.* This book was a masterly exposition of the evidence in favor of the Copernican theory, and the book was published in 1632 *with* the imprimatur of the Church censors. Nevertheless, Church authorities responded in anger when the book appeared, and Galileo was soon brought to trial before the Inquisition in Rome on charges of having violated the 1616 prohibition.

It seems clear that many churchmen were unhappy with the decision to prosecute the eminent scientist. Even under the Church law of the time, the case against Galileo was questionable, and he was given a comparatively light sentence. He was not, in fact, confined to jail at all, but merely to house arrest in his own comfortable villa in Arcetri. Theoretically, he was to have no visitors, but that provision of the sentence was not enforced. His only other punishment was the requirement that he publicly recant his view that the earth moved around the sun. This the sixty-nine-year-old scientist did in open court. (There is a famous and probably apocryphal story that after he finished making his retraction, Galileo looked down to the earth and whispered softly, "It still moves.") In Arcetri he continued to write on mechanics. He died there, in 1642.

Galileo's enormous contribution to the advancement of science has long been recognized. His importance rests in part on his scientific discoveries such as the law of inertia, his invention of the telescope, his astronomical observations, and his genius in proving the Copernican hypothesis. Of greater importance,

The Leaning Tower of Pisa, from which Galileo supposedly demonstrated the laws of falling bodies.

however, is his role in the development of the methodology of science. Most previous natural philosophers, taking their cues from Aristotle, had made qualitative observations and categorized phenomena; but Galileo measured phenomena and made quantitative observations. This emphasis on careful quantitative measurements has since become a basic feature of scientific research.

Galileo is probably more responsible than any other man for the empirical attitude of scientific research. It was he who first insisted upon the necessity of performing experiments. He rejected the notion that scientific questions could be decided by reliance upon authority, whether it be the pronouncements of the Church or the assertions of Aristotle. He also rejected reliance on complex deductive schemes that were not based on a firm foundation of experiment. Medieval scholastics had discussed at great length what *should* happen and *why* things happen, but Galileo insisted upon performing experiments to determine what actually *did* happen. His scientific outlook was distinctly non-mystical; in this respect, he was even more modern than some of his successors, such as Newton.

Galileo, it might be noted, was a deeply religious man. Despite his trial and conviction, he did not reject either religion or the church, but only the attempt of Church authorities to stifle investigation of scientific matters. Later generations have quite rightly admired Galileo as a symbol of revolt against dogmatism, and against authoritarian attempts to stifle freedom of thought. Of greater importance, however, is the role he played in founding modern scientific method.

13

ARISTOTLE

3 8 4 B.C. - 3 2 2 B.C.

Aristotle was the greatest philosopher and scientist of the ancient world. He originated the study of formal logic, enriched almost every branch of philosophy, and made numerous contributions to science.

Many of Aristotle's ideas are outmoded today. But far more important than any of his individual theories is the rational approach underlying his work. Implicit in Aristotle's writings is the attitude that every aspect of human life and society may be an appropriate object of thought and analysis; the notion that the universe is not controlled by blind chance, by magic, or by the whims of capricious deities, but that its behavior is subject to rational laws; the belief that it is worthwhile for human beings to conduct a systematic inquiry into every aspect of the natural world; and the conviction that we should utilize both empirical observations and logical reasoning in forming our conclusions. This set of attitudes—which is contrary to traditionalism, superstition, and mysticism—has profoundly influenced Western civilization.

Aristotle was born in 384 B.C., in the town of Stagira, in Macedonia. His father was a prominent physician. At seventeen,

Aristotle went to Athens to study in the Academy of Plato. He remained there for twenty years, until shortly after Plato died. From his father, Aristotle may have gained an interest in biology and in "practical science"; under Plato he cultivated an interest in philosophical speculation.

In 342 B.C., Aristotle returned to Macedonia to become the private tutor of the king's son, a thirteen-year-old boy who was to become known to history as Alexander the Great. Aristotle tutored the young Alexander for several years. In 335 B.C., after Alexander had ascended the throne, Aristotle returned to Athens, where he opened his own school, the Lyceum. He spent the next twelve years in Athens, a period roughly coinciding with Alexander's career of military conquest. Alexander did not ask his former tutor for advice, but he did provide him generously with funds for research. This was probably the first example in history of a scientist receiving large-scale government funding for his research, and it was to be the last for centuries to come.

Nevertheless, association with Alexander had its dangers. Aristotle was opposed on principle to the dictatorial style of Alexander, and when the conqueror executed Aristotle's nephew on suspicion of treason, he seems to have considered executing Aristotle as well. But if Aristotle was too democratic for Alexander's tastes, he was too closely associated with Alexander to be trusted by the Athenians. When Alexander died, in 323 B.C., the anti-Macedonian faction gained control in Athens, and Aristotle was indicted for "impiety." Aristotle, recalling the fate of Socrates seventy-six years earlier, fled the city, saying that he would not give Athens a second chance to sin against philosophy. He died in exile a few months later, in 322 B.C., at the age of sixty-two.

The sheer quantity of Aristotle's output is astonishing. Forty-seven of his works have survived, and ancient lists credit him with no fewer than 170 books. However, it is not merely the number of his works, but the enormous range of his erudition, which is amazing. His scientific works constitute a virtual encyclopedia of the scientific knowledge of his day. Aristotle wrote

Portrait of Aristotle by Raphael, detail from "The School of Athens."

on astronomy, zoology, embryology, geography, geology, physics, anatomy, physiology, and almost every other field of learning known to the ancient Greeks. His scientific works represent, in part, a compilation of knowledge already aquired by others; in part, the findings of assistants whom he hired to acquire data for him; and in part, the results of his own numerous observations.

To be a leading expert in every field of science is an incredible feat, and one not likely to be duplicated by any man in the future. But Aristotle achieved even more than that. He was also an original philosopher, and made major contributions to every area of speculative philosophy. He wrote on ethics and on metaphysics, on psychology and on economics, on theology and on politics, on rhetoric and on aesthetics. He wrote on education, poetry, barbarian customs, and the constitution of the Athenians. One of his research projects was a collection of the constitutions of a large number of different states, which he subjected to a comparative study.

Perhaps most important of all was his work on the theory of logic, and Aristotle is generally considered the founder of this important branch of philosophy. It was indeed the logical nature of his mind that enabled Aristotle to make contributions to so many fields. He had a gift for organizing thought, and the definitions that he proposed and the categories that he established have provided the basis for later thought in many different fields. Never mystical and never an extremist, Aristotle is consistently the voice of practical common sense. He made mistakes, of course, but what is surprising is how few times in this vast encyclopedia of thought Aristotle made foolish errors.

Aristotle's influence upon all later Western thought has been immense. During ancient and medieval times, his works were translated into Latin, Syriac, Arabic, Italian, French, Hebrew, German, and English. The later Greek writers studied and admired his works, and so did Byzantine philosophers. His work was a major influence on Islamic philosophy, and for centuries his writings dominated European thought. Averroës, perhaps the most famous of all Arab philosophers, attempted to create a synthesis of Islamic theology and Aristotelian rationalism. Maimonides, the most influential of medieval Jewish thinkers, achieved a similar synthesis for Judaism. But the most celebrated such work was the great *Summa Theologica* of the Christian scholar, St. Thomas Aquinas. Far too many medieval scholars were deeply influenced by Aristotle to list them all.

Admiration for Aristotle became so great that in late

medieval times it approached idolatry, and his writings became a kind of intellectual straight jacket inhibiting further inquiry, rather than a lamp to light the way. Aristotle, who liked to observe and think for himself, would doubtless have disapproved of the blind adulation that later generations gave to his writings.

Some of Aristotle's ideas seem extremely reactionary by today's standards. For example, he supported slavery as being in accord with natural law, and he believed in the natural inferiority of women. (Both of these ideas, of course, reflected the prevailing views of his time.) However, many of Aristotle's views are strikingly modern, e.g., "Poverty is the parent of revolution and crime," and "All who have meditated on the art of governing mankind are convinced that the fate of empires depends on the education of youth." (There was, of course, no public education at the time that Aristotle lived.)

In recent centuries, Aristotle's influence and reputation have declined considerably. Nevertheless, I feel that his influence was so pervasive, and lasted for so long, that I rather regret that I cannot place him higher on this list. His present ranking is primarily a consequence of the enormous importance of each of the twelve persons preceding him.

Aristotle and his pupil, Alexander.

14   E U C L I D   *fl. c.* 300 B.C.

Few persons on this list have earned such enduring fame as the great Greek geometer, Euclid. Although in their lifetimes such figures as Napoleon, Alexander the Great, and Martin Luther were much better known than Euclid, in the long run his fame will probably well outlast theirs.

Despite his reknown, almost none of the details of Euclid's life are known. We do know that he was active as a teacher in Alexandria, Egypt, in about 300 B.C. However, his dates of birth and death are uncertain, and we do not even know on which continent he was born, much less in which city. Although he wrote several other books, some of which survive, his place in history rests primarily upon his great textbook of geometry, the *Elements*.

The importance of the *Elements* does not lie in any one of the individual theorems it demonstrates. Almost all of the theorems in the book had been known before Euclid, and a good many of the proofs as well. Euclid's great contribution was his arrangement of the material, and his formulation of the overall plan of the book. This involved, in the first place, the selection of a suitable set of axioms and postulates. (This was a very difficult task, requiring extraordinary judgment and great insight.) He then carefully arranged the theorems so that each followed logically from its predecessors. Where necessary, he supplied missing steps and developed missing proofs. It is worth noting that the *Elements*, while primarily a development of plane and solid geometry, also contains large sections on algebra and number theory.

The *Elements* has been used as a textbook for more than two thousand years, and is unquestionably the most successful textbook ever written. So superbly did Euclid do his work, that with the appearance of his book all prior geometry textbooks were superseded and promptly forgotten. Originally written in Greek, the *Elements* has since been translated into many other languages. The first printed edition appeared as early as 1482, only about thirty years after Gutenberg's invention of printing. Since then, over a *thousand* different editions have been published.

As an agent for training men's minds in the nature of logical reasoning, the *Elements* has been far more influential than any of Aristotle's treatises on logic. It is the outstanding example of a complete deductive structure, and as such has fascinated thinkers ever since its creation.

It is fair to say that Euclid's book was a major factor in the rise of modern science. Science is more than just a collection of accurate observations and shrewd generalizations. The great achievements of modern science come from a combination of empiricism and experimentation on the one hand, and careful analysis and deductive reasoning on the other.

We are not certain just why science arose in Europe rather than in China or Japan, but it is safe to say that it was not merely by chance. Certainly, the roles played by such brilliant figures as Newton, Galileo, Copernicus, and Kepler were of tremendous importance. However, it seems likely that there were underlying reasons why men such as these flourished in Europe, rather than the Orient. Perhaps the most obvious historical factor predisposing western Europe to science was Greek rationalism, along with the mathematical knowledge that the Greeks had bequeathed.

To the Europeans, the idea that there were a few basic physical principles from which everything else could be deduced seemed quite natural, for they had the example of Euclid before them. (In general, Europeans did not consider the geometry of Euclid to be merely an abstract system. they believed that Euclid's postulates—and therefore his theorems—were actually true of the real world.)

All of the men just mentioned were steeped in the Euclidean tradition. Indeed, each of them had carefully studied the *Elements*, and it formed the basis of their mathematical knowledge. The influence of Euclid on Isaac Newton is particularly obvious, since Newton wrote his great book, the *Principia*, in a "geometric" form, similar to that of the *Elements*. Since then, many other Western scientists have emulated Euclid, by showing how their conclusions could all be logically derived from a small number of initial assumptions; so have many mathematicans, such as Bertrand Russell and Alfred North Whitehead; and philosophers, such as Spinoza.

The contrast with China is particularly striking. For centuries, its technology was more advanced than that of Europe. But there was never any Chinese mathematician corresponding to Euclid, and consequently the Chinese never possessed the theoretical structure of mathematics that the West did. (The Chinese had a good knowledge of practical geometry, but their geometric knowledge was never reformulated into a deductive scheme.) Euclid was not translated into Chinese until about 1600 A.D., and it took a few centuries for his conception of a deductive scheme of geometry to become widely known among educated Chinese. Until that happened, the Chinese did no serious work in science.

Similar statements might be made about Japan, where Euclid's work was unknown until the eighteenth century, and even then not appreciated for a good many years. Though there are many excellent scientists in Japan today, there were none there before Euclid became known. One cannot help wondering whether the Europeans would have been able to create modern science had Euclid not prepared the way!

Today, mathematicians have come to understand that Euclid's geometry is not the only self-consistent geometrical system which can be devised; and during the past 150 years many non-Euclidean geometries have been constructed. Indeed, since Einstein's general theory of relativity has been accepted, scientists have realized that Euclidean geometry does not always hold true in the real universe. In the vicinity of black holes and neutron stars, for example, where the gravitational fields are extremely intense, Euclid's geometry does not give an accurate picture of the world. However, these cases are rather special; in most cases Euclid's geometry provides a very close approximation of reality.

These recent advances in human knowledge, in any case, do not detract from Euclid's intellectual achievement. Nor do they detract from his historical importance in the development of mathematics and in the establishment of the logical framework necessary for the growth of modern science.

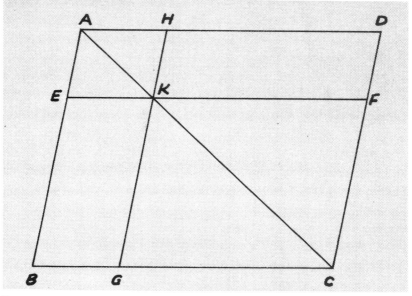

Diagram from a Euclidian geometric theorem.

15

MOSES

fl. 1 3 t h *c.* B.C.

Probably no person in history has been so widely admired as the great Hebrew prophet Moses. Furthermore, his fame, as well as the number of people who respect him, has steadily grown throughout the ages. It is most likely that Moses flourished in the thirteenth century B.C., since Ramses II, generally thought to be the pharaoh of the Exodus story, died in 1237 B.C. During Moses' lifetime, as the Book of Exodus makes clear, there were a fair number of Hebrews who disagreed with his policies. Within five centuries, however, Moses was revered by all the Jewish people. By 500 A.D., his fame and reputation had spread, along with Christianity, throughout much of Europe. A century later, Muhammad recognized Moses as a true prophet, and with the spread of Islam, Moses became an admired figure throughout the Moslem world (even in Egypt). Today, some thirty-two centuries after he lived, Moses is honored by Jews, Christians, and

Moslems alike, and is even respected by many agnostics. Thanks to modern communications, he is probably even better known today than he was in the past.

Despite his renown, reliable information concerning Moses' life is scarce. There has even been speculation (not accepted by most scholars) that Moses was an Egyptian, since his name is of Egyptian, rather than Hebrew, origin. (It means "child" or "son," and occurs as part of the name of several famous pharaohs.) The Old Testament stories concerning Moses can hardly be accepted at face value, since they involve a large number of miracles. The stories of the burning bush, or of Moses turning his staff into a serpent, for example, are basically miraculous in nature; and it does tax one's credulity, perhaps, to believe that Moses, who was already eighty years old at the time of the Exodus, still managed to lead the Hebrews in a forty-year trip through the desert. Surely, we would like to know exactly what the real Moses accomplished before his story was buried in an avalanche of legends.

Many persons have tried to give natural interpretations to the Biblical stories of the ten plagues and the crossing of the Red Sea. However, most of the favorite Old Testament stories concerning Moses are legendary, with analogues in other mythologies. The story of Moses and the bulrushes, for instance, is strikingly similar to a Babylonian story concerning Sargon of Akkad, a great king who reigned about 2360-2305 B.C.

In general, there are three major achievements attributed to Moses. First, he is credited with being the political figure who led the Hebrews in the Exodus from Egypt. On this point, at least, it is clear that he deserves credit. Second, he is the reputed author of the first five books of the Bible (Genesis, Exodus, Leviticus, Numbers, and Deuteronomy), which are often referred to as the "Five Books of Moses," and which constitute the Jewish *Torah*. These books include the Mosaic Code, the set of laws which in principle governed the conduct of the Jews in biblical times, and which include the Ten Commandments. In view of the enormous influence which the *Torah* as a whole and the Ten Commandments in particular have had, their author would surely deserve to be considered a man of great and enduring influence. However, most biblical scholars agree that Moses was *not* the sole author of these books. The books were apparently written by several authors, and the great bulk of the material was not put into writing until considerably after Moses' death. It is possible that Moses played some role in codifying existing Hebrew customs, or even in originating Hebrew laws, but there is really no way of judging how great his role was.

Third, many people consider Moses to be the founder of Jewish monotheism. In one sense, there is no basis at all for such a claim. Our only source of information concerning Moses is the Old Testament; and the Old Testament explicitly and unambiguously credits Abraham with being the founder of monotheism. Nevertheless, it is quite clear that Jewish monotheism would have died out had it not been for Moses, and he unquestionably played the crucial role in its preservation and transmission. In this, of course, lies his greatest importance, since Christianity and Islam, the two largest religions in the world, are both derived from Jewish monotheism. The idea of one true God, which Moses believed in so passionately, has eventually spread through a large part of the world.

"Moses with the Ten Commandments,"
by Guido Reni.

16 CHARLES DARWIN

1809-1882

Charles Darwin, the originator of the theory of organic evolution by means of natural selection, was born in Shrewsbury, England, on February 12, 1809 (on exactly the same day that Abraham Lincoln was born). At sixteen, he entered the University of Edinburgh to study medicine; however, he found both medicine and anatomy dull subjects, and after a while transferred to Cambridge to study for the ministry. At Cambridge, he found such activities as riding and shooting far more agreeable than his studies. Nevertheless, he managed to impress one of his professors sufficiently to be recommended for the position of naturalist on the exploratory voyage of the *H.M.S. Beagle*. His father at first objected to Charles's accepting the appointment, feeling that such a trip would simply be a further excuse for the young man to delay settling down to serious work. Fortunately, the elder Darwin was persuaded to give his consent to the trip, for this was to prove one of the most rewarding ocean voyages in the history of Western science.

Darwin set sail on the *Beagle* in 1831, at the age of twenty-two. In the course of the next five years, the *Beagle* sailed around the world, skirting the coasts of South America at a leisurely pace, exploring the lonely Galapagos Islands, and visiting other islands of the Pacific, the Indian Ocean, and the South Atlantic. During the long course of the voyage, Darwin saw many natural wonders, visited primitive tribes, discovered large numbers of fossils, and observed an enormous number of plant and animal species. Furthermore, he took voluminous notes on everything that he observed. These notes provided the basis for almost all his later work; from them, he derived many of his principal ideas, as well as the immense wealth of evidence by which he made his theories prevail.

Darwin returned home in 1836, and over the next twenty years he published a series of books which established his reputation as one of the leading biologists in England. As early as 1837, Darwin became convinced that animal and plant species were not fixed, but had evolved over the course of geologic history. At that time, however, he had no idea what might be the cause of such evolution. In 1838, however, he read *An Essay on the Principle of Population* by Thomas Malthus, and that provided him with the vital clue to his notion of natural selection through competition for survival. But even after Darwin had formulated the principle of natural selection, he did not rush to present his ideas in print. He realized that his theory was bound to arouse a good deal of opposition, and he therefore spent a long time carefully assembling the evidence and marshalling the arguments in favor of his hypothesis.

He wrote an outline of his theory as early as 1842, and by 1844 was working on a full-length book. However, in June 1858, when Darwin was still adding to and revising his great work, he received a manuscript from Alfred Russel Wallace (a British naturalist who was at that time in the East Indies) outlining Wallace's own theory of evolution. In every essential point, Wallace's theory was the same as Darwin's! Wallace had developed his theory completely independently and had sent his manuscript to Darwin in order to obtain the opinion and comments of an established scientist before publishing it. It was an embarrassing situation, which could easily have developed into an unpleasant battle over priority. Instead, Wallace's paper and an outline of Darwin's book were presented as a joint paper before a scientific body the following month.

Oddly enough, that presentation did not arouse a great deal of attention. However, Darwin's book, *The Origin of Species*, published the following year, created a furor. In fact, it is probable that no scientific book ever published has been so widely and vigorously discussed, by scientist and layman alike, as *On The Origin of Species by Means of Natural Selection, or the Preservation of Favoured Races in the Struggle for Life*. The arguments were still going strong in 1871, when Darwin published *The Descent of Man, and Selection in Relation to Sex*. That book, which propounded the idea that man was descended from ape-like creatures, added still more fuel to the raging controversy.

Darwin himself took no part in the public debates on his theories. For one thing, he had been in bad health ever since the voyage of the *Beagle* (probably the result of a recurrent ailment, Chagas' disease, which he had contracted from insect bites in South America). Furthermore, the partisans of evolution possessed, in Thomas H. Huxley, a skilled debater and a vigorous defender of Darwin's theories. The large majority of scientists had accepted the basic correctness of Darwin's theories by the time he died, in 1882.

Darwin was not the originator of the idea of the evolution of species; quite a few persons had postulated that theory before him, including the French naturalist, Jean Lamarck, and Charles's own grandfather, Erasmus Darwin. But these hypotheses had never gained the acceptance of the scientific world, because their proponents were unable to give convincing explanations of the means by which evolution occurred. Darwin's great contribution was that he was able to present not only a mechanism—natural selection—by which evolution could occur, but also a large quantity of convincing evidence to support his hypothesis.

It is worth noting that Darwin's theory was formulated without any reliance on genetic theory—or indeed, any knowledge of it. In Darwin's day, no one knew anything about the way in which particular characteristics were passed on from one generation to the next. Although Gregor Mendel was working out the laws of heredity during the same years that Darwin was writing and publishing his epoch-making books, Mendel's work—which supplements Darwin's so perfectly—was almost totally ignored until the year 1900, by which time Darwin's theories were already well established. Thus, our modern understanding of evolution, which combines the laws of genetic inheritance with natural selection, is more complete than the theory proposed by Darwin.

Darwin's influence on human thought has been immense. In the purely scientific sense, of course, he revolutionized the entire subject of biology. Natural selection is a very broad principle indeed, and attempts have been made to apply it to many other fields, such as anthropology, sociology, political science, and economics.

Even more important, perhaps, than their scientific or sociological import, has been the impact of Darwin's theories upon religious thought. In Darwin's day, and for many years thereafter, many devout Christians believed that the acceptance of Darwin's theories would undermine belief in religion. Their fears were perhaps justified, although it is obvious that many other factors have played a role in the general decline of religious sentiment. (Darwin himself became an agnostic.)

Even on a secular level, Darwin's theory has caused a great change in the way that human beings think about their world. The human race as a whole no longer seems to occupy the central position in the natural scheme of things that it once did. We now have to regard ourselves as one species among many, and we recognize the possibility that we may one day be superseded. As a result of Darwin's work, the viewpoint of Heraclitus, that "there is nothing permanent except change" has gained much wider acceptance. The success of the theory of evolution as a general explanation of the origin of man has greatly strengthened belief in the ability of science to provide answers to all physical questions (although not, alas, to all human problems). The Darwinian terms "the struggle for existence" and "the survival of the fittest" have passed into our vocabulary.

It is obvious that Darwin's theories would have been expounded even had he never lived. In fact, in view of Wallace's work, this is perhaps more obviously true of Darwin than of any other person on this list. Still, it was Darwin's writings which revolutionized biology and anthropology, and which have so altered our view of man's place in the world.

Beagle Channel was named after Darwin's ship "The Beagle."

17 SHIH HUANG TI

259 B.C.-210 B.C.

The great Chinese emperor Shih Huang Ti, who ruled from 238-210 B.C, united China by force of arms and instituted a set of sweeping reforms. Those reforms have been a major factor in the cultural unity that China has maintained ever since.

Shih Huang Ti (also known as Ch'in Shih Huang Ti) was born in 259 B.C. and died in 210 B.C. To understand his importance, it is necessary to have some knowledge of the historical background of his times. He was born in the final years of the Chou dynasty, which had been founded about 1100 B.C. Centuries before his time, however, the Chou monarchs had ceased to be effective rulers, and China had become divided into a large number of feudal states.

The various feudal lords were constantly at war with one another, and gradually, several of the smaller rulers were eliminated. One of the most powerful of the warring states was Ch'in, in the western portion of the country. The Ch'in rulers had adopted the ideas of the Legalist school of Chinese philosophers as the basis of state policy. Confucius had suggested that men should be governed primarily by the moral example of a good ruler; but according to the Legalist philosophy, most men were not good enough to be ruled in that way and could only be controlled by a strict set of laws firmly and impartially enforced. Laws were made by the ruler and could be changed at his pleasure to further state policy.

Possibly because of their adoption of Legalist ideas, possibly because of their geographical position, or possibly because of the capability of the Ch'in rulers, that state had already become the most powerful of the Chinese states at the time that Cheng (the future Shih Huang Ti) was born. Nominally, Cheng ascended the throne in 246 B.C., at the age of thirteen, but, in fact, a regent governed until Cheng came of age in 238 B.C. The new monarch chose able generals and vigorously prosecuted the wars against the remaining feudal states. The last of these were conquered in 221 B.C., and he could now have declared himself Wang (king) of all China. To emphasize, however, the complete break he was making with the past, he chose a new title, and called himself *Shih Huang Ti*, which means "the first emperor."

Shih Huang Ti immediately began to institute a large number of important reforms. Determined to avoid the disunity which had destroyed the Chou monarchy, he decided to abolish the entire feudal system of government. The territory he ruled was re-apportioned into thirty-six provinces, each with a civilian governor appointed by the emperor. Shih Huang Ti decreed that the office of provincial governor was no longer to be hereditary. Indeed, the practice soon developed of shifting governors from one province to another after a few years, to avoid the possibility of an ambitous governor attaining a strong power base of his own. Each province also had its own military leader, appointed by the emperor and removable at his pleasure, and a third, centrally-appointed official to maintain the balance between the civil and military governors. An extensive system of good roads was constructed, connecting the capital city with the provinces, and insuring that the central army could be quickly dispatched to any province besieged by a local revolt. Shih Huang Ti also decreed that the surviving members of the old aristocracy would have to move to Hsien Yang, his own capital, where he could keep an eye on them.

But Shih Huang Ti was not content with merely political and military unity in China; he sought commercial unity as well. He instituted a unified set of weights and measures throughout the country; standardized the coinage, various implements, and the axle lengths of wagons; and supervised the construction of roads and canals. He also established a system of unified laws throughout China and standardized the written language.

The emperor's most famous (or perhaps infamous) act was the decree of 213 B.C, in which he ordered the burning of all the books in China. Exceptions were made for writings on such technical topics as agriculture and medicine, the historical records of the state of Ch'in, and the philosophical works of the Legalist writers. But the writings of all the other schools of philosophy—including the doctrines of Confucius—were to be destroyed. By this Draconian decree, probably the first example of large-scale censorship in all of history, Shih Huang Ti hoped to destroy the influence of rival philosophies, and particularly that of the Confucian school. However, he did order that copies of the prohibited books were to be kept in the imperial library, in the capital city.

Shih Huang Ti's foreign policy was equally vigorous. He made extensive conquests in the southern part of the country, and the regions that he annexed were eventually absorbed into China. In the North and West also, his armies were successful, but he could not permanently conquer the peoples living there.

However, to prevent them from making raids into China, Shih Huang Ti connected the various local walls already existing on China's northern frontiers into one gigantic wall, The Great Wall of China, which has endured to the present day. These construction projects, together with the series of foreign wars, necessitated high taxes, which made the emperor unpopular. Since rebellion against his iron rule was impossible, attempts were made to assassinate him. None of these attempts succeeded, however, and Shih Huang Ti died a natural death in the year 210 B.C.

The emperor was succeeded by his second son, who took the title *Erh Shih Huang Ti*. But Erh Shih Huang Ti lacked his father's ability, and revolts soon broke out. Within four years he was killed; the palace and the imperial library were burned; and the Ch'in dynasty was totally destroyed.

But the work that Shih Huang Ti had accomplished was not to be undone. The Chinese were glad that his tyrannical rule was ended, but few of them wanted to return to the anarchy of the preceding era. The next dynasty (the Han dynasty) continued the basic administrative system set up by Ch'in Shih Huang Ti. Indeed, for twenty-one centuries the Chinese Empire continued to be organized along the lines he had established. Although the harsh system of laws of the Ch'in were soon moderated by the Han emperors, and although the whole Legalist philosophy fell into disfavor and Confucianism became the official state philosophy, the cultural and political unification which Shih Huang Ti had created was not reversed.

The critical importance of Shih Huang Ti for China and for the world as a whole should now be apparent. Westerners have always been awed at the enormous size of China; however, throughout most of history China has not really been much more populous than Europe. The difference is that Europe has always been divided into many small states, while China has been united into a single large state. This difference seems to have resulted from political and social factors rather than geography: internal barriers, such as mountain ranges, are just as prominent in China as they are in Europe. Of course, the unity of China cannot be ascribed to the work of Shih Huang Ti alone. Various other persons—for example, Sui Wen Ti—have also played important roles, but there seems no doubt of Shih Huang Ti's central importance.

No discussion of Shih Huang Ti would be complete without mention of his brilliant and celebrated chief minister, Li Ssŭ. In fact, so important was the influence of Li Ssŭ on the emperor's policies, that it is difficult to know how to divide the credit between them for the great changes instituted. Rather than attempt that, I have assigned all the credit for their joint achievement to Shih Huang Ti. (After all, although Li Ssŭ offered advice, it was the emperor who had the final say.)

Shih Huang Ti, partly because of his burning of the books, has been vilified by most later Confucian writers. They denounce him as a tyrant, superstitious, malevolent, illegitimately born, and of mediocre ability. The Chinese Communists on the other hand, generally praise him as a progressive thinker. Western writers have occasionally compared Shih Huang Ti to Napoleon; however, it seems far more appropriate to compare him to Augustus Caesar, the founder of the Roman Empire. The empires that they established were of more or less the same size and population. However, the Roman Empire endured for a far shorter period, and the territory ruled by Augustus did not in the long run retain its unity, whereas the territory governed by Shih Huang Ti did, making him the more influential of the two.

18

AUGUSTUS

CAESAR

6 3 B.C.–1 4 A.D.

Augustus Caesar, the founder of the Roman Empire, is one of the great pivotal figures in history. He ended the civil wars that had disrupted the Roman Republic during the first century B.C., and he reorganized the Roman government so that internal peace and prosperity were maintained for two centuries.

Gaius Octavius (better known as Octavian; he did not receive the title "Augustus" until he was thirty-five years old) was born in 63 B.C. He was the grandnephew of Julius Caesar, who was the leading political figure of Rome during Octavian's youth. Julius Caesar, who had no legitimate sons of his own, liked the youth, and helped prepare him for a political career. However, when Caesar was assassinated in 44 B.C., Octavian was still only an eighteen-year-old student.

The death of Caesar set off a long and bitter struggle for power between various Roman military and political figures. At first, his rivals, who were all men of long experience in the rough arena of Roman politics, did not consider the youthful Octavian a serious threat. Indeed, the young man's only visible asset was that Julius Caesar had adopted him as his son. By making skillful use of this advantage, Octavian managed to win the support of some of Caesar's legions. Many of Caesar's troops, however, chose to support Mark Antony, who had been one of Caesar's closest associates. A series of battles over the next few years eliminated all the other contestants for power; by 36 B.C., Rome, and the many territories she had already conquered, were divided between Mark Antony, who controlled the eastern portion, and Octavian, who controlled the West. For a few years, there was an uneasy truce between them. During that time, Antony seems to have paid too much attention to his romance with Cleopatra, while Octavian steadily improved his position. War broke out between the two men in 32 B.C., and the issue was decided by the great naval battle at Actium (31 B.C.), which was won by Octavian's forces. The following year, the war ended with the complete triumph of Octavian, and Antony and Cleopatra both committed suicide.

Octavian had now achieved the same position of power that Julius Caesar had attained fifteen years earlier. Caesar had been assassinated, because it had been obvious that he intended to end republican government in Rome and set himself up as a monarch. But by 30 B.C., after many years of civil war and the obvious failure of republican government in Rome, most Romans were willing to accept a benevolent despot, as long as the pretense of democratic rule was continued.

Octavian, though he had been ruthless during his fight to the top, was surprisingly conciliatory once he was established in power. In 27 B.C., to soothe senatorial feelings, he announced that he was restoring the Republic, and he offered to resign all

ATLANTIC

OCEAN

BRITAIN

GAUL

Marseilles

SPAIN

Munda

ITALY

Rome

Naples

Actiur

MAURETANIA

Carthage

M E D I T E R R A N E A N

Syracuse

Roman territory at the death of Julius Caesar, 44 B.C.

Territory added during reign of Augustus Caesar

* Battles

*The Roman Empire
at the death
of Augustus.*

his government posts. In fact, however, he retained his position
as head of the provinces of Spain, Gaul, and Syria. Since the majority of Roman troops were in these three provinces, the actual
power was securely in his hands. The Senate voted him the
honorific title of Augustus, but he never assumed the title of
king. In theory, Rome was still a republic, and Augustus was no
more than *princeps* (first citizen). In actual practice, the grateful
and docile Senate appointed Augustus to whatever positions he
chose, and for the remainder of his life he was effectively a dictator. By the time he died, in 14 A.D., Rome had completed the
transition from republic to monarchy, and his adopted son succeeded him without difficulty.

Augustus stands out as perhaps the best example in history
of a capable, benevolent despot. He was a true statesman, whose
conciliatory policies did much to heal the deep divisions resulting
from the Roman civil wars.

Augustus ruled Rome for over forty years, and his policies
influenced the Empire for many years to come. Under him,
Roman armies completed the conquest of Spain, Switzerland,
Galatia (in Asia Minor), and a large portion of the Balkans. By
the end of his rule, the northern boundary of the Empire was not
much different from the Rhine-Danube line which was to be the
northern border for most of the next few centuries.

Augustus was an extraordinarily able administrator and
played a major role in building up a capable civil service. He
revised the tax structure and financial system of the Roman state;
he reorganized the Roman army; and he established a permanent
navy. He also organized a personal bodyguard, the Praetorian
Guard, which in future centuries was to play a great role in selecting and deposing emperors.

Under Augustus, an extensive network of excellent roads
was constructed throughout the Roman Empire; many public
buildings were erected in Rome itself; and the city was greatly
beautified. Temples were constructed, and Augustus encouraged
observance of and loyalty to the old Roman religion. Laws were
passed encouraging marriage and the raising of children.

From 30 B.C. on, Rome had internal peace under Augustus. The natural result was a greatly increased prosperity. This, in turn, led to a great flourishing of the arts, and the Augustan Age was the Golden Age of Roman literature. Rome's greatest poet, Virgil, lived during this period, as did many other writers, including Horace and Livy. Ovid incurred the displeasure of Augustus, and was banished from Rome.

Augustus had no sons, and a nephew and two grandsons died before him; he therefore adopted his stepson, Tiberius, and designated him his successor. But the dynasty (which later included the infamous rulers Caligula and Nero) soon became extinct. Nevertheless, the period of internal peace that commenced with Augustus, the so-called *Pax Romana*, was to endure for some two hundred years. During this extended period of peace and prosperity, Roman culture was suffused deeply into the territories that Augustus and other Roman leaders had conquered.

The Roman Empire is the most celebrated empire of antiquity, and rightly so. For Rome was both the culmination of ancient civilization and the principal conduit by which the ideas and cultural achievements of the peoples of the ancient world (Egyptians, Babylonians, Jews, Greeks, and others) have been transmitted to western Europe.

It is interesting to compare Augustus with his granduncle, Julius Caesar. Despite Augustus's good looks, intelligence, strength of character, and military successes, he lacked his predecessor's charisma. Julius excited the imagination of his contemporaries far more than August did, and he has remained more famous ever since. In their actual influence upon history, however, Augustus was by far the more important of the two.

It is also interesting to compare Augustus with Alexander the Great. Both started their careers when quite young. But Augustus had to overcome much tougher competition in order to reach the top. His military ability was not as exceptional as Alexander's, but it was certainly impressive, and his conquests were to prove much more enduring. That, in fact, is the greatest difference between the two men. Augustus carefully built for the future, and as a result, his long-term influence on human history has been considerably larger.

Augustus might also be compared with George Washington. Both of them played important (and somewhat analogous) roles in world history; but in view of the length of Augustus's rule, the success of his policies, and the importance of the Roman Empire in world history, I believe that Augustus should be ranked the higher of the two.

Statue of Augustus Caesar at the Vatican.

19
NICOLAUS COPERNICUS
1 4 7 3 - 1 5 4 3

The great Polish astronomer Nicolaus Copernicus (Polish name: Mikolaj Kopernik), was born in 1473, in the city of Torún, on the Vistula River, in Poland. He came from a well-to-do family. As a young man, Copernicus studied at the University of Cracow, where he became interested in astronomy. In his mid-twenties he went to Italy, where he studied law and medicine at the Universities of Bologna and Padua, and later received a doctorate in canon law from the University of Ferrara. Copernicus spent most of his adult life on the staff of the cathedral at Frauenburg (Polish: Frombork), where he was a canon. Copernicus was never a professional astronomer, and the great work which has made him famous was accomplished in his spare time.

During his stay in Italy, Copernicus had become acquainted with the idea of the Greek philosopher, Aristarchus of Samos (third century B.C.), that the earth and the other planets revolved about the sun. Copernicus became convinced of the correctness of this heliocentric hypothesis, and when he was about forty he began to circulate among his friends a short, handwritten manuscript setting forth in preliminary form his own ideas on the subject. Copernicus spent many years taking the observations and making the calculations that were necessary for the composition of his great book, *De revolutionibus orbium coelestium (On the Revolution of the Celestial Spheres)*, in which he describes his theory in detail, and sets forth the evidence for it.

In 1533, when he was sixty years old, Copernicus delivered a series of lectures in Rome, in which he presented the principal points of his theory, without incurring papal disapproval. However, it was not until he was in his late sixties that Copernicus finally decided to have his book published; and it was not until the day he died, May 24, 1543, that he received the first copy of his book from the printer.

In his book, Copernicus correctly stated that the earth rotates on its axis; that the moon revolves around the earth; and that the earth and the other planets all revolve about the sun. However, like his predecessors, he badly underestimated the scale of the solar system. Also, he was wrong in believing that the orbits consist of circles or of epicycles. Thus, his theory was not only complicated mathematically, but inexact as well. Nevertheless, his book promptly aroused great interest. It also motivated other astronomers, most notably the great Danish astronomer, Tycho Brahe, to make more accurate observations of planetary motions. It was from the observational data accumulated by Tycho that Johannes Kepler was finally able to deduce the correct laws of planetary motion.

Though Aristarchus of Samos had propounded the heliocentric hypothesis more than seventeen centuries before Copernicus, it is appropriate that Copernicus has received the bulk of the credit. Aristarchus had made an inspired guess, but had never

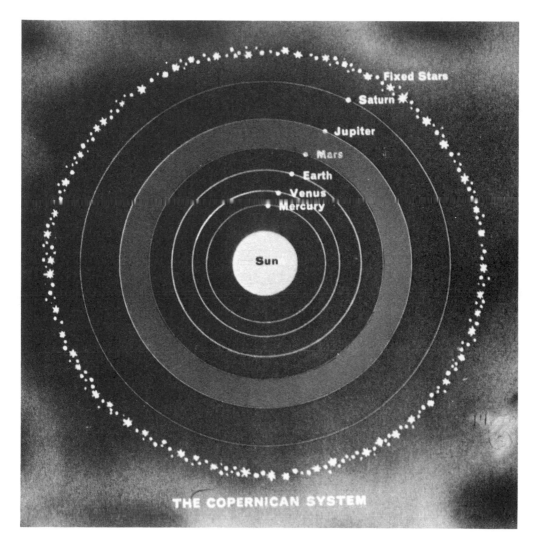

The Copernican system of the universe.

presented his theory in sufficient detail to make it scientifically useful. When Copernicus worked out the mathematics of the hypothesis in detail, he transformed it into a useful scientific theory—one that could be used for prediction, that could be checked against astronomical observations, and that could be meaningfully compared with the older theory that the earth was the center of the universe.

It is clear that the Copernican theory has revolutionized our conception of the universe, and has led to major changes in our whole philosophical outlook. But in evaluating the importance of Copernicus, it should be remembered that astronomy does not have the great range of practical applications that physics, chemistry, and biology do. In principle, one could construct such devices as a television set, an automobile, or a modern chemical factory without the slightest knowledge or application of Copernicus's theories. (One could not do so without applying the ideas of Faraday, Maxwell, Lavoisier, and Newton.)

But to consider only the *direct* influence on Copernicus on technology would be to completely miss his true significance. Copernicus's book was the indispensable prologue to the work of both Galileo and Kepler. They in turn were the major predecessors of Newton, and it was their discoveries which enabled Newton to formulate his laws of motion and gravitation. Historically, the publication of *De revolutionibus orbium coelestium* was the starting point of modern astronomy—and, more importantly, the starting point of modern science.

20

ANTOINE LAURENT LAVOISIER

1 7 4 3 - 1 7 9 4

The great French scientist Antoine Laurent Lavoisier was the most important figure in the development of chemistry. At the time of his birth, in Paris, in 1743, the science of chemistry lagged far behind physics, mathematics, and astronomy. Large numbers of individual facts had been discovered by chemists, but there was no adequate theoretical framework in which to fit these isolated bits of information. At that time, it was incorrectly believed that air and water were elementary substances. Worse still, there was a complete misunderstanding of the nature of fire. It was believed that all combustible materials contained a hypothetical substance called "phlogiston," and that during combustion the inflammable substance released its phlogiston into the air.

In the interval from 1754 to 1774, talented chemists such as Joseph Black, Joseph Priestley, Henry Cavendish, and others had isolated such important gases as oxygen, hydrogen, nitrogen, and carbon dioxide. However, since these men accepted the phlogiston theory, they were quite unable to understand the nature or significance of the chemical substances they had discovered. Oxygen, for example, was referred to as dephlogisticated air, i.e., air from which all the phlogiston had been removed. (It was known that a sliver of wood burned better in oxygen than in ordinary air; presumably, this was because dephlogisticated air could more readily absorb phlogiston from the burning wood.) Obviously, real progress in chemistry could not be made until the fundamentals were correctly understood.

It was Lavoisier who managed to put the pieces of the puzzle together correctly, and to get chemical theory started on the correct path. In the first place, Lavoisier said, the phlogiston theory is. completely incorrect: there is no such substance as phlogiston. The process of combustion consists of the chemical combination of the burning substance with oxygen. In the second place, water is not an elementary substance at all but a chemical compound of oxygen and hydrogen. Air is not an elementary substance either, but consists primarily of a mixture of the two gases, oxygen and nitrogen. All of these statements seem quite obvious today. However, they were not at all obvious to Lavoisier's predecessors and contemporaries. Even after Lavoisier formulated his theories and presented the evidence for them, many leading chemists refused to accept his ideas. But Lavoisier's excellent textbook, *Elements of Chemistry* (1789), so clearly presented his hypotheses, and so convincingly marshalled the evidence in their behalf, that the younger generation of chemists was quickly convinced.

Having shown that water and air were not chemical elements, Lavoisier included in his book a list of those substances that he did believe to be elementary. Although his list contains a few errors, a modern list of the chemical elements is basically an enlarged version of Lavoisier's table.

Lavoisier had already (in conjunction with Berthollet, Fourcroi, and Guyton de Morveau) devised the first well-organized system of chemical nomenclature. In Lavoisier's system (which forms the basis of the one used today), the composition of a chemical is described by its name. The adoption, for the first time, of a uniform system of nomenclature enabled chemists throughout the world to clearly communicate their discoveries to each other.

Lavoisier was the first person to clearly state the principle of conservation of mass in chemical reactions: A chemical reaction might *rearrange* the elements present in the original substances, but no matter is destroyed thereby, and the end products weigh the same as the original components. Lavoisier's insistence on the importance of carefully weighing the chemicals involved in a reaction helped turn chemistry into an exact science, and prepared the way for much of the subsequent progress in chemistry.

Lavoisier also made some minor contributions to the study of geology, and a major contribution in the field of physiology. By careful experiments (working in conjunction with Laplace), he was able to show that the physiological process of respiration is basically equivalent to a slow combustion. In other words, human beings and other animals derive their energy from a slow, internal burning of organic material, using the oxygen in the air they inhale. That discovery alone—which is perhaps comparable in significance to Harvey's discovery of the circulation of the blood—might well entitle Lavoisier to a place on this list. Still, Lavoisier is primarily important because his formulation of chemical theory started the science of chemistry firmly on the correct path. He is generally referred to as "the father of modern chemistry," and he richly deserves that title.

Like quite a few other persons on this list, Lavoisier studied law as a young man. Although he received a law degree and was admitted to the French bar, Lavoisier never practiced law. He did, though, engage in much administrative work and public service. He was active in the French Royal Academy of Sciences. He was also a member of the *Ferme Générale*, an organization involved in the collection of taxes. As a consequence, after the French Revolution in 1789, the Revolutionary government was very suspicious of him. Eventually, he was arrested, along with twenty-seven other members of the *Ferme Générale*. Revolutionary justice may not have been too accurate, but it was certainly speedy. On a single day (May 8, 1794), all of the twenty-eight persons were tried, convicted, and guillotined. Lavoisier was survived by his wife, a brilliant woman who had assisted him in his researches.

At the trial, an appeal was made to spare Lavoisier, citing his numerous services to his country and to science. The judge rejected the plea with the curt remark that, "The Republic has no need of geniuses." Somewhat closer to the truth was the remark of his colleague, the great mathematician Lagrange: "It took but a moment to sever that head, though a hundred years may not produce another like it."

Lavoisier in his laboratory at the Royal Arsenal.

21

CONSTANTINE THE GREAT

c. 280-337

Constantine the Great was the first Christian emperor of Rome. By his adoption of Christianity, and by his various policies encouraging its growth, he played a major role in transforming it from a persecuted sect into the dominant religion of Europe.

Constantine was born about 280, in the town of Naissus (present day Niš), in what is now Yugoslavia. His father was a high-ranking army officer, and Constantine spent his younger days in Nicomedia, where the court of the Emperor Diocletian was situated.

Diocletian abdicated in 305, and Constantine's father, Constantius, became the ruler of the western half of the Roman Empire. When Constantius died the following year, Constantine was proclaimed emperor by his troops. Other generals, however, disputed his claim, and a series of civil wars followed. These ended in 312 when Constantine defeated his remaining rival, Maxentius, at the Battle of the Milvian Bridge, near Rome.

Constantine was now the undisputed ruler of the western half of the Empire; however, another general, Licinius, ruled the eastern half. In 323, Constantine attacked and defeated Licinius also, and from then until his death in 337 was sole ruler of the Roman Empire.

It is uncertain just when Constantine became converted to Christianity. The most usual story is that on the eve of the Battle of the Milvian Bridge, Constantine saw a fiery cross in the sky, together with the words "By this sign shalt thou conquer." Regardless of how or when he was converted, Constantine became deeply dedicated to the advancement of Christianity. One of his early actions was the Edict of Milan, under which Christianity became a legal and tolerated religion. The Edict also provided for the return of Church property which had been confiscated during the preceding period of persecution, and it established Sunday as a day of worship.

The Edict of Milan was not motivated by general feelings of religious toleration. On the contrary, Constantine's reign may be said to mark the beginning of the official persecution of the Jews that was to persist in Christian Europe for so many centuries.

Constantine never established Christianity as the official state religion. However, by his legislation and other policies, he did much to encourage its growth. During his reign it became obvious that conversion to Christianity enhanced one's prospects for promotion to a high government position, and his decrees gave the Church various useful privileges and immunities. Also, construction of several of the world's most famous church buildings—such as the Church of the Nativity in Bethlehem, and the Church of the Holy Sepulchre in Jerusalem—was commenced during his reign.

Constantine's role as the first Christian emperor of Rome

would by itself entitle him to a place on this list. However, several of his other actions have also had far-reaching consequences. For one thing, he rebuilt and greatly expanded the old city of Byzantium, renamed it Constantinople, and made it his capital. Constantinople (which is today called Istanbul) was to become one of the great cities of the world; it remained the capital of the Eastern Roman Empire until 1453, and for centuries thereafter was the capital of the Ottoman Empire.

Constantine also played a significant role in the internal history of the Church. To deal with a dispute between the followers of Arius and Athanasius (two Christian theologians who had advanced conflicting doctrines), Constantine convoked the Council of Nicaea (in 325), the first general council of the Church. The council, in which Constantine took an active part, resolved the dispute by its adoption of the Nicene Creed, which became orthodox Church doctrine.

More important still was some of his civil legislation. Constantine introduced laws which made certain occupations (e.g., butchers, bakers) hereditary. He also issued a decree under which *coloni* (a class of tenant farmers) were forbidden to leave their land. In modern terms, this decree converted the *coloni* into serfs, permanently attached to the land. This and similar legislation helped to lay the foundations for the entire social structure of medieval Europe.

Constantine chose not to be baptized until he was on his deathbed, but it is clear that he had been converted to Christianity long before that. It is equally plain that the spiritual content of Christianity had eluded him completely. Even by the standards of the day, he was ruthless and cruel—and not merely to his enemies. For reasons that are unclear, he had his wife and his eldest son put to death in 326.

It might be argued that Constantine's adoption of Christianity did not really change the course of history, but merely ratified the inevitable. After all, although the Emperor Diocletian (who ruled 284-305) had conducted a vigorous persecution of Christianity, his attempt to suppress the religion was unsuccessful, for by that time Christianity was far too strong to be stamped out by even the fiercest measures. When one considers the failure of Diocletian's efforts to extirpate Christianity, one suspects that Christianity might eventually have triumphed even without Constantine's intervention.

Such speculations are interesting, but inconclusive. It is hard to be sure what might have happened without Constantine. It is quite plain, though, that *with* his encouragement, Christianity rapidly expanded in both numbers and influence. From the creed of a small minority it became, within a century, the predominant and established religion of the largest empire on earth.

Clearly, Constantine was one of the great pivotal figures of European history. He has been ranked higher than better known figures such as Alexander the Great, Napoleon, and Hitler because of the enduring influence of his policies.

"Constantine Fighting the Lion," from Constantine tapestry designed by Pietro Da Cortona.

22
JAMES
WATT

1736-1819

The Scottish inventor James Watt, the man who is often described as the inventor of the steam engine, was the key figure of the Industrial Revolution.

Actually, Watt was not the first man to build a steam engine. Similar devices were described by Hero of Alexandria in the 1st century. In 1698, Thomas Savery patented a steam engine that was used for pumping water, and in 1712 an Englishman, Thomas Newcomen, patented a somewhat improved version. Still, the Newcomen engine had such a low efficiency that it was useful only for pumping water out of coal mines.

Watt himself became interested in the steam engine in 1764, while repairing a model of Newcomen's device. Watt, although he had received only one year's training as an instrument maker, had great inventive talent. The improvements which he made upon Newcomen's invention were so important that it is fair to consider Watt the inventor of the first practical steam engine.

Watt's first great improvement, which he patented in 1769,

was the addition of a separate condensing chamber. He also insulated the steam cylinder, and in 1782 he invented the double-acting engine. Together with some smaller improvements, these innovations resulted in an increase in the efficiency of the steam engine by a factor of four or more. In practice, this increase of efficiency meant the difference between a clever but not really very useful device, and an instrument of enormous industrial utility.

Watt also invented (in 1781) a set of gears for converting the reciprocal motion of the engine into a rotary motion. This device greatly increased the number of uses to which steam engines could be put. Watt also invented a centrifugal governor (1788), by which the speed of the engine could be automatically controlled; a pressure gauge (1790); a counter; an indicator; and a throttle valve, in addition to various other improvements.

Watt himself did not have a good head for business. However, in 1775 he formed a partnership with Matthew Boulton, who was an engineer and a very capable businessman. Over the next twenty-five years, the firm of Watt and Boulton manufactured a large number of steam engines, and both partners became wealthy men.

It would be difficult to exaggerate the importance of the steam engine. True, there were many other inventions which played a role in the Industrial Revolution. There were developments in mining, in metallurgy, and in many sorts of industrial machinery. A few of the inventions, such as the fly shuttle (John Kay, 1733) or the spinning jenny (James Hargreaves, 1764) had even preceded Watt's work. The majority of the other inventions, however, represented small improvements, and no one of them alone was vital to the Industrial Revolution. It was quite different with the steam engine, which played an absolutely crucial role, and without which the Industrial Revolution would have been vastly different. Previously, although some use had been made of windmills and waterwheels, the main source of power had always been human muscles. This factor severely limited the productive capacity of industry. With the invention of the steam engine, however, this limitation was removed. Large quantities of energy were now available for production, which accordingly increased enormously. The oil embargo of 1973 made us aware of how severely a shortage of energy can

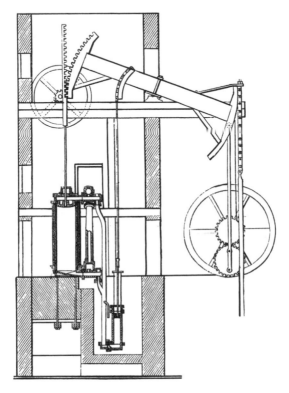

Watt's double-acting steam engine, 1769.

hamper an industrial system, and this experience might, in some slight degree, give us an idea of the importance to the Industrial Revolution of Watt's inventions.

Aside from its usefulness as a source of power for factories, the steam engine had many other important applications. By 1783, the Marquis de Jouffroy d'Abbans had successfully used a steam engine to power a boat. In 1804, Richard Trevithick built the first steam locomotive. Neither of those early models was commercially successful. Within a few decades, however, the steamboat and the railroad were to revolutionize both land and water transportation.

The Industrial Revolution occurred at about the same time in history as the American and French revolutions. Though it might not have seemed obvious at the time, today we can see that the Industrial Revolution was destined to have a far greater impact on the daily lives of human beings than either of those important political revolutions. James Watt, accordingly, has been one of the most influential persons in history.

Watt, as a boy, notices the condensation of steam.

23 MICHAEL FARADAY

1791-1867

This is the age of electricity. It is true that our era is sometimes called the space age and sometimes called the atomic age; however, space travel and atomic weapons, whatever their potential importance, have relatively little impact upon our everyday lives. But we use electrical devices constantly. In fact, it seems safe to say that no technological feature so completely permeates the modern world as does the use of electricity.

Many men have contributed to our mastery of electricity:

Charles Augustine de Coulomb, Count Alessandro Volta, Hans Christian Oersted, and André Marie Ampère are among the most important. But towering far above the others are two great British scientists, Michael Faraday and James Clerk Maxwell. Though the work of the two men was in part complementary, they were in no sense collaborators, and each man's individual achievements entitle him to a high place on this list.

Michael Faraday was born in 1791, in Newington, England. He came from a poor family and was largely self-educated. Apprenticed to a bookbinder and bookseller at the age of fourteen, he used the opportunity to read extensively. When he was twenty, he attended lectures given by the famous British scientist, Sir Humphry Davy, and was fascinated. He wrote to Davy, and eventually got a job as his assistant. Within a few years, Faraday was making important discoveries of his own. Although he lacked a good background in mathematics, as an experimental physicist he was unsurpassed.

Faraday's first important innovation in electricity was made in 1821. Two years earlier, Oersted had found that the needle of an ordinary magnetic compass would be deflected if an electric current flowed in a nearby wire. This suggested to Faraday that if the magnet were to be held fixed, the wire might move instead. Working on this hunch, he succeeded in constructing an ingenious device, in which a wire would rotate continuously in the vicinity of a magnet as long as an electric current flowed through the wire. In fact, what Faraday had invented was the first electric motor, the first device to use an electric current to make a material object move. Primitive as it was, Faraday's invention was the ancestor of all the electric motors in use in the world today.

This was a tremendous breakthrough. However, its practical usefulness was limited, as long as there was no method of generating electric currents other than the primitive chemical batteries of the day. Faraday was convinced that there must be some way of using magnetism to generate electricity, and he kept looking for such a method. Now, a stationary magnet will *not* induce an electric current in a nearby wire. But in 1831, Faraday discovered that if a magnet is passed through a closed loop of wire, a current will flow in the wire *while the magnet is moving*. This effect is called electromagnetic induction, and the discovery of the law governing it ("Faraday's law") is generally considered to be Faraday's greatest single achievement.

This was a monumental discovery, for two reasons. First, Faraday's law is of fundamental importance in our theoretical understanding of electromagnetism. Second, electromagnetic induction can be used to generate continuous electric currents, as Faraday himself demonstrated by building the first electric dynamo. Although the modern electric generators that supply power to our cities and factories are far more sophisticated than Faraday's device, they are all based on the same principle of electromagnetic induction.

Faraday also made contributions to the field of chemistry. He devised methods for liquefying gases, and he discovered various chemical substances, including benzene. Of greater importance is his work in electrochemistry (the study of chemical effects of electric currents). Faraday's careful experiments established the two laws of electrolysis which are named after him, and which form the foundations of electrochemistry. He also popularized much of the important terminology used in that field, such as anode, cathode, electrode, and ion.

It was Faraday who introduced into physics the important idea of magnetic lines of force and electric lines of force. By emphasizing not the magnets themselves but rather the *field* between them, he helped prepare the way for many advances in modern physics, including Maxwell's equations. Faraday also discovered that if polarized light is passed through a magnetic field, its polarization will be altered. This discovery is significant, because it was the first indication that there is a relationship between light and magnetism.

Faraday was not only brilliant, but also handsome, and he was a very popular lecturer on science. Nevertheless, he was modest and singularly indifferent to fame, money, and honors.

He declined a knighthood, and also declined an offer to become president of the British Royal Society. He had a long, happy marriage, but no children. He died in 1867, near London.

Faraday lectures at the Royal Institution on December 27, 1855.

24 JAMES CLERK MAXWELL

1 8 3 1 - 1 8 7 9

The great British physicist James Clerk Maxwell is best known for his formulation of the set of four equations that express the basic laws of electricity and magnetism.

Those two fields had been investigated extensively for many years before Maxwell, and it was well known that they were closely related. However, although various laws of electricity and magnetism had been discovered that were true in special circumstances, before Maxwell there was no overall, unified theory. In his set of four short (though highly sophisticated) equations, Maxwell was able to describe exactly the behavior and interaction of the electric and magnetic fields. By so doing, he transformed a confusing mass of phenomena into a single, comprehensive theory. Maxwell's equations have been employed extensively for the past century in both theoretical and applied science.

The great virtue of Maxwell's equations is that they are *general* equations, which hold under all circumstances. All the previously known laws of electricity and magnetism can be derived from Maxwell's equations, as well as a large number of other, previously unknown results.

The most important of these new results was deduced by Maxwell himself. From his equations it can be shown that periodic oscillations of the electromagnetic field are possible. Such oscillations, called electromagnetic waves, when once started will propagate outward through space. From his equations, Maxwell was able to show that the speed of such electromagnetic waves would be approximately 300,000 kilometers (186,000 miles) per second. Maxwell recognized that this was the same as the measured speed of light. From this, he correctly concluded that light itself consists of electromagnetic waves.

Thus, Maxwell's equations are not only the basic laws of electricity and magnetism, but are also the basic laws of optics! Indeed, all the previously known laws of optics can be deduced from his equations, as well as many facts and relationships previously undiscovered.

Visible light is not the only possible type of electromagnetic radiation. Maxwell's equations indicated that other electromagnetic waves, differing from visible light in their wavelength and frequency, might exist. These theoretical conclusions were later spectacularly confirmed by Heinrich Hertz, who was able both to produce and to detect the invisible waves whose existence Maxwell had predicted. A few years later, Guglielmo Marconi demonstrated that those invisible waves could be employed for wireless communication, and radio became a reality. Today, we use them for television as well.

X-rays, gamma rays, infrared rays, and ultraviolet rays are other examples of electromagnetic radiation. All can be studied by means of Maxwell's equations.

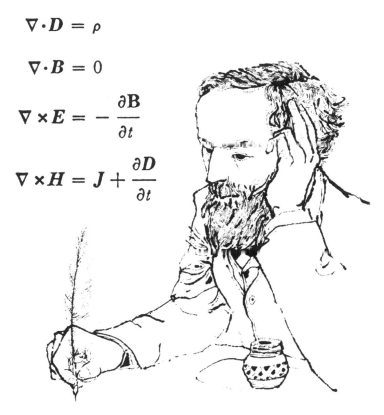

$$\nabla \cdot \boldsymbol{D} = \rho$$

$$\nabla \cdot \boldsymbol{B} = 0$$

$$\nabla \times \boldsymbol{E} = -\frac{\partial \boldsymbol{B}}{\partial t}$$

$$\nabla \times \boldsymbol{H} = \boldsymbol{J} + \frac{\partial \boldsymbol{D}}{\partial t}$$

Maxwell's equations are the basic laws of electricity and magnetism.

Although Maxwell's primary fame rests on his spectacular contributions to electromagnetism and optics, he made important contributions to many other fields of science, including astronomical theory and thermodynamics (the study of heat). One of his special interests was the kinetic theory of gases. Maxwell realized that not all of the molecules of a gas move at the same speed. Some molecules move slowly, some rapidly, some at extremely high speeds. Maxwell worked out the formula which specifies (for any given temperature) what fraction of the molecules of a given gas will be moving at any specified velocity. This formula, called "the Maxwell distribution," is one of the most widely used of scientific equations, and has important applications in many branches of physics.

Maxwell was born in 1831, in Edinburgh, Scotland. He was extremely precocious: when only fifteen years old he presented a scientific paper to the Edinburgh Royal Society. He attended the University of Edinburgh and graduated from Cambridge University. Maxwell spent most of his adult life as a college professor, his last position being at Cambridge. He was married, but had no children. Maxwell is generally considered to be the greatest theoretical physicist in the whole interval between Newton and Einstein. His brilliant career was ended prematurely, in 1879, when he died of cancer, shortly before his forty-eighth birthday.

25

MARTIN

LUTHER

1483-1546

Martin Luther, the man whose defiance of the Roman Catholic Church inaugurated the Protestant Reformation, was born in 1483, in the town of Eisleben, in Germany. He received a good university education, and for a while (apparently at his father's suggestion) he studied law. However, he did not complete his legal education, but instead chose to become an Augustinian monk. In 1512, he received the degree of Doctor of Theology from the University of Wittenberg, and soon thereafter joined its faculty.

Luther's grievances against the Church arose gradually. In 1510, he had taken a trip to Rome, and had been shocked at the venality and worldliness of the Roman clergy. But the immediate issue that stimulated his protest was the Church practice of selling indulgences. (An indulgence was a remission, granted by the Church, of the penalties for sin; it might include a reduction of the time that a sinner would have to spend in purgatory.) On October 31, 1517, Luther posted on the door of the church at Wittenberg his celebrated Ninety-five Theses, in which he strongly denounced Church venality in general, and the practice of selling indulgences in particular. Luther sent a copy of his Ninety-five Theses to the Archbishop of Mainz. In addition, the Theses were printed, and copies were widely distributed in the area.

The scope of Luther's protests against the Church rapidly broadened, and he soon came to deny the authority of the Pope, and of general Church councils, insisting that he would be guided only by the Bible and by plain reason. Not surprisingly, the Church did not look kindly upon these views. Luther was summoned to appear before Church officials, and after various hearing and orders to recant, he was finally pronounced a heretic and an outlaw by the Diet of Worms (1521), and his writings were proscribed.

The normal outcome would have been for Luther to be burned at the stake. However, his views had found widespread support among the German people, and among quite a few of the German princes. Though Luther had to go into hiding for a period of about a year, his support in Germany was strong enough to enable him to avoid any serious criminal penalties.

Luther was a prolific author, and many of his writings proved widely influential. One of his most important works was a translation of the Bible into German. This, of course, made it possible for any literate person to study the Scriptures himself, without relying on the Church or its priests. (Incidentally, the superb prose of Luther's translation had an enormous influence on German language and literature.)

Luther's theology, of course, cannot be fully described in a short space. One of his key ideas was the doctrine of justification by faith alone, an idea derived from the writings of St. Paul. Luther believed that man was by nature so tarnished with sin that good works alone could not save him from eternal damnation. Salvation comes only through faith, and only by the grace of God. If this were so, it was obvious that the Church practice of selling indulgences was improper and ineffective. Indeed, the traditional view that the Church was the necessary mediator between the individual Christian and God was in error. If one followed Luther's doctrines, the whole *raison d'être* of the Roman Catholic Church was wiped out at a stroke.

In addition to questioning the essential role of the Church, Luther also protested against a variety of specific Church beliefs and practices. For example, he denied the existence of purgatory, and he denied that the clergy should be celibate. He himself, in 1525, married a former nun, and they had six children together. Luther died in 1546 while on a visit to his home-town of Eisleben.

Martin Luther, of course, was not the first Protestant thinker. He had been preceded a century earlier by Jan Hus in Bohemia, and by the fourteenth-century English scholar John Wycliffe. Indeed, the twelfth-century Frenchman Peter Waldo might well be considered an early Protestant. But the effect of

Luther nails the Ninety-five Theses to the door of the church at Wittenberg.

each of those earlier movements had been basically local. By 1517, however, discontent with the Catholic Church was so common that Luther's words promptly ignited a chain of protests that spread rapidly through a large part of Europe. Luther, therefore, is rightly considered to be the man chiefly responsible for the commencement of the Reformation.

The most obvious consequence of the Reformation, of course, is the formation of the various Protestant sects. While Protestantism is only one branch of Christianity, and not the most numerous branch at that, it still has more adherents than Buddhism, or, in fact, than most other religions.

A second important consequence of the Reformation was the widespread religious warfare in Europe which followed it. Some of these religious wars (for example, the Thirty Years' War in Germany, which lasted from 1618 to 1648) were incredibly bloody. Even aside from the wars, political conflicts between Catholics and Protestants were to play a major role in European politics for the next few centuries.

The Reformation also played a subtle but very important role in the intellectual development of western Europe. Before 1517, there had been a single established church, the Roman Catholic Church, and dissenters were branded as heretics. Such an atmosphere was certainly not conducive to independent thinking. After the Reformation, as various countries accepted the principle of freedom of religious thought, it became safer to speculate on other subjects as well.

Another point is perhaps worth noting. More persons on this list come from Great Britain than from any other country. Germans are the next most numerous people. Indeed, the list as a whole is strongly dominated by persons coming from the Protestant countries of northern Europe and America. However, one notices that only two of those persons (Gutenberg and Charlemagne) lived before 1517. Prior to that date, most of the persons on this list came from other parts of the world, and the peoples living in what are now Protestant countries made a comparatively small contribution to human culture and history. This

"Luther before the Diet of Worms," by E. Delperee.

obviously suggests that Protestantism or the Reformation may in some way be responsible for the fact that there have been such a large number of eminent persons from these regions in the last 450 years. Perhaps the greater intellectual freedom existing in these areas has been an important factor.

Luther was not without his faults. Though himself a rebel against religious authority, he could be extremely intolerant of those who disagreed with him on religious matters. Possibly, it was partly due to the example set by Luther's intolerance that the religious wars were far fiercer and bloodier in Germany than they were, say, in England. In addition, Luther was ferociously anti-Semitic, and the extraordinary viciousness of his writings about the Jews may have helped to pave the way for the Hitler era in twentieth-century Germany.

Luther frequently stressed the importance of obedience to lawful civil authority. Probably, his principal motivation for this was his objection to the Church's interfering in civil government. (It should be borne in mind that the Reformation was not just a theological dispute. To a considerable extent, it was a nationalist German revolt against the influence of Rome, and it was partly for this reason that Luther received so much support from German princes.) Regardless of Luther's intentions, however, his statements seem to have led many German Protestants to accept absolutism in political matters. In this way, too, Luther's writings may have helped prepare the way for the Hitler era.

Some people may question why Martin Luther is not placed even higher on this list. In the first place, although Luther may seem very important to Europeans and Americans, he seems far less important to the inhabitants of Asia and Africa, relatively few of whom are Christians. As far as most Chinese, Japanese, or Indians are concerned, the differences between Catholics and Protestants are quite insignificant. (Similarly, not many Europeans are interested in the differences between the Sunni and the Shiite branches of Islam.) In the second place, Luther is a comparatively recent figure in history, and has influenced a much smaller span of human history than have Muhammad, Buddha, or Moses. Furthermore, during the past few centuries religious belief has been declining in the West, and the influence of religion on human affairs is likely to be far smaller during the next thousand years than it was during the preceding thousand. If religious belief continues to decline, Luther is apt to appear far less important to future historians than he does today.

Finally, one should remember that the religious disputes of the sixteenth and seventeenth centuries did not, in the long run, affect as many persons as did the scientific advances which occurred during the same period. That is the main reason why Luther has been ranked behind Copernicus (who was his contemporary), even though Luther played a larger *individual* role in the Protestant Reformation than Copernicus played in the scientific revolution.

26 GEORGE WASHINGTON

1732-1799

George Washington was born in 1732, in Wakefield, Virginia. The son of a wealthy planter, he inherited a substantial estate when he was twenty years old. From 1753 to 1758, Washington served in the army, taking an active part in the French and Indian War, and gaining military experience and prestige. He returned to Virginia in late 1758, and resigned his commission. Shortly thereafter, he married Martha Dandridge Custis, a wealthy widow with two children. (He had no children of his own.)

Washington spent the next fifteen years managing his estates, and did so in a very capable fashion. By 1774, when he was chosen as a delegate from Virginia to the First Continental Congress, he was one of the richest men in the colonies. Washington had not been an early advocate of independence; nevertheless, in June 1775, the Second Continental Congress (of which he was also a member) unanimously chose him to command the Continental armies. His military experience; his wealth and reputation; physical appearance (he was a well-built man, 6'2" in height) and tough constitution; his administrative talents; and, above all, his determination and strength of character made him the logical choice for that position. Throughout the war, he served without pay, and with exemplary dedication.

Washington's most significant achievements were accomplished between June 1775, when he took command of the Continental armies, and March 1797, when his second term as President ended. He died at his home in Mount Vernon, Virginia, in December 1799.

Washington's position as the predominant figure in the establishment of the United States of America derives from three important roles which he played.

First, he was the successful military leader in the American War of Independence. It is true that Washington was by no means a military genius. Certainly, he was not remotely in the class of generals such as Alexander the Great or Julius Caesar, and his ultimate success seems to have been due at least as much to the astonishing incompetence of the British commanders who opposed him as to his own abilities. Nevertheless, it should be remembered that several other American commanders were severely defeated, while Washington, though he suffered several small defeats, managed to prosecute the war to a successful conclusion.

Second, Washington was the president of the Constitutional Convention. Although Washington's ideas did not play a major role in shaping the American Constitution, his support, and the prestige of his name, played a major role in the ratification of that document by the state governments. There was, at the time, considerable opposition to the new Constitution, and had it not been for Washington's influence, it is far from certain that it would have been adopted.

In the third place, Washington was the first President of the United States of America. The United States was fortunate indeed in having as its first president a man of the caliber and character of George Washington. As can be seen from the history of many South American and African nations, it is all too easy for a new nation—even if it starts out with a democratic constitution—to soon degenerate into a military dictatorship. While Washington was a firm enough leader to keep the new nation from disintegrating, he had no ambition to hold power indefinitely. He did not wish to be either a king or a dictator, and he set a precedent for the peaceful relinquishment of power—a precedent which has been followed in the United States to this day.

George Washington was not as original and incisive a thinker as some of the other American leaders of the day, such as Thomas Jefferson, James Madison, Alexander Hamilton, and Benjamin Franklin. Nevertheless, he was far more important than any of those more brilliant men; for Washington, both in war and in peace, supplied the vital ingredient of executive leadership, without which no political movement can succeed. Madison's contribution to the formation of the United States of America was important; Washington's was well-nigh indispensable.

George Washington's place on this list depends to a large extent on one's view of the historical importance of the United States of America. An impartial estimate of that importance is naturally difficult for a contemporary American to make. Although the United States attained, in the mid-twentieth century, a position of military strength and political influence even greater than that possessed by the Roman Empire at its height, its political power may not endure as long as Rome's did. On the other hand, it seems clear that several of the technological developments achieved in the United States will be considered of great significance by other cultures and in other times. The invention of the airplane, for example, and the landing of men on the moon represent achievements that past ages have dreamed about, and it seems inconceivable that the invention of nuclear weapons will ever be deemed an unimportant development.

Since George Washington is the American political figure who roughly corresponds to Augustus Caesar in Rome, it seems reasonable to rank him fairly close to Augustus on this list. If Washington has been ranked somewhat lower, it is principally because the period of his leadership was so much briefer than that of Augustus, and because so many other men (such as Thomas Jefferson and James Madison) also played important roles in the formation of the United States of America. However, Washington ranks higher than such figures as Alexander the Great and Napoleon because his accomplishments have been so much more enduring.

27 KARL MARX

1818-1883

Karl Marx, the principal originator of "scientific socialism," was born in 1818, in the town of Trier, Germany. His father was a lawyer, and at seventeen Karl entered the University of Bonn to study law himself. Later, however, he transferred to the University of Berlin, and he eventually was awarded a Ph.D. in philosophy from the University of Jena.

Marx then turned to journalism, and for a while he was the editor of the *Rheinische Zeitung* in Cologne. But his radical political views soon got him into trouble, and he moved to Paris. There he met Friedrich Engels, and the close personal and political friendship they formed was to endure for the rest of their lives. Though each wrote several books in his own name, their intellectual collaboration was so close that their combined output can reasonably be treated as a single joint achievement. Indeed, Marx and Engels are being treated as a joint entry in this book, though listed under Marx's name alone, as he is generally (and I think rightly) considered to have been the dominant partner.

Marx was soon expelled from France, and he then moved to Brussels. It was there, in 1847, that he published his first significant work, *The Poverty of Philosophy*. The following year, he and Engels co-authored the *Communist Manifesto*, their most widely read work. Later that year, Marx returned to Cologne, but was expelled in a matter of months. He then moved to London, where he spent the rest of his life.

Although he earned some money as a journalist, Marx spent the bulk of his time in London doing research and writing books on politics and economics. (During those years, Marx and his family were supported primarily by generous contributions from Engels.) The first volume of *Das Kapital*, Marx's most important work, appeared in 1867. When Marx died, in 1883, the other two volumes had not yet been completed; they were edited and published by Engels from the notes and manuscripts that Marx left behind.

Marx's writings form the theoretical basis of Communism, as well as many modern forms of socialism. At the time Marx died, no country had yet put his ideas into practice. In the century since then, however, Communist governments were established in many places, including Russia and China; and in dozens of other countries movements based on his teachings have arisen and have attempted to gain power. The activities of those Marxist parties—activities which have included propaganda, assassinations, terrorism, and rebellions in order to achieve power, plus wars, brutal repression, and bloody purges after reaching power—kept the world in turmoil for decades and have caused roughly *100 million* deaths! No philosopher in history has had so great an impact on the world in the century after he wrote. You may believe—as I do—that Marxism has been a disaster, both economically and politically; but surely it has not been an insignificant movement. Indeed, the only reason Marx has not been ranked even higher in this book is that he must share the credit—or rather, the blame—

for what has occurred with many other persons, including such notable figures as Lenin, Stalin, and Mao Zedong.

In view of the foregoing, it is clear that Marx deserves a high place on this list. The question is, how high should he be ranked? Even if one acknowledges the enormous influence that Communism has had, one may still question the importance of Marx himself within the Communist movement. The actual conduct of the Soviet government was never rigidly controlled by the works of Marx. He wrote about concepts such as the Hegelian dialectic and the surplus value of labor, and such abstractions seem to have had little effect on the day-to-day policies of the Russian or Chinese governments.

It has often been pointed out that the Marxist theory of economics is badly in error. Certainly, many of Marx's specific predictions have turned out to be incorrect. For example, he predicted that in capitalistic countries the working people would become progressively poorer as time went on; clearly, this has not happened. Marx also predicted that the middle class would be eliminated, with most of its members falling back into the proletariat, and only a few rising into the capitalist class. Obviously, this has not happened either. He also seemed to believe that increased mechanization would diminish the profits of the capitalists, a prediction that is not only wrong, but seems quite foolish. Whether his economic theories are right or wrong, however, has little to do with Marx's influence. A philosopher's importance lies not in the correctness of his views, but in whether his ideas move people to action. Judged on that basis, Marx was unquestionably of enormous importance.

Marxist movements have generally stressed four main ideas: (1) A few rich persons live in great wealth, while most workers live in comparative poverty. (2) The way to rectify this injustice is to set up a socialist system; that is, a system where the means of production are owned by the government rather than by private individuals. (3) In most cases, the only practical way to establish this system is by a violent revolution. (4) To preserve this socialist system, the dictatorship of the Communist party must be maintained for a considerable time.

Each of the first three ideas had been clearly stated long be-fore Marx. The fourth statement is derived in part from Marx's idea of "the dictatorship of the proletariat." However, the duration of the Soviet dictatorship appears to have been more a result of the practices of Lenin and Stalin than of the writings of Marx. It has therefore been claimed by some that Marx's influence on Communism has been more nominal than real, and that the re-spect paid to his writings is mere window dressing, an attempt to claim "scientific" justification for ideas and policies that would have been adopted anyway.

While there is some truth in such claims, they are surely much too extreme. Lenin, for example, did not merely claim to follow Marx's teachings; he had actually read them, fully accepted them, and believed that he was following them. The same is true

Chinese citizens at a cadre school in Beijing receive instruction in Marxism.

of Mao Zedong and of many other Communist leaders. True, Marx's ideas may have been misunderstood or reinterpreted; however, the same could be said for the ideas of Jesus, Buddha, or Muhammad. If *all* the main policies of the various Marxist governments and movements had been directly derived from the writings of Karl Marx, he would be even higher on this list.

Some of Marx's ideas—for example, his interesting notion of "the economic interpretation of history"—are apt to remain influential even if Communism itself dies out. Plainly, though, a major factor in deciding how high Marx should be ranked will be one's estimate of the importance of Communism in the long-term history of the world. A century after Marx's death, there were well over a billion persons who were at least nominally his followers. This was a greater number of adherents than any other ideology has ever had—not just in absolute numbers, but also as a fraction of the total world population. That fact led many Communists to hope (and anti-Communists to fear) that the future might well see the eventual worldwide triumph of Marxism.

In the first edition of this book I wrote, "though one cannot be sure just how far Communism will go and just how long it will last, it should be apparent by now that the ideology is solidly entrenched, and will be a major influence in the world for at least a few centuries to come." It now appears that that estimate was unduly pessimistic. With the renunciation of Communism by Russia, by the other republics of the former Soviet Union, and by most of the countries that had been client states of the Soviet Union, the role of Marxism in the world has declined precipitously over the past few years; and one certainly gets the impression that that decline is irreversible.

If that is indeed the case—and I suspect that it is—then it would seem that the interval during which Marxism was a major force will turn out to be only about a century, rather than many centuries. The overall influence of Karl Marx will therefore be a good deal less than I had estimated in the first edition of this book. Even then, he will still be a significantly more important figure than either Napoleon or Hitler: The impact of those men was both briefer than Marx's and less extensive geographically.

28 ORVILLE WRIGHT

1871-1948

&

WILBUR WRIGHT

1867-1912

Since the achievements of these two brothers are so closely inter-twined, they have been combined as a single entry, and their stories will be told together. Wilbur Wright was born in 1867, in Millville, Indiana. Orville Wright, his brother, was born in 1871, in Dayton, Ohio. Both boys received high school educa-tions, although neither actually received his diploma.

Both boys were mechanically gifted, and both were in-terested in the subject of manned flight. In 1892, they opened a shop where they sold, repaired, and manufactured bicycles. This provided funds for their overriding interest, which was aeronautical research. They eagerly read the writings of other workers in aeronautics — Otto Lilienthal, Octave Chanute, and Samuel P. Langley. In 1899, they started working on the pro-blem of flight themselves. By December 1903, after a little more than four years' work, their efforts were crowned with success.

One may wonder why the Wright brothers were able to suc-ceed where so many others had failed. There were several reasons for their success. In the first place, two heads are much better than one. The Wright brothers always worked together and cooperated perfectly with each other. In the second place, they wisely decided that they would first learn how to fly before attempting to build a powered airplane. This sounds a bit paradoxical: how can you learn to fly unless you first have an airplane? The answer is that the Wright brothers learned how to fly by using gliders. They started working with kites and gliders in 1899. The next year, they brought their first full-scale glider (that is, large enough to carry a man) to Kitty Hawk, in North Carolina, to test it out. It was not too satisfactory. They built and tested a second full-scale glider in 1901, and a third in 1902. The third glider incorporated some of their most important innova-tions. (Some of their basic patents, applied for in 1903, relate to that glider rather than to their first powered plane.) In the third glider, they made more than a thousand successful flights. The Wright brothers were already the best and most experienced glider pilots in the world before they started to build a powered aircraft.

Their experience with glider flights provides a third clue to their success. Most persons who had previously attempted to construct airplanes had worried chiefly about how to get their contraptions off the ground. The Wright brothers correctly realized that the biggest problem would be how to control the aircraft after it was in the air. They therefore spent most of their time and effort designing ways to maintain the stability and control of the aircraft during flight. They succeeded in devising means for three-axis control of their craft, and this enabled them to achieve complete maneuverability.

The Wright brothers also made important contributions to wing design. They soon realized that the previously published data on this subject were unreliable. They therefore built their own wind tunnel, and in it tested more than two hundred differently shaped wing surfaces. On the basis of these experiments, they were able to construct their own tables describing how the pressure of the air upon a wing depended on the wing shape. This information was then used to design wings for their aircraft.

The Wright brothers' original biplane.

Despite all these achievements, the Wright brothers could not have succeeded if they had not appeared at the right moment in history. Attempts at powered flight in the first half of the nineteenth century were inevitably doomed to failure. Steam engines were simply too heavy in proportion to the power that they produced. By the time the Wright brothers came along, efficient internal combustion engines had already been invented. However, those internal combustion engines in common use had far too high a ratio of weight to power to be usable in a flying machine. As no manufacturer seemed able to design an engine with a low enough weight-to-power ratio, the Wright brothers (with the help of a mechanic) designed their own. It is an indication of their genius that, although they spent relatively little time on the design of the engine, they were still able to construct an engine superior to those which most manufacturers could design. In addition, the Wright brothers had to design their own propellers. The one that they used in 1903 had about a 66 percent efficiency.

The first flight was made on December 17, 1903, at Kill Devil Hill, near Kitty Hawk, North Carolina. The brothers each made two flights on that day. The first flight, made by Orville Wright, lasted 12 seconds and covered 120 feet. The final flight, made by Wilbur Wright, lasted 59 seconds and covered 852 feet. Their plane, which they called the *Flyer I* (it is today popularly called the *Kitty Hawk)*, cost less than a thousand dollars to build. It had a wing span of about 40 feet and weighed about 750 pounds. It had a 12-horsepower engine, which weighed only 170 pounds. Incidentally, the original airplane is now in the National Air and Space Museum, in Washington, D.C.

Although there were five witnesses to those first flights, relatively few newspapers reported it the next day (and generally not very accurately). Their hometown paper in Dayton, Ohio, ignored it completely. It was, in fact, almost five years before it was generally realized in the world at large that manned flight had actually been achieved.

After their flights at Kitty Hawk, the Wright brothers returned to Dayton, where they built a second airplane, the *Flyer II*. They made 105 flights in that airplane in 1904, without, however, attracting much attention. *Flyer III*, an improved and very practical model, was built in 1905. Even though they had made many flights near Dayton, most people still did not believe that the airplane had been invented. In 1906, for example, the Paris edition of the *Herald Tribune* carried an article on the Wright brothers with the headline "Flyers or Liars?"

In 1908, however, the Wright brothers put an end to the public's doubts. Wilbur Wright took one of their planes to France, gave a series of public demonstrations of the aircraft in

The historic first flight of the Wright brothers' airplane at Kitty Hawk.

action, and organized a company there to market their invention. Meanwhile, back in the United States, Orville Wright was giving similar public displays. Unfortunately, on September 17, 1908, the plane he was flying crashed. It was the only serious accident that either of them ever had. A passenger was killed, and Orville broke a leg and two ribs, but recovered. His successful flights, however, had already persuaded the United States government to sign a contract for the supply of airplanes to the U.S. War Department, and in 1909 the Federal budget included an allocation of $30,000 for Army aviation.

For a while there was considerable patent litigation between the Wright brothers and rival claimants, but in 1914 the courts ruled in their favor. Meanwhile, Wilbur Wright contracted typhoid fever and died in 1912, at the age of forty-five. Orville Wright, who in 1915 sold his financial interests in the airplane company, lived on till 1948. Neither of the brothers ever married.

Despite a lot of earlier research in the field, and many prior attempts and claims, there is no question that the Wright brothers deserve the lion's share of the credit for the invention of the airplane. In deciding where to rank them on this list, therefore, the main factor is one's assessment of the importance of the airplane itself. It seems to me that the airplane is a far less important invention than either the printing press or the steam engine, each of which has revolutionized the entire mode of human existence. Still, it is unquestionably an invention of great significance, with applications in both peace and war. In a few decades, the airplane has shrunk our once vast planet and turned it into a small world. Furthermore, the successful achievement of manned flight was an essential preliminary to the development of space travel.

For untold centuries men had dreamed of flying. But practical persons had always believed that the "flying carpets" of the Arabian Nights were only dreams, and could never exist in the real world. The genius of the Wright brothers fulfilled the age-old dream of mankind, and turned a fairy tale into reality.

29

GENGHIS KHAN

c. 1162 - 1227

Genghis Khan, the great Mongol conqueror, was born about 1162. His father, a petty Mongol chieftain, named the boy Temujin, after a defeated rival chieftain. When Temujin was nine, his father was killed by members of a rival tribe, and for some years the surviving members of the family lived in constant danger and privation. This was an inauspicious beginning, but Temujin's situation was to become a lot worse before it got better. When he was a young man, he was captured in a raid by a rival tribe. To prevent his escaping, a wooden collar was placed around his neck. From this extremity of helplessness, as an illiterate prisoner in a primitive, barren country, Temujin rose to become the most powerful man in the world.

144

His rise started when he managed to escape from his captors. He then allied himself with Toghril, a friend of his father's, and chieftain of one of the related tribes living in the area. There followed many years of internecine warfare among these various Mongol tribes, in the course of which Temujin gradually fought his way to the top.

The tribesmen of Mongolia had long been known as skilled horsemen and fierce warriors. Throughout history, they had made sporadic raids into northern China. However, before the rise of Temujin, the various tribes had always spent most of their energy in fighting each other. By a combination of military prowess, diplomacy, ruthlessness, and organizational ability, Temujin managed to weld all of these tribes together under his leadership, and in 1206 an assembly of the Mongol chieftains proclaimed him Genghis Khan, or "the universal emperor."

The formidable military machine that Genghis Khan had assembled was then turned outward upon neighboring nations. He first attacked the Hsi Hsia state in northwestern China and the Chin Empire in northern China. While these battles were going on, a dispute arose between Genghis Khan and the Khwarezm Shah Muhammad, who ruled a considerable empire in Persia and central Asia. In 1219, Genghis led his armies against the Khwarezm Shah. Central Asia and Persia were overrun, and the Khwarezm Shah's empire was completely destroyed. While other Mongol armies were attacking Russia, Genghis Khan himself led a raid into Afghanistan and northern India. He returned to Mongolia in 1225, and died there in 1227.

Shortly before his death, Genghis Khan requested that his third son, Ogadai, be named to succeed him. It was a wise choice, for Ogadai became a brilliant general in his own right. Under his leadership, the Mongol armies continued to advance in China, completely overran Russia, and advanced into Europe. In 1241, a series of Polish, German, and Hungarian armies were completely routed by the Mongols, who advanced well past Budapest. However, in that year Ogadai died, and the Mongol armies withdrew from Europe, never to return.

There was a substantial interruption while the Mongol chieftains argued about the succession. However, under the next two Khans (Genghis's grandsons, Mangu Khan and Kublai Khan) the Mongol advance in Asia was resumed. By 1279, when Kublai Khan completed the conquest of China, the Mongols ruled the largest land empire in all of history. Their domains included China, Russia, and Central Asia, in addition to Persia and most of Southwest Asia. Their armies had raided successfully from Poland to northern India, and Kublai Khan's sovereignty was recognized in Korea, Tibet, and parts of Southeast Asia.

An empire of this size, given the primitive means of transportation existing at the time, could not possibly be held together for long, and the Mongol empire soon split up. But Mongol rule lasted for a long time in several of the successor states. The Mongols were expelled from most of China in 1368. In Russia, however, their rule lasted much longer. The Golden Horde, the name ususally given to the Mongol kingdom set up in Russia by Genghis's grandson Batu, endured until the sixteenth century, and the Khanate of the Crimea survived until 1783. Other sons or grandsons of Genghis established dynasties that ruled in central Asia and in Persia. Both of these areas were conquered in the fourteenth century by Timur (Tamerlane), who was himself of Mongol blood, and who claimed descent from Genghis. Tamerlane's dynasty was finally brought to an end in the fifteenth century. However, even this was not the end of Mongol conquests and rule. Tamerlane's great-great-grandson, Baber, invaded India, there to found the Mogul (Mongol) dynasty. The Mogul rulers, who eventually conquered almost all of India, remained in power until the mid-eighteenth century.

In the course of history, there has been a succession of men—madmen, if you will—who set out to conquer the world and who achieved a considerable measure of success. The most notable of these megalomaniacs were Alexander the Great, Genghis Khan, Napoleon Bonaparte, and Adolf Hitler. Why do all four of these men rank so highly on this list? Are not ideas ultimately more important than armies? I would certainly agree that in the long run the pen is mightier than the sword. However, the short run matters, too. Each of these four men controlled such a large territory and population, and exerted such an enormous influence on the lives of their contemporaries, that they cannot be curtly dismissed as common bandits.

The Mongol conquests.

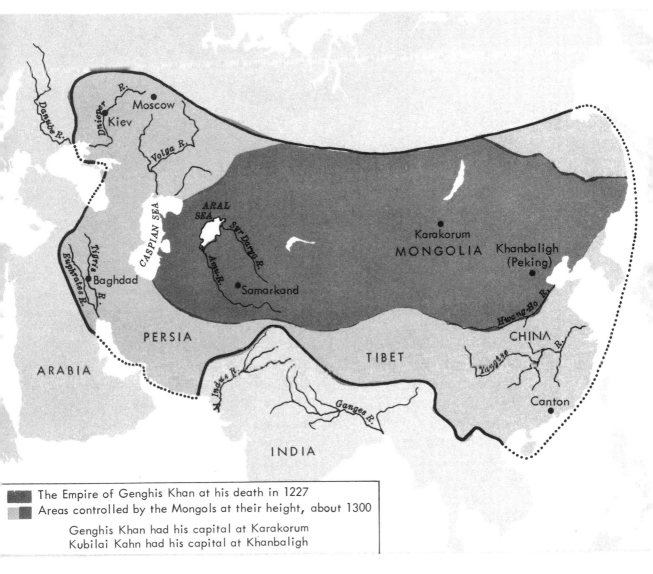

The Empire of Genghis Khan at his death in 1227
Areas controlled by the Mongols at their height, about 1300

Genghis Khan had his capital at Karakorum
Kubilai Kahn had his capital at Khanbaligh

30 ADAM SMITH

1723-1790

Adam Smith, the leading figure in the development of economic theory, was born in 1723, in the town of Kirkcaldy, Scotland. As a young man, he studied at Oxford University, and from 1751 to 1764 he was a professor of philosophy at Glasgow University. While there, he published his first book, *Theory of Moral Sentiments*, which established his reputation in intellectual circles. However, his lasting fame rests primarily on his great work, *An Inquiry Into the Nature and Causes of the Wealth of Nations*, which was published in 1776. The book was an immediate success, and for the rest of his life Smith enjoyed fame and respect. He died in Kirkcaldy, in 1790. Smith had no children and never married.

Adam Smith was not the first person to devote himself to economic theory, and many of his best-known ideas were not original. But he was the first to present a comprehensive and systematic theory of economics that was sufficiently correct to serve as a foundation for future progress in the field. For this reason, it may fairly be said that *The Wealth of Nations* is the starting point of the modern study of political economy.

One of the book's great achievements was that it cleared away many past misconceptions. Smith argued against the older mercantilist theory, which stressed the importance of a state having large supplies of gold bullion. Similarly, his book rejected the view of the physiocrats that land was the principal source of value, and instead asserted the basic importance of labor. Smith heavily stressed the great increase in production that could be brought about through the division of labor, and he attacked the whole set of antiquated and arbitrary government restrictions that were hampering industrial expansion.

The central idea of *The Wealth of Nations* is that the seemingly chaotic free market is actually a self-regulating mechanism, which automatically tends to produce the type and quantity of goods that are most desired and needed by the community. For example, suppose some desirable product is in short supply. Naturally, its price will increase, and the higher price will lead to higher profits for those who manufacture it. Because of the high profits, other manufacturers will be eager to produce the article also. The resultant increase in production will alleviate the original shortage. Furthermore, the increased supply, in conjunction with competition between various manufacturers, will tend to reduce the price of the commodity to its "natural price," i.e., its production cost. No one has deliberately set out to help society by eliminating the shortage; nevertheless, the problem has been solved. Each person, in Smith's words, "intends only his own gain," but he is, as it were, "led by an invisible hand to promote an end which was no part of his intention...By pursuing his own interest he frequently promotes that of the society more effectually than when he really intends to promote it" (*The Wealth of Nations*, Book IV, Chapter II).

The "invisible hand," however, cannot do the job properly

if there are obstructions to free competition. Smith therefore believed in free trade and argued strongly against high tariffs. In fact, he strongly opposed most government interference with business and the free market. Such interference, he claimed, almost always decreases economic efficiency, and ultimately results in the public paying higher prices. (Smith did not invent the term "laissez faire," but he did more than any other man to promote the concept.)

Some people have the impression that Adam Smith was a mere apologist for business interest, but such a view is incorrect. He repeatedly, and in the strongest terms, denounced monopolistic business practices and urged their elimination. Nor was Smith naive regarding actual business practices. Here is a typical observation from *The Wealth of Nations:* "People of the same trade seldom meet together but the conversation ends in a conspiracy against the public, or in some diversion to raise prices."

So well did Adam Smith organize and present his system of economic thought, that within a few decades the earlier schools of economic thought were abandoned. Virtually all of their good points had been incorporated into Smith's system, while he had systematically exposed their shortcomings. Smith's successors, including such important economists as Thomas Malthus and David Ricardo, elaborated and refined his system (without changing its basic outlines) into the structure that is today referred to as classical economics. Although modern economic theory has added new concepts and techniques, it is largely a natural outgrowth of classical economics.

In *The Wealth of Nations*, Smith partly anticipated the views of Malthus on overpopulation. However, while Ricardo and Karl Marx both insisted that population pressure would prevent wages from rising above the subsistence level (the so-called "iron law of wages"), Smith stated that under conditions of increasing production wages would be able to increase. Quite obviously, events have proved that Smith was correct on this point, while Ricardo and Marx were wrong.

Quite aside from any question of the correctness of Smith's

views, or of his influence upon later theorists, is the matter of his influence upon legislation and government policies. *The Wealth of Nations* was written with great skill and clarity, and it was widely read. Smith's arguments against government interference in business and commercial affairs, and in favor of low tariffs and free trade, had a decided influence upon governmental policies during the entire nineteenth century. Indeed, his influence on such policies is still felt today.

Since economic theory has advanced greatly since Smith's day, and since some of his ideas have been superseded, it is easy to underrate Adam Smith's importance. The fact is, though, that he was the principal originator and founder of economic theory as a systematic study, and as such is a major figure in the history of human thought.

Smith is commemorated on the Scots penny.

Edward de Vere, the Seventeenth Earl of Oxford

From the portrait attributed to Marcus Gheeraedts, formerly in the collection of His Grace, The Duke of St. Albans. Reproduced by permission of Susan L. Hanson, David J. Hanson, and Trustees of the Minos D. Miller Sr. Trust, LA, U.S.A.

152

31

EDWARD DE VERE
better known as
"WILLIAM SHAKESPEARE"

1 5 5 0 - 1 6 0 4

The great British playwright and poet, William Shakespeare, is generally acknowledged to be the greatest writer who ever lived. There is a good deal of dispute about his identity (which will be discussed below), but the talent and achievements of the author are agreed to by all.

Shakespeare wrote at least thirty-six plays, including such masterpieces as *Hamlet, Macbeth, King Lear, Julius Caesar,* and *Othello,* a magnificent set of 154 sonnets, and a few longer poems. In view of his genius, accomplishments, and deserved fame, it may seem a bit odd that his name does not appear higher on this list. I have ranked Shakespeare this low not because I am unappreciative of his artistic accomplishments, but only because of my belief that, in general, literary and artistic figures have had comparatively little influence on human history

The activities of a religious leader, scientist, politician, explorer, or philosopher frequently influence developments in many other fields of human endeavor. For example, scientific advances have had tremendous impact upon economic and political affairs, and have also affected religious beliefs, philosophical attitudes, and developments in art.

However, a famous painter, though he may have a great deal of influence upon the work of subsequent painters, is likely to have very little influence upon the development of music and literature, and virtually none upon science, exploration, or other fields of

human endeavor. Similar statements can be made concerning poets, playwrights, and composers of music. In general, artistic figures influence only art, and indeed, only the particular field of art
in which they work. It is for this reason that no figure in the literary,
musical, or visual arts has been ranked in the top twenty, and only
a handful appear on this list at all.

Why, then, are there *any* artistic figures on this list? One
answer is that our general culture—in the sociological sense—is in
part created by art. Art helps to form the connective glue of society.
It is no accident that art is a feature of *every* human civilization
that has ever existed.

Furthermore, the enjoyment of art plays a direct part in the
life of each individual person. In other words, an individual may
spend part of his time reading books, part of his time looking at
paintings, etc. Even if the time we spent listening to music had no
effect whatsoever upon our other activities that time would still
represent some not insignificant fraction of our lives. However, art
does affect our other activities, and in some sense our whole life.
Art connects us to our souls; it expresses our deepest feelings and
validates them for us.

In some cases, artistic works have a more or less explicit philosophical content, which can influence our attitudes on other topics.
This, of course, occurs more frequently in the case of literary compositions than in the case of music or paintings. For example, when
in *Romeo and Juliet* (Act III, scene 1) Shakespeare has the prince
say, "Mercy but murders, pardoning those that kill," an idea is
presented that (whether or not one accepts it) has obvious philosophical content, and is more likely to influence political attitudes
than is, say, viewing the "Mona Lisa."

It seems beyond dispute that Shakespeare is preeminent
among all literary figures. Relatively few people today read the
works of Chaucer, Virgil, or even Homer, except when those works
are assigned reading in school. However, a performance of one of
Shakespeare's plays is certain to be well attended. Shakespeare's
gift for a well-turned phrase is without parallel, and he is frequently quoted—even by persons who have never seen or read his

plays. Furthermore, it is plain that his popularity is not a mere passing fad. His works have given pleasure to readers and viewers for almost four centuries. As they have already stood the test of time, it seems reasonable to assume that the works of Shakespeare will continue to be popular for a good many centuries to come.

In assessing Shakespeare's importance, one should take into account that had he not lived, his plays would never have been written at all. (Of course, a corresponding statement could be made regarding every artistic or literary figure, but that factor does not seem particularly important in evaluating the influence of minor artists.)

Although Shakespeare wrote in English, he is truly a world figure. If not quite a universal language, English is closer to being one than any other language ever has been. Moreover, Shakespeare's works have been very widely translated, and his works have been read and performed in a very large number of countries.

There are, of course, some popular authors whose writings are disdained by literary critics Not so with Shakespeare, whose works have received unstinting praise from literary scholars. Generations of playwrights have studied his works and have attempted to emulate his literary virtues. This combination of enormous influence on other writers and continued worldwide popularity makes it plain that William Shakespeare is entitled to a high position in this book. However, there has long been a controversy as to the identity of the man who wrote under that name.

The orthodox view (which I accepted uncritically when writing the first edition of this book) is that he was the same person as William Shakspere, who was born in Stratford-on-Avon in 1564 and died there in 1616. However, on carefully evaluating the arguments of the skeptics and the counter-arguments of the orthodox, I have concluded that the skeptics have much the better of the argument and have reasonably established their case.

The bulk of the evidence indicates that "William Shakespeare" was a pseudonym used by Edward de Vere, the 17th Earl of Oxford, and that William Shakspere (or *Shaxpere*, or *Shakspeyr*, or *Shagspere*, or *Shaxbere*: the family name was spelled several ways in

Stratford, but almost always without the first "e"; it was therefore pronounced quite differently—with a short "a"—than Shakespeare) was merely a prosperous merchant whose business took him to London, but who had nothing to do with the writing of the plays.

I am not suggesting that de Vere was a ghostwriter for Shakspere, who took public credit for the plays at the time. During his lifetime, Shakspere was *not* considered to be the author, nor did he ever claim to be! The notion that Shakspere was the great playwright William Shakespeare did not arise until 1623—seven years after Shakspere died!—when the First Folio edition of Shakespeare's plays appeared. The editors of that book included some prefatory material in which it was strongly hinted (though never said directly) that the man from Stratford-on-Avon was the author.

To understand why it is so unlikely that Shakspere was the playwright it is first necessary to present the orthodox version of his biography, which goes as follows:

Shakspere's father, John, had once been fairly prosperous, but he fell on hard times, and young William was reared in difficult financial circumstances. Nevertheless, he attended the Stratford Grammar School, where he studied Latin and classical literature.

When William was eighteen he made a young woman named Anne Hathaway pregnant. He duly married her, and she gave birth a few months later. Two and one-half years later she gave birth to twins: so William had a wife and three children to support before he was twenty-one years old.

We have no knowledge of his activities or whereabouts for the next six years, but in the early 1590s he was present in London as a member of an acting troup. He was a successful actor, but soon branched out into writing plays and poetry. By 1598 he was already being hailed as the greatest of all English writers, living or dead. Shakspere stayed in London for about twenty years, during which time he wrote at least thirty-six plays, 154 sonnets, and a few longer poems. Within a few years he became prosperous, and in 1597 was able to purchase an expensive home ("New Place") in Stratford. His family remained behind in Stratford the whole time, but he continued to support them.

Oddly, he never published any of the great plays he was writing. But unscrupulous printers, realizing their commercial value, published pirated editions of nearly half of them. Although the pirated editions are often rather garbled, Shakspere made no attempt to interfere.

About 1612, when he was forty-eight years old, he suddenly retired from writing, returned to Stratford, and resumed living with his wife. He died there in April 1616, and was buried in the church courtyard. The stone over his supposed grave does not bear his name; however, some time later a monument was erected on the wall nearby. Three weeks before his death he executed a will, leaving most of his property to his elder daughter Susanna. She and her descendants continued to live at New Place until the last of them died, in 1670.

Hedingham Castle, the birthplace and childhood home of Edward de Vere.

It should be pointed out that a good deal of the foregoing biography is pure conjecture on the part of orthodox biographers. For example, there is no actual record of Shakspere ever being a student at Stratford Grammar School. Nor did any student or teacher there ever claim to have been a classmate or instructor of the famous playwright. Similarly, it is unclear that he ever had an acting career.

Nevertheless, at first sight, the official story may sound plausible. However, as soon as we examine it closely, grave difficulties arise.

The first problem—mentioned even by many orthodox biographers—is that we have so little information about the life of Shakspere, *very* much less than we would expect to have about so prominent a person. In an attempt to explain this surprising paucity of data people sometimes say, "He lived almost four hundred years ago. Naturally most of the documents by and about him have been lost." But that view greatly underestimates the amount of information we have about the era Shakspere lived in.

He was not living in a backward country or a barbaric age, but in England during the reign of Queen Elizabeth, a well-documented era where there were printing presses, where writing materials were commonplace, and where very many persons knew how to read and write. Of course, many papers have been lost; but several *million* original documents from that era still survive.

Because of the great interest in William Shakespeare, an army of scholars has spent three generations scouring that data, searching for information about the world's most renowned literary genius. As a by-product of that search they have uncovered reams of information about every other major poet of the day—and about many minor poets as well. But all they have uncovered about Shakspere are about three dozen minor references, not one of which describes him as a poet or playwright!

We know incomparably more about the lives of Francis Bacon, Queen Elizabeth, Ben Jonson, or Edmund Spencer than we do about Shakspere's life. Indeed, we know far more about even such a minor poet as John Lyly than we do of Shakspere.

The contrast with Isaac Newton—history's foremost scientific genius—is particularly striking. We have many *thousands* of original documents by and about Newton (who, like Shakspere, came from a small town in England). Admittedly, Newton was born seventy-eight years after Shakspere. But we also have much more detailed information about Galileo (born the same year as Shakspere), about Michelangelo (born eighty-nine years earlier), or even about Boccaccio (born in 1313) than we do about Shakspere.

A related problem is the fact that during his years in London the great playwright was virtually invisible. Shakspere is supposed to have spent roughly twenty years in London (1592–1612). But we cannot find a *single* record, during that whole twenty-year stretch, of anyone seeing the great actor and playwright in the flesh. When people saw the famous actor Richard Burbage or met the playwright Ben Jonson, they marked it down as a notable event. But if anyone in London, during the whole twenty years of his greatest prominence, saw Shakspere on stage, or discussed poetry with him, or corresponded with him, or met him at a party or on the street, they did not think the encounter worthy of mention!

The only plausible explanation for the above facts is that the name "William Shakespeare" was a pseudonym used by the author in a successful attempt to keep his identity secret, and that those persons who did meet the author therefore did not know they were meeting the great William Shakespeare. (Obviously, Shakspere, whose name was so similar, could not have successfully hidden behind such a pen-name.)

Perhaps an even graver difficulty with the official story is the attitude towards Shakspere in Stratford-on-Avon. Though Shakspere is supposed to have been the greatest writer in England— and a well-known actor to boot—nobody in his home town seemed to be aware that he was a famous man, nor that there was anything unusual about him! This is even more amazing when one recalls that he was poor when he left Stratford and wealthy when he returned, a change which would naturally tend to make friends and neighbors curious. Yet the fact is that during his lifetime, *not one of his friends, or neighbors in Stratford*—not even his own family!—*ever referred to Shakspere as an actor, a playwright, a poet, or a literary figure of any sort*!

Well, what about the manuscripts of the plays in Shakspere's own handwriting? Surely they prove that he was the author. Unfortunately, there are no manuscripts of the plays in his handwriting, or any early drafts, or any fragments, or any unpublished or unfinished works. In fact, aside from six signatures on legal documents, there is NOTHING in his handwriting! No notes, no notebooks, no memoranda, no diaries. Not a single personal letter by him survives, nor a single business letter. (Nor do even his earliest biographers report having seen a single line in his handwriting.) Judging from the record, it appears that Shakspere, far from being an author, was barely literate, or even illiterate!

A related point is that Shakspere's parents, wife, and children were all illiterate. Now a man does not choose his parents, and he might select a mate for reasons other than her reading ability, but it seems scarcely believable that a man to whom the written word meant so much would allow his own daughters to grow up unable to read and write. If Shakspere was indeed Shakespeare, then he is the *only* prominent author in history whose children are known to have been illiterate!

Then there is the question of Shakspere's will. The original document survives: it is three pages long, and lists his property in considerable detail, with many specific bequests. Nowhere does it mention any poems, any plays, any manuscripts, any works in progress, or any literary rights. Nor does it make mention of any personal books or papers. There is no hint that he would like to see his remaining plays published (although at least twenty of them had not yet appeared in print), or that he had ever written a play or poem in his life. It is the will of an unschooled, possibly illiterate, merchant.

We might also note that, in an era when the English poets typically arranged gaudy funerals and composed lengthy poetic eulogies when one of their members died, the death of Shakspere in 1616 went completely unmentioned by every writer in England. Not even Ben Jonson—who later claimed to have been a great admirer and friend of William Shakespeare—expressed the slight-

Monsieur treshonorable

Monsieur i'ay receu voz lettres, plaines d'humanité et courtoysie, et fort resemblantes
à vostre grand'amour et singuliere affection enuers moy. comme vrais enfans
denement procreez d'une telle mere. pour la quelle ie me trenne de iour en iour
plus tenu a v.h. voz bons admonestements pour l'observation du bon ordre
selon voz appointemens, ie me delibere dieu aidant le garder en tout à à venir
comme chose que ie cognois et considere tendre especialement a mon propre
bien et profit, usant en cela l'aduis et authorité de ceux qui sont aupres
de moy. la discretion desquels i'estime si grande (s'il me conuient parler
quelque chose a leur aduange) qui non seulement ils se porteront
selon qu'un tel temps le requiert. ains que plus est feront tant que
ie me gouuerne selon que vous aues ordonné et commandé. Quant a l'ordre
de mon estude pour ce que il requiert un long discours a l'expliquer par
le me menu, et le temps est court à ceste heure, ie vous prie affectueuse-
ment m'en excuser pour le present. vous asseurant que par le premier
passant ie le vous feray scauoir bien au long cependant ie prie a dieu
vous donner santé.

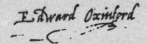

Edward Oxinford

Letter written (in French) by Edward de Vere when he was 13 years old.

est regret when Shakspere died, or mentioned the event at all. Clearly, the other poets of the day saw no connection between the Stratford man and the great playwright.

To my mind, the foregoing arguments are already conclusive, and no further proof is needed that Shakspere was not the play- wright and that "William Shakespeare" was a pseudonym used to conceal the true author's identity. However, there are additional strong arguments against Shakspere being the author, although their persuasiveness is not crucial to the case against him.

For example, it has been pointed out that most dramatists and writers of fiction include in their writings many incidents from their own lives. (Often, such events form a major part of the story.) But the plays of Shakespeare are virtually devoid of any incidents or circumstances which can be traced back to Shakspere's own experiences.

Another argument is that the author, William Shakespeare, was obviously an extremely well educated man; witness his enor- mous vocabulary (*much* larger than that of any other playwright), his familiarity with both Latin and French, his accurate knowledge of legal terminology, and his voluminous knowledge of classical literature. But everyone agrees that Shakspere never attended a university, and (as explained above) it is doubtful whether he even attended grammar school.

Still another point is that Shakespeare (the author) seems to be of aristocratic sympathies and background, very familiar with the sports of the aristocracy (such as fox-hunting and falconry) and familiar with court life and court intrigues. Shakspere, on the other hand, came from a small town and had a petit bourgeois back- ground.

There are many other aspects of the life of Shakspere that do not fit in with the hypothesis that he was the famous author, Wil- liam Shakespeare, and I could easily write many pages describing additional difficulties with that theory. (The reader who wants more details can find them in the excellent book, *The Mysterious William Shakespeare*, by Charlton Ogburn.) Of course, orthodox biographers have constructed hypothetical explanations for each of those difficulties, and for each of the problems I have already described. Some of those explanations are rather unlikely, but each one individually is at least possible.

For example, it is *possible*—although people tend to save letters that they receive from famous men—that by the merest coincidence *every* personal or business letter that Shakspere ever wrote has vanished without a trace, together with all his notes, notebooks, and manuscripts. It is *possible* that the greatest of English poets composed for his own epitaph the childish piece of doggerel that we see on Shakspere's gravestone. It is *possible* that a man whose plays show that he admired intelligent, educated women let his own daughters grow up illiterate. And it is *possible* that, although Shakspere was the most celebrated writer in England, not a single one of his friends, family, or neighbors in Stratford ever referred to him as an actor, poet, or playwright. It's not very likely, but it's *possible*!

However, in this case, as in most, the whole is greater than any of its parts. Were there just one or two difficulties with the official story, we might accept even rather far-fetched explanations for them. But after a while we can't help noticing that *nothing* seems to fit the official story naturally. Everything about that story seems to require an ad hoc, and often far-fetched, explanation. The problem is that William Shakspere of Stratford-on-Avon was a barely literate small-town merchant, and neither his education, nor his character, nor his actions, nor what his family and neighbors said about him, are consistent with his being the great author, William Shakespeare.

Well, if Shakspere was not the author of the plays, who was? Many other persons have been suggested, of which the best known is the famous philosopher Francis Bacon. But in recent years, the accumulation of evidence has swung opinion strongly towards Edward de Vere.

We know a lot about Edward de Vere: he led an adventurous life, and many events in his life are mirrored in the plays. He was born in 1550, the son and heir of the 16th Earl of Oxford, a wealthy and high-ranking aristocrat. As befit the heir to a title which went back to the Norman Conquest, young Edward received training in all the customary skills of a young lord: riding, hunting, military arts, and also such milder pursuits as music and dancing. Nor was his academic education ignored. He had private tutors for both French and Latin, as well as other subjects. Eventually he obtained a bachelor's degree from Cambridge University and a master's degree from Oxford. Afterwards, he studied law for a year at Gray's Inn, one of the famed Inns of Court in London.

His father died when Edward was only twelve, and his mother subsequently remarried. However, Edward did not remain with his mother for long. Instead, he became a royal ward, and a guardian was appointed for him. The guardian chosen was William Cecil, Lord Treasurer of England, and a member of Queen Elizabeth's privy council for many years. As the Queen's oldest and most trusted adviser, Cecil was one of the most powerful men in England.

Young de Vere, as befitted his high rank, was treated as a family member in Cecil's household. (A somewhat mysterious incident, in which he killed one of Cecil's servants, was kept out of the courts due to Cecil's influence.) In his late teens he was introduced to Court, where he met all the leading figures, including the Queen herself. She was much taken with the young man who, in addition to being brilliant, athletic, and charming, was also very good-looking, and he soon became a favorite of hers.

When he was twenty-one, de Vere married Anne Cecil, his guardian's daughter. Since they had been reared together, and she was almost his "kid sister," such a marriage was quite unusual. (But Posthumus Leonatus, the hero of *Cymbeline*, was also a royal ward who married his guardian's daughter, and there are many other resemblances between his story and de Vere's.)

When he was twenty-four, de Vere embarked on a lengthy trip through Europe. He visited France and Germany, spent about ten months in Italy, and then returned to England via France. On the trip back across the English Channel his ship was attacked by pirates, who planned to hold their captives for ransom. But de

Vere informed the pirates of his personal friendship with Queen Elizabeth, and the pirates decided it was prudent to release him promptly without demanding a ransom. (A very similar incident occurs to the hero of *Hamlet*.)

Meanwhile, his wife Anne had given birth to a daughter. Though the girl had been born only eight months after de Vere left England, he insisted that the child was not his, and, claiming that Anne was an adulteress, he refused to live with her. Most historians feel that his charge was ill-founded. Apparently de Vere eventually reached this conclusion also, as after a five-year separation he dropped his charges and resumed living with Anne. (False charges of the adultery of a blameless young wife are a common theme in Shakespeare's plays. For example: *All's Well That Ends Well, Cymbeline, The Winter's Tale*, and *Othello*. And in every case the grievously wronged wife forgives her husband.)

During the five-year separation from his wife, de Vere had an affair with a court lady, which resulted in her pregnancy. Queen Elizabeth, angered at this, had de Vere arrested and sent to the Tower of London. He was released after a few months; but a friend of the young woman, resentful of de Vere's actions, attacked him, and de Vere was badly injured. Street brawls between the two families continued for a while, until the Queen threatened to jail them all unless the fighting stopped. (Reminds one of *Romeo and Juliet*.)

After de Vere resumed living with his wife, they had five children together. Then Anne, still only thirty-two years old, died suddenly. Four years later de Vere remarried, and his second wife outlived him.

Meanwhile, de Vere's financial affairs—which had been in bad shape, due to his spendthrift habits—had improved radically. In 1586, when de Vere was thirty-six years old, Queen Elizabeth granted him a lifetime pension in the extraordinary amount of 1,000 pounds a year. That is equivalent to about $100,000 a year today, tax-free! A remarkable sum, especially considering that Elizabeth was notoriously tight-fisted with money! Curiously, the grant made no mention of any duties which de Vere must perform in return, nor of any past services for which he was being rewarded. The grant, however, was paid regularly for the rest of her life, and her successor (King James I) continued to pay it after her death in 1603.

De Vere had always been intensely interested in poetry and the theatre, was friends with many literary figures, and as a young man is known to have written poetry and plays in his own name. (Those early plays have been lost, but several of the poems survive. Some of them are quite good, though well below the standard of the mature William Shakespeare.) However he did not publish any of them, due to the prevailing notion that it was discreditable for an aristocrat to write poetry for publication. (Such an attitude seems very peculiar nowadays; but historians agree that such an attitude was common at the time, and that the taboo was rarely violated.)

After the grant by Queen Elizabeth, though, de Vere never wrote another line in his own name. But within a few years, poems and plays started appearing by the invisible author "William Shakespeare."

Why did Elizabeth grant this extraordinarily generous pension to de Vere? Although no reason was ever stated, the obvious explanation is that she—like so many other monarchs before her—was patronizing a talented artist in the hopes that his achievements would glorify her reign. If that was her motive, she certainly got her money's worth. Indeed, no ruler before or since seems to have made a better choice!

After being awarded the pension by the Queen, the formerly very active Edward de Vere retired completely from court life. Presumably, he spent the last eighteen years of his life writing and revising the great plays and poetry that have made "William Shakespeare" famous. He died in 1604, during an epidemic of the plague, and was buried near his country home at Hackney, near the village of Stratford. (There were two towns in England named Stratford; and at the time that one was larger than Stratford-on-Avon.)

Unlike Shakspere—or any of the other persons suggested as the author—Edward de Vere seems to fit perfectly the requirements for the mysterious William Shakespeare.

He had an excellent education, had studied law, and was well-versed in foreign languages. (He certainly knew Latin and French, and possibly other languages as well.)

He was an aristocrat, and had an insider's knowledge of court life and court intrigue.

He had the large amount of free time necessary to compose the plays.

He was repeatedly described by others as brilliant and talented.

He had a lifelong interest in the theatre, and is known to have written poetry and plays in his own name when he was younger. Indeed, he was *specifically* named, during his lifetime, as one of those noblemen who had written poetry but (because of the taboo mentioned above) had not published it under his own name. Moreover, he was praised as the most skillful and excellent of the gentlemen who had done so. (These descriptions are in documents surviving from that era.)

The plays of William Shakespeare contain a large number of incidents and characters which can be clearly identified as relating to events, personalities, and situations in the life of Edward de Vere. (A few of them have been noted above, but there are many others.)

The only problem at all with accepting de Vere as the author of the plays is the question: Why did he keep his identity a secret? There are several possible explanations.

1) There was a strong taboo at that time against noblemen writing poetry for publication, or plays for the commercial theatre.

2) De Vere was known to be an insider at court. Since many of the plays dealt with court life, if he admitted authorship people would naturally (and probably correctly!) have assumed that various characters in the plays were intended as insulting parodies of various real people in court. Today, such writing is accepted as commonplace and, though hardly friendly, not a cause for action. By the standards of those days, however, it would at least have been grounds for a lawsuit, and more likely for a duel. By hiding his identity, de Vere avoided such problems.

3) Many of the sonnets of William Shakespeare are addressed

to a female lover. His admission of authorship, therefore, would be embarrassing to his wife.

4) Far worse, many of the other sonnets are addressed to a *male*, and have often been interpreted as showing that the author was homosexual or bisexual. Whether or not that interpretation is correct (and the majority of critics believe it is not), admitting that he was the author of the sonnets would have caused gossip that would have been very embarrassing to his family.

Perhaps no one of these answers is entirely convincing by itself. Taken together, though, they might indeed be the full explanation for de Vere's concealing his identity. However, it is certainly possible that he had additional reasons which we do not know of. (For example, it is possible that, as a condition of the pension granted him, Elizabeth had insisted that he follow the social norms—and avoid possible duels between her courtiers—by not publishing anything in his own name.)

Whether or not we know the full explanation for de Vere's concealing his authorship, he matches the requirements for Shakespeare perfectly in all other respects—and remember: nobody else even comes close! To me, it seems virtually certain that he is the author.

One final question: How did Shakspere ever get to be considered the author of the plays? That belief seems to have its origin in three references, each made a few years after Shakspere had died, and each somewhat ambiguous. Unless an unusual coincidence is postulated, it appears that someone (or ones) deliberately committed a hoax. Why was that done, and by whom?

We cannot be certain of the answer to that question; but the most likely explanation is that the hoax was perpetrated by de Vere's family when they decided (about 1620) to have his collected works published and chose to continue to keep his identity secret. Their motives were probably quite similar to his: fear of scandal (and perhaps other motives, such as a promise to the monarch). To make the deception more complete, they decided to present another person as the author. Shakspere was the obvious choice as the stand-in, because of the similarity of names. Also, since he had been dead for several years he could not expose the fraud; and since he was little known in London, and even less remembered, there were very few others in town who would realize that the story was a hoax.

The deception was probably fairly easy to carry out. Ben Jonson, who provided a prefatory poem to the First Folio edition, was persuaded to include a couple of ambiguous lines that strongly hinted (without saying so directly, or telling any other flat-out lies) that the author came from Stratford-on-Avon. They also arranged for a monument to be erected there, near Shakspere's grave, with an inscription which includes strong (though vague) words of praise. Since the identity of William Shakespeare had always been kept a secret, a few hints that he was the man from Stratford sufficed to get the story started. Nobody at the time was very interested in checking the story carefully. (There was much less interest in literary biography then than there is now.) By the time the first biography of Shakespeare was written (by William Rowe: 1709) those who knew the truth had long been dead, and the myth of Shakspere's authorship long accepted.

32 JOHN DALTON

1766-1844

John Dalton was the English scientist who, in the early nineteenth century, introduced the atomic hypothesis into the mainstream of science. By so doing, he provided the key idea that made possible the enormous progress in chemistry since his day.

To be sure, he was not the first person to suggest that all material objects are composed of vast numbers of exceedingly small, indestructible particles called atoms. That notion had been suggested by the ancient Greek philosopher, Democritus (460-370 B.C.?), and probably even earlier. The hypothesis was adopted by Epicurus (another Greek philosopher), and was brilliantly presented by the Roman writer, Lucretius (died: 55 B.C.), in his famous poem *De rerum natura (On the Nature of Things)*.

Democritus's theory (which had not been accepted by Aristotle) was neglected during the Middle Ages, and had little effect on modern science. Still, several leading scientists of the seventeenth century (including Isaac Newton) supported similar notions. But none of the earlier atomic theories were expressed quantitatively, nor were they used in scientific research. Most important, nobody saw the connection between the philosophical speculations about atoms and the hard facts of chemistry.

That was where Dalton came in. He presented a clear, quantitative theory, which could be used to interpret chemical experiments, and could be precisely tested in the laboratory.

Though his terminology was slightly different from the one we use now, Dalton clearly expressed the concepts of *atoms, molecules, elements,* and *chemical compounds*. He made it clear that although the total number of atoms in the world is very large, the number of different *types* of atoms is rather small. (His original book listed twenty elements, or species of atoms; today, slightly over a hundred elements are known.)

Though different types of atoms differ in weight, Dalton insisted that any two atoms of the same species are identical in all their properties, including mass. (Sophisticated modern experiments show that there are exceptions to this rule. For any given chemical element there exist two or more types of atoms—called *isotopes*—which differ slightly in mass, though their chemical properties are almost identical.) Dalton included in his book a table listing the relative weights of different kinds of atoms the first such table ever prepared, and a key feature of any quantitative atomic theory.

Dalton also stated clearly that any two molecules of the same chemical compound are composed of the same combination of atoms. (For example, each molecule of nitrous oxide consists of two atoms of nitrogen and one atom of oxygen.) From this it follows that a given chemical compound—no matter how it may be prepared, or where found—always contains the same elements in exactly the same proportion by weight. This is the "law of definite proportions," which had been discovered experimentally by Joseph Louis Proust a few years earlier.

So convincingly did Dalton present his theory that within twenty years it was adopted by the majority of scientists. Furthermore, chemists followed the program that his book suggested: determine exactly the relative atomic weights; analyze chemical compounds by weight; determine the exact combination of atoms which constitutes each species of molecule. The success of that program has, of course, been overwhelming.

It is difficult to overstate the importance of the atomic hypothesis. It is the central notion in our understanding of chemistry.

Dalton's table of atomic weights.

In addition, it is an indispensable prologue to much of modern physics. It is only because atomism had been so frequently discussed before Dalton that he does not appear even higher on this list.

Dalton was born in 1766, in the village of Eaglesfield, in northern England. His formal schooling ended when he was only eleven years old, and he was almost entirely self-taught in science. He was a precocious young man, and when he was twelve years old he became a teacher himself. He was to be a teacher or private tutor for most of his remaining years. When he was fifteen, he moved to the town of Kendal, and when he was twenty-six he moved to Manchester, where he dwelled until his death in 1811. He never married.

Dalton became interested in meteorology in 1787, when he was twenty-one years old. Six years later, he published a book on the subject. The study of air and the atmosphere aroused his interest in the properties of gases in general. By performing a series of experiments, he discovered two important laws governing the behavior of gases. The first, which Dalton presented in 1801, states that the volume occupied by a gas is proportional to its temperature. (It is generally known as Charles's law, after the French scientist who had discovered it several years before Dalton, but who had failed to publish his results.) The second, also presented in 1801, is known as Dalton's law of partial pressures.

By 1804, Dalton had formulated his atomic theory and prepared a list of atomic weights. However, his principal book, *A New System of Chemical Philosophy,* did not come out till 1808. That book made him famous, and in later years, many honors were accorded him.

Incidentally, Dalton suffered from a form of color blindness. Characteristically, the condition aroused his curiosity. He studied the subject and eventually published a scientific paper on color blindness—the first ever written on the topic!

33

ALEXANDER THE GREAT

3 5 6 B.C.- 3 2 3 B.C.

Alexander the Great, the most celebrated conqueror of the ancient world, was born in 356 B.C, in Pella, the capital city of
Macedonia. His father, King Philip II of Macedon, was a man of
truly outstanding ability and foresight. Philip enlarged and
reorganized the Macedonian army, and converted it into a
fighting force of the highest caliber. He first used this army to
conquer surrounding regions to the north of Greece, and then
turned south and conquered most of Greece itself. Next, Philip
created a federation of the Greek city-states, with himself as
leader. He was planning to make war on the vast Persian Empire
to the east of Greece; indeed, the invasion had already commenced, in 336 B.C, when Philip, still only forty-six years old, was
assassinated.

174

Alexander was only twenty years old when his father died, but he succeeded to the throne without difficulty. Philip had carefully prepared his son to succeed him, and the young Alexander already had considerable military experience. Nor had his father neglected his intellectual education. Alexander's tutor had been the brilliant philosopher Aristotle, perhaps the greatest scientist and philosopher of the ancient world.

In both Greece and the northern territories, the peoples conquered by Philip saw the occasion of his death as a good opportunity to throw off the Macedonian yoke. However, Alexander, in the two years following his accession to the throne, was able to subdue both regions. He then turned his attention to Persia.

For two hundred years, the Persians had governed a vast territory that stretched all the way from the Mediterranean to India. Although Persia was no longer at the height of its powers, it was still a formidable adversary—the largest, mightiest, and wealthiest empire on Earth.

Alexander launched his invasion of the Persian Empire in 334 B.C. Since he had to leave part of his army at home to maintain control of his European possessions, Alexander had only 35,000 troops with him when he set out on his audacious quest—a very small force compared with the Persian armies. In spite of the numerical disadvantage, Alexander won a series of crushing victories over the Persian forces. There were three main reasons for his success. In the first place, the army which Philip had left him was better trained and organized than the Persian forces. In the second place, Alexander was a general of outstanding genius, perhaps the greatest of all time. The third factor was Alexander's own personal courage. Although he would direct the early stages of each battle from behind the lines, Alexander's policy was to lead the decisive cavalry charge himself. This was a risky procedure, and he was frequently wounded. But his troops saw that Alexander was sharing their danger, and was not asking them to take any risks that he himself would not take. The effect on their morale was enormous.

Alexander first led his troops through Asia Minor, defeating the smaller Persian armies stationed there. Then, moving into northern Syria, he routed an immense Persian army at Issus. Alexander then moved further south, and after a difficult seven-month siege, conquered the Phoenician island-city of Tyre, in present-day Lebanon. While Alexander was besieging Tyre, he received a message from the Persian king offering to cede Alexander half of his empire in return for a peace treaty. One of Alexander's generals, Parmenio, thought the offer rather good. "I would take that offer, if I were Alexander," he said. "And so would I," Alexander replied, "if I were Parmenio."

After the fall of Tyre, Alexander continued south. Gaza fell after a two-month siege. Egypt surrendered to him without a fight. Alexander then paused for a while in Egypt to rest his troops. There, though still only twenty-four years old, he was crowned pharaoh and declared a god. He then led his armies back into Asia, and at the decisive battle of Arbela, in 331 B.C., he completely routed a much larger Persian army.

After that victory Alexander led his troops into Babylon, and into the Persian capitals of Susa and Persepolis. The Persian king, Darius III (not to be confused with his predecessor, Darius the Great), was assassinated by his officers in 330 B.C., to prevent him from surrendering to Alexander. Nevertheless, Alexander defeated and killed Darius's successor, and in three years of fighting, subdued all of eastern Iran and pushed on into Central Asia.

With the whole Persian Empire now subject to him, Alexander might now have returned home and reorganized his new dominions. But his thirst for conquest was still unslaked, and he continued on, into Afghanistan. From there he led his army across the Hindu Kush mountains into India. He won a series of victories in western India, and intended to continue on to eastern India. His troops, however, exhausted by years of fighting, refused to go any farther, and Alexander reluctantly returned to Persia.

After returning to Persia, Alexander spent the next year or so reorganizing his empire and army. And a major reorganization it was. Alexander had been brought up to believe that Greek culture represented the only true civilization, and that all of the non-Greek peoples were barbarians. Such, of course, was the prevailing view throughout the Greek world, and even Aristotle had shared it. But, despite the fact that he had thoroughly defeated the Persian armies, Alexander had come to realize that the Persians were not barbarians at all, and that individual Persians could be as intelligent, capable, and worthy of respect as individual Greeks. He therefore conceived the notion of fusing the two parts of his empire together, thereby creating a joint Graeco-Persian culture and kingdom, with himself, of course, as ruler So far as we can determine, he really intended the Persians to be equal partners with the Greeks and Macedonians. To implement this plan, he took large numbers of Persians into his army. He

The Empire of Alexander the Great.

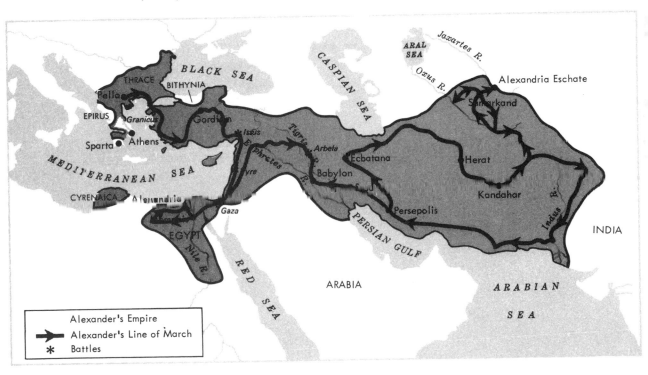

also held a great feast, "the marriage of East and West," at which several thousand Macedonian troops were formally married to Asian women. He himself, although he had previously married an Asian princess, married the daughter of Darius.

It is plain that Alexander intended to make additional conquests with this reorganized army. We know that he planned to invade Arabia, and probably also the regions north of the Persian Empire. He may also have intended another invasion of India, or the conquest of Rome, Carthage, and the western Mediterranean. Whatever his plans may have been, as it turned out, there were to be no further conquests. In early June, in the year 323 B.C., while in Babylon, Alexander suddenly fell ill of a fever, and he died ten days later. He was not yet thirty-three years old.

Alexander had named no successor, and soon after his death a fight for power ensued. In the struggle that followed, Alexander's mother, wives, and children were all killed. His empire was eventually divided among his generals.

Because Alexander died young and undefeated, there has been much speculation as to what might have occurred had he lived. If he had led his forces into an invasion of the western Mediterranean lands, he would most likely have been successful, and in that case, the entire history of western Europe might have been vastly different. But such speculations, however interesting, have little relevance to an assessment of Alexander's actual influence.

Alexander was perhaps the most dramatic figure in history, and his career and personality have remained a source of fascination. The true facts of his career are dramatic enough, and dozens of legends have grown up around his name. It was plainly his ambition to be the greatest warrior of all time, and he seems to deserve that title. As an individual fighter, he combined ability and courage. As a general, he was supreme, and in eleven years of fighting, he never lost a single battle.

At the same time, however, he was an intellectual who had studied under Aristotle and treasured the poetry of Homer. Indeed, in his realization that non-Greeks were not necessarily bar-

*Alexander on horseback, detail from "The Battle of
Alexander," mosaic at Pompei from the 2nd century,* B.C.

barians, he showed far more vision than most Greek thinkers of
his day. In other ways, however, he was surprisingly short-
sighted. Although he repeatedly risked his life in battle, he made
no provisions for a successor, and his failure to do so was in large
part responsible for the rapid breakup of his empire after his
death.

Alexander reputedly could be very charming, and he was
often extremely conciliatory and charitable to defeated enemies.

On the other hand, he was also an egomaniac with a ferocious temper. On one occasion, in a drunken argument, he killed a close associate of his, Cleitus, a man who had once saved his life.

Like Napoleon and Hitler, Alexander had an overwhelming effect upon his own generation. His short-term influence, however, was less than theirs, simply because the limited means of travel and communication existing at the time restricted his influence to a smaller portion of the globe.

In the long run, the most important effect of Alexander's conquests was to bring the Greek and Middle Eastern civilizations into close contact with each other, and thereby to greatly enrich both cultures. During and immediately after Alexander's career, Greek culture spread rapidly into Iran, Mesopotamia, Syria, Judea, and Egypt; before Alexander, Greek culture had been entering these regions only slowly. Also, Alexander spread Greek influence into India and Central Asia, areas which it had never reached before. But the cultural influence was by no means a one-way affair. During the Hellenistic Age (the centuries immediately following Alexander's career), eastern ideas—particularly religious ideas—spread into the Greek world. It was this Hellenistic culture—predominantly Greek but with strong oriental influences—that eventually affected Rome.

In the course of his career, Alexander founded more than twenty new cities. The most famous of these was Alexandria, in Egypt, which soon became one of the leading cities of the world, and a notable center of learning and culture. A few others, such as Herat and Kandahar in Afghanistan, also developed into cities of importance.

Alexander, Napoleon, and Hitler seem fairly close in overall influence. One gets the impression, though, that the influence of the other two men will be less enduring than that of Alexander. On that basis, he has been ranked slightly above them, even though his short-term influence was somewhat less than theirs.

34 NAPOLEON BONAPARTE

1769-1821

The celebrated French general and emperor, Napoleon I, was born in Ajaccio, Corsica, in 1769. His original name was Napoleone Buonaparte. France had acquired Corsica only some fifteen months before his birth, and in his early years, Napoleon was a Corsican nationalist who considered the French to be oppressors. Nevertheless, Napoleon was sent to military academies in France, and when he graduated in 1785, at the age of sixteen, he became a second lieutenant in the French army.

Four years later, the French Revolution erupted, and within a few years, the new French government was involved in wars with several foreign powers. Napoleon's first opportunity to distinguish himself came in 1793, at the siege of Toulon (in which the French recaptured the city from the British), where he was in charge of the artillery. (By this time he had abandoned his Corsican nationalist ideas and considered himself a Frenchman.) His accomplishments at Toulon won him promotion to brigadier general, and in 1796, he was given the command of the French army in Italy. There, in 1796-97, Napoleon achieved a spectacular series of victories. A hero, he then returned to Paris.

In 1798, Napoleon headed a French invasion of Egypt. The campaign was a disaster. On the land, Napoleon's armies were generally successful. But the British navy, under the leadership of Lord Nelson, destroyed the French fleet, and in 1799 Napoleon abandoned his army in Egypt and returned to France.

Back in France, Napoleon found that the public remembered the successes of his Italian campaign rather than the debacle of the Egyptian expedition. Capitalizing on this, a month after his return, Napoleon took part in a *coup d' etat*, together with the Abbé Sièyes and others. The coup resulted in a new government, the Consulate, with Napoleon holding the office of first consul. Although an elaborate constitution was adopted, and was ratified by a popular plebiscite, it was only a mask for the military dictatorship of Napoleon, who had soon gained the ascendancy over the other conspirators.

Napoleon's rise to power was, thus, incredibly rapid. In August 1793, before the siege of Toulon, Napoleon had been a totally unknown twenty-four-year-old minor officer of not-quite French birth. Less than six years later, Napoleon, still only thirty, was the undisputed ruler of France—a position he was to hold for over fourteen years.

During his years in power, Napoleon instituted major revisions in the administration of France and in the French legal system. For example, he reformed the financial structure and the judiciary; he created the Bank of France and the University of

Napoleon before the Sphinx ("L'Oedipe") by J. L. Gerome.

France; and he centralized the French administration. Although each of these changes had a significant, and in some cases enduring, impact on France itself, they had little impact on the rest of the world.

One of Napoleon's reforms, however, was destined to have an impact far beyond the borders of France. That was the creation of the French civil code, the famous *Code Napoleon*. In many ways the code embodied the ideals of the French Revolution. For example, under the code there were no privileges of birth, and all men were equal under the law. At the same time, the code was sufficiently close to the older French laws and customs to be acceptable to the French public and the legal profession. On the whole, the code was moderate, well organized, and written with commendable brevity and outstanding lucidity. As a result, the code has not only endured in France (the French civil code today is strikingly similar to the original *Code Napoleon)* but has been adopted, with local modifications, in many other countries.

It was always Napoleon's policy to insist that he was the defender of the Revolution. Nevertheless, in 1804 he had himself proclaimed Emperor of France. In addition, Napeoleon installed three of his brothers on the thrones of other European states. These actions doubtless aroused the resentment of some French republicans—who considered such behavior a complete betrayal of the ideals of the French Revolution—but Napoleon's only serious difficulties were to result from his foreign wars.

In 1802, at Amiens, Napoleon had signed a peace treaty with England, giving France a respite after more than a decade of almost continuous warfare. However, the following year the peace treaty broke down, and a long series of wars with England and her allies followed. Though Napoleon's armies repeatedly won victories on the land, England could not be conquered unless her navy was defeated. Unfortunately for Napoleon, at the crucial battle of Trafalgar, in 1805, the English navy won an overwhelming victory; thereafter, England's control of the seas was not seriously disputed. Although Napoleon's greatest victory (at Austerlitz, against the armies of Austria and Russia) came only six weeks after Trafalgar, it did not really compensate for the naval disaster.

In 1808, Napoleon foolishly involved France in a long and pointless war on the Iberian peninsula, in which French armies were bogged down for years. Napoleon's decisive blunder, however, was his Russian campaign. In 1807, Napoleon had met with the Czar, and in the Treaty of Tilsit, they had vowed eternal friendship. But the alliance gradually deteriorated, and in June 1812, Napoleon led his *Grande Armée* into Russia.

The results are well known. The Russian army generally avoided fighting pitched battles against Napoleon, and he was able to advance rapidly. By September, he had occupied

Moscow. However, the Russians set fire to the city, and most of it was destroyed. After waiting five weeks in Moscow (in a vain hope that the Russians would sue for peace), Napoleon finally decided to retreat. But by then it was too late. The combination of the Russian army, the Russian winter, and the inadequate supplies of the French army soon turned the retreat into a rout. Less than 10 percent of the *Grande Armée* got out of Russia alive.

Other European countries, such as Austria and Prussia, realized that they now had an opportunity to throw off the French yoke. They joined forces against Napoleon, and at the battle of Leipzig, in October 1813, Napoleon suffered another crushing defeat. The following year he resigned and was banished to Elba, a small island off the Italian coast.

In 1815, he escaped from Elba and returned to France, where he was welcomed and restored to power. But the other European powers promptly declared war, and a hundred days after his restoration, he met his final defeat at Waterloo. After Waterloo, Napoleon was imprisoned by the British on St. Helena, a small island in the south Atlantic. He died there, of cancer, in 1821.

Napoleon's military career presents a surprising paradox. His genius at tactical maneuvering was dazzling, and if he were to be judged only by that, he might perhaps be considered the greatest general of all time. In the field of grand strategy, however, he was prone to making incredibly gross blunders, such as the invasions of Egypt and Russia. His strategic errors were so egregious that Napoleon should not be placed in the first rank of military leaders. Is this unfair second-guessing? I think not. Certainly, one criterion of a general's greatness is his ability to avoid disastrous errors. It is very hard to second-guess the very greatest generals, such as Alexander the Great, Genghis Khan, and Tamerlane, whose armies were never defeated. Because Napoleon was defeated in the end, all of his foreign conquests proved ephemeral. After his final defeat, in 1815, France possessed less territory than she had in 1789, at the outbreak of the Revolution.

Napoleon was, of course, an egomaniac, and he has often been compared to Hitler. But there is a crucial difference between the two men. Whereas Hitler was motivated in large part by a hideous ideology, Napoleon was merely an ambitious opportunist, and he had no particular interest in perpetrating horrible massacres. Nothing in Napoleon's regime remotely compares with the Nazi concentration camps.

Napoleon's very great fame makes it easy to overestimate his influence. His *short-term* influence was indeed enormous, probably larger than Alexander the Great's had been, though much less than Hitler's. (It has been estimated that approximately 500,000 French soldiers died during the Napoleonic Wars; however, in comparison, it has been estimated that 8,000,000 Germans died during the Second World War.) By any standard, Napoleon's activities disrupted far fewer of his contemporaries' lives than did Hitler's.

In regard to long-term influence, Napoleon seems more important than Hitler, though less so than Alexander. Napoleon made extensive administrative changes in France, but France comprises less than one-seventieth of the world's population. In any event, such administrative changes should be viewed in proper prospective. They have had far less effect upon the lives of individual Frenchmen than the numerous technological changes of the last two centuries.

It has been said that the Napoleonic era provided time for the changes instituted during the French Revolutionary era to become established, and for the gains made by the French bourgeoisie to be consolidated. By 1815, when the French monarchy was finally re-established, these changes were so well entrenched that a return to the social patterns of the *ancien régime* was unthinkable. The most important changes, however, had been instituted before Napoleon; by 1799, when Napoleon took office, it was probably already too late for any return to the *status quo ante*. However, Napoleon, despite his own monarchical ambitions, did play a role in spreading the ideals of the French Revolution throughout Europe.

Napoleon also had a large, though indirect, effect on the

history of Latin America. His invasion of Spain so weakened the Spanish government that for a period of several years it lost effective control of its colonies in Latin America. It was during this period of *de facto* autonomony that the Latin American independence movements commenced.

Of all Napoleon's actions, however, the one that has perhaps had the most enduring and significant consequences was one that was almost irrelevant to his main plans. In 1803, Napoleon sold a vast tract of land to the United States. He realized that the French possessions in North America might be difficult to protect from British conquest, and besides he was short of cash. The Louisiana Purchase, perhaps the largest peaceful transfer of land in all of history, transformed the United States into a nation of near-continental size. It is difficult to say what the United States would have been like without the Louisiana Purchase; certainly it would have been a vastly different country than it is today. Indeed, it is doubtful whether the United States would have become a great power without the Louisiana Purchase.

Napoleon, of course, was not solely responsible for the Louisiana Purchase. The American government clearly played a role as well. But the French offer was such a bargain that it seems likely that any American government would have accepted it, while the decision of the French government to sell the Louisiana territory came about through the arbitrary judgment of a single individual, Napoleon Bonaparte.

Napoleon at the Battle of Waterloo.

35 THOMAS EDISON

1847-1931

The versatile inventor Thomas Alva Edison was born in 1847, in the town of Milan, Ohio. He had only three months of formal education, and his schoolmaster considered him to be retarded!

Edison created his first invention, an electric vote-recorder, when he was only twenty-one years old. It did not sell, and thereafter Edison concentrated on inventing objects that he expected would be readily marketable. Not long after the vote-recorder, he invented an improved stock ticker system which he sold for forty thousand dollars, a tremendous sum in those days. A series of other inventions followed, and Edison was soon both wealthy and famous. Probably his most original invention was the phonograph, which he patented in 1877. More important to the world, however, was his development of a practical incandescent light bulb in 1879.

Edison was not the first to invent an electrical lighting system. A few years earlier, electric arc lamps had been utilized for street lighting in Paris. But Edison's bulb, together with the system of distributing electric power that he developed, made electric lighting practical for ordinary home use. In 1882, his company started producing electricity for homes in New York City, and thereafter the home use of electricity spread rapidly throughout the world.

By setting up the first distribution company that carried electrical power into private homes, Edison laid the groundwork for the development of an enormous industry. It is, after all, not only the electric light which uses this power source today, but the whole array of home electrical appliances, from the TV set to the washing machine. Furthermore, the availability of electric power from the distribution network that Edison had established greatly stimulated the use of electricity by industry.

Edison contributed enormously to the development of motion-picture cameras and projectors. He made important improvements in the telephone (where his carbon transmitter markedly improved audibility), in the telegraph, and in the typewriter. Among his other inventions were a dictating machine, a mimeograph machine, and a storage battery. All told, Edison patented more than a thousand separate inventions—a truly incredible total.

One reason for Edison's astonishing productivity is that early in his career he set up a research laboratory at Menlo Park, New Jersey, where he employed a group of capable assistants to help him. This was the prototype of the large research laboratories that so many industrial firms have since established. Edison's origination of the modern, well-equipped research laboratory, where many persons work together as a team, was one of his most important inventions—though, of course, one which he could not patent.

Edison was not merely an inventor; he also engaged in manufacturing and organized several industrial companies. The most important of these eventually became the General Electric Company.

Although not by temperament a pure scientist, Edison did make one significant scientific discovery. In 1882, he discovered that in a near-vacuum, an electric current could be made to flow between two wires that did *not* touch each other. This phenomenon, called the Edison effect, is not only of considerable theoretical interest, but has important practical applications as well. It led, in time, to the development of the vacuum tube and to the foundation of the electronics industry.

For most of his life, Edison suffered from seriously impaired hearing. However, he more than compensated for that handicap by his astonishing capacity for hard work. Edison was married twice (his first wife died young) and had three children by each marriage. He died in West Orange, New Jersey, in 1931.

There is no dispute concerning Edison's talent. Everyone agrees that he was the greatest inventive genius who ever lived. His parade of useful inventions is awe-inspiring, even though it is probable that most of them would have been developed by others within thirty years. However, if we consider his inventions individually, we see that no one of them was of really critical importance. The incandescent light bulb, for example, although widely used, is not an irreplaceable part of modern life. In fact, fluorescent light bulbs, which operate on a completely different scientific principle, are also widely used, and our everyday life would not be much different if we had no incandescent bulbs at all. Indeed, before electric lights came into use, candles, oil lamps, and gaslights were generally regarded as reasonably satisfactory sources of light.

The phonograph is certainly an ingenious device, but no one would claim that it has transformed our daily life to the extent that radio, television, or the telephone have. Futhermore, in recent years, quite different methods of recording sound have been developed, such as the magnetic tape recorder, and today it would make relatively little difference if there were no phonographs or record players at all. Many of Edison's patents related to improvements of devices that other persons had already invented and that were already in quite usable form. Such improvements, although helpful, cannot be considered of major importance in the overall sweep of history.

But although no single one of Edison's inventions was of overwhelming importance, it is worth remembering that he did not invent just one device, but more than one thousand. It is for this reason that I have ranked Edison higher than such renowned inventors as Guglielmo Marconi and Alexander Graham Bell.

Edison in his laboratory at Menlo Park.

36 ANTONY VAN LEEUWENHOEK

1632-1723

Antony van Leeuwenhoek, the man who discovered microbes, was born in 1632, in the town of Delft, in the Netherlands. He came from a middle-class family, and for most of his adult life held a minor post with the town government.

Leeuwenhoek's great discovery came about because he had taken up microscopy as a hobby. In those days, of course, one could not purchase microscopes in a store, and Leeuwenhoek constructed his own instruments. He was never a professional lens grinder, nor did he ever receive formal instruction in the field; but the skill he developed was truly remarkable, far exceeding that of any of the professionals of his day.

Although the compound microscope had been invented a generation before he was born, Leeuwenhoek did not make use of it. Instead, by very careful and accurate grinding of small lenses of very short focal length, Leeuwenhoek was able to attain a resolving power greater than that of any of the early compound microscopes. One of his surviving lenses has a magnifying power of about 270 times, and there are indications that he had made even more powerful ones.

Leeuwenhoek was an extremely patient and careful observer, and he was possessed of keen eyesight and unbounded curiosity. With his minute lenses, he examined a wide variety of materials, from human hair to dog's semen; from rain water to small insects; as well as muscle fibers, skin tissues, and many other specimens. He took careful notes, and he made meticulous drawings of the things he observed.

From 1673 on, Leeuwenhoek was in correspondence with the Royal Society of England, the leading scientific society of his day. Despite his lack of advanced education (he had attended an elementary school, but knew no language except Dutch), he was elected a fellow of the society in 1680. He also became a corresponding member of the Academy of Sciences in Paris.

Leeuwenhoek married twice and had six children, but no grandchildren. He enjoyed good health, and was able to continue working in his later years. Many dignitaries came to visit him, including both the Czar of Russia (Peter the Great) and the Queen of England. He died in 1723, in Delft, at the age of ninety.

Leeuwenhoek made many significant discoveries. He was the first person to describe spermatozoa (1677), and one of the earliest to describe red blood corpuscles. He opposed the theory of spontaneous generation of lower forms of life, and presented much evidence against it. He was able to show, for example, that fleas propagate in the usual manner of winged insects.

His greatest discovery came in 1674, when he made the first observations of microbes. It was one of the great seminal discoveries in human history. Inside a small drop of water,

Leeuwenhoek had discovered an entire new world, a totally un-suspected new world, teeming with life. And although he did not know it yet, this new world was of very great importance to human beings. Indeed, those "very little animalcules" that he had observed often held the power of life and death over humans. Once he had studied them, Leeuwenhoek was able to find microbes in many different places: in wells and ponds, in rain water, in the mouths and intestines of human beings. He described various types of bacteria, as well as protozoa, and calculated their sizes.

Applications of Leeuwenhoek's great discovery were not to come until the time of Pasteur, almost two centuries later. In fact, the entire subject of microbiology remained practically dor-mant until the nineteenth century, when improved microscopes were developed. One might therefore argue that had Leeuwenhoek never lived, and his discoveries not been made un-til the nineteenth century, it might have made little difference to the progress of science. However, there is no denying that Leeuwenhoek did discover microbes, and that it was through him that the scientific world actually became aware of their ex-istence.

Leeuwenhoek is sometimes regarded as a man who by sheer luck happened to stumble on an important scientific discovery. Nothing could be further from the truth. His discovery of microorganisms was a natural consequence of his careful con-struction of microscopes of unprecedented quality, and of his pa-tience and accuracy as an observer. In other words, his discovery resulted from a combination of skill and hard work—the very an-tithesis of mere luck.

The discovery of microbes is one of the few really important scientific discoveries that is largely attributable to the work of a single person. Leeuwenhoek worked alone. His discovery of pro-tozoa and bacteria was unanticipated and—unlike most other advances in biology—was in no sense a natural outgrowth of previous biological knowledge. It is that factor, together with the importance of the eventual applications of his discovery, which account for his high place on this list.

37 WILLIAM T. G. MORTON

1819-1868

The name of William Thomas Green Morton may not ring a bell in the minds of most readers. He was, however, a far more influential person than many more famous men, for Morton was the man principally responsible for the introduction of the use of anesthesia in surgery.

Few inventions in all of history are so highly valued by individual human beings as anesthetics, and few have made as profound a difference in the human condition. The grimness of surgery in the days when a patient had to be awake while a surgeon sawed through his bones is frightful to contemplate. The ability to put an end to this kind of pain is certainly one of the greatest gifts that any man ever gave to his fellows.

195

Morton was born in 1819, in Charlton, Massachusetts. As a young man, he studied at the Baltimore College of Dental Surgery. In 1842, he began the practice of dentistry. For a while, in 1842 and 1843, he was the partner of Horace Wells, a slightly older dentist who was himself interested in anesthesia. It seems, however, that their partnership was not profitable, and it ended in late 1843.

A year later, Wells began experimenting with nitrous oxide ("laughing gas") as an anesthetic. He was able to use it effectively in his dental practice in Hartford, Connecticut. Unfortunately, however, a public demonstration that he attempted in Boston was unsuccessful.

In his own dental practice, Morton specialized in fitting people for artificial teeth. To do this properly, it was necessary to extract the roots of the old teeth first. Such extraction, in the days before anesthesia, was extremely painful, and the desirability of some means of anesthesia was apparent. Morton correctly judged that nitrous oxide would not be sufficiently effective for his purposes, and he searched for a more powerful agent.

Charles T. Jackson, a learned doctor and scientist whom Morton knew, suggested that he try using ether. That ether had anesthetic properties had been discovered more than three hundred years earlier by Paracelsus, a famous Swiss physician and alchemist; one or two similar reports had also been printed during the first part of the nineteenth century. But neither Jackson, nor any of the persons who had written about ether, had ever used the chemical in a surgical operation.

Ether sounded like a promising possibility to Morton, and he experimented with it, first on animals (including his pet dog) and then on himself. Finally, on September 30, 1846, a perfect opportunity arose for testing ether on a patient. A man named Eben Frost walked into Morton's office with a terrible toothache and a willingness to try anything which might relieve the pain of the necessary extraction. Morton administered ether to him and then pulled his tooth. When Frost regained consciousness, he reported that he had felt no pain. A better result could hardly have been hoped for, and Morton could see success, fame, and fortune in front of him.

Although the operation had been witnessed, and was reported in Boston newspapers the next day, it did not attract widespread attention. Clearly, a more dramatic demonstration was needed. Morton therefore asked Dr. John C. Warren, senior surgeon at Massachusetts General Hospital in Boston, for an opportunity to give a practical demonstration—before a group of doctors—of his method of preventing pain. Dr. Warren agreed, and a demonstration was scheduled at the hospital. There, on October 16, 1846, before a considerable audience of doctors and medical students, Morton administered ether to a surgical patient, Gilbert Abbott; Dr. Warren then removed a tumor from Abbott's neck. The anesthetic proved completely effective, and the demonstration was an overwhelming success. That demonstration, which was promptly reported in many newspapers, was directly responsible for the widespread use of anesthetics in surgical operations over the course of the next few years.

Several days after the operation on Abbott, an application for a patent was filed by Morton and Jackson. Although a patent was granted to them the following month, it did not prevent a series of priority fights from arising. Morton's claim that he was entitled to most of the credit for the introduction of anesthesia was contested by a few other persons, particularly by Jackson. Furthermore, Morton's expectation that his innovation would make him rich was not fulfilled. Most doctors and hospitals who made use of ether did not bother to pay any royalties. The costs of litigation and of his struggle for priority soon exceeded the money that Morton received for his invention. Frustrated and impoverished, he died in 1868, in New York City. He was not quite forty-nine years old.

The usefulness of anesthesia in dentistry and in major surgery is obvious. In estimating Morton's overall importance, therefore, the main difficulty is in deciding to what extent credit for the introduction of anesthesia should be divided between

Morton and the various other men involved. The principal other
persons to be considered are: Horace Wells, Charles Jackson, and
Crawford W. Long, a Georgia doctor. On considering the facts,
it appears to me that Morton's contribution was far more important that any of the others', and I have ranked him accordingly.

It is true enough that Horace Wells had started using
anesthesia in his dental practice almost two years before Morton's successful use of ether. But the anesthetic that Wells used,
nitrous oxide, did not and could not have revolutionized surgery.
Despite some desirable qualities, nitrous oxide is simply not a
powerful enough anesthetic to be used alone in major surgery. (It
is useful today when employed in a sophisticated combination
with other drugs, and also in some dental work.) Ether, on the
other hand, is an amazingly effective and versatile chemical, and
its use revolutionized surgery. In most individual cases today, a

Morton anesthetizes a patient.

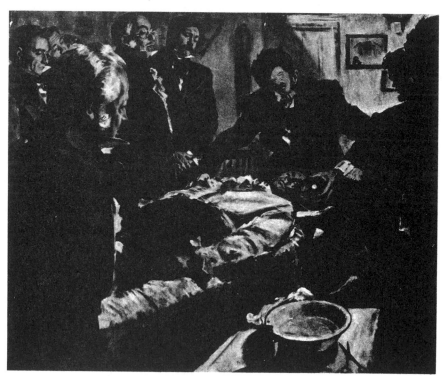

more desirable drug, or combination of drugs, than ether can be found; but for roughly a century after its introduction, ether was the anesthetic most usually employed. Despite its disadvantages (it is inflammable, and nausea is a common after-effect of its use), it is still perhaps the most versatile single anesthetic ever discovered. It is easy to transport and to administer; and, most important of all, combines safety and potency.

Crawford W. Long (born 1815, died 1878) was a Georgian doctor who had used ether in surgical operations as early as 1842, which was four years before Morton's demonstration. However, Long did not publish his results until 1849, which was long after Morton's demonstration had made the usefulness of ether in surgery well known to the medical world. As a result, Long's work benefited only a handful of patients, whereas Morton's work benefited the world at large.

Charles Jackson suggested the use of ether to Morton, and he also gave Morton helpful advice on how to administer ether to patients. On the other hand, Jackson himself never made any significant use of ether in a surgical operation; nor, prior to Morton's successful demonstration, did Jackson make any attempt to inform the medical world of what he did know about ether. It was Morton, not Jackson, who risked his reputation by making a public demonstration. If Gilbert Abbott had died on the operating table, it seems exceedingly unlikely that Charles T. Jackson would have claimed any responsibility for the demonstration.

Where does William Morton belong on this list? An apt comparison could be made between Morton and Joseph Lister. Both were medical men; both are famous for introducing a new technique or procedure that revolutionized surgery and childbearing; both of the innovations seem, in hindsight, to have been fairly obvious; neither man was actually the first to employ the technique or procedure which was publicized and popularized through his efforts; and each must share the credit for his innovation with others. I have ranked Morton higher than Lister principally because I believe that in the long run the introduction of anesthesia was a more important development than the introduction of antiseptic surgery. After all, to some extent, modern antibiotics can substitute for the lack of antiseptic measures during surgery. Without anesthesia, delicate or prolonged operations were not feasible, and even simple operations were often avoided until it was too late for them to be of help.

The public demonstration of a practical means of anesthesia that Morton gave on that October morning in 1846 is one of the great dividing points in human history. Perhaps nothing sums up Morton's achievement better than the inscription on his monument:

William T. G. Morton
Inventor and revealer of anesthetic inhalation,
By whom pain in surgery was averted and annulled;
Before whom surgery was at all times agony,
Since whom science has control of pain.

With this glass container, Morton first administered sulphuric ether to a patient in 1846.

38

GUGLIELMO MARCONI

1874-1937

Guglielmo Marconi, the inventor of the radio, was born in
Bologna, Italy, in 1874. His family was quite well-to-do, and he
was educated by private tutors. In 1894, when he was twenty
years old, Marconi read of the experiments that Heinrich Hertz
had performed a few years earlier. Those experiments had clearly demonstrated the existence of invisible electromagnetic waves,
which move through the air with the speed of light.

Marconi was immediately fired by the idea that these waves
could be used to send signals across great distances without
wires. This would provide many possibilities of communication
that were not possible with the telegraph. For example, by this
method messages might be sent to ships at sea.

By 1895, after only a year's work, Marconi succeeded in pro-

ducing a working device. In 1896, he demonstrated his device in
England, and received his first patent on the invention. Marconi
soon formed a company, and the first "Marconigrams" were sent
in 1898. The following year, he was able to send wireless
messages across the English Channel. Although his most important patent was granted in 1900, Marconi continued to make and
patent many improvements on his invention. In 1901, he succeeded in sending a radio message across the Atlantic Ocean,
from England to Newfoundland.

The importance of the new invention was dramatically
illustrated in 1909, when the *S.S. Republic* was damaged in a
collision and sank at sea. Radio messages brought help, and all
but six persons were rescued. That same year, Marconi won a
Nobel Prize for his invention. The following year, he succeeded
in transmitting radio messages from Ireland to Argentina, a
distance of over six thousand miles.

All these messages, by the way, were sent in the dot-and-
dash system of Morse code. It was known that the voice could
also be transmitted by radio, but this was not done until 1906.

Marconi in his floating laboratory, the yacht "Elettra."

Radio broadcasting on a commercial scale only began in the early 1920s, but then its popularity and importance grew very quickly.

An invention to which the patent rights were so extremely valuable was certain to stimulate legal disputes. However, this litigation died out after 1914, when the courts recognized Marconi's clear priority. In his later years, Marconi did significant research in shortwave and microwave communication. He died in Rome, in 1937.

Since Marconi is famous only as an inventor, it is clear that his influence is proportional to the importance of radio and its direct offshoots. (Marconi did not invent television. However, the invention of radio was a very important precursor of television, and it therefore seems just to give Marconi part of the credit for the development of television as well.) Obviously, wireless communication is enormously important in the modern world. It is used for the transmission of news, for entertainment, for military purposes, for scientific research, and in police work, as well as for other purposes. Although for some purposes the telegraph (which had been invented more than half a century earlier) would serve almost as well, for a large number of uses the radio is irreplaceable. It can reach automobiles, ships at sea, airplanes in flight, and even spacecraft. It is plainly a more important invention than the telephone, since a message sent by telephone might be sent by radio instead, whereas radio messages can be sent to places that cannot be reached by telephone.

Marconi has been ranked higher on this list than Alexander Graham Bell, simply because wireless communication is a more important invention than the telephone. I have ranked Edison slightly above Marconi because of the vast number of his inventions, even though no one of them is nearly as important as the radio. Since radio and television are only a small part of the practical applications of the theoretical work of Michael Faraday and James Clerk Maxwell, it seems fair that Marconi should be ranked considerably below those two men. It seems equally clear that only a handful of the most important political figures have had as much influence on the world as Marconi has had, and therefore, he is entitled to a fairly high place on this list.

39 ADOLF HITLER

1889 - 1945

I must confess that it is with a feeling of disgust that I include Adolf Hitler in this book. IIis influence was almost entirely pernicious, and I have no desire to honor a man whose chief importance lies in his having caused the deaths of some thirty-five million people. However, there is no getting away from the fact that Hitler had an enormous influence upon the lives of a very great number of persons.

Adolf Hitler was born in 1889, in Braunau, Austria. As a young man, he was an unsuccessful artist, and sometime during his youth he became an ardent German nationalist. During

World War I, he served in the German army, was wounded, and received two medals for bravery.

Germany's defeat left him shocked and angered. In 1919, when he was thirty, he joind a tiny, right-wing party in Munich, which soon changed its name to the National Socialist German Workers' Party (the Nazi party, for short). Within two years he had become its undisputed leader (in German: Fuehrer).

Under Hitler's leadership, the Nazi party rapidly increased in strength, and in November 1923, it attempted a coup d'etat known as "the Munich Beer Hall Putsch." When the putsch failed, Hitler was arrested, tried for treason, and convicted. However, he was released from jail after serving less than one year of his sentence.

In 1928, the Nazi party was still small. However, the advent of the Great Depression caused a general public disaffection with the established German political parties. The Nazis rapidly gained strength, and in January 1933, at the age of forty-four, Hitler became chancellor of Germany.

Upon becoming chancellor, Hitler rapidly established a dictatorship by using the government apparatus to crush all opposition. It should not be thought that this process consisted of a gradual erosion of civil liberties and the rights of criminal defendants. It was accomplished very quickly, and the Nazis frequently did not bother with trials at all. Many political opponents were beaten up, or simply murdered outright. Still, in the pre-war years, Hitler gained the genuine support of most Germans, because he was able to reduce unemployment and generate economic recovery.

Hitler then set Germany on a path of conquest that was to produce World War II. He achieved his first territorial gains without actually going to war. England and France, beset with their own economic problems, so desperately desired peace that they did not intervene when Hitler violated the Treaty of Versailles by building up the German army, nor when his troops occupied and fortified the Rhineland (March 1936), nor when he forcibly annexed Austria (March 1938). They even acquiesced

(September 1938) to his annexation of the Sudetenland, the well-fortified border region of Czechoslovakia. An international agreement known as the Munich Pact, which the British and French hoped would buy "peace in our time," left Czechoslovakia helpless, and Hitler took over the rest of that country a few months later. At each stage, Hitler cleverly combined arguments justifying his actions with the threat that he would go to war if his desires were thwarted, and at each stage, the Western democracies timidly backed down.

England and France, however, were determined to defend Poland, Hitler's next target. Hitler first protected himself by signing, in August 1939, a "non-aggression" pact with Stalin (actually an offensive alliance, in which the two dictators agreed on how to divide Poland between them). Nine days later, Germany attacked Poland, and sixteen days after that, the Soviet Union did also. Though England and France declared war on Germany, Poland was quickly defeated.

Hitler's greatest year was 1940. In April, his armies gobbled up Denmark and Norway. In May, they overran Holland, Belgium, and Luxembourg. In June, France capitulated. But later that year, the British withstood a long series of attacks by the German air force—the celebrated "Battle of Britain"—and Hitler was never able to launch an invasion of England.

Hitler's armies conquered Greece and Yugoslavia in April 1941. In June 1941, Hitler tore up his non-aggression pact with the Russians and attacked them, too. His armies conquered enormous stretches of Soviet territory, but were unable to eliminate the Russian armies before winter. Though already fighting both England and Russia, Hitler nevertheless declared war on the United States in December 1941, a few days after the Japanese had attacked the United States naval base at Pearl Harbor.

By the middle of 1942, Germany ruled a larger portion of Europe than had ever been controlled by any nation in history; in addition, she ruled much of North Africa. The turning point of the war came in the last half of 1942, when Germany lost the crucial battles of El Alamein in Egypt and Stalingrad in Russia.

After those setbacks, German military fortunes declined steadily. But although Germany's eventual defeat should now have seemed inevitable, Hitler refused to give up. Despite fearful casualties, Germany continued fighting for more than two years after Stalingrad. The bitter end came in the spring of 1945. Hitler committed suicide in Berlin on April 30; seven days later, Germany surrendered.

During his years in power, Hitler engaged in a policy of genocide without parallel in history. He was a fanatical racist, with a particularly virulent animosity toward the Jews. He made it his specific, publicly-stated goal to kill every Jew in the world. During his regime, the Nazis constructed large extermination camps, equipped with massive gas chambers for this purpose. In every territory that came under his control, innocent men, women, and children were rounded up and shipped off in cattle cars to be killed in those chambers. In the space of just a few years, almost 6,000,000 Jews died in this way.

The Jews were not Hitler's only victims. During his regime, staggering numbers of Russians and gypsies were also massacred, as well as many others who were deemed to be either racially inferior or enemies of the state. It should never be imagined that these murders were spontaneous acts, performed in the heat and passion of battle: Hitler's death camps were organized as carefully as a great business enterprise. Records were kept, quotas set, and the bodies of the dead systematically searched for such valuables as gold tooth fillings and wedding rings. The bodies of many of the victims were also utilized for the manufacture of soap. So intent upon this program of murder was Hitler, that even late in the war, when Germany was short of fuel for domestic and military use, the cattle cars were kept rolling to the death camps on their grisly—but militarily useless—mission.

For several reasons, it seems obvious that Hitler's fame will last. In the first place, he is widely considered to be the most evil man in all of history. If men like Nero and Caligula, whose misdeeds were small in comparison with Hitler's, have remained well-known for twenty centuries as symbols of cruelty, it seems

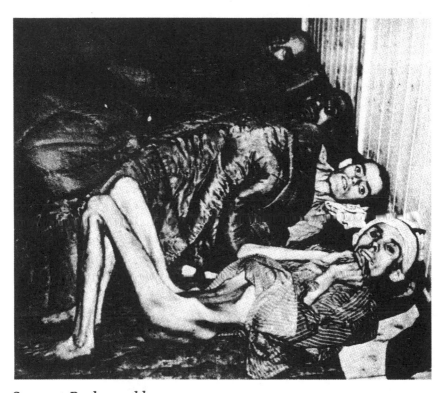

Scene at Buchenwald.

safe to predict that Hitler, whose reputation as the most evil person in history is uncontested, will remain famous for many, many centuries. In addition, of course, Hitler will be remembered as the principal instigator of World War II, the largest war the world has yet seen. The advent of nuclear weapons makes it very unlikely that there will be many such large-scale wars in the future. Therefore, even two or three thousand years from now, World War II will probably be considered a major event in history.

Furthermore, Hitler will remain famous because his entire story is so bizarre and so interesting. That a foreigner (Hitler was born in Austria, not Germany) without political experience, money, or political connections could, in a period of less than fourteen years, become the head of a major world power, is truly amazing. His ability as an orator was extraordinary. Judged by his ability to move people to significant action, it is likely that Hitler was the most effective orator in all of history. Finally, the fiendish uses to which he put his power, once he had attained it, will not soon be forgotten.

It is probable that no figure in history has had more influence upon his own generation than Adolf Hitler. In addition to the tens of millions of people who died in the war that he instigated, or in the Nazi concentration camps, there were millions more who were made homeless or whose lives were entirely disrupted as a result of the fighting.

Any estimate of Hitler's influence must take into consideration two other factors. First, much of what actually occurred under his leadership would probably not have occurred at all had it not been for Hitler. (In this respect, he stands in sharp contrast to such persons as, say, Charles Darwin or Simón Bolívar.) It is true, of course, that the situation in Germany and in Europe provided Hitler with an opportunity. His militaristic and anti-Semitic remarks, for example, certainly struck a responsive chord in many of his listeners. There is no sign, however, that most Germans in the 1920s or 1930s either wanted or intended their government to follow a policy nearly as extreme as Hitler's proved, and there is little indication that other potential German leaders would have done the same thing. Nor, in fact, were the actual events of the Hitler era even approximately predicted by any outside observer.

Second, the entire Nazi movement was dominated by a single leader to an extraordinary degree. Marx, Lenin, Stalin, and others all played major roles in the rise of Communism. But National Socialism had no significant leader before Hitler, and none after him. He led the Nazis to power, and maintained his leadership throughout their period in power. When he died, the Nazi party and the government it headed died with him.

But though Hitler's influence on his own generation was so enormous, the effects of his actions upon future ages seem to be

Nazi soldiers, 1933.

rather slight. Hitler totally failed to accomplish any of his major goals, and what little effect he appears to have had on later generations seems to be in the opposite direction from what he intended. For example, Hitler was interested in expanding German influence and territory. But his territorial conquests, although very large, were ephemeral, and today Germany has less territory than it did when Hitler took office. It was Hitler's consuming passion to destroy the Jews; but fifteen years after Hitler took office, an independent Jewish state came into existence for the first time in 2,000 years. Hitler hated both Communism and Russia. However, at his death, and partly as a result of the war he started, the Russians were able to extend their control over a large part of eastern Europe, and Communist influence in the world was greatly expanded. Hitler despised democracy and hoped to destroy it, not just in other nations, but in Germany, too. Nevertheless, Germany is a functioning democracy today, and her citizens appear to have far less tolerance for authoritarian rule than any generation of Germans before Hitler's time ever had.

What does this strange combination of enormous influence in his own day and relatively little influence on future generations add up to? Hitler's effect upon the world of his day was so enormous that it is obvious that he must be ranked fairly high on this list. But he surely must be placed well behind such figures as Shih Huang Ti, Augustus Caesar, and Genghis Khan, whose actions influenced the world for centuries after they lived. The closest parallels are with Napoleon and Alexander the Great. In the short run, Hitler disturbed the world even more than those two men did; he has been ranked slightly below them because of their greater long-term influence.

40

PLATO

4 2 7 B.C.- 3 4 7 B.C.

The ancient Greek philosopher Plato represents the starting point of Western political philosophy, and of much of our ethical and metaphysical thought as well. His speculations on these subjects have been read and studied for over 2,300 years. Plato stands, therefore, as one of the great fathers of Western thought.

Plato was born into a distinguished Athenian family, in about 427 B.C. As a young man, he made the acquaintance of the noted philosopher Socrates, who became his friend and mentor. In 399 B.C., Socrates, then seventy years old, was tried on rather vague charges of impiety and of corrupting the youth of Athens. Socrates was condemned, sentenced to death, and executed. The execution of Socrates—whom Plato calls "the wisest, the justest, and the best of all the men whom I have ever known"—left Plato with an enduring distaste for democratic government.

Not long after the death of Socrates, Plato left Athens and spent the next ten or twelve years in foreign travel. About 387

B.C., he returned to Athens and founded a school there, the Academy, which continued in operation for over nine hundred years. Plato spent most of his remaining forty years in Athens, teaching and writing philosophy. His most famous pupil was Aristotle, who came to the Academy when he was seventeen years old and Plato sixty. Plato died in 347 B.C., at the age of eighty.

Plato wrote thirty-six books, mostly on political and ethical questions, but also on metaphysics and theology. Obviously, it is not possible to summarize these works in a few short sentences. However, at the risk of oversimplifying his thought, I will try to summarize the main political ideas expressed in Plato's most famous book, *The Republic*, which represents his concept of an ideal society.

The best form of government, Plato suggests, is an aristocracy. By this he means not an hereditary aristocracy, or a monarchy, but an aristocracy of merit—that is, rule by the best and wisest persons in the state. These persons should be chosen not by a vote of the citizens, but by a process of co-optation. The persons who are already members of the ruling, or *guardian* class should admit additional persons to their ranks purely on the basis of merit.

Plato believed that all persons, both male and female, should be given the chance to demonstrate their fitness to be members of the guardian class. (Plato was the first major philosopher, and for a long time virtually the only one, to suggest the basic equality of the sexes.) To insure equality of opportunity, Plato advocated the rearing and education of all children by the state. Children should first receive a thorough physical training; but music, mathematics, and other academic disciplines should not be neglected. At several stages, extensive examinations should be given. The less successful persons should be assigned to engage in the economic activity of the community, while the more successful persons should continue to receive further training. This additional education should include not only the normal academic subjects, but also the study of "philosophy," by which Plato means the study of his metaphysical doctrine of ideal forms.

At age thirty-five, those persons who have convincingly demonstrated their mastery of theoretical principles are to receive an additional fifteen years of training, which should consist of practical working experience. Only those persons who show that they can apply their book learning to the real world should be admitted into the guardian class. Moreover, only those persons who clearly demonstrate that they are primarily interested in the public welfare are to become guardians.

Membership in the guardian class would not appeal to all persons. The guardians are not to be wealthy. They should be permitted only a minimal amount of personal property, and no land or private homes. They are to receive a fixed (and not very large) salary, and may not own either gold or silver. Members of the guardian class should not be permitted to have separate families, but are to eat together, and are to have mates in common. The compensation of these philosopher-kings should not be material wealth, but rather the satisfaction of public service. Such, in brief, was Plato's view of the ideal republic.

The Republic has been widely read for many centuries. It should be noted, however, that the political system advocated therein has not been used as the model for any actual civil government. During most of the interval between Plato's day and our own, most European states have been governed by hereditary monarchies. In recent centuries, several states have adopted democratic forms of government; there have also been instances of military rule, or of demagogic tyrannies, such as those of Hitler and Mussolini. None of those forms of government is similar to Plato's ideal republic. Plato's theories have never been adopted by any political party, nor have they formed the basis of a political movement in the way that the theories of Karl Marx have. Should we therefore conclude that Plato's works, though spoken of with respect, have been completely ignored in practice? I think not.

It is true that no civil government in Europe has been patterned directly on Plato's model; nevertheless, there is a striking similarity between the position of the Catholic Church in medieval Europe and that of Plato's guardian class. The medieval Church consisted of a self-perpetuating elite, whose members had all received training in an offical philosophy. In principle, all males, regardless of family background, were eligible to enter the priesthood (although females were excluded). In principle, too, the clergy had no families, and it was intended that they should be motivated primarily by concern for their flock, rather than by a desire for self-aggrandizement.

Plato's ideas have also influenced the structure of the United States government. Many members of the American Constitutional Convention were familiar with Plato's political ideas. It was intended, of course, that the United States Constitution would provide a means of discovering and giving effect to the popular will. But it was also intended as a means for selecting the wisest and best persons to govern the nation.

The difficulty in assessing Plato's importance is that his influence through the ages, while broad and pervasive, has been subtle and indirect. In addition to his political theories, his discussions of ethics and metaphysics have influenced many subsequent philosophers. If Plato has been ranked considerably lower than Aristotle on the present list, it is principally because Aristotle was an important scientist as well as a philosopher. On the other hand, Plato has been ranked higher than such thinkers as Thomas Jefferson and Voltaire, because their political writings have so far affected the world for only two or three centuries, while the influence of Plato has endured for over twenty-three centuries.

41 OLIVER CROMWELL

1599 - 1658

Oliver Cromwell, the brilliant and inspiring military leader who led the Parliamentary forces to victory in the English Civil War, is the man most responsible for the eventual establishment of parliamentary democracy as the English form of government.

Cromwell was born in 1599, in Huntingdon, England. As a young man, he lived in an England torn by religious dissensions and governed by a king who believed in and wished to practice absolute monarchy. Cromwell himself was a farmer and a country gentleman, and a devout Puritan. In 1628, he was elected to Parliament; but he served only briefly, because the following year King Charles I decided to dismiss Parliament and govern the country alone. Not until 1640, when he was in need of money to prosecute a war against the Scots, did the king call a new Parliament. This new Parliament, of which Cromwell was also a member, demanded assurances and protections against a resumption of arbitrary rule by the king. But Charles I was unwilling to be subservient to Parliament, and in 1642, war broke out between forces loyal to the king and those loyal to Parliament.

Cromwell chose the parliamentary side. Returning to Huntingdon, he raised a cavalry troop to fight against the king. During the four-year duration of the war, his remarkable military ability won increasing recognition. Cromwell played the leading role at both the critical Battle of Marston Moor (July 2, 1644), which was the turning point of the war, and at the decisive Battle of Naseby (June 14, 1645). In 1646, the war ended with Charles I a prisoner, and with Cromwell recognized as the most successful general on the parliamentary side.

But peace did not come, because the parliamentary side was divided into factions whose goals differed substantially, and because the king, knowing this, avoided a settlement. Within a year, a second civil war had begun, precipitated by the escape of King Charles and his attempt to rally his forces. The outcome of this renewed conflict was the defeat of the king's forces by Cromwell, the elimination of the more moderate members from Parliament, and the execution of the king in January 1649.

England now became a republic (called the Commonwealth), ruled temporarily by a Council of State, of which Cromwell was chairman. But royalists soon gained control in Ireland and Scotland, and gave their support to the dead king's son, the future Charles II. The result was the successful invasion of both Ireland and Scotland by Cromwell's armies. The long series of wars finally ended in 1652 with the complete defeat of the royalist forces.

Now that the fighting had ended, it was time for the establishment of a new government. There remained, however, the problem of the constitutional form that government should take. This problem was never to be solved during Cromwell's lifetime. The Puritan general had been able to lead to victory the forces that opposed absolute monarchy; but neither his power nor his prestige were sufficient to resolve the social conflicts of his supporters and enable them to agree on a new constitution, for these conflicts were intricately interwoven with the religious conflicts that divided Protestants from each other, as well as from Roman Catholics.

When Cromwell came to power, all that remained of the Parliament of 1640 was a small, unrepresentative, extremist minority, the so-called Rump. At first, Cromwell tried to negotiate for the holding of new elections. When the negotiations broke down, however, he dissolved the Rump by force (April 20, 1653). From then until Cromwell's death in 1658, three different Parliaments were formed and disbanded. Two different constitutions were adopted, but neither functioned successfully. Throughout this period, Cromwell ruled with the support of the army. In effect, he was a military dictator. However, his repeated attempts to institute democratic practices, as well as his refusal of the throne when it was offered to him, indicate that dictatorship was not what he sought; it was forced upon him by the inability of his supporters to establish a workable government.

From 1653 to 1658, Cromwell, under the title of Lord Protector, ruled England, Scotland, and Ireland. During those five years, Cromwell provided Britain with a generally good government and an orderly administration. He ameliorated various harsh laws, and he supported education. Cromwell was a believer in religious toleration, and he permitted the Jews to resettle in England and to practice their religion there. (They had been expelled from England more than three centuries earlier by King Edward I.) Cromwell also conducted a successful foreign policy. He died in London, in 1658, of malaria.

Cromwell's eldest son, Richard Cromwell, succeeded him, but ruled only briefly. In 1660, Charles II was restored to the throne. The remains of Oliver Cromwell were dug up and hung from the gibbet. But this vindictive act could not hide the fact that the struggle for royal absolutism had been lost. Charles II fully realized this, and did not attempt to contest Parliament's supremacy. When his successor, James II, tried to restore royal absolutism, he was soon deposed in the bloodless revolution of 1688. The result was just what Cromwell had wanted in 1640, a constitutional monarchy with the king clearly subservient to Parliament, and with a policy of religious toleration.

In the three centuries since his death, the character of Oliver Cromwell has been the subject of considerable dispute. Numerous critics have denounced him as a hypocrite, pointing out that whereas he always claimed to favor parliamentary supremacy, and to be opposed to arbitrary executive rule, he in fact established a military dictatorship. The majority view, though, is that Cromwell's devotion to democracy was quite sincere, although circumstances beyond his control sometimes compelled him to exercise dictatorial powers. It has been observed that Cromwell was never devious, nor did he ever accept the throne or the establishment of a permanent dictatorship. His rule was usually moderate and tolerant.

How shall we assess Cromwell's overall influence on history? His chief importance, of course, was as a brilliant military leader who defeated the royalist forces in the English Civil War. Since the parliamentary forces had been getting somewhat the worst of it in the early stages of the war, before Cromwell came to the fore, it seems quite possible that their ultimate victory would not have occurred without him. The result of Cromwell's victories was that democratic government was maintained and strengthened in England.

This should not be thought of as something that would have occurred in any event. In the seventeenth century, most of Europe was moving in the direction of greater royal absolutism; the triumph of democracy in England was an event running counter to the overall trend. In later years, the example of English democracy was an important factor in the French Enlightenment, in the French Revolution, and in the eventual establishment of democratic governments in western Europe. It is also obvious that the triumph of the democratic forces in England played a vital role in the establishment of democracy in the United States and in other former English colonies, such as Canada and Australia. Although England itself occupies only a small part of the world, democracy has flowed from England to regions that are not small at all.

Oliver Cromwell would have been ranked higher, except that almost equal credit for the establishment of democratic institutions in England and the United States should be accorded to the philosopher John Locke. It is difficult to assess the relative importance of Cromwell, who was basically a man of action, and Locke, who was a man of ideas. However, given the intellectual climate of Locke's day, political ideas closely similar to his would probably have been presented fairly soon, even had Locke himself never lived. On the other hand, had Cromwell never lived, there is a strong chance that the parliamentary forces would have lost the English Civil War.

Cromwell refuses the crown of England.

42   ALEXANDER GRAHAM BELL

1847 - 1922

Alexander Graham Bell, the inventor of the telephone, was born in Edinburgh, Scotland, in 1847. Although he had only a few years of formal schooling, he was well-educated by his family and himself. Bell's interest in the reproduction of vocal sounds arose quite naturally, since his father was an expert in vocal physiology, speech correction, and the teaching of the deaf.

Bell moved to Boston, Massachusetts, in 1871. It was there, in 1875, that he made the discoveries leading to his invention of the telephone. He filed a patent claim for his invention in February 1876, and it was granted a few weeks later. (It is interesting to note that another man, Elisha Gray, had filed a patent claim for a similar device on the same day as Bell, but at a slightly later hour.)

Shortly after his patent was granted, Bell exhibited the

telephone at the Centennial Exposition in Philadelphia. His invention aroused great public interest, and received an award. Nevertheless, the Western Union Telegraph Company, which was offered the rights to the invention for $100,000, declined to purchase it. Bell and his associates therefore, in July 1877, formed a company of their own, the ancestor of today's American Telephone and Telegraph Company. The telephone met with prompt—and enormous—commercial success, and AT&T eventually became the largest private business corporation in the world. (It has since been broken up into several smaller companies.)

Bell and his wife, who in March 1879 owned about 15 percent of the shares in the telephone company, seem to have had little idea of just how fantastically profitable the company would be. Within seven months, they had sold the majority of their stock at an average price of about $250 a share. By November, the stock was already selling at $1,000 a share! (Back in March, when the stock was selling at $65 a share, Bell's wife had pleaded with him to sell immediately, since she feared the stock would never go that high again!) In 1881, they unwisely sold off one-third of their remaining stock. Nevertheless, by 1883 they were worth about one million dollars.

Though the invention of the telephone made Bell a wealthy man, he never discontinued his research activities, and he succeeded in inventing several other useful (though less important) devices. His interests were varied, but his primary concern always was to help the deaf. His wife, in fact, was a deaf girl whom he had formerly tutored. They had two sons and two daughters, but both boys died as infants. In 1882, Bell became a United States citizen. He died in 1922.

Any estimate of Bell's influence rests upon the degree of importance one ascribes to the telephone. In my view, this is very great, since few inventions are so widely used and have had such a tremendous impact upon everyday life.

I have ranked Bell below Marconi because the radio is a more versatile device than the telephone. That is, a conversation conducted over the telephone could, in principle, be conducted by radio instead, but there are many situations (such as communication with an airplane in flight), in which a telephone could not possibly replace a radio. Were that the only factor involved, Bell would be ranked a *lot* lower than Marconi. However, there are two other points to be considered. First, although an *individual* phone conversation could be conducted by radio, it would be extremely difficult to replace our entire telephone *system* by an equivalent network of radio communication. Second, Bell was the first person to devise a method for reproducing sounds; furthermore, that method was later adapted and utilized by the inventors of the radio receiver, the record player, and various similar devices. I therefore consider Alexander Graham Bell to have been only slightly less influential than Marconi.

Bell opens the telephone line between New York and Chicago in 1892.

43 ALEXANDER FLEMING

1881-1955

Alexander Fleming, the discoverer of penicillin, was born in 1881, in Lochfield, Scotland. After graduating from the medical school of St. Mary's Hospital in London, Fleming engaged in immunological research. Later, as an army doctor in World War I, he studied wound infections, and he noticed that many antiseptics injured the body cells even more than they injured the microbes. He realized that what was needed was some substance that, while it would harm bacteria, would not be harmful to human cells.

After the war, Fleming returned to St. Mary's Hospital. In 1922, while doing research there, he discovered a substance which he called lysozyme. Lysozyme, which is produced by the human body, and which is a component of both mucus and tears, is not harmful to human cells. It destroys certain microbes, but unfortunately, not those that are particularly harmful to man. The discovery, therefore, although interesting, was not of major importance.

It was in 1928 that Fleming made his great discovery. One of his laboratory cultures of staphylococcus bacteria was exposed to the air and became contaminated by a mold. Fleming noticed that in the region of the culture just surrounding the mold, the bacteria had been dissolved. He correctly inferred that the mold was producing some substance which was toxic to the staphylococcus bacteria. He was soon able to show that the same substance inhibited the growth of many other types of harmful bacteria. The substance—which he named *penicillin* after the mold (penicillium notatum) that produced it—was not toxic to either human beings or animals.

Fleming's results were published in 1929, but they did not at first attract much notice. Fleming had suggested that penicillin could have important medical use. However, he himself was unable to develop a technique for purifying penicillin, and for more than ten years the marvelous drug remained unused.

Finally, in the later 1930s, two British medical researchers, Howard Walter Florey and Ernst Boris Chain, came across Fleming's article. They repeated his work and verified his results. They then purified penicillin, and tested the substance on laboratory animals. In 1941, they tested penicillin on sick human beings. Their tests clearly showed that the new drug was astoundingly potent.

With the encouragement of the British and American governments, pharmaceutical companies now entered the field, and rather quickly developed methods for producing large quantities of penicillin. At first, penicillin was reserved only for the use of war casualties, but by 1944, it was available for the treatment of civilians in Britain and America. When the war ended, in 1945, the use of penicillin spread all over the world.

The discovery of penicillin greatly stimulated the search for other antibiotics, and that research has resulted in the discovery of many other "miracle drugs." Nevertheless, penicillin remains the most widely used antibiotic.

One reason for its continued supremacy is that penicillin is effective against a very large variety of harmful microorganisms. The drug is useful in the treatment of syphilis, gonorrhea, scarlet fever, and diphtheria, as well as some forms of arthritis, bronchitis, meningitis, blood poisoning, boils, bone infections, pneumonia, gangrene, and various other ailments.

Another advantage of penicillin is the wide margin of safety in its use. Doses of 50,000 units of penicillin are effective against some infections; but injections of 100 *million* units of penicillin a day have been given without ill effects. Although a small percentage of people are allergic to penicillin, for most persons the drug provides an ideal combination of potency and safety.

Since penicillin has already saved many millions of lives and will surely save many more in the future, few persons would dispute the importance of Fleming's discovery. His exact placement on a list such as this would depend, of course, upon how much credit one feels should be allocated to Florey and Chain. I feel that the bulk of the credit should go to Fleming, who made the essential discovery. Without him, it might have been many years before penicillin was ever discovered. Once he had published his results, however, it was inevitable that sooner or later improved techniques of production and purification would be devised.

Fleming was happily married and had one child. In 1945, he was awarded a Nobel Prize for his discovery, sharing the award with Florey and Chain. Fleming died in 1955.

44

JOHN

LOCKE

1 6 3 2 - 1 7 0 4

The famous English philosopher John Locke was the first writer to put together in coherent form the basic ideas of constitutional democracy. His ideas strongly influenced the founding fathers of the United States, as well as many leading philosophers of the French Enlightenment.

Locke was born in 1632, in Wrington, England. He was educated at Oxford University, where he received a bachelor's degree in 1656 and a master's degree in 1658. As a young man, he was very much interested in science, and at thirty-six was elected to the Royal Society. He became good friends with the famous chemist Robert Boyle, and later in his life became friends with Isaac Newton. He was also interested in medicine, and received a bachelor's degree in that field, though he only practiced occasionally.

A turning point in Locke's life was his acquaintance with the Earl of Shaftesbury, to whom he became secretary and family physician. Shaftesbury was an important spokesman for liberal political ideas, and for a while was imprisoned by King Charles II because of his political activities. In 1682, Shaftesbury fled to Holland, where he died the following year. Locke, who because of his close association with Shaftesbury was likewise under suspicion, fled to Holland in 1683. He remained there until after Charles's successor, King James II, had been removed by the successful revolution of 1688. Locke returned home in 1689; thereafter, he lived in England. Locke, who never married, died in 1704.

The book that first made Locke famous was *An Essay Concerning Human Understanding* (1690), in which he discussed the origin, nature, and limits of human knowledge. Locke's views were basically empiricist, and the influence of Francis Bacon and René Descartes upon his thought is obvious. Locke's ideas, in turn, influenced philosophers such as Bishop George Berkeley, David Hume, and Immanuel Kant. Although the *Essay* is Locke's most original work, and is one of the famous classics of philosophy, it has had less influence upon historical developments than his political writings.

In *A Letter Concerning Toleration* (first published anonymously, in 1689), Locke maintained that the state should not interfere with the free exercise of religion. Locke was not the first Englishman to suggest religious toleration of all Protestant sects; however, the strong arguments he presented in favor of toleration were a factor in the growth of public support for this policy. Furthermore, Locke extended the principle of toleration to non-Christians: "...neither Pagan, nor Mahometan, nor Jew, ought to be excluded from the civil rights of the commonwealth because of his religion." However, Locke believed that this toleration should not be extended to Catholics, because he believed that they owed their allegiance to a foreign potentate, nor to atheists. By today's standards, he would therefore be considered very intolerant, but it is reasonable to judge him in relation to the ideas of his own times. In fact, the arguments he presented in favor of religious toleration were more convincing to his readers than the exceptions he made. Today, thanks in part to Locke's writings, religious toleration is extended even to those groups that he would have excluded.

Of still greater importance was Locke's *Two Treatises of Government* (1689), in which he presented the basic ideas underlying liberal constitutional democracy. That book's influence upon political thought throughout the English-speaking world has been profound. Locke firmly believed that each human being possessed natural rights, and that these included not only life, but personal liberty and the right to hold property. The main purpose of government, Locke asserted, was to protect the persons and property of the subjects. This view has sometimes been called the "night-watchman theory of government."

Rejecting the notion of the divine right of kings, Locke maintained that governments obtained their authority only from the consent of the governed. "The liberty of man in society is to be under no other legislative power but that established by consent in the commonwealth..." Locke strongly emphasized the idea of a social contract. This notion was derived in part from the writings of an earlier English philosopher, Thomas Hobbes (1588-1679). But whereas Hobbes had used the idea of a social contract to justify absolutism, in Locke's view the social contract was revokable:

> *...whenever the legislators endeavor to take away and destroy the property of the people, or to reduce them to slavery under arbitrary power, they put themselves into a state of war with the people, who are thereupon absolved from any further obedience, and are left to the common refuge which God hath provided for all men against force and violence.*

Also, "...there remains still in the people a supreme power to remove or alter the legislative when they find the legislative act contrary to the trust reposed in them..." Locke's defense of the right of revolution strongly influenced Thomas Jefferson and other American revolutionaries.

Locke believed in the principle of separation of powers; however, he felt that the legislature should be superior to the executive (and therefore to the judiciary, which he considered a part of the executive branch.) A believer in legislative supremacy, Locke would almost certainly have opposed the right of courts to declare legislative acts unconstitutional.

Though Locke firmly believed in the principle of majority rule, he nevertheless made it clear that a government did not possess unlimited rights. A majority must not violate the natural rights of men, nor was it free to deprive them of their property rights. A government could only rightfully take property with the consent of the governed. (In America, this idea was eventually expressed by the slogan, "No taxation without representation.")

It is evident from the foregoing that Locke had expressed virtually all the major ideas of the American Revolution almost a century before that event. His influence upon Thomas Jefferson is particularly striking. Locke's ideas penetrated to the European mainland as well—particularly to France, where they were an indirect factor leading to the French Revolution and the French *Declaration of the Rights of Man*. Although such figures as Voltaire and Thomas Jefferson are more famous than Locke, his writings preceded theirs and strongly influenced them. It therefore seems reasonable that he should precede them on this list.

45 LUDWIG VAN BEETHOVEN

1770-1827

Ludwig van Beethoven, the greatest of all musical composers, was born in 1770, in the city of Bonn, Germany. He exhibited talent at an early age, and his first published works date from 1783. As a young man, he visited Vienna, where he was introduced to Mozart; however, their acquaintance was fairly brief. In 1792, Beethoven returned to Vienna, and for a while he studied under Haydn, then the leading Viennese composer (Mozart had died the year before). Beethoven was to remain in Vienna, at that time the music capital of the world, for the remainder of his life.

Beethoven's immense virtuosity as a pianist impressed everyone, and he was successful both as a performer and a teacher. He soon became a prolific composer as well. His works were well received, and from his mid-twenties on, he was able to sell them to publishers without difficulty.

When Beethoven was in his late twenties, the first signs of his deafness appeared. Not surprisingly, the young composer was deeply disturbed by this ominous development. For a while, he even contemplated suicide.

The years from 1802 to 1815 are sometimes considered the middle period of Beethoven's career. During this interval, as his deafness steadily progressed, he began to withdraw socially. His increasing deafness caused people to form the unwarranted impression that he was a misanthrope. He had several romantic attachments with young ladies, but all appear to have ended unhappily, and he never married.

Beethoven's musical output continued to be prolific. As the years went by, however, he paid less and less attention to what would be popular with the musical audiences of his day. Nevertheless, he continued to be successful.

In his late forties, Beethoven became totally deaf. As a consequence, he gave no more public performances and became even more withdrawn socially. His works were fewer and harder to understand. By now, he was composing primarily for himself and some ideal future audience. He is alleged to have said to one critic, "They are not for you, but for a later age."

It is one of the cruelest ironies of fate that the most talented composer of all times should have been afflicted with the disability of deafness. Had Beethoven, by a superhuman effort of will, managed to maintain the quality of his compositions despite his deafness, it would have been an inspiring and near-incredible feat. But truth is stranger than fiction: in fact, during his years of total deafness, Beethoven did more than merely equal the level of his earlier compositions. The works that he produced during those last years are generally considered to be his greatest masterpieces. He died in Vienna in 1827, at the age of fifty-seven.

Beethoven's large output included nine symphonies, thirty-two piano sonatas, five piano concertos, ten sonatas for the piano and violin, a series of magnificent string quartets, vocal music, theater music, and much more. More important, however, than the quantity of his work is its quality. His works superbly com-

bine intensity of feeling with perfection of design. Beethoven
demonstrated that instrumental music could no longer be considered an art form of secondary importance, and his own compositions raised such music to the very highest level of art.

Beethoven was a highly original composer, and many of the
changes that he introduced have had a lasting effect. He expanded the size of the orchestra. He extended the length of the sym-
phony and widened its scope. By demonstrating the enormous
possibilities of the piano, he helped to establish it as the foremost
musical instrument. Beethoven marked the transition from the
classical to the romantic style of music, and his works were an inspiration for much that characterized romanticism.

Beethoven had a very great influence upon many later com-
posers, including persons with such diverse styles as Brahms,
Wagner, Schubert, and Tchaikovsky. He also paved the way for
Berlioz, Gustav Mahler, Richard Strauss, and many others.

An original manuscript by Ludwig van Beethoven.

It seems plain that Beethoven must outrank any other musician on this list. Although Johann Sebastian Bach is almost equally prestigious, Beethoven's works have been more widely and frequently listened to than Bach's. Furthermore, the numerous innovations that Beethoven made have had a more profound influence on subsequent developments in music than Bach's works have.

In general, political and ethical ideas can be more easily and clearly expressed in words than in music, and literature is thus a more influential field of art than is music. It is for this reason that Beethoven, though the preeminent figure in the history of music, has been ranked somewhat lower than Shakespeare. In comparing Beethoven with Michelangelo, I have been strongly influenced by the fact that most persons spend far more time listening to music than they do looking at painting or sculpture. For this reason, I think that musical composers are generally more influential than painters or sculptors whose eminence in their own field is equivalent. All in all, it seems appropriate to rank Beethoven roughly halfway between Shakespeare and Michelangelo.

46

WERNER HEISENBERG

1901-1976

In 1932, the Nobel Prize in physics was awarded to Werner Karl Heisenberg, a German physicist, for his role in the creation of quantum mechanics, one of the most important achievements in the entire history of science.

Mechanics is that branch of physics which deals with the general laws governing the motion of material objects. It is the most fundamental branch of physics, which in turn is the most fundamental of the sciences. In the early years of the twentieth century, it gradually became apparent that the accepted laws of mechanics were unable to describe the behavior of extremely minute objects, such as atoms and subatomic particles. This was both distressing and puzzling, since the accepted laws worked superbly when applied to macroscopic objects (that is, to objects which were much larger than individual atoms).

In 1925, Werner Heisenberg proposed a new formulation of physics, one that was radically different in its basic concepts from the classical formulation of Newton. This new theory—after some modification by Heisenberg's successors—has been brilliantly successful, and is today accepted as being applicable to *all* physical systems, of whatever type or size.

It can be demonstrated mathematically that where only macroscopic systems are involved, the predictions of quantum mechanics differ from those of classical mechanics by amounts which are far too small to measure. (For this reason, classical mechanics—which is mathematically much simpler than quantum mechanics—can still be used for most scientific computations.) However, where systems of atomic dimensions are involved, the predictions of quantum mechanics differ substantially from those of classical mechanics; experiments have shown that in such cases the predictions of quantum mechanics are correct.

One of the consequences of Heisenberg's theory is the famous "uncertainty principle," which he himself formulated in 1927. That principle is generally considered to be one of the most profound and far-reaching principles in all of science. What the uncertainty principle does is to specify certain theoretical limits on our ability to make scientific measurements. The implications of this principle are enormous. If the basic laws of physics prevent a scientist, *even in the most ideal circumstances,* from obtaining accurate knowledge of the system that he is attempting to investigate, it is obvious that the future behavior of that system cannot be completely predicted. According to the uncertainty principle, no improvements in our measuring apparatus will ever permit us to surmount this difficulty!

The uncertainty principle insures that physics, in the very nature of things, is unable to make more than statistical predictions. (A scientist studying radioactivity, for example, might be able to predict that out of a trillion radium atoms, two million will emit gamma rays during the next day. He is, however, unable to predict whether any *particular* radium atom will do so.) In many practical circumstances, this is not a grave restriction. Where very large numbers are involved, statistical methods can often provide a very reliable basis for action; but where small numbers are involved, statistical predictions are unreliable indeed. In fact, where small systems are involved, the uncertainty principle forces us to abandon our ideas of strict physical causality. This represents a most profound change in the basic philosophy of science; so profound, indeed, that a great scientist like Einstein was never willing to accept it. "I cannot believe," Einstein once said, "that God plays dice with the universe." That, however, is essentially the view that most modern physicists have felt it necessary to adopt.

It is clear that from a theoretical point of view the quantum theory, to a greater extent perhaps than even the theory of relativity, has altered our basic conception of the physical world. However, the theory's consequences are not only philosophical.

Among its practical applications are such modern devices as electron microscopes, lasers, and transistors. Quantum theory also has wide applications in nuclear physics and atomic energy. It forms the basis of our knowledge of spectroscopy, and is employed extensively in astronomy and chemistry. It is also used in theoretical investigations of such diverse topics as the properties of liquid helium, the internal constitution of the stars, ferromagnetism, and radioactivity.

Werner Heisenberg was born in Germany, in 1901. He received a doctorate in theoretical physics from the University of Munich in 1923. From 1924 to 1927, he worked in Copenhagen with the great Danish physicist, Niels Bohr. His first important paper on quantum mechanics was published in 1925, and his formulation of the uncertainty principle appeared in 1927. Heisenberg died in 1976, at the age of seventy-four. He was survived by his wife and seven children.

In view of the importance of quantum mechanics, the reader may wonder why Heisenberg has not been ranked even higher on this list. However, Heisenberg was not the only important scientist involved in the development of quantum mechanics. Significant contributions had been made by his predecessors, Max Planck, Albert Einstein, Niels Bohr, and the French scientist, Louis de Broglie. In addition, many other scientists, including the Austrian, Erwin Schrödinger, and the Englishman, P.A.M. Dirac, made major contributions to quantum theory in the years immediately following the publication of Heisenberg's seminal paper. Nevertheless, I think that Heisenberg was the principal figure in the development of quantum mechanics, and that—even when the credit is distributed—his contributions entitle him to a high spot on this list.

47 LOUIS DAGUERRE

1787-1851

Louis Jacques Mandé Daguerre was the man who, in the late 1830s, succeeded in developing the first practical method of photography.

Daguerre was born in 1787, in the town of Cormeilles, in northern France. As a young man, he was an artist. In his mid-thirties, he designed the Diorama, a spectacular array of panoramic paintings exhibited with special lighting effects. While engaged in this work, he became interested in developing a mechanism for automatically reproducing views of the world without brushes and paint—in other words, a camera.

His early attempts to devise a workable camera were unsuccessful. In 1827, he met Joseph Nicéphore Niepce, who had likewise been trying (and up till then with somewhat greater success) to invent a camera. Two years later they became partners.

In 1833, Niepce died, but Daguerre persisted in his efforts. By 1837, he had succeeded in developing a practical system of photography, called the daguerreotype.

In 1839, Daguerre made his process public, without patenting it; in return, the French government granted lifetime pensions both to Daguerre and to Niepce's son. The announcement of Daguerre's invention created a great public sensation. Daguerre was the hero of the day and was showered with honors, while the daguerreotype method rapidly came into widespread use. Daguerre himself soon retired. He died in 1851, at his country home near Paris.

Few inventions have as many uses as photography does. It is widely employed in virtually every field of scientific research. It has a wide variety of industrial and military applications. It is a serious art form for some people, and an enjoyable hobby for millions more. Photographs impart information (or misinformation) in education, journalism, and advertising. Because photographs are capable of vividly recalling the past, they have become the most common of all souvenirs and mementos. Cinematography, of course, is an important subsidiary development that—besides serving as a major entertainment medium— has virtually as many applications as still photography.

No invention derives entirely from the work of a single man, and certainly, the earlier work of many other men had prepared the way for Daguerre's achievement. The camera obscura (a device similar to a pinhole camera, but without any film) had been invented at least eight centuries before Daguerre. In the sixteenth century, Girolamo Cardano took the important step of placing a lens in the opening of the camera obscura. That made it an interesting preliminary to the modern camera; however, since the image it produced had no permanence at all, it can hardly be considered a type of photography. Another important preliminary discovery was made in 1727, by Johann Schulze, who discovered that silver salts were sensitive to light. Although he used this discovery to make some temporary images, Schulze did not really pursue the idea.

The predecessor who came closest to Daguerre's achievement was Niepce, who later became Daguerre's partner. About 1820, Niepce discovered that bitumen of Judea, a type of asphalt, was sensitive to light. By combining this light-sensitive substance with a camera obscura, Niepce succeeded in making the world's first photographs. (One that he took in 1826 still exists.) For that reason, some people feel that Niepce should rightly be considered the inventor of photography. However, Niepce's method of photography was totally impractical, since it required about eight hours' exposure time, and even then resulted in a rather fuzzy picture.

In Daguerre's method, the image was recorded on a plate coated with silver iodide. An exposure time of fifteen to twenty minutes was sufficient, which made the method, although cumbersome, of practical utility. Within two years after Daguerre made his method public, other persons proposed a slight modification: the addition of silver bromide to the silver iodide used as a light-sensitive material. This slight change had the important effect of greatly reducing the exposure time needed, and thereby making it practical to make portraits by photography.

In 1839, not long after Daguerre announced his invention of photography, William Henry Fox Talbot, an English scientist, announced that he had developed a different method of photography, one that involved making negative prints first, as is done today. It is interesting to note that Talbot had actually produced his first photographs in 1835, two years before the first daguerreotype. Talbot, who was engaged in several other projects, did not promptly follow up his photographic experiments. Had he done so, he would probably have developed a commercially feasible system of photography before Daguerre did, and would today be considered the inventor of photography.

In the years following Daguerre and Talbot, there have been enormous improvements in photography: the wet-plate process, the dry-plate process, modern roll film, color photographs, motion pictures, Polaroid photography, and xerography.

Despite the many persons involved in the development of photography, I feel that Louis Daguerre made by far the most important contribution. There was no feasible system of photography before him, whereas the technique that he devised was practical and soon became widely used. Furthermore, his well-publicized invention provided a great impetus to subsequent developments. It is true that the methods of photography that we use today are very different from the daguerreotype method; however, even had none of these later techniques ever been developed, the daguerreotype would provide us with a usable technique of photography.

The official Daguerre camera produced by Daguerre's brother-in-law, Alphonse Giroux, carried a label that says: "No apparatus guaranteed if it does not bear the signature of M. Daguerre and the seal of M. Giroux."

48 SIMÓN BOLÍVAR

1783-1830

Simón Bolívar is often called "the George Washington of South America" because of his role in the liberation of five South American countries (Colombia, Venezula, Ecuador, Peru and Bolivia) from Spanish rule. Few, if any, political figures have played so dominant a role in the history of an entire continent as he did.

Bolívar was born in 1783, in Caracas, Venezuela, into an aristocratic family of Spanish descent. He was orphaned at the age of nine. During his formative years, Bolivar was strongly influenced by the ideas and ideals of the French Enlightenment. Among the philosophers whose works he read were John Locke, Rousseau, Voltaire, and Montesquieu.

As a young man, Bolívar visited several European countries. In Rome, in 1805, at the top of the Aventine Hill, Bolívar made his celebrated vow that he would not rest until his fatherland had been liberated from Spain.

In 1808, Napoleon Bonaparte invaded Spain and placed his own brother at the head of the Spanish government. By dislodging the Spanish royal family from effective political power, Napoleon provided the South American colonies with a golden opportunity to strike out for their own political independence.

The revolution against Spanish rule in Venezuela commenced in 1810, when the Spanish governor of Venezuela was deposed. A formal declaration of independence was made in 1811, and that same year Bolívar became an officer in the revolutionary army. But the following year the Spanish troops regained control of Venezuela. The leader of the revolution, Francisco Miranda, was jailed, and Bolívar fled the country.

The succeeding years witnessed a series of wars, in which temporary victories were followed by crushing defeats. Nevertheless, Bolívar's resolution never wavered. The turning point came in 1819, when Bolívar led his small, ragtag army across rivers, plains, and the high passes of the Andes in order to attack the Spanish troops in Colombia. There he won the crucial Battle of Boyaca (August 7, 1819), the true turning point of the struggle. Venezuela was liberated in 1821, and Ecuador in 1822.

Meanwhile, the Argentine patriot José de San Martín had secured the freedom of Argentina and Chile from Spanish rule, and had undertaken the liberation of Peru. The two liberators met in the city of Guayaquil, Ecuador, in the summer of 1822. However, they were unable to agree on a plan for cooperating and coordinating their efforts against the Spanish. Since San Martín was unwilling to engage in a power struggle with the ambitious Bolívar (which would only have aided the Spanish), he decided to resign his command and withdraw from South America completely. By 1824, Bolívar's armies had completed the liberation of what is now Peru, and in 1825, the Spanish troops in Upper Peru (present-day Bolivia) were routed.

The remaining years of Bolívar's career were less successful. He had been impressed by the example of the United States of

America, and looked forward to a federation of the new South American nations. In fact, Venezuela, Colombia, and Ecuador had already been formed into a Republic of Greater Colombia, with Bolívar as president. Unfortunately, the centrifugal tendencies in South America were far greater than they had been in the North American colonies. When Bolívar convoked a Congress of Spanish American States in 1826, only four nations attended. Indeed, rather than more nations joining Greater Colombia, the republic itself soon began to break up. Civil war broke out, and in 1828, an attempt was made to assassinate Bolívar. By 1830, Venezuela and Ecuador had seceded. Bolívar, realizing that he himself was an obstacle to peace, resigned in April 1830. When he died, in December 1830, he was discouraged, impoverished, and exiled from his native Venezuela.

Bolívar was clearly a very ambitious man, and under the exigencies of the times, he sometimes assumed dictatorial powers. Nevertheless, when it came to a choice, he was willing to subordinate his personal ambitions to the public welfare and the ideal of democracy, and he invariably relinquished his dictatorial powers. He was once offered a throne, but declined it. Doubtless, he felt that the name "El Libertador" (the Liberator), which had already been bestowed upon him, was a greater honor than any kingly title.

There is no doubt that Bolívar was the dominant figure in the liberation of Spanish America from colonial rule. He provided the ideological leadership for the movement—writing articles, issuing a newspaper, making speeches, and writing letters. He was tireless in raising funds to support the struggle. And he was the principal military leader of the revolutionary forces.

Still, it would be a mistake to think of Bolívar as a great general. The armies he defeated were neither large nor well-led. Bolívar himself was not particularly talented in either strategy or tactics. (This is hardly surprising, since he had never received any military training.) But Bolívar made up for all his other shortcomings by his indomitable spirit in the face of adversity. After each defeat by the Spanish, when others were willing to abandon the fight, Bolívar resolutely reassembled an army and continued the struggle.

In my opinion, Bolívar was far more influential than such famous figures as Julius Caesar or Charlemagne, both because the changes resulting from his career have proven more permanent, and because the regions affected cover a larger area. However, Bolívar has been ranked below Alexander the Great, Adolf Hitler, and Napoleon, since many of the things that those three men did would not have occurred without them, while it is difficult to believe that the South American countries would not eventually have achieved their independence anyway.

The most interesting and significant comparison to make is between Bolívar and George Washington. Like Washington, Bolívar commanded small and poorly-trained armies. Money was short, and it frequently required an inspiring leader to keep the army together at all.

Unlike Washington, Bolívar freed all his own slaves during his lifetime. In addition, by proclamation and by constitutional provision, he actively tried to abolish slavery in the lands he liberated. His attempts were not wholly successful, and slavery still existed in the region when he died.

Bolívar had a complex and interesting personality—dramatic, daring, and romantic. A handsome man, he had numerous love affairs. He was a far-sighted idealist, but had less administrative ability than Washington, and enjoyed flattery more. He was far more ambitious than Washington—to the disadvantage of the regions that he liberated. On the other hand, Bolívar was utterly uninterested in financial gain. He was wealthy when he entered politics, poor when he retired.

The territory that Bolívar freed from colonial rule was considerably larger than that of the original United States. Nevertheless, it is clear that he is a considerably less important figure than Washington, simply because the United States has played a far more important role in history than the countries liberated by Bolívar.

49 RENÉ DESCARTES

1 5 9 6 - 1 6 5 0

René Descartes, the famous French philosopher, scientist, and mathematician, was born in 1596, in the village of La Haye. In his youth he attended a fine Jesuit school, the College of La Flèche. When he was twenty, he obtained a law degree from the University of Poitiers; however, he never practiced law. Though he had received an excellent education, Descartes was convinced that there was very little reliable knowledge in any field, with the exception of mathematics. Rather than continuing his formal education, he decided to travel throughout Europe and see the world for himself. As his family was well-to-do, Descartes's income was sufficient to enable him to travel freely.

From 1616 to 1628, Descartes traveled extensively. He served briefly in three different armies (those of Holland, Bavaria,

248

and Hungary), though apparently he was not involved in any combat. He also visited Italy, Poland, Denmark, and other countries. During these years, he formulated what he considered to be a general method for discovering truth. When he was thirty-two years old, Descartes decided to apply his method in an attempt to construct a comprehensive picture of the world. He then settled in Holland, where he was to live for the next twenty-one years. (He chose Holland because there was more intellectual liberty there, and also because he preferred to be away from the social distractions of Paris.)

About 1629, he wrote *Rules for the Direction of the Mind*, a book in which his method was outlined. (However, the book is incomplete and was probably never intended for publication; it was first published more than fifty years after Descartes's death.) In the years from 1630 through 1634, Descartes applied his method to the study of the sciences. To learn more about anatomy and physiology, he performed dissections. He engaged in major independent research in optics, meteorology, mathematics, and several other branches of science.

It was Descartes's intention to present his scientific results in a book to be called *Le Monde* (the world). However, in 1633, when the book was almost finished, he learned that church authorities in Italy had convicted Galileo for advocating Copernicus's theory that the earth revolved about the sun. Though in Holland he was not subject to the Catholic authorities, Descartes nevertheless decided that it would be prudent of him not to issue his book, as in it, he, too, defended the Copernican theory. Instead, in 1637, he published his most famous work, his *Discourse on the Method for Properly Guiding the Reason and Finding Truth in the Sciences* (usually abbreviated to *Discourse on Method*).

The *Discourse* was written in French rather than Latin, so that all intelligent persons could read it, including those who had not had a classical education. Appended to the *Discourse* were three essays in which Descartes gave examples of the discoveries he had made by the use of his method. In the first such appendix, the *Optics*, Descartes presented the law of refraction of light (which had, however, been discovered earlier by Willebrord Snell). He also discussed lenses and various optical instruments; described the functioning of the eye and various malfunctions; and presented a theory of light that is a preliminary version of the wave theory later formulated by Christiaan Huygens. His second appendix comprised the first modern discussion of meteorology. He discussed clouds, rain, and wind, and gave a correct explanation for the rainbow. He argued against the notion that heat consists of an invisible fluid, and he correctly concluded that heat is a form of internal motion. (But this idea had already been presented by Francis Bacon and others.) In the third appendix, the *Geometry*, Descartes presented his most important contribution of all, his invention of analytic geometry. This was a major mathematical advance that prepared the way for Newton's invention of calculus.

Perhaps the most interesting part of Descartes's philosophy is the way he begins. Mindful of the large number of incorrect notions that were generally accepted, Descartes decided that in order to reach the truth he must make a fresh start. He therefore begins by doubting everything—everything his teachers had told him, all of his most cherished beliefs, all his commonsense ideas—even the existence of the external world, even his own existence—in a word, *everything*.

This, of course, leads to a problem: how is it possible to overcome such universal doubt and obtain reliable knowledge of *anything*? Descartes, however, by a series of ingenious metaphysical arguments, was able to prove to his own satisfaction that he himself existed ("I think, therefore I am"), that God exists, and that the external world exists. These were the starting points of Descartes's theory.

The importance of Descartes's method is twofold. First, he placed at the center of his philosophical system the fundamental epistemological question, "What is the origin of human knowledge?" Earlier philosophers had tried to describe the nature of the world. Descartes has taught us that such a question cannot be answered satisfactorily except in conjunction with the question "How do I know?"

Second, Descartes suggested that we should start not with *faith* but with *doubt*. (This was the exact reverse of the attitude of St. Augustine, and most medieval theologians, that faith must come first.) It is true that Descartes then proceeded to reach orthodox theological conclusions. However, his readers paid far more attention to the method he advocated than to the conclusions he reached. (The Church's fears that Descartes's writings would in the end prove subversive were quite justified.)

In his philosophy, Descartes stresses the distinction between the mind and material objects, and in this respect advocates a thoroughgoing dualism. This distinction had been made before, but Descartes's writings stimulated philosophical discussion of the subject. The questions he raised have interested philosophers ever since, and have still not been resolved.

Also highly influential was Descartes's conception of the physical universe. He believed that the entire world — aside from God and the human soul—operated mechanically, and that therefore all natural events could be explained by mechanical causes. For this reason, he rejected the claims of astrology, magic, and other forms of superstition. He likewise rejected all teleological explanations of events. (That is, he looked for direct mechanical causes and rejected the notion that events occurred in order to serve some remote final purpose.) From Descartes's outlook, it followed that animals were, in essence, complicated machines, and that the human body, too, was subject to the ordinary laws of mechanics. This has since become one of the fundamental ideas of modern physiology.

Descartes favored scientific research and believed that its practical applications could be beneficial to society. He felt that scientists should avoid vague notions and should attempt to describe the world by mathematical equations. All this sounds very modern. However, Descartes, though he made observations himself, never really stressed the crucial importance of experimentation in the scientific method.

The famous British philosopher Francis Bacon had proclaimed the need for scientific investigation, and the benefits to be expected therefrom, several years before Descartes. Nor was Descartes's celebrated argument, "I think, therefore I am," original; it had been stated more than 1200 years earlier (in different words, of course) by St. Augustine. Similarly, Descartes's "proof" of the existence of God is merely a variation of the ontological argument first presented by St. Anselm (1033-1109).

In 1641, Descartes published another famous book, the *Meditations*. His *Principles of Philosophy* appeared in 1644. Both were originally written in Latin, but French translations appeared in 1647.

Although Descartes was a polished writer, with a charming prose style, the *tone* of his writings is surprisingly old-fashioned. Indeed, he often sounds (perhaps because of his rationalist approach) like a medieval scholastic. By contrast, Francis Bacon, though born thirty-five years before Descartes, has a quite modern tone.)

As his writings make clear, Descartes was a firm believer in God. He considered himself a good Catholic; however, Church authorities disliked his views, and his works were placed on the Catholic *Index* of forbidden books. Even in Protestant Holland (at that time, probably the most tolerant country in Europe), Descartes was accused of atheism and had trouble with the authorities.

In 1649, Descartes accepted a generous financial offer from Queen Christina of Sweden to come to Stockholm and become her private tutor. Descartes liked warm rooms, and had always enjoyed sleeping late. He was much distressed to learn that the queen wanted her lessons given at five o'clock in the morning! Descartes feared that the cold morning air would be the death of him, and indeed it was: it was not long before he caught pneumonia. He died in February 1650, only four months after arriving in Sweden.

Descartes never married. However he had one child, a daughter, who unfortunately died young.

Descartes's philosophy was strongly criticized by many of his contemporaries, in part because they felt that it involved circular reasoning. Subsequent philosophers have pointed out many shortcomings in his system, and few people today would defend it wholeheartedly. But the importance of a philosopher does not depend solely on the correctness of his system: of greater significance is whether his ideas—or rather, the ideas that others extract from his writings—prove widely influential. On that basis, there is little doubt that Descartes was an important figure.

At least five of Descartes's ideas had an important impact on European thought: (a) his mechanical view of the universe; (b) his positive attitude towards scientific investigation; (c) the stress he laid on the use of mathematics in science; (d) his advocacy of initial skepticism; and (e) the attention he focused on epistemology.

In assessing Descartes's overall importance I have also taken into account his impressive scientific achievements, in particular his invention of analytic geometry. It is that factor which has persuaded me to rank Descartes substantially higher than such eminent philosophers as Voltaire, Rousseau, and Francis Bacon.

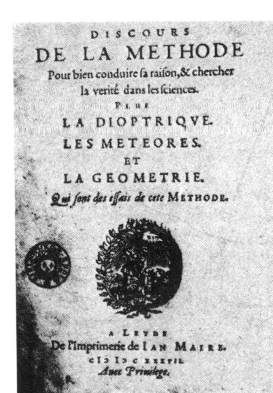

Title page from the first edition of Discourse on Method, *1637.*

50 MICHELANGELO

1475-1564

The great Renaissance artist Michelangelo Buonarroti is the outstanding figure in the history of the visual arts. A brilliant painter, sculptor, and architect, Michelangelo left behind an assortment of masterpieces which have impressed viewers for over four centuries. His work profoundly influenced the subsequent development of European painting and sculpture.

Michelangelo was born in 1475, in the town of Caprese, Italy, about forty miles from Florence. He showed talent at an early age, and at thirteen he was apprenticed to the famous painter Ghirlandaio, in Florence. When Michelangelo was fifteen, he was taken to live in the Medici palace, almost as a member of the family, by Lorenzo the Magnificent, the ruler of Florence, who became his patron. Throughout his career, Michelangelo's enormous talent was obvious, and he was frequently commissioned by popes and secular rulers alike, to design and produce works of art. Although he lived in various places, most of his life was spent in Rome and Florence. He died in Rome, in 1564, shortly before his eighty-ninth birthday. He never married.

Although he was not quite as universal a genius as his older contemporary, Leonardo da Vinci, Michelangelo's versatility is still extremely impressive. He was the only artist, indeed, perhaps the only person, ever to reach the highest peaks of achievement in two separate fields of human endeavor. As a painter, Michelangelo ranks at or near the very top, both in the quality of his finest work and in the influence he has had upon later painters. The enormous set of frescoes with which he decorated the ceiling of the Sistine Chapel in Rome is justly celebrated as one of the greatest artistic achievements of all time. Nevertheless, Michelangelo considered himself to be primarily a sculptor, and many critics consider him the greatest sculptor who ever lived. His statues of David and of Moses, for example, and the famous *Pietà*, are all works of unexcelled artistry.

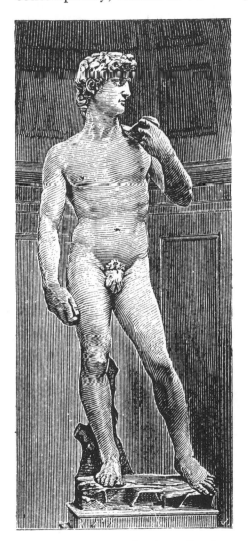

The "David," in the Accademia in Florence.

The "Pietà," in the Vatican in Rome.

Michelangelo was also a highly talented architect. Among his well-known achievements in this field is the design of the Medici Chapel in Florence. For a good many years, he was also the chief architect of St. Peter's in Rome.

Michelangelo composed many poems during his lifetime, some 300 of which survive. His numerous sonnets and other poems were not published until well after his death. They provide considerable insight into his personality, and clearly show that he was a talented poet.

As I have explained in the article on Shakespeare, it is my belief that art and artists in general have had comparatively little influence upon human history and everyday life. It is for that reason that Michelangelo, despite his eminence as an artistic genius, appears lower on this list than many scientists and inventors, many of whom are far less famous than he.

"God Dividing the Waters from the Earth," section of the Sistine Chapel ceiling.

51 POPE URBAN II

1042-1099

Not many people today remember Pope Urban II. Yet there have been few men whose impact on human history has been so obvious and so direct, for Urban II was the pope whose call for a Christian war to recapture the Holy Land from the Moslems inaugurated the Crusades.

Urban, whose original name was Odo de Lagery, was born about 1042, near the city of Châtillon-sur-Marne in France. He came from a great family of French nobles, and he received a good education. As a young man, he was an archdeacon at Reims. Later, he became successively a Cluniac monk, a prior, and a cardinal-bishop, before his election as pope in 1088.

Urban was a strong, effective, and politically astute pope, but this is not what has earned him a place in this book. The action for which Urban II is principally remembered occurred on November 27, 1095. He had convoked a great church council, held at the city of Clermont in France. There, before a crowd of thousands, Urban delivered what was perhaps the single most effective speech in history—one that was to influence Europe for centuries to come. In his speech, Urban protested that the Seljuk Turks, who were occupying the Holy Land, were defiling the Christian holy places and molesting Christian pilgrims. Urban urged that all Christendom join together in a holy war—a great crusade to recapture the Holy Land for Christianity. But Urban was far too clever to appeal to altruistic motives alone. He pointed out that the Holy Land was fruitful and wealthy—far richer than the overcrowded lands of Christian Europe. Finally, the Pope announced, participation in the crusade would take the place of all penances and assure the crusader of remission of all his sins.

Urban's brilliant speech, which appealed at the same time to his listeners' highest motives and to their most selfish ones, aroused passionate enthusiasm in his audience. Before he had finished, the multitude was shouting, *"Deus le volt!"* (God wills it), which was soon to become the battle cry of the crusaders. Within a few months, the First Crusade was under way. It was to be followed by a long series of holy wars (there were eight major crusades and many smaller ones), which took place over a period of roughly two hundred years.

As for Urban himself, he died in 1099, two weeks after the First Crusade succeeded in capturing Jerusalem, but before news of that capture had reached him.

It hardly seems necessary to explain the importance of the Crusades. Like all wars, they had a direct influence upon the participants, and upon the civilian populations caught in their path. In addition, however, the Crusades had the effect of bringing western Europe into close contact with the Byzantine and Islamic civilizations, which at that time were considerably more advanced than western Europe. That contact helped prepare the way for the Renaissance, which in turn led to the full flowering of modern European civilization.

Pope Urban II is on this list not only because of the enormous significance of the Crusades, but also because it is unlikely that they would have taken place without his inspiration. Obviously, conditions were ripe; otherwise his speech would have fallen upon deaf ears. However, to start a general European movement, the leadership of some central figure was needed. No national king could have done it. (Had a German emperor, for example, declared a holy war against the Turks, and led his armies on a crusade, it is doubtful that many English knights would have joined him.) There was only one figure in western Europe whose authority transcended national boundaries. Only the Pope could propose a project for all western Christendom to engage in, with a hope that large numbers of persons would follow his suggestion. Without the leadership of the Pope, and the dramatic speech which he made, the Crusades, as a mass European movement, would probably never have begun.

Nor were circumstances such that virtually any person holding the papal office would have proposed a crusade to liberate the Holy Land. On the contrary, it was in many ways an impractical suggestion. Most prudent leaders would be very reluctant to make an unusual proposal, the consequences of which were so difficult to predict. But Urban II dared to do so; and by so doing he had a greater and more enduring effect on human history than many far more famous men.

Mosque in Cairo named after 'Umar ibn al-Khattab.

52 'UMAR IBN AL-KHATTAB

c. 5 8 6 - 6 4 4

'Umar ibn al-Khattab was the second, and probably the greatest, of the Moslem caliphs. He was a younger contemporary of Muhammad, and like the Prophet, was born in Mecca. The year of his birth is unknown, but was perhaps about 586.

'Umar was originally one of the most bitter opponents of Muhammad and his new religion. Rather suddenly, however, 'Umar became converted to Islam, and thereafter was one of its strongest supporters. (The parallel with the conversion of St. Paul to Christianity is striking.) 'Umar became one of the closest advisors of the prophet Muhammad, and remained so throughout Muhammad's life.

In 632, Muhammad died without having named a successor. 'Umar promptly supported the candidacy of Abu Bakr, a close associate and father-in-law of the Prophet. This avoided a power struggle and enabled Abu Bakr to be generally recognized

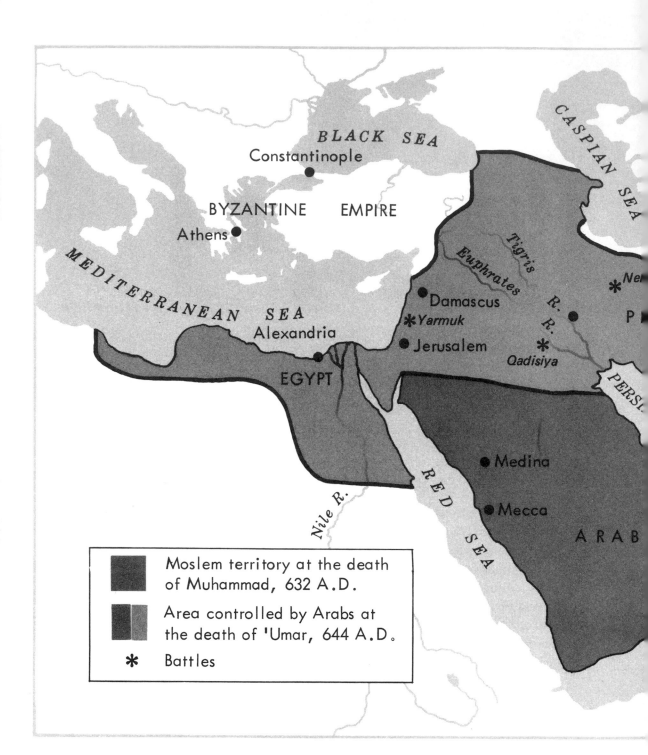

Arab expansion under 'Umar ibn al-Khattab.

as the first caliph (i.e., as the "successor" of Muhammad). Abu Bakr was a successful leader, but he died after serving as caliph for only two years. He had, however, specifically named 'Umar (who was also a father-in-law of the Prophet) to succeed him, so once again a power struggle was avoided. 'Umar became caliph in 634, and retained power until 644, when he was assassinated in Medina by a Persian slave. On his deathbed, 'Umar named a committee of six persons to choose his successor, thereby again averting an armed struggle for power. The committee chose Othman, the third caliph, who ruled from 644 to 656.

It was during the ten years of 'Umar's caliphate that the most important conquests of the Arabs occurred. Not long after 'Umar's accession, Arab armies invaded Syria and Palestine, which at that time were part of the Byzantine Empire. At the Battle of the Yarmuk (636), the Arabs won a crushing victory over the Byzantine forces. Damascus fell the same year, and Jerusalem surrendered two years later. By 641, the Arabs had conquered all of Palestine and Syria, and were advancing into present-day Turkey. In 639, Arab armies invaded Egypt, which had also been under Byzantine rule. Within three years, the Arab conquest of Egypt was complete.

Arab attacks upon Iraq, at that time part of the Sassanid Empire of the Persians, had commenced even before 'Umar took office. The key Arab victory, at the battle of Qadisiya (637) occurred during 'Umar's reign. By 641, all of Iraq was under Arab control. Nor was that all: Arab armies invaded Persia itself, and at the battle of Nehavend (642) they decisively defeated the forces of the last Sassanid emperor. By the time 'Umar died, in 644, most of western Iran had been overrun. Nor had the Arab armies run out of momentum when 'Umar died. In the East, they fairly soon completed the conquest of Persia, while in the West they continued their push across North Africa.

Just as important as the extent of 'Umar's conquests is their permanence. Iran, though its population became converted to Islam, eventually regained its independence from Arab rule. But Syria, Iraq, and Egypt never did. Those countries became thoroughly Arabized and remain so to this day.

'Umar, of course, had to devise policies for the rule of the great empire that his armies had conquered. He decided that the Arabs were to be a privileged military caste in the regions they had conquered, and that they should live in garrison cities, apart from the natives. The subject peoples were to pay tribute to their Moslem (largely Arab) conquerors, but were otherwise to be left in peace. In particular, they were *not* to be forcibly converted to Islam. (From the above, it is clear that the Arab conquest was more a nationalist war of conquest than a holy war, although the religious aspect was certainly not lacking.)

'Umar's achievements are impressive indeed. After Muhammad himself, he was the principal figure in the spread of Islam. Without his rapid conquests, it is doubtful that Islam would be nearly as widespread today as it actually is. Furthermore, most of the territory conquered during his reign has remained Arab ever since. Obviously, of course, Muhammad, who was the prime mover, should receive the bulk of the credit for those developments. But it would be a grave mistake to ignore 'Umar's contribution. The conquests he made were not an automatic consequence of the inspiration provided by Muhammad. Some expansion was probably bound to occur, but not to the enormous extent that it did under 'Umar's brilliant leadership.

It may occasion some surprise that 'Umar—a figure virtually unknown in the West—has been ranked higher than such famous men as Charlemagne and Julius Caesar. However, the conquests made by the Arabs under 'Umar, taking into account both their size and their duration, are substantially more important than those of either Caesar or Charlemagne.

Asoka issued edicts on stone pillars, such as this one which stands at Lauriya-Nandangarh.

53
ASOKA

c. 3 0 0 B.C.- *c.* 2 3 2 B.C.

Asoka, who was probably the most important monarch in the history of India, was the third ruler of the Mauryan dynasty and the grandson of its founder, Chandragupta Maurya. Chandragupta was an Indian military leader, who in the years subsequent to the campaign of Alexander the Great, conquered most of northern India, and thereby established the first major empire in Indian history.

The year of Asoka's birth is unknown; probably it was close to 300 B.C. Asoka ascended the throne about 273 B.C. At first he followed in his grandfather's footsteps and sought to extend his territory through military action. In the eighth year of his reign,

266

he concluded a successful war against Kalinga, a state on the east coast of India (about where the present state of Orissa is). But when he realized the horrible human cost of his triumph, Asoka was appalled. One hundred thousand persons had been killed, and an even larger number wounded. Shocked and remorseful, Asoka decided that he would not complete the military conquest of India, but would instead renounce all aggressive warfare. He adopted Buddhism as his religious philosophy, and attempted to practice the virtues of *dharma*, which include truthfulness, mercy, and nonviolence.

On a personal level, Asoka gave up hunting and became a vegetarian. Of more significance were the various humane and political policies that he adopted. He established hospitals and animal sanctuaries, mitigated many harsh laws, built roads, and promoted irrigation. He even appointed special government officials, *dharma* officers, to instruct people in piety and to encourage friendly human relationships. All religions were tolerated in his realm, but Asoka particularly promoted Buddhism, which naturally enjoyed a great increase in its popularity. Buddhist missions were sent to many foreign countries, and were especially successful in Ceylon.

Asoka ordered descriptions of his life and policies inscribed on rocks and pillars throughout his large realm. Many of these monuments survive to the present day. Their geographic distribution provides us with reliable information concerning the extent of Asoka's domain, and the inscriptions on them are our main source of knowledge of his career. Incidentally, these pillars are also considered to be superb works of art.

Within fifty years of Asoka's death, the Mauryan Empire fell apart, and it was never revived. However, through his support of Buddhism, Asoka's long-term influence upon the world has been very large. When he ascended the throne, Buddhism was a small, local religion, popular only in northwest India. By the time of his death, it had adherents throughout India and was spreading rapidly to neighboring countries. More than any one man, except Gautama himself, Asoka is responsible for the development of Buddhism into a major world religion.

54 ST. AUGUSTINE

354-430

Augustine, who lived during the declining years of the Roman Empire, was the greatest theologian of his era. His writings profoundly influenced Christian doctrines and attitudes throughout the Middle Ages, and indeed still have influence today.

Augustine was born in 354, in the town of Tagaste (now Souk-Ahras, in Algeria), about forty-five miles south of the large coastal town of Hippo (now Annaba). His father was a pagan; his mother a devout Christian. He was not baptized as an infant.

Even in his adolescence, Augustine's intelligence was impressive, and at sixteen he was sent to Carthage to study. There he took a mistress and had an illegitimate child. At nineteen, he decided to study philosophy. He soon converted to Manichaeism, the religion founded about 240 by the prophet Mani. To the young Augustine, Christianity seemed unsophisticated, while Manichaeism appealed to his reason. However, over the course of the next nine years, he gradually became disillusioned with Manichaeism. When Augustine was twenty-nine, he moved to Rome. A bit later he moved to Milan, in northern Italy, where he became a professor of rhetoric. There he became familiar with Neoplatonism, a modified version of Plato's philosophy that had been developed by Plotinus in the third century.

The bishop in Milan at that time was St. Ambrose. Augustine listened to some of his sermons, which introduced him to a new, more sophisticated aspect of Christianity. At the age of thirty-two, Augustine was converted, and the one-time skeptic became an ardent proponent of Christianity. In 387, Augustine was baptized by Ambrose, and soon thereafter he returned home to Tagaste.

In 391, Augustine became the assistant to the bishop of Hippo. Five years later the bishop died, and Augustine, then forty-two years old, became the new bishop of Hippo. He remained at that post for the rest of his life.

Although Hippo was not an important city, Augustine's brilliance was so obvious that he soon became one of the most respected leaders in the church. Although he had a weak constitution, with the help of stenographers he was able to compose a large number of religious writings. About 500 of his sermons survive, as do more than 200 of his letters. Of his books, the two most famous and influential are *The City of God* and his *Confessions*. The latter, which is one of the most famous autobiographies ever written, was composed when he was in his forties.

Many of Augustine's letters and sermons are devoted to refuting the beliefs of the Manichaeans, the Donatists (a schismatic Christian sect), and the Pelagians (another heretical Christian group of the day). His dispute with the Pelagians forms an important part of Augustine's religious doctrines. Pelagius was an English monk who came to Rome about 400, and there expounded several interesting theological doctrines. We are each, Pelagius claimed, without original sin, and are free to choose good or evil. By righteous living and good works, an individual can attain salvation.

Partly through the influence of St. Augustine's writings, the views of Pelagius were declared heretical, and Pelagius himself (who had already been banished from Rome) was excommunicated. According to Augustine, all men are stained with Adam's sin. Human beings are unable to attain salvation solely through their own efforts and good works: the grace of God is necessary for salvation. Similar ideas had been expressed previously; however, Augustine amplified the earlier statements, and his writings solidified the Church's position on these points, which thereafter became fixed.

Augustine maintained that God already knows who will be saved and who will not, and that some of us are therefore *predestined* to be saved. This idea of predestination was to greatly influence later theologians, such as St. Thomas Aquinas and John Calvin.

Probably even more important than the doctrine of predestination were St. Augustine's attitudes concerning sex. When he converted to Christianity, Augustine had decided that it was necessary for him to renounce sex. (He once wrote, "Nothing is so much to be shunned as sex relations.") However, the actual renunciation proved quite difficult for St. Augustine; both his personal struggle and his views on the subject are described at some length in his *Confessions*. The views he expressed there, because of Augustine's great reputation, exerted a strong influence upon medieval attitudes toward sex. Augustine's writings also linked together the notion of original sin and sexual desire.

During Augustine's life, the Roman Empire was rapidly declining. In fact, in 410, the city of Rome was sacked by the Visigoths under Alaric. Naturally, the remaining Roman pagans claimed that the Romans were thereby being punished for their desertion of their ancient gods in favor of Christianity. St.

Augustine dictates to a scribe.

Augustine's most famous book, *The City of God*, is in part a defense of Christianity against that charge. However, the book also includes an entire philosophy of history, one that was to have considerable influence upon later developments in Europe. Augustine expressed the view that the Roman Empire was not of any basic importance, nor was the city of Rome, nor any earthly city. What was really important was the growth of the "heavenly city"—in other words, the spiritual progress of mankind. The vehicle for this progress was, of course, the Church. ("There is no salvation outside the Church.") It therefore followed that emperors, whether pagan or Christian or barbarian, were not as important as the Pope and the Church were.

Although Augustine himself did not take the final step, the thrust of his argument leads easily to the conclusion that temporal rulers should be subordinate to the Pope. Medieval popes were glad to draw that conclusion from Augustine, and his doctrines therefore laid the foundation for the long conflict between Church and State that was to characterize European history for many centuries.

Augustine's writings were a factor in the transmission of certain aspects of Greek philosophy to medieval Europe. In particular, Neoplatonism strongly influenced Augustine's mature thought, and through Augustine it influenced medieval Christian philosophy. It is also interesting to note that Augustine expressed the idea behind Descartes' famous statement, "I think, therefore I am," though in different words, of course.

Augustine was the last great Christian theologian before the Dark Ages, and his writings left Church doctrine, in all its major outlines, in roughly the form it was to keep throughout the Middle Ages. He was the most eminent of the Latin Church fathers, and his writings were widely read by the clergy. His views on salvation, sex, original sin, and many other points were correspondingly influential. Many later Catholic theologians, such as St. Thomas Aquinas, as well as Protestant leaders such as Luther and Calvin, were strongly influenced by him.

Augustine died in Hippo, in 430 A.D., in his seventy-sixth year. The Vandals, one of the barbarian tribes which had invaded the disintegrating Roman Empire, were besieging Hippo at the time. A few months later, they captured the town and burned most of it; however, Augustine's library and the cathedral escaped destruction.

55

WILLIAM HARVEY

1578-1657

William Harvey, the great English physician who discovered the circulation of the blood and the function of the heart, was born in 1578, in the town of Folkestone, England. Harvey's great book, *An Anatomical Treatise on the Movement of the Heart and Blood in Animals,* published in 1628, has rightly been called the most important book in the entire history of physiology. It is, in fact, the starting point of the modern science of physiology. Its primary importance lies not in its direct applications, but rather in the basic understanding it provides of how the human body works.

For us today, who have been brought up with the knowledge that the blood circulates, and therefore take that fact for granted, Harvey's theory seems completely obvious. But what now appears so simple and evident was not obvious at all to earlier biologists. Leading writers on biology had expounded views such as: (a) food is turned into blood in the heart; (b) the heart heats up the blood; (c) the arteries are filled with air; (d) the heart manufactures "vital spirits"; (e) blood in both the veins and the arteries ebbs and flows, sometimes going toward the heart and sometimes away.

Galen, the greatest physician of the ancient world, a man who personally performed many dissections and thought carefully about the heart and blood vessels, never suspected that the blood circulates. Nor for that matter did Aristotle, though biology was one of his major interests. Even after the publication of Harvey's book, many physicians were unwilling to accept his idea that the blood in the human body is constantly being recirculated through a closed system of blood vessels, with the heart supplying the force to move the blood.

Harvey first formed the notion that the blood circulates by making a simple arithmetic calculation. He estimated that the quantity of blood that was ejected by the heart every time it beat was about two ounces. Since the heart beats about 72 times per minute, simple multiplication led to the conclusion that about 540 pounds of blood were ejected each hour from the heart into the aorta. But 540 pounds far exceeds the total body weight of a normal human being, and even more greatly exceeds the weight of the blood alone. It therefore seemed obvious to Harvey that the same blood was constantly recycled through the heart. Having formulated this hypothesis, he spent nine years performing experiments and making careful observations to determine the details of the circulation of the blood.

In his book, Harvey clearly stated that the arteries carry blood away from the heart, while the veins return the blood to the heart. Lacking a microscope, Harvey was unable to see the capillaries, the minute blood vessels that transport the blood from the smallest arteries to the veins, but he correctly inferred their existence. (The capillaries were discovered by the Italian biologist, Malpighi, a few years after Harvey died.)

Harvey also stated that the function of the heart was to

pump the blood into the arteries. On this, as on every other major point, Harvey's theory was essentially correct. Furthermore, he presented a wealth of experimental evidence, with careful arguments to support his theory. Though his theory at first encountered strong opposition, by the end of his life it had been generally accepted.

Harvey also did work on embryology, which, though less important than his research on blood circulation, was not insignificant. He was a careful observer, and his book, *On the Generation of Animals*, published in 1651, marks the real begin-

Harvey explains his ideas to Charles I.

ning of the modern study of embryology. Like Aristotle, by whom he was strongly influenced, Harvey opposed the theory of preformation—the hypothesis that an embryo, even in its earliest stages, had the same overall structure as the adult animal, though on a much smaller scale. Harvey correctly asserted that the final structure of an embryo developed gradually.

Harvey had a long, interesting, and successful life. In his teens, he attended Caius College at the University of Cambridge. In 1600, he went to Italy to study medicine at the University of Padua, at that time perhaps the best medical school in the world. (It might be noted that Galileo was a professor at Padua while Harvey was there, although it is not known whether the two ever met.) Harvey received his medical degree from Padua in 1602. He then returned to England, where he had a long and very successful career as a physician. Among his patients were two kings of England (James I and Charles I), as well as the eminent philosopher Francis Bacon. Harvey lectured on anatomy at the College of Physicians in London, and in fact was once elected president of the College. (He declined the post.) In addition to his private practice, he was for many years the chief physician at St. Bartholomew's Hospital in London. When his book on the circulation of the blood was published, in 1628, it made him famous throughout Europe. Harvey was married, but had no children. He died in 1657, in London, at the age of seventy-nine.

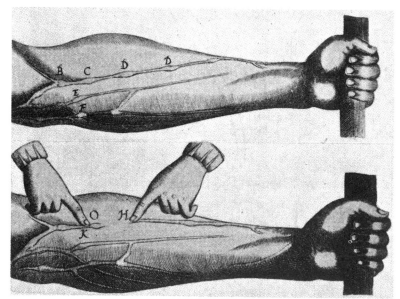

Illustration from William Harvey's book On the Movement of the Heart and Blood in Animals.

56

ERNEST
RUTHERFORD

1871–1937

Ernest Rutherford is generally considered to have been the greatest experimental physicist of the twentieth century. He is the central figure in our knowledge of radioactivity, and is also the man who originated the study of nuclear physics. In addition to their enormous theoretical importance, his discoveries have had a wide range of important applications including: nuclear weapons, nuclear power plants, radioactive tracers, and radioactive dating. His influence on the world has therefore been profound, is probably still growing, and will likely be enduring.

Rutherford was born and raised in New Zealand. He attended Canterbury College there, obtaining three degrees (B.A., M.A., B.Sc.) by the time he was twenty-three. The following year he was awarded a scholarship to Cambridge University in England, where he spent three years as a research student under J. J. Thomson, one of the leading scientists of the day. When he was twenty-seven he became professor of physics at McGill University in Canada, where he stayed for nine years. He went back to England in 1907 to head the physics department at Manchester University. In 1919 he returned to Cambridge, this time as Director of the Cavendish Laboratory, and he remained there for the rest of his life.

Radioactivity had been discovered in 1896 by the French scientist Antoine Henri Becquerel, while he was doing some experiments with uranium compounds. But Becquerel soon lost interest in the subject, and most of our basic knowledge in the field comes from Rutherford's extensive research. (Marie and Pierre Curie found two more radioactive elements—polonium and radium—but made no discoveries of fundamental importance.)

One of Rutherford's first findings was that the radioactive emissions from uranium consist of two quite different components, which he called alpha rays and beta rays. He later demonstrated the nature of each component (they consist of fast-moving particles) and showed that there is also a third component, which he called gamma rays.

An important feature of radioactivity is the energy involved. Becquerel, the Curies, and most other scientists had thought that the energy had an external source. But Rutherford proved that the energy involved—which was much greater than that released in chemical reactions—was coming from the interior of the individual uranium atoms! By so doing, he originated the important concept of atomic energy.

Scientists had always assumed that individual atoms were indestructible and unchangeable. But Rutherford (with the aide of a very talented young assistant, Frederick Soddy), was able to show that whenever an atom emits alpha or beta rays it is transformed

into an atom of a different sort. At first, chemists found this hard
to believe; but Rutherford and Soddy worked out the whole series
of radioactive decays that transform uranium to lead. He also measured the rates of decay and formulated the important concept of
"half-life." This soon led to the technique of radioactive dating,
which has become one of the most useful of scientific tools, with
important applications in geology, archaeology, astronomy, and
many other fields.

This stunning set of discoveries earned Rutherford a Nobel
prize in 1908 (Soddy later received a Nobel prize also), but his
greatest achievement was yet to come. He had noticed that fast-
moving alpha particles could go right through a thin foil of gold
(leaving no visible puncture!), although they were slightly deflected
by the passage. This suggested that gold atoms, rather than being
hard, impenetrable objects, like "tiny billiard balls"—as scientists
had previously believed—were soft inside! It seemed as if the
smaller, harder alpha particles could go right through the gold
atoms like a high-speed bullet going through jello.

But Rutherford (working with Geiger and Marsden, two
younger associates) found that some of the alpha particles were
sharply deflected when they struck the gold foil; in fact, some even
bounced right back! Rutherford, sensing that something important
was involved, had the experiment repeated many times, carefully
counting the number of particles scattered in each direction. Then,
by a very difficult but utterly convincing mathematical analysis, he
showed that there was only one way of explaining the experimental
results: A gold atom consisted almost entirely of empty space, with
almost all of the atom's mass concentrated in a minute "nucleus"
in the center!

At a single blow, Rutherford's paper (1911) shattered forever
our common-sense picture of the world. If even a piece of metal—
seemingly the solidest of objects—was mostly empty space, then
everything which we had regarded as substantial had suddenly
dissolved into tiny specks rushing about in an immense void!

Rutherford's discovery of the atomic nucleus is the foundation of all modern theories of atomic structure. When Niels Bohr, two years later, published his famous paper describing the atom as a miniature solar system governed by quantum mechanics, he used Rutherford's nuclear atom as the starting point of his model. So did Heisenberg and Schrodinger when they constructed their more sophisticated atomic models using matrix mechanics and wave mechanics.

Rutherford's discovery also led to a new branch of science: the study of the nucleus itself. In this field too, Rutherford proved to be a pioneer. In 1919, he succeeded in transforming nitrogen nuclei into oxygen nuclei by bombarding them with fast-moving alpha particles. It was an achievement to dazzle the dreams of the ancient alchemists.

It was soon realized that nuclear transformations might be the source of the Sun's energy. Furthermore, inducing the transformation of atomic nuclei is the key process in atomic weapons, and also in nuclear power plants. Rutherford's discovery has therefore been of far more than academic interest.

Rutherford's "larger than life" personality constantly impressed those who met him. He was a big man, with a loud voice, boundless energy and confidence, and a conspicuous lack of modesty. When a colleague commented on Rutherford's uncanny ability to always be "on the crest of the wave" of scientific research, he replied promptly, "Well, why not? After all, I made the wave, didn't I!" Few scientists would disagree with that assessment.

57

JOHN CALVIN

1509-1564

The famous Protestant theologian and moralist John Calvin is one of the major figures of European history. His views on such diverse subjects as theology, government, personal morality, and work habits have, over a period of more than 400 years, influenced the lives of hundreds of millions of people.

John Calvin (original name: Jean Cauvin) was born in 1509, in the town of Noyon, in France. He received a good education. After attending the Collège de Montaigu in Paris, he went to the University of Orléans to study law. He also studied law at Bourges.

Calvin was only eight years old when Martin Luther posted his Ninety-five Theses on the church door in Wittenberg, and thereby inaugurated the Protestant Reformation. Calvin was brought up as a Catholic, but as a young man he converted to Protestantism. To avoid persecution, he soon left Paris, where he had been living, and after traveling about for a while, settled in

Basel, Switzerland. There he lived under a pseudonym while he studied theology intensively. In 1536, when he was twenty-seven years old, he published his best-known work, the *Institutes of the Christian Religion*. This book, which summarized the essential Protestant beliefs and presented them in comprehensive and systematic form, made him famous.

Later in 1536, he visited Geneva, Switzerland, where Protestantism was rapidly gaining in strength. He was asked to stay there as a teacher and leader of the Protestant community. But conflicts soon arose between the fiercely puritanical Calvin and the Genevans, and in 1538, he was forced to leave the city. In 1541, however, he was invited to return. He did so, and he became not only the religious leader of the city, but also its effective political leader until his death in 1564.

In theory, Calvin was never a dictator in Geneva: many of the townspeople had voting rights, and much of the formal political authority was held by a council which consisted of twenty-five persons. Calvin was not a member of this council. He was subject to removal at any time (and was, in fact, expelled in 1538) if he did not have the consent of the majority. In practice, though, Calvin dominated the city, and after 1555 he was a virtual autocrat.

Under Calvin's leadership, Geneva became the leading Protestant center of Europe. Calvin consistently tried to promote the growth of Protestantism in other countries, particularly in France, and for a while Geneva was referred to as the "Protestant Rome." One of the first things that Calvin did after his return to Geneva was to draw up a set of ecclesiastical regulations for the Reformed Church there. These were to set a pattern for many other Reformed Churches in Europe. While in Geneva, Calvin wrote many influential religious tracts, and continued to revise the *Institutes of the Christian Religion*. He also gave many lectures on theology and the Bible.

Calvin's Geneva was a rather austere and puritanical place. Not only were adultery and fornication considered serious crimes, but gambling, drunkenness, dancing, and the singing of ribald songs were all prohibited, and could result in severe punishment. Attendance at church during prescribed hours was required by law, and lengthy sermons were customary.

Calvin strongly encouraged diligence in work. He also encouraged education, and it was during his administration that the University of Geneva was founded.

Calvin was an intolerant man, and those whom he considered heretics received short shrift in Geneva. His most famous victim (there were quite a few) was Michael Servetus, a Spanish physician and theologian who did not believe in the doctrine of the Trinity. When Servetus came to Geneva, he was arrested, tried for heresy, and burnt at the stake (in 1553). In addition, several persons suspected of witchcraft were burnt at the stake during Calvin's administration.

Calvin died in Geneva, in 1564. He had married, but his wife had died in 1549, and their only child had died at birth.

Calvin's principal importance lies not in his direct political activities, but rather in the ideology he promulgated. He stressed the authority and importance of the Bible, and like Luther, denied the authority and importance of the Roman Catholic Church. Like Luther, St. Augustine, and St. Paul, Calvin held that all men are sinners, and that salvation comes not through good works, but through faith alone. Particularly striking were Calvin's ideas on predestination and reprobation. According to Calvin, God has already decided—and without regard to merit—who is to be saved and who is to be damned. Why, then, should an individual bother to behave morally? Calvin's answer was that the "elect" (that is, those persons whom God has chosen to accept Christ and thereby achieve redemption) have also been selected by God to behave righteously. We are not saved because we do good, but we do good because we have been chosen for salvation. Although such a doctrine may seem strange to some, there seems little doubt that it has inspired many Calvinists to lead unusually pious and upright lives.

Calvin has exerted great influence on the world. His theological doctrines ultimately gained even more adherents than Luther's did. Though northern Germany and Scandinavia became predominantly Lutheran, Switzerland and the Netherlands became Calvinist. There were significant Calvinist minorities in Poland, Hungary, and Germany. The Presbyterians in Scotland were Calvinists, as were the Huguenots in France and the Puritans in England. Puritan influence in America, of course, has been both long and strong.

Calvin's Geneva may have been more a theocracy than a democracy, but the net effect of Calvinism has nevertheless been to increase democracy. Perhaps the fact that in so many countries the Calvinists were a minority made them inclined to favor restrictions on established power; or perhaps the comparatively democratic internal organization of the Calvinist churches was a factor. Whatever the reason, the original Calvinist strongholds (Switzerland, Holland, and Great Britain) became strongholds of democracy as well.

It has been claimed that Calvinist doctrines were a major factor in the creation of the so-called "Protestant work ethic," and in the rise of capitalism. It is difficult to judge the extent to which that claim is justified. The Dutch, for example, were

This monument in Geneva commemorates the Reformation; a statue of Calvin is at the extreme left.

reputed to be an industrious people long before Calvin had ever been born. On the other hand, it seems unreasonable to assume that Calvin's firmly expressed attitude toward hard work had no influence upon his followers. (It might be noted that Calvin did permit the charging of interest, a practice which had been condemned by most earlier Christian moralists, but one that was important to the development of capitalism.)

How high on this list should Calvin be ranked? The influence of Calvin has been confined primarily to western Europe and North America. Furthermore, it is plain that his influence has been sharply declining during the last century. In any case, much of the credit for the existence of Calvinism has already been assigned to earlier figures such as Jesus, St. Paul, and Luther.

Although the Protestant Reformation was an event of great historical importance, it is plain that Martin Luther was the person most responsible for that upheaval. Calvin himself was only one of several influential Protestant leaders who arose after Luther. It is therefore quite clear that Calvin must be ranked far below Luther. On the other hand, Calvin must be ranked well ahead of such philosophers as Voltaire and Rousseau, partly because his influence has extended over twice as long a period as theirs, and partly because his ideas have had such a profound effect on the lives of his followers.

58 GREGOR MENDEL

1822-1884

Gregor Mendel is famous today as the man who discovered the basic principles of heredity. During his lifetime, however, he was an obscure Austrian monk and amateur scientist, whose brilliant research was ignored by the scientific world.

Mendel was born in 1822, in the town of Heinzendorf, at that time within the Austrian Empire, but now part of Czechoslovakia. In 1843, he entered an Augustinian monastery in Brünn, Austria (now Brno, Czechoslovakia). He was ordained a priest in 1847. In 1850, he took an examination for teacher certification. He failed, receiving his lowest marks in biology and geology! Nevertheless, the abbot in charge of his monastery sent Mendel to the University of Vienna, where, from 1851 to 1853, he studied mathematics and science. Mendel never did get a regular teacher's license, but from 1854 to 1868, he was a substitute teacher of natural science at the Brünn Modern School.

Meanwhile, starting in 1856, he performed his famous experiments in plant breeding. By 1865, he had derived his famous laws of heredity and presented them in a paper given before the Brünn Natural History Society. In 1866, his results were published in the *Transactions* of that society, in an article entitled "Experiments with Plant Hybrids." A second article was published in the same journal three years later. Although the *Transactions* of the Brünn Natural History Society was not a prestigious journal, it was carried by major libraries. In addition, Mendel sent a copy of his paper to Karl Nägeli, a leading authority on heredity. Nägeli read the paper and replied to Mendel, but failed to comprehend the paper's enormous importance. Thereafter, Mendel's articles were generally ignored and, indeed, almost forgotten for over thirty years.

In 1868, Mendel was appointed abbot of his chapter, and from then on his administrative duties left him little time to continue his plant experiments. When he died, in 1884, at the age of sixty-one, his brilliant research had been nearly forgotten, and he had received no recognition for it.

Mendel's work was not rediscovered until the year 1900, when three different scientists (a Dutchman, Hugo de Vries; a German, Carl Correns; and an Austrian, Erich von Tschermak), working independently, came across Mendel's article. Each of the three men had performed his own botanical experiments; each had independently discovered Mendel's Laws; each, before publishing his results, had researched the literature and come across Mendel's original article; and each carefully cited Mendel's paper and stated that his own work confirmed Mendel's conclusions. An astounding triple coincidence! Moreover, in that same year, William Bateson, an English scientist, came across Mendel's original article and promptly drew it to the attention of other scientists. By the end of the year, Mendel was receiving the acclaim that he had so richly deserved during his lifetime.

What were the facts about heredity that Mendel discovered?

In the first place, Mendel learned that in all living organisms there were basic units, today called genes, by which inherited characteristics were transmitted from parent to offspring. In the plants that Mendel studied, each individual characteristic, such as seed color or leaf shape, was determined by a pair of genes. An individual plant inherited one gene of each pair from each parent. Mendel found that if the two genes inherited for a given trait were different (for example, one gene for green seeds and another gene for yellow seeds) then, normally, only the effect of the dominant gene (in this case for yellow seeds) would manifest itself in that individual. Nevertheless, the recessive gene was not destroyed and might be transmitted to the plant's descendants. Mendel realized that each reproductive cell, or gamete (corresponding to sperm or egg cells in human beings) contained only one gene of each pair. He also stated that it was completely a matter of chance which gene of each pair occurred in an individual gamete and was transmitted to an individual offspring.

Mendel's laws, although they have been modified slightly, remain the starting point of the modern science of genetics. How is it that Mendel, an amateur scientist, was able to discover those important principles that had eluded so many eminent professional biologists before him? Fortunately, he had selected for his investigations a species of plant whose most striking characteristics are each determined by a single set of genes. Had the characteristics he investigated each been determined by several sets of genes, his research would have been immensely more difficult. But this piece of good luck would not have helped Mendel had he not been an extremely careful and patient experimenter, nor would it have helped him had he not realized that it was necessary to make a *statistical* analysis of his observations. Because of the random factor mentioned above, it is generally not possible to predict which traits an individual offspring will inherit. Only by performing a large number of experiments (Mendel had recorded results for over 21,000 individual plants!), and by analyzing his results statistically was Mendel able to deduce his laws.

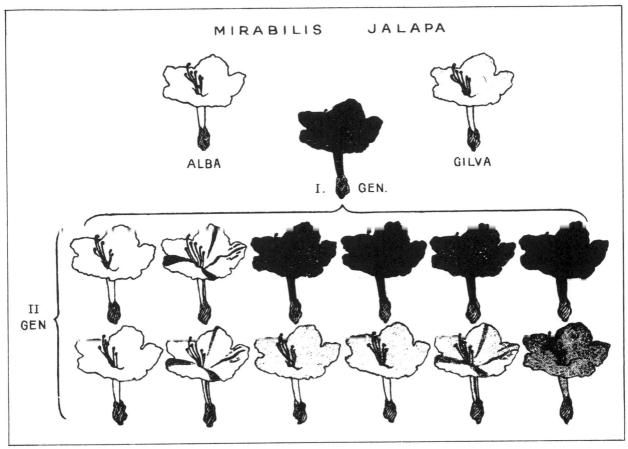

MIRABILIS   JALAPA

ALBA

GILVA

I. GEN.

II GEN

The genetic patterns of the flower mirabilis jalapa.

It is obvious that the laws of heredity are an important addition to human knowledge, and our knowledge of genetics will probably have even more applications in the future than it has had so far. There is, however, another factor to be considered when deciding where Mendel should be placed. Since his discoveries were ignored during his lifetime, and his conclusions were rediscovered independently by later scientists, Mendel's research might be deemed expendable. If that argument is pushed to its limit, one might conclude that Mendel should be left off this list entirely, just as Leif Ericson, Aristarchus, and Ignaz

Semmelweiss have been omitted in favor of Columbus, Copernicus, and Joseph Lister.

There are, however, differences between Mendel's case and the others. Mendel's work was forgotten only briefly, and once rediscovered, quickly became widely known. Furthermore, de Vries, Correns, and Tschermak, though they rediscovered his principles independently, eventually did read his paper and cite his results. Finally, one cannot rightly say that Mendel's work would have had no influence if de Vries, Correns, and Tschermak had never lived. Mendel's article had already been included in a widely circulated bibliography (by W. O. Focke) of works on heredity. That listing ensured that sooner or later some serious student in the field would come across Mendel's article. It might be noted that none of the other three scientists ever claimed credit for the discovery of genetics; also, the scientific principles discovered are universally referred to as "Mendel's Laws."

Mendel's discoveries seem comparable, both in originality and importance, with Harvey's discovery of the circulation of the blood, and he has been ranked accordingly.

59 MAX PLANCK

1858-1947

In December 1900, the German physicist Max Planck startled the scientific world with his bold hypothesis that radiant energy (that is, the energy of light waves) is not emitted in a continuous flow, but rather consists of small chunks or lumps, which he called *quanta*. Planck's hypothesis, which conflicted with the classical theories of light and electromagnetism, provided the starting point for the quantum theories which have since revolutionized physics and provided us with a deeper understanding of the nature of matter and radiation.

Planck was born in 1858, in Kiel, Germany. He studied in the Universities of Berlin and Munich, and received his doctor's degree in physics *(summa cum laude)* from the University of Munich when he was twenty-one years old. For a while he taught at the University of Munich, and then at Kiel University. In 1889, he became a professor at the University of Berlin, where he remained until his retirement in 1928, at the age of seventy.

Planck, like several other scientists, was interested in the subject of black body radiation, which is the name given to the electromagnetic radiation emitted by a perfectly black object when it is heated. (A perfectly black object is defined as one that does not reflect any light, but completely absorbs all light falling on it.) Experimental physicists had already made careful measurements of the radiation emitted by such objects, even before Planck started working on the problem. Planck's first achievement was his discovery of the fairly complicated algebraic formula that correctly describes the black body radiation. This formula, which is frequently used in theoretical physics today, neatly summarized the experimental data. But there was a problem: the accepted laws of physics predicted a quite different formula.

Planck pondered deeply on this problem and finally came up with a radically new theory: radiant energy is only emitted in exact multiples of an elementary unit that Planck called the *quantum*. According to Planck's theory, the magnitude of a quantum of light depends on the frequency of the light (i.e., on its color), and is also proportional to a physical quantity that Planck abbreviated h, but that is now called Planck's constant. Planck's hypothesis was quite contrary to the then prevalent concepts of physics; however, by using it he was able to find an exact theoretical derivation of the correct formula for black body radiation.

Planck's hypothesis was so revolutionary that it doubtless would have been dismissed as a crackpot idea, had not Planck been well-known as a solid, conservative physicist. Although the hypothesis sounded very strange, in this particular case it did lead to the correct formula.

At first, most physicists (including Planck himself) regarded his hypothesis as no more than a convenient mathematical fiction. After a few years, though, it turned out that Planck's concept of the quantum could be applied to various physical phenomena other than black body radiation. Einstein used the concept in 1905 to explain the photoelectric effect, and Niels Bohr used it in 1913 in his theory of atomic structure. By 1918, when Planck was awarded the Nobel Prize, it was clear that his hypothesis was basically correct, and that it was of fundamental importance in physical theory.

Planck's strong anti-Nazi views placed him in considerable danger during the Hitler era. His younger son was executed in early 1945 for his role in the unsuccessful officers' plot to assassinate Hitler. Planck himself died in 1947, at the age of eighty-nine.

The development of quantum mechanics is probably the most important scientific development of the twentieth century, more important even than Einstein's theories of relativity. Planck's constant, h, plays a vital role in physical theory, and is now recognized as one of the two or three most fundamental physical constants. It appears in the theory of atomic structure, in Heisenberg's uncertainty principle, in radiation theory, and in many scientific formulas. Planck's original estimate of its numerical value was within 2 percent of the figure accepted today.

Planck is generally considered to be the father of quantum mechanics. Although he played little part in the later development of the theory, it would be a mistake to rank Planck too low. The initial breakthrough which he provided was very important. It freed men's minds from their earlier misconceptions, and it thereby enabled his successors to construct the far more elegant theory we have today.

60 JOSEPH LISTER

1827-1912

Joseph Lister, the British surgeon who introduced the use of antiseptic measures in surgery, was born in 1827, in Upton, England. In 1852, he received a medical degree from University College in London, where he had been an excellent student. In 1861, he became surgeon at the Glasgow Royal Infirmary, a position he was to hold for eight years. It was primarily during this period that he developed his method of antiseptic surgery.

At the Glasgow Royal Infirmary, Lister was in charge of the wards in the new surgical block. He was appalled by the high rate of postoperative mortality that occurred there. Serious infections, such as gangrene, were a common aftermath of surgery. Lister tried to keep his wards generally clean; however, this did not prove sufficient to prevent a high mortality rate. Many doctors maintained that "miasmas" (noxious vapors) about the hospital were the cause of these infections. However, this explanation did not satisfy Lister.

Then, in 1865, he read a paper by Louis Pasteur, which introduced him to the germ theory of disease. This provided Lister with his key idea. If infections were caused by microbes, then the best method of preventing postoperative infections would be to kill the microbes before they got into the open wound. Using carbolic acid as a germ-killer, Lister instituted a new set of antiseptic procedures. He not only cleaned his hands carefully before every operation, but made sure that the instruments and the dressings that were used were also rendered completely sanitary. Indeed, for a while he even sprayed carbolic acid into the air in the operating room. The result was a dramatic drop in postoperative fatalities. During the period 1861-1865, the postoperative mortality rate in the male accident ward had been 45 percent. By 1869, it had been reduced to 15 percent.

Lister's first great paper on antiseptic surgery was published in 1867. His ideas were not immediately accepted. However, he was offered the Chair of Clinical Surgery at Edinburgh University in 1869, and during his seven-year stay there his fame spread. In 1875, he toured Germany, lecturing on his ideas and methods; the following year, he made a similar tour in the United States. But the majority of doctors were not yet convinced.

In 1877, Lister was given the Chair of Clinical Surgery at King's College in London, a position that he held for over fifteen years. His demonstrations of antiseptic surgery in London aroused great interest in medical circles, and resulted in increased acceptance of his ideas. By the end of his life, Lister's principles of antiseptic surgery had won virtually universal acceptance among physicians.

Lister received many honors for his pioneering work. He was president of the Royal Society for five years, and was Queen Victoria's personal surgeon. Married, but childless, Lister lived to be almost eighty-five. He died in 1912, in Walmer, England.

Lister's innovations have completely revolutionized the field of surgery, and have saved many millions of lives. Not only do far fewer people die today from postoperative infections, but today surgery saves many persons who would be unwilling to undergo operations if the danger of infection were as great now as it was a century ago. Furthermore, surgeons are now able to undertake complicated operations that they would never have attempted in earlier days, when the risk of infection was so great. A century ago, for example, operations that involved opening the chest cavity were not normally contemplated. Although present-day techniques of aseptic surgery are different from the antiseptic methods that Lister used, they involve the same basic ideas, and are an extension of Lister's principles.

One might claim that Lister's ideas were such obvious corollaries of Pasteur's that Lister is not entitled to any significant credit. However, despite Pasteur's writings, someone was required to develop and popularize the techniques of antiseptic surgery. Nor does the inclusion of both Lister and Pasteur in this book amount to counting the same discovery twice. The applications of the germ theory of disease are of such significance that, even when the credit is divided up, Pasteur, Leeuwenhoek, Fleming and Lister all are fully entitled to a place on this list.

There is another possible objection to Lister's being placed so high on this list. Almost twenty years before Lister did his work, the Hungarian doctor, Ignaz Semmelweiss (1818-1865), working in the Vienna General Hospital, had clearly demonstrated the advantages of antiseptic procedures, both in obstetrics and in surgery. However, although Semmelweiss became a professor and wrote an excellent book setting forth his ideas, he was by and large ignored. It was Joseph Lister whose writings, talks, and demonstrations actually convinced the medical profession of the necessity for antiseptic procedures in medical practice.

61

NIKOLAUS AUGUST OTTO

1832-1891

Nikolaus August Otto was the German inventor who, in 1876, built the first four-stroke internal combustion engine, the prototype of the hundreds of millions that have been built since then.

The internal combustion engine is a versatile device: it is used to power motorboats and motorcycles; it has had many industrial applications; and it was the vital requisite for the invention of the airplane. (Until the first jet plane flew, in 1939, virtually all aircraft were powered by internal combustion engines working on the Otto cycle.) However, by far the most important use of the internal combustion engine is to power automobiles.

There had been many attempts to construct automobiles before Otto developed his engine. Some inventors, such as Siegfried Marcus (in 1875), Étienne Lenoir (in 1862), and Nicolas Joseph Cugnot (about 1769), had even succeeded in building models that ran. But lacking a suitable type of engine—one capable of combining low weight with high power—none of those models was practical. However, within fifteen years of the invention of Otto's four-stroke engine, two different inventors,

Karl Benz and Gottlieb Daimler, each constructed practical, marketable automobiles. Various other types of engines have since been used to power automobiles, and it is quite possible that in the future, cars powered by steam, or by electric batteries, or by some other device, will ultimately prove superior. But of the hundreds of millions of cars built in the past century, 99 percent have used the four-stroke internal combustion engine. (The Diesel engine, an ingenious form of internal combustion engine which is used to power many trucks, buses, and ships, employs a four-stroke cycle basically similar to Otto's, but the fuel is admitted at a different stage.)

The great majority of scientific inventions (with the important exceptions of weapons and explosives) are generally conceded to be beneficial to mankind. It is rare, for example, that anyone suggests that we abandon refrigerators or penicillin, or that we seriously restrict their use. The drawbacks of the widespread use of private automobiles, however, are glaringly obvious. They are noisy, they cause air pollution, they consume scarce fuel resources, and each year they cause a ghastly toll of dead and injured persons.

Clearly, we would never consider putting up with the automobile if it did not provide us with enormous advantages as well. Private automobiles are infinitely more flexible than public transportation. Unlike railroads and subway trains, for example, a private automobile will leave whenever you wish, will take you wherever you want to go, and will provide door-to-door service. It is fast, comfortable, and carries luggage easily. By providing us with an unprecedented degree of choice about where we live and how we spend our time, it has considerably increased individual freedom.

Whether all these advantages are worth the price that the automobile exacts from society may be debatable, but no one denies that the automobile has had a major impact on our civilization. In the United States alone there are over 180 million cars in use. Together, they account for approximately three *trillion* passenger miles a year—more than the combined mileage traveled on foot, in airplanes, in trains, in boats, and by all other forms of transportation.

To accommodate the automobile, we have built acres of parking lots and endless miles of superhighways, altering the whole landscape in the process. In return, the automobile provides us with a mobility scarcely dreamed of by earlier generations. Most car owners now have a vastly larger range of activities and facilities readily available than they could possibly have had without the automobile. It widens our choice of where we work and where we can live. Thanks to the automobile, numerous facilities that previously were only available to urban dwellers are now available to those who live in the suburbs. (This has perhaps been the principal underlying cause of the growth of the suburbs in recent decades and the concomitant decline of the inner cities in the United States.)

Nikolaus August Otto was born in 1832, in the town of Holzhausen, in Germany. His father died when he was an infant. Otto was a good student; however, he dropped out of high school at the age of sixteen to get a job and to gain business experience. For a while, he worked in a grocery store in a small town. Later, he was a clerk in Frankfurt. After that, he became a traveling salesman.

About 1860, Otto heard of the gas engine recently invented by Étienne Lenoir (1822-1900), the first workable internal combustion engine. Otto realized that the Lenoir engine would have many more applications if it could run on liquid fuel, since in that case it would not have to be attached to a gas outlet. Otto soon devised a carburetor; his patent application was denied by the patent office, however, because similar devices had already been invented.

Undiscouraged, Otto devoted his efforts to improving the Lenoir engine. As early as 1861, he hit upon the idea of a basically new type of engine, one operating on a four-stroke cycle (unlike Lenoir's primitive engine which operated on a two-stroke cycle). In January 1862, Otto built a working model of his four-stroke engine. But he ran into difficulties, especially with the ignition, in making this new engine practical, and soon put it aside. Instead, he developed his "atmospheric engine," an improved two-stroke engine, which ran on gas. He patented it in 1863, and soon found a partner, Eugen Langen, to finance him. They built a small factory, and continued to improve the engine. In 1867, their two-stroke engine won a gold medal at the Paris World's Fair. Thereafter, sales were brisk, and the company's profits soared. In 1872, they hired Gottlieb Daimler, a brilliant engineer with experience in factory management, to help produce their engine.

Although profits from the two-stroke engine were good, Otto could not get out of his mind the four-stroke engine that he had conceived originally. He was convinced that a four-stroke engine, which *compressed* the mixture of fuel and air before igniting it, could be much more efficient than any modification of Lenoir's two-stroke engine. In early 1876, Otto finally devised an improved ignition system, and with it was able to construct a practical four-stroke engine. The first such model was built in May 1876, and a patent was granted the following year. The superior efficiency and performance of the four-stroke engine were obvious, and it was an immediate commercial success. Over 30,000 were sold in the next ten years alone, and all versions of the Lenoir engine soon became obsolete.

Otto's German patent on his four-stroke engine was overturned in 1886 in a patent suit. It turned out that a Frenchman, Alphonse Beau de Rochas, had thought of a basically similar device in 1862, and had patented it. (One should not, however, think of Beau de Rochas as an influential figure. His invention was never marketed, and, indeed, he never built a single model. Nor did Otto get the idea of his invention from him.) Despite the loss of the valuable patent, Otto's firm continued to make money. When he died, in 1891, he was prosperous.

Meanwhile, in 1882, Gottlieb Daimler left the firm. He was determined to adapt the Otto engine for vehicular use. By 1883, he had developed a superior ignition system (*not*, however, the one in general use today), which enabled the engine to operate at

Otto's engine was employed by automobile pioneers Gottlieb Daimler and Karl Benz. The first Royal Daimler was a 6-horsepower car supplied to the Prince of Wales.

Smithsonian #30, 399

The original "Benzine Buggy."

700-900 revolutions per minute. (Otto's models had a top speed of 180-200 rpm.) Furthermore, Daimler took pains to construct a very light engine. In 1885, he attached one of his engines to a bicycle, thereby constructing the world's first motorcycle. The following year, Daimler constructed his first four-wheel automobile. It turned out, though, that Karl Benz had beat him to the punch. Karl Benz had built *his* first automobile—a three-wheeler, but undeniably an automobile—just a few months earlier. Benz's car, like Daimler's, was powered by a version of Otto's four-stroke engine. Benz's engine ran at well under 400 rpm, but that was enough to make his automobile practical. Benz steadily improved his automobile, and within a few years he succeeded in marketing it. Gottlieb Daimler started marketing his cars a bit later than Benz, but he, too, was successful. (Eventually, the Benz and Daimler firms merged together. The famous Mercedes-Benz automobile is manufactured by the resulting firm.)

One more figure in the development of the automobile must be mentioned: the American inventor and industrialist, Henry Ford, who was the first to mass-produce inexpensive automobiles.

The internal combustion engine and the automobile were inventions of staggering importance, and if a single person were entitled to exclusive credit for them he would rank near the top of this list. The principal credit for these inventions must, however, be divided among several men: Lenoir, Otto, Daimler, Benz, and Ford. Of all these men, Otto made the most significant contribution. The Lenoir engine was intrinsically neither powerful nor efficient enough to power automobiles. Otto's engine was. Before 1876, when Otto invented his engine, development of a practical automobile was almost impossible; after 1876, it was virtually inevitable. Nikolaus August Otto is, therefore, one of the true makers of the modern world.

62

FRANCISCO PIZARRO

c. 1 4 7 5 - 1 5 4 1

Francisco Pizarro, the illiterate Spanish adventurer who conquered the Inca Empire in Peru, was born about 1475, in the city of Trujillo, Spain. Like Hernando Cortés, whose career parallels his in many ways, Pizarro came to the New World to seek fame and fortune. From 1502 to 1509, Pizarro lived on Hispaniola, the Caribbean island on which Haiti and the Dominican Republic are now situated. In 1513, he was a member of the expedition, led by Vasco Núñez de Balboa, which discovered the Pacific Ocean. In 1519, he settled in Panama. In 1522, when Pizarro was about forty-seven years old, he learned of the existence of the Inca Empire from Pascual de Andagoya, a Spanish explorer who had visited it. Pizarro, doubtless inspired by the recent conquest of Mexico by Hernando Cortés, decided to conquer the Inca Empire. His first attempt, in 1524-25, was unsuccessful, and his two ships had to turn back before reaching Peru. On his second attempt, 1526-28, he managed to reach the coast of Peru and return with gold, llamas, and Indians.

In 1528, he returned to Spain. There, the following year, the emperor Charles V authorized him to conquer Peru for Spain, and supplied him with funds for an expedition. Pizarro returned to Panama, where he assembled the expedition. It sailed from Panama in 1531, at which time Pizarro was already fifty-six years old. The force which he had assembled included fewer than 200 men, while the empire that he had set out to conquer had a population of over six million!

Pizarro reached the coast of Peru the following year. In September 1532, taking with him only 177 men and 62 horses, he marched inland. Pizarro led his small force high into the Andes mountains to reach the town of Cajamarca, where the Incan ruler, Atahualpa, was staying with an army of forty thousand warriors. Pizarro's troops arrived at Cajamarca on November 15, 1532. The following day, at Pizarro's request, Atahualpa left the bulk of his troops behind, and accompanied only by about five thousand unarmed retainers, came to parley with Pizarro.

In the light of what Atahualpa must have known, his behavior is baffling. From the time that they had first landed on the coast, the Spaniards had plainly demonstrated both their hostile intent and their utter ruthlessness. It is therefore hard to understand why Atahualpa permitted Pizarro's forces to approach Cajamarca unhindered. Had the Indians attacked him on the narrow mountain roads, where Pizarro's horses were almost useless, they could easily have annihilated the Spanish forces. Atahualpa's behavior after Pizarro reached Cajamarca was still more amazing. To approach a hostile army while himself unarmed was incredibly stupid. The mystery is only heightened by the fact that ambush was a common tactic of the Incas.

Pizarro did not let his golden opportunity pass. He ordered his troops to attack Atahualpa and his unarmed escort. The battle—or rather massacre—lasted only about half an hour. Not a single Spanish soldier was killed; the only one wounded was Pizarro himself, who suffered a minor wound while protecting Atahualpa, whom he succeeded in capturing alive.

Pizarro's strategy worked perfectly. The Inca Empire was a highly centralized structure, with all authority flowing from the Inca, or emperor, who was believed to be semi-divine. With the Inca held prisoner, the Indians were unable to react to the Spanish invasion. In the hope of regaining his freedom, Atahualpa paid Pizarro an enormous ransom in gold and silver, probably worth more than 28 million dollars. Nevertheless, within a few months Pizarro had him executed. In November 1533, a year after the capture of Atahualpa, Pizarro's troops entered the Inca capital, Cuzco, without a fight. There, Pizarro installed a new Inca as his puppet. In 1535, he founded the city of Lima, which became the new capital of Peru.

In 1536, however, the puppet Inca escaped and led an Indian revolt against the Spanish. For a while the Spanish forces were besieged in Lima and Cuzco. The Spanish managed to regain control of most of the country the following year, but it was not until 1572 that the revolt was finally crushed. By then, however, Pizarro himself was dead.

Pizarro's downfall came about because the Spanish started fighting among themselves. One of Pizarro's closest associates, Diego de Almagro, revolted in 1537, claiming that Pizarro was not giving him his rightful share of the booty. Almagro was captured and executed; but the issue was not really settled, and in 1541, a group of Almagro's followers broke into Pizarro's palace in Lima and assassinated the sixty-six-year-old leader, only eight years after he had entered Cuzco victoriously.

Francisco Pizarro was brave, determined, and shrewd. By his own lights, he was a religious man, and it is reported that the dying Pizarro drew a cross on the ground with his own blood, and that his last word was "Jesus." However, he was also an incredibly avaricious man, cruel, ambitious, and treacherous: perhaps the most brutal of the conquistadors.

But Pizarro's harsh character should not blind us to the

*Pizarro's audience with
Charles V before
embarking for Peru.*

magnitude of his military achievement. When, in 1967, the
Israelis won a dramatic victory over Arab nations which greatly
outnumbered them, and which possessed far more military
equipment, many persons were surprised. It was an impressive
triumph; but history is studded with examples of military victories won against sizable numerical odds. Napoleon and Alexander the Great repeatedly won victories against larger armies.
The Mongols, under the successors of Genghis Khan, managed to
conquer China, a country which had at least thirty times their
population.

However, Pizarro's conquest of an empire of over six million with a force of only 180 men is the most astonishing military feat in history. The numerical odds he overcame were considerably higher than those which faced Cortés, who invaded an empire of roughly five million with a force of 600 men. Could even Alexander the Great or Genghis Khan have matched Pizarro's accomplishment? I doubt it, since neither of them would ever have been so reckless as to attempt a conquest when faced with such overwhelming odds.

But, one might ask, did not Spanish firearms give them an overwhelming tactical advantage? Not at all. Arquebuses, the primitive firearms of the time, had a small range and took a long time to reload. Although they made a frightening noise, they were actually less effective than good bows and arrows. In any event, when Pizarro entered Cajamarca, only three of his men had arquebuses, and no more than twenty had crossbows. Most of the Indians were killed by conventional weapons such as swords and spears. Despite their possession of a few horses and firearms, it is plain that the Spanish entered the conflict at an overwhelming military disadvantage. Leadership and determination, rather than weaponry, were the chief factors in the Spanish victory. Of course, Pizarro had good luck as well; but it is an old saying that fortune favors the brave.

Francisco Pizarro has been condemned by some writers as little more than a courageous thug. But few if any thugs have had his impact on history. The empire which he overthrew ruled most of present-day Peru and Ecuador, as well as the northern half of Chile, and part of Bolivia. Its population was considerably larger than all the rest of South America combined. As a result of Pizarro's conquests, the religion and culture of Spain were imposed on the entire region. Furthermore, after the fall of the Inca Empire, no other part of South America had any chance of successfully resisting European conquest. Millions of Indians still inhabit South America. But in most parts of the continent the Indians have never regained political power, and European language, religion, and culture remain dominant.

Cortés and Pizarro, each leading only small forces, succeeded in rather quickly overthrowing the empires of the Aztecs and the Incas. This has led many people to suspect that the conquest of Mexico and Peru by Europeans was inevitable. Indeed, it does seem that the Aztec Empire had no real chance of maintaining its independence. Its location (near the Gulf of Mexico, and a comparatively short sail from Cuba) left it vulnerable to Spanish attack. Even if the Aztecs had succeeded in defeating Cortés's small forces, larger Spanish armies were sure to follow fairly soon.

The Inca Empire, on the other hand, was far better situated for defense. The only ocean bordering it was the Pacific, which was less accessible to Spanish ships than the Atlantic. The Incas maintained large armies, and their empire was populous and well organized. Furthermore, the terrain of Peru is rugged and mountainous, and in many sections of the world, the European colonial powers found it very difficult to conquer mountainous regions. Even in the late nineteenth century, when European arms were far more advanced than they had been in the early sixteenth century, an Italian attempt to conquer Ethiopia was unsuccessful. Similarly, the British had almost endless difficulties with the tribes on the mountainous northwest frontier of India. And the Europeans were never able to colonize such mountainous countries as Nepal, Afghanistan, and Iran. Had Pizarro's invasion failed, and had the Incas thereby had the opportunity to gain some knowledge of European weapons and tactics, they might well have been able to fight off substantially larger European forces afterwards. As it was, it took the Spanish thirty-six years to suppress the Indian revolt of 1536, even though the Indians had very few guns and were never able to muster more than a small fraction of the troops which they could have assembled before Pizarro's conquest. The Spanish might have conquered the Inca Empire even without Pizarro, but that conclusion seems far from certain.

Thus, Pizarro has been ranked slightly higher than Cortés on this list. Cortés speeded up history; Pizarro may possibly have altered its course.

63 HERNANDO CORTÉS

1485-1547

Hernando Cortés, the conqueror of Mexico, was born in 1485, in Medellín, Spain. His father was a minor noble. In his youth, Cortés attended the University of Salamanca, where he studied law. At the age of nineteen, he left Spain to seek his fortune in the newly-discovered Western Hemisphere. He arrived in Hispaniola in 1504, and spent several years there as a gentleman farmer and local Don Juan. In 1511, he took part in the Spanish conquest of Cuba. Following this adventure, he married the sister-in-law of the Imperial Governor of Cuba, Diego Velásquez, and was appointed mayor of Santiago.

In 1518, Velásquez chose Cortés to be the captain of an expedition to Mexico. The governor, fearing Cortés's ambition, soon reversed his order, but it was too late to stop Cortés. He sailed in February 1519, with 11 ships, 110 sailors, 553 soldiers (including only 13 with hand guns and 32 with crossbows), 10 heavy cannons, 4 light cannons, and 16 horses. The expedition disembarked on Good Friday at the site of the present city of Veracruz. Cortés remained near the coast for a while, gathering information about the situation in Mexico. He learned that the Aztecs, who ruled Mexico, had a great capital which lay inland; that they had great stores of precious metals; and that they were hated by many of the other Indian tribes whom they had subdued.

Cortés, who was bent on conquest, decided to march inland and invade the Aztec territory. Some of his men were frightened by the enormous numerical odds which they would have to overcome; so before marching inland, Cortés destroyed the expedition's boats, thus leaving his men no choice but to either follow him to victory or be killed by the Indians.

Proceeding inland, the Spaniards encountered fierce resistance from the Tlaxcalans, an independent tribe of Indians. But after their large army had been defeated by the Spanish in some hard-fought battles, the Tlaxcalans decided to join forces with Cortés against the Aztecs, whom they hated. Cortés then advanced to Cholula, where the Aztec ruler, Montezuma II, had planned a surprise attack on the Spanish. However, Cortés, who had obtained advance information of the Indians' intentions, struck first, and massacred thousands of them at Cholula. He then advanced toward the capital, Tenochtitlán (now Mexico City), and on November 8, 1519, entered the city without opposition. He soon imprisoned Montezuma, whom he made a puppet, and it looked as though the conquest was almost complete.

But then another Spanish force, under Pánfilo de Narváez, arrived on the coast with orders to arrest Cortés. Cortés left some of his forces in Tenochtitlán, and hastily led the rest of his troops back to the coast. There, he defeated the troops of Narváez and persuaded the survivors to join him. However, by the time he was able to return to Tenochtitlán, the subordinate whom he had left there had antagonized the Aztecs beyond endurance. On June 30, 1520, there was an uprising in Tenochtitlán, and the Spanish forces, suffering severe casualties, retreated to Tlaxcala. However, Cortés obtained additional troops, and the following May he returned and laid siege to Tenochtitlán. The city fell on August 13. After that, Spanish control of Mexico was reasonably secure, although Cortés had to spend some time consolidating the conquest of the outlying regions. Tenochtitlán was rebuilt and renamed Mexico City, and it became the capital of the Spanish colony of New Spain.

Considering the small number of troops with which Cortés started, his conquest of an empire of five million was a truly remarkable military feat. The only example in history of a conquest against greater numerical odds is that of Francisco Pizarro over the Incas in Peru. It is natural to be curious about how and why Cortés succeeded. Certainly, his possession of horses and firearms was a factor; however, the very small numbers of those which he possessed were not in themselves nearly sufficient compensation for his enormous numerical disadvantage. (It is worth noting that neither of the two previous Spanish expeditions to the Mexican coast had succeeded in establishing a settlement or in making any permanent conquests.) Certainly, the leadership which Cortés provided, and his courage and determination were major factors in his success. An equally important factor was his skillful diplomacy. Cortés not only avoided inspiring an Indian coalition against him, but he successfully persuaded substantial numbers of Indians to join with him against the Aztecs.

Cortés was also aided by Aztec legends concerning the god Quetzalcoatl. According to Indian legend, this god had instructed the Indians in agriculture, metallurgy, and government; he had been tall, with white skin, and a flowing beard. After promising to revisit the Indians, he had departed over the "Eastern Ocean," that is, the Gulf of Mexico. To Montezuma, it seemed very possible that Cortés was the returning god, and this fear seems to have markedly influenced his behavior. Certainly,

Montezuma's reaction to the Spanish invasion was weak and indecisive.

One last factor in the Spaniards' success was their religious fervor. To us, of course, Cortés's invasion seems an inexcusable act of aggression. Cortés, however, was convinced that his invasion was morally justified. He could, and did, quite sincerely tell his men that they would win because their cause was just, and because they were fighting under the banner of the Cross. Cortés's religious motivation was quite sincere: more than once, he risked the success of his expedition by heavy-handed attempts to convert his Indian allies to Christianity.

Although Cortés was an excellent diplomat when dealing with the Indians, he was not equally successful in the political infighting with his Spanish rivals. The Spanish king rewarded him richly with lands and made Cortés a marquis, but removed him from his post as Governor of Mexico. Cortés returned to Spain in 1540, and spent the last seven years of his life vainly petitioning the king to restore his authority in New Spain. When Cortés died, in 1547, near Seville, Spain, he was an embittered though wealthy man. His large estates in Mexico were inherited by his son.

That Cortés was greedy and ambitious is obvious. An admirer who knew Cortés personally described him as ruthless, haughty, mischievous, and quarrelsome. But Cortés had many admirable qualities as well. He was courageous, determined, and intelligent. He had a generally cheerful disposition. Though a firm military leader, he was not wantonly cruel. Unlike Pizarro, who was universally hated, Cortés got along well with many of the Indians and tried not to govern them harshly. Incidentally, Cortés was apparently handsome and charming; he was always a great ladies' man.

In his will, Cortés stated that he was uncertain whether it was morally right to own Indian slaves. The question had troubled him, and he requested his son to consider the matter carefully. For his times, this was a rare attitude; one can hardly conceive of Francisco Pizarro (or Christopher Columbus), being

Cortés and Montezuma meet.

troubled by such a question. All in all, one gets the impression
that of all the Spanish conquistadors, Cortés was the most decent
human being.

Cortés and Pizarro were born within fifty miles of each
other, and only about ten years apart. The achievements of the
two men (who appear to have been relatives) are strikingly
similar. Between them, they conquered a region of virtually continental size, and imposed on that region the language, religion,
and culture of the conquerors. Throughout most of that region,
political power has ever since remained with persons of European ancestry.

The combined influence of Cortés and Pizarro was considerably greater than that of Simón Bolívar. Their conquests

transferred political power in South America from the Indians to the Europeans. Bolivar's victories merely succeeded in transferring power from the Spanish government to persons of European ancestry born in South America.

It might seem, at first, that Cortés should be ranked higher than Pizarro because his conquests took place earlier and inspired those of Pizarro. Furthermore, Indian resistance in Peru had not ended when Pizarro died, whereas Cortés essentially completed the conquest of Mexico. But in my opinion, those points are slightly overbalanced by another consideration. The conquering zeal of the Spanish, and the superiority of their weapons, obviously posed a serious threat to both the Aztecs and the Incas. Peru, protected by its mountainous terrain, had some chance of retaining its independence. Pizarro's bold and successful attack may, therefore, actually have changed the course of history.

But the Aztec dominions were less mountainous than Peru; furthermore, Mexico (unlike Peru) borders on a portion of the Atlantic Ocean and was therefore relatively accessible to Spanish forces. It therefore appears that the conquest of Mexico by Spain was virtually inevitable: the principal result of Cortés's daring and able leadership was to hasten the process.

64 THOMAS JEFFERSON

1743-1826

Thomas Jefferson, the third President of the United States of America, and the author of the Declaration of Independence, was born in 1743, in Shadwell, Virginia. His father was a surveyor and a successful planter who eventually left a large estate to his son. Jefferson attended the College of William and Mary for two years, but left without receiving a degree. Afterward, he studied law for several years, and in 1767, he was admitted to the Virginia bar. Jefferson spent the next seven years as a practicing lawyer and a planter. He also became a member of the House of Burgesses, the lower house of the Virginia legislature.

Jefferson's first important essay, *A Summary View of the*

Rights of British America, was written in 1774. The following year, he was chosen as one of Virginia's delegates to the Second Continental Congress, and in 1776, he drafted the Declaration of Independence. Later that year, he returned to the Virginia legislature, where he played a leading role in the adoption of several major reforms. Two of his important proposals were the *Statute of Virginia for Religious Freedom* and a *Bill for the More General Diffusion of Knowledge*, which concerned public education.

Jefferson's proposals on education included: public elementary education available to all; a state university in which the more gifted could receive a higher education; and a system of scholarships. His educational plan was not adopted by the state of Virginia at that time, although similar plans were later instituted by virtually all the states.

The statute concerning religious liberty is noteworthy in that it provided for complete religious toleration and for the complete separation of Church and State. (Previously, the Anglican Church had been the established church in Virginia.) There was considerable opposition to Jefferson's proposal, but it was eventually passed by the Virginia legislature (1786). The same ideas were soon adopted in the bills of rights of other states, and later in the United States Constitution as well.

Jefferson served as governor of Virginia from 1779 to 1781. He then "retired" from political life. During his retirement, he wrote his only book, *Notes on the State of Virginia*. The book contains, among other things, a clear statement of Jefferson's opposition to the institution of slavery. In 1782, Jefferson's wife died. (They had been married ten years and had six children.) Though he was still fairly young, Jefferson never remarried.

Jefferson soon came out of retirement and entered Congress. There, a proposal of his for a decimal system of coinage was adopted. However, a similar proposal of his for a decimal system of weights and measures (this was *before* the metric system had been devised) was not approved. He also introduced a proposal which would have prohibited slavery in all new states; however it was defeated by a single vote.

In 1784, Jefferson went to France on a diplomatic mission. There, he soon succeeded Benjamin Franklin as the American ambassador. He stayed in France for five years, and was therefore absent from the United States during the entire period in which the United States Constitution was drafted and ratified. Jefferson favored adoption of the Constitution, though like many others he strongly believed that a bill of rights should be included.

Jefferson returned to America in late 1789, and was soon appointed the country's first Secretary of State. Within the Cabinet, a clash soon developed between Jefferson and Alexander Hamilton, who was Secretary of the Treasury and whose political outlook was quite different from Jefferson's. In the nation, supporters of Hamilton's policies eventually came together to form the Federalist party. Supporters of Jefferson's policies joined together to form the Democratic-Republican party, which eventually became known as the Democratic party.

In 1796, Jefferson was a candidate for President, but he came in second to John Adams. Under the constitutional provisions prevailing at that time, he thereby became Vice-President. In 1800, he ran for President again, this time defeating Adams.

As President, Jefferson was moderate and conciliatory towards his former opponents, thereby setting a valuable precedent for the United States. From the standpoint of lasting effect, the most notable governmental action during his term in office was the Louisiana Purchase, which roughly doubled the area of the United States. The Louisiana Purchase, perhaps the largest peaceful transfer of territory in recorded history, helped turn the United States into a great power, and was an event of far-reaching importance. If I thought that Thomas Jefferson were the person principally responsible for the Lousiana Purchase, he would be ranked considerably higher on this list. However, I believe that the French leader, Napoleon Bonaparte, by making the crucial decision to sell the territory to the United States, was actually chiefly responsible for the transfer. If any individual American deserves special credit for the Louisiana Purchase, it would not be Jefferson, who had never envisaged such an extensive purchase, but rather the American envoys in Paris, Robert Livingston and James Monroe, who when they saw the opportunity for an extraordinary bargain, exceeded their diplomatic instructions and negotiated the acquisition of the enormous territory. (It is noteworthy that Jefferson, who wrote his own epitaph, did *not* include the Louisiana Purchase as one of his principal achievements.)

Jefferson was re-elected President in 1804; however, in 1808, he chose not to run for a third term, thereby reinforcing the precedent which George Washington had set. Jefferson retired in 1809, and his only subsequent governmental activity was in connection with the founding of the University of Virginia (chartered in 1819). He thereby saw a portion of the educational program he had suggested to the Virginia legislature forty-three years earlier finally put into practice. Jefferson died on July 4, 1826, the fiftieth anniversary of the Declaration of Independence, after more than eighty-three years of a full and well-spent life.

Jefferson had many other talents besides his obvious political gifts. He knew five or six foreign languages; he was interested in natural science and mathematics; he was a successful planter who engaged in scientific farming. He was also a manufacturer, minor inventor, and skilled architect.

Because Jefferson's talents and personal qualities were so outstanding, it is easy to overestimate the actual influence he has had on history. In assessing his true importance, we should perhaps start by considering the Declaration of Independence, since drafting that is usually considered to be his outstanding achievement. The first thing to note is that the Declaration of Independence is not part of the governing law of the United States of America; its primary importance is as a statement of American ideals. Furthermore, the ideas expressed in it were not original with Jefferson, but were largely derived from the writings of John Locke. The Declaration was not original philosophy, nor was it intended to be; rather, it was meant to be a concise statement of beliefs already held by many Americans.

Nor was Jefferson's magnificent phrasing of the Declaration

Jefferson's home in Charlottesville, Virginia—the historic Monticello—was built from his own designs.

responsible for the American decision to declare independence. The Revolutionary War had actually commenced in April 1775 (more than a year before the Declaration of Independence), with the battles of Lexington and Concord. In the months following those battles, the American colonies faced a critical decision: should they demand outright independence, or should they seek a compromise with the English government? In the spring of 1776, sentiment in the Continental Congress was running strongly toward the former alternative. It was not Jefferson, but rather Richard Henry Lee of Virginia, who on June 7 formally proposed that the colonies declare their independence from Great Britain. The Congress decided to postpone a vote on Lee's resolution for a few weeks, and appointed a committee, headed by Jefferson, to meanwhile prepare a public statement of the reasons for declaring independence. (The other committee members wisely permitted Jefferson to draft the statement almost singlehandedly.) Congress took up Lee's motion again on July 1, and the following

319

day it was brought to a vote and carried unanimously. It was that vote, on July 2, in which the critical decision in favor of independence was made. It was not until after that vote that the text of Jefferson's draft was debated. It was adopted by Congress (with some modifications) two days later, on July 4, 1776.

Even if the Declaration of Independence was not really as important as most people think, would not Jefferson's other achievements still entitle him to a higher position on this list? In his epitaph, Jefferson mentioned the two other achievements for which he most wished to be remembered. One of those, his role as the founder of the University of Virginia, although certainly very praiseworthy, is hardly of sufficient importance to greatly affect his overall position on this list. The other accomplishment, his authorship of the *Statute of Virginia for Religious Freedom*, is quite significant indeed. Of course, the general idea of religious freedom had been expressed by several prominent philosphers before Jefferson, including John Locke and Voltaire. However, Jefferson's statute went considerably further than the policies which had been advocated by Locke. Furthermore, Jefferson was an active politician who succeeded in having his proposals enacted into law, and Jefferson's proposal influenced other states when they drew up bills of rights.

That brings up another question: to what extent was Thomas Jefferson responsible for the adoption of the Federal Bill of Rights? Jefferson was certainly representative of those persons who wanted to have a bill of rights; indeed, he was one of the intellectual leaders of that group. But Jefferson, who was out of the country from 1784 until late 1789, was unable to lead the fight for a bill of rights during the crucial period immediately following the Constitutional Convention, and it was James Madison who played the principal role in actually getting the amendments through Congress. (Congress passed the amendments on September 25, 1789, before Jefferson returned to the United States.)

It might be said that it was not Jefferson's official actions, but rather his attitudes, which have most deeply affected the United States. However, it is rather doubtful to what extent Jefferson's ideas are actually accepted by the American people. Many persons who honor the name of Thomas Jefferson support policies quite contrary to his. For example, Jefferson strongly believed in what we today would call "small government." A characteristic phrase (taken from his inaugural address) is, "...a wise and frugal government, which shall restrain men from injuring one another, which shall leave them otherwise free to regulate their own pursuits of industry and improvement...." Possibly Jefferson's viewpoint was right, but the elections of the last fifty years indicate that his words have not convinced the majority of the American public. As a second example, Jefferson was strongly opposed to the view that the final power to interpret the Constitution rested with the Supreme Court, which could therefore declare a law unconstitutional even though it had been passed by Congress. Such a view, he felt, was contrary to principles of democratic government.

The preceding paragraphs perhaps make it sound as if Thomas Jefferson had rather little influence, and does not belong in this book at all. But too great a concern with details can sometimes cause one not to see the forest for the trees. If, instead, one steps back and tries to view Jefferson's career as a whole, one can readily see why he has been described as the "preeminent spokesman for human liberty."

Should Thomas Jefferson be ranked higher or lower than George Washington? American independence and democratic institutions were created by the combined efforts of men of ideas and men of action. While both were essential, I believe that in general the ideas were the more important contribution. On the executive side, George Washington plainly played the dominant role. Credit for the ideas, however, must be divided between a large number of men, including Americans such as Jefferson and James Madison, and Europeans such as John Locke, Voltaire, and many others. It is for that reason that Thomas Jefferson, despite his enormous talents and prestige, has been ranked substantially below George Washington on this list.

65
QUEEN
ISABELLA I
1451-1504

Today, most people only remember Isabella I of Castile as the queen who financed Christopher Columbus's voyage across the Atlantic. In reality, she was an energetic and capable ruler, who made a whole series of crucial decisions which profoundly influenced Spain and Latin America for centuries, and which indirectly affect many millions of persons today.

Since most of her policies were decided upon after consultation with her shrewd and equally capable husband, Ferdinand of Aragon, and since they were carried out with his close cooperation, it seems reasonable to consider them as a joint entry in this book. However, Isabella's name has been chosen to head this article because it was her suggestions which were adopted in their most important decisions.

Isabella was born in 1451, in the town of Madrigal, in the kingdom of Castile (now part of Spain). As a young girl, she received a strict religious training and became a very devout Catholic. Her half-brother, Henry IV, was king of Castile from 1454 until he died, in 1474. At that time, there was no kingdom of Spain. Instead, the present territory of Spain was divided among four kingdoms: Castile, which was the largest; Aragon, in the northeast portion of present-day Spain; Granada, in the south; and Navarre, in the north.

In the late 1460s, Isabella, who was the probable heir to the throne of Castile, was the richest heiress in Europe, and various princes sought her hand. Her half-brother, Henry IV, wished her to marry the King of Portugal. However, in 1469, when she was eighteen years old, Isabella slipped off, and despite the opposition of King Henry, married Ferdinand, the heir to the throne of Aragon. Angered at Isabella's disobedience, Henry named his daughter Juana to succeed him. Nevertheless, when Henry died, in 1474, Isabella claimed the throne of Castile. The supporters of Juana did not accept this, and a civil war followed. By February 1479, Isabella's forces were triumphant. King John II of Aragon died that same year, and Ferdinand became the king of Aragon. Thereafter, Ferdinand and Isabella ruled most of Spain together.

In theory, the two kingdoms of Aragon and Castile were still separate, and most of their governmental institutions remained separate. In practice, however, Ferdinand and Isabella made all their decisions together, and to the best of their ability acted as the joint rulers of Spain. Throughout the twenty-five years of their combined rule, their basic policy was to create a unified Spanish kingdom governed by a strong monarchy. One of their first projects was the conquest of Granada, the only portion of the Iberian peninsula which was still under Moslem rule. The war commenced in 1481; it ended in January 1492, with the complete victory of Ferdinand and Isabella. With the conquest of Granada, Spain assumed almost exactly the same territorial boundaries that it has today. (The small kingdom of Navarre was annexed by Ferdinand in 1512, after Isabella had died.)

Very early in their reign, Ferdinand and Isabella instituted the Spanish Inquisition. The Inquisition was an ecclesiastical tribunal which combined the powers of judge, jury, prosecuting attorney, and police investigators. It was notorious both for the ferocity of its punishments and for the gross unfairness of its procedures. Suspects had little or no opportunity to refute the charges against them. They were not informed of the full testimony against them, or even of the names of their accusers. Suspects who denied the charges brought against them were often subjected to gruesome tortures until they confessed. At a conservative estimate, at least two thousand persons were burnt at the stake during the first twenty years of the Spanish Inquisition, and many times that number received lesser punishments.

The Spanish Inquisition was headed by the ultra-fanatical monk, Tomás de Torquemada, who was the personal confessor of Isabella. Although the Inquisition had been authorized by the Pope, it actually was under the control of the Spanish monarchs. The Inquisition was used partly to establish religious conformity, and partly to stamp out political opposition to the monarchs. In England, the feudal lords always retained enough strength to check the power of the king. The Spanish feudal lords also had once been powerful; however, the Spanish monarchs were able to use the Inquisition as a weapon against defiant feudal lords, and were thereby able to establish a centralized and absolute monarchy. They also used it to gain greater control over the Spanish clergy.

However, the principal targets of the Inquisition were those persons suspected of religious deviation, and in particular, Jews and Moslems who had become nominally converted to Catholicism, but who continued to practice their former religions in secret.

At its inception, the Inquistion was not directed against professing Jews. However, in 1492, at the insistence of the fanatical Torquemada, Ferdinand and Isabella signed a decree ordering all Spanish Jews to either convert to Christianity or leave the country within four months, leaving their property behind. For the roughly 200,000 Spanish Jews, this order of expulsion was a disaster, and many died before reaching a safe haven. For Spain, the loss of a high proportion of the country's most industrious and skilled tradesmen and artisans proved a severe economic setback.

When Granada had surrendered, the peace treaty provided that the Moslems living in Spain were to be permitted to continue practicing their religion. In fact, however, the Spanish government soon violated this agreement. The Moors therefore rebel-led, but were defeated. In 1502, all Moslems living in Spain were forced to choose either conversion to Christianity or exile—the same choice that had been presented to the Jews ten years earlier.

Although Isabella was a devout Catholic, she never permit-ted her orthodoxy to interfere with her Spanish nationalism. She and Ferdinand struggled hard and successfully to insure that the Catholic Church in Spain was controlled by the Spanish monar-chy, rather than by the Pope. This was one of the reasons why the Protestant Reformation in the sixteenth century never made any headway in Spain.

The most notable event of Isabella's reign, of course, was the discovery of the new world by Christopher Columbus, which also occurred in the fateful year 1492. Columbus's expedition was sponsored by the kingdom of Castile. (However, the story that Isabella had to pawn her jewels to pay for the expedition is not true.)

Isabella died in 1504. During her lifetime, she had given birth to one son and four daughters. The son, Juan, died in 1497. The best known of her daughters was Juana. Ferdinand and Isabella arranged for Juana to marry Philip I (the Handsome), who was the son of the Austrian Hapsburg emperor and was also the heir to the kingdom of Burgundy. As a result of this extraor-dinary dynastic marriage, Isabella's grandson, the Emperor Charles V, inherited one of the largest empires in European history. He was also elected Holy Roman Emperor, and was the wealthiest and most powerful European monarch of his time. The territories which he either nominally or actually ruled in-cluded Spain, Germany, Holland, Belgium, Austria, Switzer-land, most of Italy, and parts of France, Czechoslovakia, Po-land, Hungary, and Yugoslavia, in addition to a large portion of the Western Hemisphere. Both Charles V and his son Philip II were ardent Catholics who, during their long reigns, used the wealth of the New World to finance wars against the Protestant states of northern Europe. Thus, the dynastic marriage arranged by Ferdinand and Isabella influenced the history of Europe for almost a century after their deaths.

Let me try to summarize the accomplishments and influence of Ferdinand and Isabella. By their joint efforts, they largely succeeded in creating a united kingdom of Spain with essentially the same boundaries that Spain has retained for the last five centuries; they created a centralized, absolute monarchy in Spain; the expulsion of the Moors and the Jews had important consequences both for the exiles and for Spain herself; and their religious bigotry and establishment of the Inquisition had profound effects on the entire future history of Spain.

This last point merits some discussion. In the simplest terms, one might say that the Inquisition placed Spain in an intellectual strait jacket. In the centuries following 1492, most of western Europe underwent an enormous intellectual and scientific flowering. Not so Spain. In a society where the expression of any deviant thoughts placed one in danger of arrest by the Inquisition, it is not surprising that originality was lacking. Other European countries allowed some diversity of opinion. In Spain, the Inquisition permitted only a rigidly orthodox Catholicism. By 1700, Spain was an intellectual backwater compared with the rest of western Europe. Indeed, although it is five centuries since Ferdinand and Isabella established the Spanish Inquisition, and over 150 years since the Inquisition was finally abolished, Spain has still not fully recovered from its effects.

Furthermore, Isabella's sponsorship of Columbus's expedition insured that most of South and Central America became Spanish colonies. This meant that Spanish culture and institutions—including the Inquisition—were established throughout a large portion of the Western Hemisphere. It is hardly surprising, therefore, that just as Spain was intellectually backward compared with most of western Europe, so the Spanish colonies in South America became intellectually less advanced than the English colonies in North America.

In considering where Isabella should be ranked on this list, one factor to be considered is whether much the same events would have occurred without her. It is true that the crusading spirit was already very strong in Spain, because of the 700-year-long struggle to reconquer the Iberian peninsula from the Moslems. However, when that struggle ended successfully in 1492, Spain had a choice of directions in which to go. It was Ferdinand and Isabella—particularly Isabella—who set the course of Spain in the direction of uncompromising religious orthodoxy. Without her influence, it seems quite possible that Spain would have remained a reasonably pluralistic society.

It is perhaps natural to compare Isabella with the more famous Queen Elizabeth I of England. Elizabeth was at least as capable as Isabella; furthermore, because of her comparatively humane and tolerant policies, she seems a far more admirable ruler. But she was less of an innovator than Isabella, and none of her actions had as profound an influence as did Isabella's establishment of the Inquisition. Although some of Isabella's policies were quite abhorrent, few monarchs in history have had as far-reaching an influence as she had.

66

JOSEPH STALIN

1879 - 1953

Stalin, whose original name was Iosif Vissarionovich Dzhugash-vili, was for many years the dictator of the Soviet Union. He was born in 1879, in the town of Gori, in Georgia, in the Caucasus. His native language was Georgian—a very different language from Russian, which he learned later, and which he always spoke with a marked Georgian accent.

Stalin was reared in poverty. His father, a cobbler who drank excessively and beat his son brutally, died when Iosif was eleven years old. As a youth, Iosif attended a church school in Gori, and as a teenager, he attended a theological seminary in Tiflis; however, in 1899, he was expelled from the seminary for spreading subversive ideas. He joined the underground Marxist movement, and in 1903, when there was a party split, he sided with the Bolshevik wing. In the years leading up to 1917, he was an active party member, and was arrested at least six times.

(However, since his sentences were generally light, and since he managed to escape on more than one occasion, it seems possible that he was actually a double agent for part of that time.) It was during this period that he adopted the not inappropriate pseudonym "Stalin" (man of steel).

Stalin did not play a really major role in the Communist revolution of 1917. However, he was very active during the next two years, and in 1922, became Secretary General of the Communist Party. This post gave him a great deal of influence in the administration of the party and was a major factor in his success in the struggle for power that occurred after Lenin died.

It is clear that Lenin wished Leon Trotsky to be his successor. In fact, in his political testament, Lenin stated that Stalin was too ruthless and ought to be removed from his post as Secretary General. However, after Lenin's death in early 1924, Stalin succeeded in having Lenin's testament suppressed. Furthermore, Stalin was able to join forces with Lev Kamenev and Grigori Zinoviev, two important members of the Politburo, to form a "troika," or triumvirate. Together they succeeded in defeating Trotsky and his followers. Then Stalin, a genius at political infighting, turned on Zinoviev and Kamenev and defeated them. Having defeated the "left-wing opposition" (i.e., Trotsky, Kamenev, Zinoviev, and their followers) in the power struggle, Stalin proceeded to adopt several of their main political proposals. Not long after that, Stalin turned on the leaders of the right wing of the Communist party—his erstwhile allies—and defeated them too. By the early 1030s, he was the sole dictator of the Soviet Union.

From this position of power, starting in 1934, Stalin unleashed a drastic series of political purges. The event that nominally set off those purges was the assassination, on December 1, 1934, of Sergei Kirov, a high Communist official and one of Stalin's advisors. However, it seems quite likely that Stalin himself ordered Kirov's assassination, partly in order to get rid of Kirov, but mostly in order to furnish a pretext for the purges that followed.

In the course of the next few years, a high proportion of the men who had been Communist party leaders during the 1917 Revolution, and, under Lenin's administration, were charged with treason by Stalin and executed. Many of them openly confessed in large public trials. It was as if Thomas Jefferson, while President, had arrested most of the signers of the Declaration of Independence and the Constitution, charged them all with treason, and executed them after their "confessions" in public trials. In 1938, the man who had headed the earlier purges, Genrikh Yagoda, was himself brought to trial, confessed to treason, and was duly executed. For that matter, his successor, Nicolai Yezhov, was also eventually purged and executed.

The purges of the mid-1930s extended throughout the Communist party and the Soviet armed forces. They were not directed primarily against anti-Communists or counter-revolutionaries. (Most of those had been crushed during Lenin's administration.) Rather, they were directed against the Communist party itself. Stalin was far more successful in killing Communists than the Czarist police had ever been. For example, of the members of the Central Committee elected at the Party Congress of 1934, more than two thirds were killed during the subsequent purges. From this, it is clear that Stalin's primary motive was to preclude the establishment of any independent power within the country.

Stalin's ruthless use of the secret police, and his program of arbitrary arrests and executions, and long terms in prison or labor camps for anyone even slightly critical of his rule, succeeded in cowing the population into submission. By the end of the 1930s he had created perhaps the most totalitarian dictatorship of modern times, a government structure which intruded into every aspect of life and under which there were no civil liberties.

Among the economic policies instituted by Stalin was the forced collectivization of agriculture. This policy was highly unpopular with the peasants, and many of them resisted it. In the early 1930s, however, by Stalin's orders, millions of peasants were either killed or starved to death, and in the end his policy prevailed.

Another policy that Stalin pushed was the rapid industrialization of the Soviet Union. This was accomplished in part by a series of "Five-Year Plans," since imitated by many countries outside the

*Scene from one of the spectacular Russian treason trials of
the thirties, which established Stalin's reputation as a
tyrant.*

Soviet Union. Despite various inefficiencies, Stalin's program of
industrialization was, in the short run, a success. In spite of its
enormous material losses during World War II, the Soviet Union
emerged from that war as the world's second largest industrial
power. (In the long run, though, the agricultural and industrial
policies which he instituted have severely damaged the Soviet
economy.)

In August 1939, Hitler and Stalin signed their famous "nonag-
gression" pact. Within two weeks, Hitler invaded Poland from the

331

west, and a few weeks later the Soviet Union invaded Poland from the east and took over the eastern half of the country. Later that year, the Soviet Union threatened the three independent nations of Latvia, Lithuania, and Estonia with armed invasion. All three surrendered without a fight and were eventually annexed to the USSR. Similarly, part of Romania was annexed by the threat of force. Finland refused to submit to threats; however, a Russian invasion resulted in the conquest of Finnish territory. An excuse often given for these annexations is that the territory was needed by the Soviet Union for defense against the expected attack from Nazi Germany. However, when the war was over, and Germany thoroughly defeated, Stalin did not relinquish control over any of the occupied territories.

At the end of World War II, Soviet armies occupied much of eastern Europe, and Stalin utilized the opportunity to set up Communist governments, subservient to the Soviet Union, throughout that region. A Marxist government also emerged in Yugoslavia; however, as there were no Russian troops in that country, Yugoslavia did not become a Russian satellite. To prevent the other Communist countries in eastern Europe from following the Yugoslav example, Stalin had purges instituted in the east European satellite states. It was during the immediate postwar era that the Cold War commenced. Although some people have attempted to blame this on Western leaders, it seems abundantly clear that the principal cause of the Cold War was the expansionist policies of Stalin, and his implacable desire to spread the Communist system—and Soviet power—throughout the world.

In January 1953, the Soviet government announced that a group of doctors had been arrested for plotting the deaths of high-ranking Soviet officials. This sounded very much as if Stalin was planning still another set of sweeping purges. However, on March 5, 1953, the seventy-three-year-old dictator died in the Kremlin in Moscow. His body was preserved and put on display in a position of honor, next to the body of Lenin in the mausoleum in Red Square. In later years, however, Stalin's reputation was downgraded very sharply; and today he is generally abhorred as a tyrant throughout the lands he once ruled.

Stalin's family life was not very successful. He married in 1904, but three years later his wife died of tuberculosis. Their only child, Jacob, was captured by the Germans in World War II. The Germans offered to exchange him, but Stalin turned the offer down, and Jacob died in a German prison camp. In 1919, Stalin married a second time. His second wife died in 1932, reportedly by her own hand, although there have been rumors that Stalin himself killed her or had her killed. There were two children by the second marriage. The son, an officer in the Soviet Air Force, became an alcoholic. He died in 1962. Stalin's daughter, Svetlana, defected from the Soviet Union, and in 1967 came to the United States.

The outstanding characteristic of Stalin's personality was his total ruthlessness. No consideration of sentiment or pity seems to have influenced him in the slightest. He was also an intensely suspicious person, verging on paranoia. He was, however, an immensely capable man: energetic, persistent, and shrewd, with an unusually powerful mind.

As the dictator of the Soviet Union for approximately a quarter of a century, Stalin had a great deal of influence on a great many lives. In fact, if the overall influence of a dictator upon his own generation is deemed to be proportional to the number of people he controls, to the degree of his individual control, and to the time he remains in power, then Stalin was perhaps the foremost dictator in history. During his lifetime, Stalin sent millions of persons to their deaths, or to forced labor camps, or had them starved to death. (There is no way of knowing just how many people died as a result of his various purges, but it was probably in the neighborhood of 30 million.)

There is therefore no doubt that Stalin's short-term influence was immense. However, like his contemporary, Adolf Hitler (with whom he is often compared), it is unclear how great his permanent influence will be.

During his lifetime, Stalin expanded the borders of the Soviet Union, set up a satellite empire in eastern Europe, and transformed the USSR into a great power, with influence in every portion of the globe. But in the past few years the imposing Soviet empire in eastern Europe has crumbled away, and the Soviet Union itself has fractured into fifteen independent states.

During Stalin's lifetime, the USSR was a vast police state. However, the fearful grip of the secret police was gradually curbed after Stalin's death. Today, Russians enjoy more individual liberty than at any time in their country's history.

Stalin's economic program was derived from the ideas of Marx and Lenin. But while Marx had suggested those policies, and Lenin had started to put them into effect, it was really Stalin who succeeded in largely eliminating private farming and private business enterprises within the Soviet Union. However, those policies have proven to be disastrous, and are now being abandoned entirely.

Despite this, I cannot help but feel that the foregoing greatly underestimates Stalin's overall influence. Joseph Stalin was not just another power-mad dictator who ruled a large country for twenty-five years. By instituting the Cold War, he dominated the history of the entire world for many years after he died. No war in history—not even World War II—had such a global effect as did the Cold War. It was not just the USSR and the USA which were affected: Every country on earth was caught up in the diplomatic and economic aspects of the struggle, and in many parts of the world there were shooting wars as well. The arms race between the two superpowers—which, although the largest and costliest arms race in history, was only one aspect of the struggle—cost many *trillions* of dollars. Worst of all, perhaps, for many years the entire world lived under the threat of a nuclear holocaust which might entirely destroy civilization.

The Cold War was widely detested, and most people devoutly wished for its end. But for decades the dead, denounced Stalin had more power—more actual effect on the world—than any living political figure. Of him, more perhaps than of any other man in history, it could truly be said that, "the evil that men do lives after them."

The Cold War is over now, and Stalin's pernicious influence may finally be ending. We should also remember that some of the blame for Stalin's crimes must be accorded to Lenin, who preceded Stalin and set the stage for him. Nevertheless, Stalin was one of the titans of history: a cruel genius who will not soon be forgotten.

Stalin meets with M.I. Kalinin, President of the Soviet Union 1923-1946.

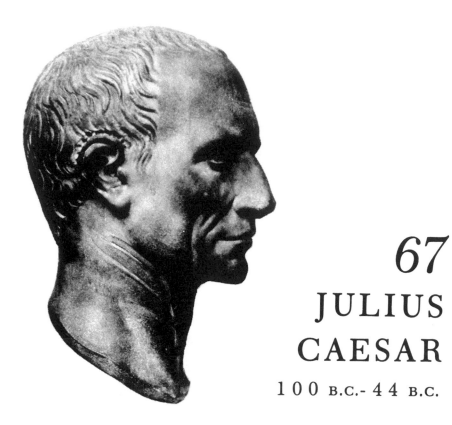

67
JULIUS CAESAR
100 B.C.- 44 B.C.

Gaius Julius Caesar, the famous Roman military and political leader, was born in Rome in 100 B.C., during a period of extraordinary political turmoil.

In the second century B.C., following their victory over Carthage in the Second Punic War, the Romans had created a large empire. This conquest had made many Romans very rich. However, the wars had badly disrupted the social and economic fabric of Rome, and many of the peasantry had been dispossessed. The Roman Senate, in origin a sort of board of aldermen for a small city, proved unable to fairly and efficiently govern a large empire. Political corruption was rampant, and the entire Mediterranean world was suffering from misgovernment by Rome. In Rome itself, starting in about 133 B.C., there had been a protracted period of disorder. Politicians, generals, and demagogues struggled for power, and partisan armies (such as that of Marius in 87 B.C. and that of Sulla in 82 B.C.) marched through Rome itself. Though the fact of misgovernment was obvious to all, most Roman citizens wanted to retain republican government. Julius Caesar was probably the first important political leader to clearly see that democratic government in Rome was no longer worth saving, and indeed was already past saving.

Caesar himself was descended from an old patrician family. He had received a good education, and as a young man, entered political life. The details of the various offices which he held, his sundry alliances, and his political rise are very involved, and no attempt will be made to recount them here. However, in 58 B.C., when he was forty-two years old, Julius was appointed the governor of three foreign provinces ruled by Rome: Cisalpine Gaul (northern Italy); Illyricum (the coastal regions of present-day Yugoslavia); and Narbonese Gaul (the southern coast of France). Under his command at that time were four Roman legions, totaling about twenty thousand men.

During the years 58-51 B.C., Caesar used those forces to invade and conquer all the rest of Gaul—a region comprising, roughly, present-day France and Belgium, together with parts of Switzerland, Germany, and Holland. Although his forces were badly outnumbered, he succeeded in completely defeating the Gallic tribes and in adding all the territory up to the Rhine River to the Roman dominions. He also sent two expeditions to Britain, but achieved no permanent conquests there.

The conquest of Gaul made Caesar, who was already a leading political figure, a popular hero back in Rome; in the opinion of his political opponents, far too popular and powerful. When his military command ran out, he was ordered by the Roman Senate to return to Rome as a private citizen—that is, without his army. Caesar feared, probably correctly, that if he returned to Rome without his troops, his political opponents would use the opportunity to destroy him. Therefore, on the

night of January 10-11, 49 B.C., in open defiance of the Roman
Senate, Caesar led his troops across the Rubicon River in northern Italy and marched on Rome. This plainly illegal act started
a civil war between Caesar's legions on the one hand and forces
loyal to the Senate on the other hand. The war lasted four years
and ended in a complete victory for Caesar, the final battle being
fought at Munda, in Spain, on March 7, 45 B.C.

Caesar had already concluded that the efficient, enlightened despotism which Rome required could best be supplied by
himself. He returned to Rome in October of 45 B.C., and was
soon made dictator for life. In February of 44 B.C., he was offered a crown but turned it down. However, since he was
already a military dictator, this did not greatly reassure his
republican opponents. On March 15, 44 B.C., (the famous Ides of
March) Caesar was assassinated at a Senate meeting by a group
of conspirators.

During the last years of his life, Caesar had embarked on a
vigorous program of reform. He had instituted a plan to resettle
army veterans and the urban poor of Rome in new communities
throughout the empire. He had extended Roman citizenship to
several additional groups of persons. He planned to institute a
uniform system of municipal government for Italian cities. He
also planned a vast building program, and a codification of
Roman law. He instituted various other reforms as well. But he
did not succeed in setting up a satisfactory constitutional system
of government for Rome, and this was perhaps the principal
cause of his downfall.

Since it was only a year between Caesar's victory at Munda
and his assassination in Rome, many of his plans were never im-
plemented, and it is hard to be sure just how enlightened or efficient his administration would have been had he lived. Of all his
reforms, the one which had the most lasting effect was the adoption of a new calendar. The calendar he introduced has, with only minor modifications, remained in use ever since.

Julius Caesar was one of the most charismatic political
figures in history, and possessed a wide variety of talents. He was

a successful politician, a brilliant general, and an excellent orator and writer. The book he wrote (*De bello Gallico*) describing the conquest of Gaul has long been considered a literary classic: in the opinion of many students, the most readable and interesting of all the Latin classics. Caesar was bold, vigorous, and handsome. He was a notorious Don Juan, and even by the permissive standards of his day was considered promiscuous. (His most famous affair, of course, was his celebrated romance with Cleopatra.)

Caesar's character has often been criticized. He was ambitious for power, and he certainly used his political offices to become rich. However, unlike most ambitious politicians, he was in general neither devious nor deceitful. Caesar was ruthless and

The Ides of March: the assassination of Julius Caesar.

brutal when fighting the Gauls. On the other hand, he was remarkably magnanimous to his defeated Roman opponents.

It is an indication of the prestige attached to his name that both the German imperial title, *Kaiser*, and the Russian imperial title, *Czar*, are derived from the word "Caesar." He has always been far more famous than his grandnephew Augustus Caesar, the true founder of the Roman Empire. However, Julius Caesar's actual influence upon history is not equal to his enormous fame. It is true that he played a significant role in the downfall of the Roman Republic. But his importance in that respect should not be exaggerated, since republican government in Rome was already tottering.

Caesar's most important accomplishment was his conquest of Gaul. The territories he conquered there were to remain under Roman rule for approximately five centuries. During that interval, they became thoroughly Romanized. Roman laws, customs, and language were adopted, and later, Roman Christianity as well. Present-day French is derived to a substantial extent from the colloquial Latin of those times.

Caesar's conquest of Gaul was also an important influence on Rome itself, providing Italy for several centuries with security against attacks from the north. Indeed, the conquest of Gaul was a factor in the security of the whole Roman Empire.

Would the Romans sooner or later have conquered Gaul, even without Caesar? They had no technological or numerical advantage over the Gallic tribes. On the other hand, Rome was rapidly expanding in the period before Caesar's conquest of Gaul, and for sometime afterward. Given the high military effectiveness of the Roman armies of that time, the proximity of Gaul to Rome, and the disunity of the Gallic tribes, it appears that Gaul had little chance of remaining independent. In any event, it is indisputable that Caesar was the general who actually defeated the large Celtic armies and conquered Gaul, and he is in this book chiefly for that accomplishment.

68

WILLIAM
THE CONQUEROR

c. 1 0 2 7 - 1 0 8 7

In the year 1066, Duke William of Normandy, with only a few thousand troops behind him, crossed the English Channel in an attempt to become ruler of England. His bold attempt succeeded—the last time that any foreign invasion of England has been successful. The Norman Conquest did far more than obtain the throne of England for William and his successors. It profoundly influenced all subsequent English history—in ways and to an extent that William himself could scarcely have envisioned.

William was born about 1027, in Falaise, a town in Normandy, France. He was the illegitimate, but only son of Robert I, Duke of Normandy. Robert died in 1035, while returning from a pilgrimage to Jerusalem. Before his departure, he had designated William to be his heir. Thus, at the age of eight, William became Duke of Normandy.

Far from assuring him of a comfortable position of wealth and power, the succession put William in a precarious position. He was only a little boy, and he was the overlord of feudal barons who were grown men. Not surprisingly, the barons' ambition was stronger than their loyalty, and a period of severe anarchy followed, during which three of William's guardians died violent deaths, and his personal teacher was murdered. Even with the help of King Henry I of France, his nominal overlord, William was lucky to survive those early years.

In 1042, when William was in his mid-teens, he was knighted. Thereafter, he took a personal role in political events. After a long series of wars against the feudal barons of Normandy, William finally succeeded in gaining firm control of his duchy. (Incidentally, his illegitimate birth was a distinct political handicap, and his opponents frequently referred to him as "the Bastard.") In 1063, he succeeded in conquering the neighboring province of Maine, and in 1064, he was also recognized as the overlord of the neighboring province of Brittany.

From 1042 to 1066, the King of England was Edward the Confessor. Since Edward was childless, there was much maneuvering for the succession to the English throne. From the standpoint of consanguinity, William's claim to succeed Edward was rather weak: Edward's mother was a sister of William's grandfather. However, in 1051, Edward, perhaps influenced by William's manifest ability, promised William the succession.

In 1064, Harold Godwin, the most powerful of the English lords, and a close associate and brother-in-law of Edward the Confessor, fell into William's hands. William treated Harold well, but detained him until Harold swore a solemn oath to support William's claim to the English throne. Many people would not consider a promise extorted in this fashion to be either legally or morally binding, and certainly Harold did not. When Edward died in 1066, Harold Godwin claimed the throne of England for himself, and the Witan (a council of English lords which often took part in deciding the succession) chose him to be the new king. William, ambitious to extend his realm and angered at

Harold's breach of his oath, decided to invade England in order to impose his claim by force of arms.

William assembled a fleet and an army on the French coast, and in early August of 1066, he was ready to set sail. However, the expedition was delayed for several weeks by unrelenting north winds. Meanwhile, Harald Hardraade, the King of Norway, launched a separate invasion of England from across the North Sea. Harold Godwin had been keeping his army in the south of England, prepared to oppose William's invasion. Now he had to march his army to the north, to meet the Norwegian attack. On September 25, at the Battle of Stamford Bridge, the Norwegian king was killed and his forces routed.

Just two days later, the wind changed in the English Channel, and William promptly transported his troops to England. Perhaps Harold should have let William march toward him, or at least he should have fully rested his troops before offering battle. Instead, he quickly marched his troops back south to fight William. The two armies met on October 14, 1066, at the celebrated Battle of Hastings. By the end of the day, William's cavalry and archers had succeeded in routing the Anglo-Saxon forces. Near nightfall, King Harold himself was killed. His two brothers had been killed earlier in the battle, and there was no English leader remaining with the stature to raise a new army or to contest William's claim to the throne. William was crowned in London that Christmas day.

Over the next five years, there were a series of scattered revolts, but William suppressed them all. William used these revolts as a pretext to confiscate all of the land in England and to declare it his own personal property. Much of it was then dispensed to his important Norman followers, who held the land under feudal tenure as his vassals. As a result, virtually the entire Anglo-Saxon aristocracy was dispossessed and replaced by Normans. (As dramatic as this sounds, only a few thousand people were directly involved in this transfer of power. For the peasants tilling the soil, there was simply a change of overlords.)

William always contended that he was the rightful King of

England, and during his lifetime most English institutions were retained. As William was interested in obtaining information concerning his new holdings, he ordered that a detailed census of the population and property of England be taken. The results were recorded in the enormous *Domesday Book*, which has been an invaluable source of historical information. (The original manuscripts still exist; they are now in the Public Record Office in London.)

William was married and had four sons and five daughters. He died in 1087, in the city of Rouen, in northern France. Every monarch of England since then has been his direct descendant. Curiously, although William the Conqueror is perhaps the most important of all the kings of England, he himself was not English, but French. He was born and died in France, lived almost his entire life there, and spoke only French. (He was, incidentally, illiterate.)

In assessing William's influence upon history, the most important thing to remember is that the Norman conquest of England would not have occurred without him. William was not the natural successor to the English throne, and save for his personal ambition and ability, there was no historical reason or necessity for the Norman invasion. England had not been invaded from France since the Roman conquest a thousand years earlier. It has not been successfully invaded from France (or from anywhere else) in the nine centuries since William's day.

The question then is: just how great was the effect of the Norman Conquest? The Norman invaders were relatively small in number, but they had a great influence upon English history. In the five or six centuries before the Norman Conquest, England had been invaded repeatedly by Anglo-Saxon and Scandinavian peoples, and her culture was basically Teutonic. The Normans were themselves of Viking descent, but their language and culture were French. The Norman Conquest, therefore, had the effect of bringing English culture into close contact with French culture. (Today that may seem a natural thing; however, in the centuries before William the Conqueror, most of England's cultural contacts had been with northern Europe.) What resulted in England was a blend of the French and Anglo-Saxon cultures, a blend which might not have occurred otherwise.

William introduced into England an advanced form of feudalism. The Norman kings, unlike their Anglo-Saxon predecessors, thereby had at their command a force of several thousand armed knights—a powerful army by medieval standards. The Normans were skilled administrators, and the English government became one of the most powerful and effective governments in Europe.

William the Conqueror at the Battle of Hastings.

Another interesting result of the Norman Conquest was the development of a new English language. As a result of the Norman Conquest, there was a large infusion of new words into English—so large, in fact, that modern English dictionaries include more words of French or Latin origin than of Anglo-Saxon derivation. Furthermore, during the three or four centuries immediately following the Norman Conquest, English grammar changed very rapidly, largely in the direction of greater simplicity. Had it not been for the Norman Conquest, present-day English might be only slightly different from Low German and Dutch. This is the only known instance in which a major language would not exist in anything like its present form, were it not for the career of a single individual. (It is worth noting that English is today quite plainly the foremost language in the world.)

One might also mention the effect of the Norman Conquest upon France. For roughly four centuries thereafter, there was a long series of wars between the English kings (who, because of their Norman origin, held substantial land in France) and the French kings. These wars are directly traceable to the Norman Conquest; prior to 1066, there had been no wars between England and France.

In many ways, England is substantially different from all the continental European countries. Both by her acquisiton of a great empire and by her democratic institutions, England has had a profound influence upon the rest of the world, completely out of proportion to her own size. To what extent are these aspects of British political history a consequence of William's activities?

Historians are not agreed on just why modern democracy developed originally in England, rather than, say, in Germany. But English culture and institutions were a blend of the Anglo-Saxon and Norman, and this blend resulted from the Norman Conquest. On the other hand, I hardly think it reasonable to give the despotic William too much of the credit for the later growth of English democracy. Certainly, there was precious little democracy in England in the century following the Norman Conquest.

With regard to the formation of the British empire, William's influence seems more clear. Prior to 1066, England had invariably been on the receiving end of invasions. After 1066, the roles were reversed. Thanks to the strong central government which William established and which his successors maintained, and to the military resources which this government commanded, England was never invaded again. Instead, she was continually engaged in overseas military operations. It was therefore natural that when the power of Europe expanded overseas, England eventually acquired more colonies than any other European state.

One cannot, of course, give William the Conqueror the credit for *all* later developments in English history; but surely the Norman Conquest was an indirect factor in much of what later occurred. The long-term influence of William is therefore very great.

The first known painting of the Battle of Hastings.

69 SIGMUND FREUD

1856-1939

Sigmund Freud, the originator of psychoanalysis, was born in 1856, in the town of Freiberg, which is now in Czechoslovakia but was then part of the Austrian empire. When he was four years old, his family moved to Vienna, where he lived almost his entire life. Freud was an outstanding student in school, and he received his medical degree from the University of Vienna in 1881. During the next ten years, he did research in physiology, joined the staff of a psychiatric clinic, engaged in private practice in neurology, worked in Paris with the eminent French neurologist, Jean Charcot, and also worked with the Viennese physician, Josef Breuer.

Freud's ideas on psychology developed gradually. It was not until 1895 that his first book, *Studies in Hysteria*, appeared, with Breuer as co-author. His next book, *The Interpretation of Dreams*, appeared in 1900, and was one of his most original and most significant works. Although the book sold very slowly at first, it greatly enhanced his reputation. Other important works followed, and by 1908, when he gave a series of lectures in the United States, Freud was already famous. In 1902, he had organized a psychology discussion group in Vienna. One of the earliest members was Alfred Adler, and a few years later, Carl Jung joined. Both men were to become world-famous psychologists in their own right.

Freud was married and had six children. In his later life, he developed cancer of the jaw, and from 1923 on, he underwent more than thirty operations in an attempt to correct the condition. Nevertheless, he continued working, and some important works were produced during these later years. In 1938, the Nazis entered Austria, and the 82-year-old Freud, who was Jewish, was forced to flee to London, where he died the following year.

Freud's contributions to psychological theory were so extensive that it is difficult to summarize them briefly. He stressed the enormous importance of unconscious mental processes in human behavior. He showed how such processes affect the content of dreams, and cause commonplace mishaps such as slips of the tongue and forgetting names, as well as self-inflicted accidents and even diseases.

Freud developed the technique of psychoanalysis as a method of treating mental illness. He formulated a theory of the structure of the human personality. He also developed or popularized psychological theories concerning anxiety, defense mechanisms, the castration complex, repression, and sublimation, to name just a few. His writings greatly stimulated interest in psychological theory. Many of his ideas were, and are, highly controversial, and have provoked heated discussion ever since he proposed them.

Freud is perhaps best known for proposing the idea that

repressed sexual feelings often play a causative role in mental illness or neurosis. (Actually, Freud did *not* originate this idea, although his writings did much to give it scientific currency.) He also pointed out that sexual feelings and desires begin in early childhood, rather than in adolescence.

Because many of Freud's ideas are still so controversial, it is very difficult to assess his place in history. He was a pioneer and a trailblazer, with a remarkable talent for coming up with new ideas. However, Freud's theories (unlike those of Darwin or Pasteur) have never won the general endorsement of the scientific community, and it is hard to tell what fraction of his ideas will ultimately be considered correct.

Despite the continuing controversy over his ideas, there seems little doubt that Freud is a towering figure in the history of human thought. His ideas on psychology have completely revolutionized our conception of the human mind, and many of the ideas and terms which he introduced have become common usage—e.g., the id, the ego, the superego, the Oedipus complex, and the death wish.

It is true that psychoanalysis is an extremely expensive mode of treatment, and that it quite often fails. But it is also true that the technique has a great many successes to its credit. Future psychologists may well conclude that repressed sexual feelings play a lesser role in human behavior than many Freudians have claimed. However, such feelings surely play a greater role than most psychologists before Freud had believed. Similarly, the majority of psychologists are now convinced that unconscious mental processes play a decisive role in human behavior—one that was greatly underestimated before Freud.

Freud was certainly not the first psychologist, and in the long run probably will not be considered the one whose ideas were most nearly correct. Still, he was clearly the most influential and important figure in the development of modern psychological theory, and in view of the enormous importance of his field, he certainly deserves a place on this list.

70 EDWARD JENNER

1749-1823

The English physician Edward Jenner was the man who developed and popularized the technique of vaccination as a preventive measure against the dreaded disease of smallpox.

Today, when, thanks to Jenner, smallpox has been wiped off the face of the earth, we tend to forget just how frightful were the casualties it caused in earlier centuries. Smallpox was so contagious that a substantial majority of the people living in Europe caught the disease at some time during their lives. And it was so virulent that at least 10 to 20 percent of those who contracted the disease died from it. Of those who survived, another 10 or 15 percent were permanently disfigured by severe pockmarks. Smallpox was not confined to Europe, of course, but raged throughout North America, India, China, and many other parts of the world. Everywhere, children were the most frequent victims.

For many years, attempts had been made to find a reliable means of preventing smallpox. It had been known for a very long time that a person who survived an attack of smallpox was thereafter immune, and would not catch the disease a second time. In the Orient, this observation had led to the practice of inoculating healthy people with material taken from someone who had a mild case of smallpox. This was done in the hope that the person so inoculated would himself contract only a mild case of the disease and, after recovering, would be immune.

This practice was introduced into England in the early eighteenth century by Lady Mary Wortley Montagu, and it had become fairly common there a good many years before Jenner. Jenner himself, in fact, had been inoculated with smallpox when he was eight years old. However, this ingenious preventive measure had a grave drawback: a fair number of persons so inoculated developed not a minor attack of the disease but a virulent attack which left them badly pockmarked. In fact, roughly 2 percent of the time inoculation itself resulted in a fatal attack of smallpox! Clearly, a superior method of prevention was badly needed.

Jenner was born in 1749, in the small town of Berkeley, in Gloucestershire, England. As a boy of twelve, he was apprenticed to a surgeon. Later, he studied anatomy and worked in a hospital. In 1792, he received a medical degree from St. Andrew's University. In his mid-forties, he was well established as a physician and surgeon in Gloucestershire.

Jenner was familiar with the belief, which was common among dairymaids and farmers in his region, that people who contracted cowpox—a minor disease of cattle, which can, however, be transmitted to humans—never got smallpox afterward. (Cowpox itself is not dangerous to human beings, although its symptoms somewhat resemble those of an extremely mild attack of smallpox.) Jenner realized that if the farmers' belief was correct, then inoculating people with cowpox would provide a *safe* method of immunizing them against smallpox. He investigated the matter carefully, and by 1796, became convinc-

Jenner administers the first vaccination.

ed that the belief was indeed correct. He therefore decided to test it directly.

In May 1796, Jenner inoculated James Phipps, an eight-year-old boy, with matter taken from a cowpox pustule on a dairymaid's hand. As expected, the boy developed cowpox, but soon recovered. Several weeks later, Jenner inoculated Phipps with smallpox. As he had hoped, the child developed no signs of the disease.

After some further investigations, Jenner set forth his results in a short book, *An Inquiry into the Causes and Effects of the Variolae Vaccinae*, which he published privately in 1798. It was that book which was primarily responsible for the rapid adoption of the practice of vaccination. Jenner subsequently wrote five other articles concerning vaccination, and for years devoted much of his time to disseminating knowledge of his technique, and working for its adoption.

The practice of vaccination spread rapidly in England, and was soon made compulsory in the British army and navy. Eventually it was adopted throughout most of the world.

Jenner freely offered his technique to the world and made no attempt to profit from it. However, in 1802, the British Parliament, in gratitude, granted him an award of £10,000. A few years later, Parliament granted him an additional £20,000. He became world-famous, and many honors and medals were bestowed upon him. Jenner was married and had three children. He lived to be seventy-three, dying in early 1823, in his home town of Berkeley.

As we have seen, Jenner did not originate the idea that an attack of cowpox would confer immunity against smallpox; he heard it from others. It even appears, in fact, that a few persons had deliberately been vaccinated with cowpox before Jenner came along.

But although Jenner was not a strikingly original scientist, there are few men who have done as much to benefit mankind. By his investigations, his experiments, and his writings, he transformed a folk belief, which the medical profession had never taken seriously, into a standard practice which has saved countless millions of lives. Although Jenner's technique could only be applied to the prevention of a single disease, that disease was a major one. He richly deserves the honors which his own and all subsequent generations have accorded him.

71
WILHELM CONRAD RÖNTGEN

1845-1923

Wilhelm Conrad Röntgen, the discoverer of X-rays, was born in 1845, in the town of Lennep, in Germany. He received his Ph.D. in 1869 from the University of Zurich. During the next nineteen years, Röntgen worked at a number of different universities, gradually acquiring a reputation as an excellent scientist. In 1888, he was appointed professor of physics and director of the Physical Institute at the University of Würzburg. It was there, in 1895, that Röntgen made the discovery which made him famous.

On November 8, 1895, Röntgen was doing some experiments with cathode rays. Cathode rays consist of a stream of electrons. The stream is produced by applying a high voltage between electrodes placed at each end of a closed glass tube from which almost all of the air has been removed. Cathode rays themselves are not particularly penetrating, and are readily stopped by a few centimeters of air. On this occasion, Röntgen had completely covered his cathode-ray tube with heavy black paper, so that even when the electric current was turned on, no light could be seen coming from the tube. However, when Röntgen turned on the current in the cathode-ray tube, he was surprised to see that a fluorescent screen lying on a bench nearby started glowing, just as though a light had stimulated it. He turned off the tube, and the screen (which was coated with barium platino-cyanide, a fluorescent substance) stopped glowing. Since the cathode-ray tube was completely covered, Röntgen soon realized that some invisible form of radiation must be coming from the tube when the electric current was on. Because of its mysterious nature, he called this invisible radiation "X-rays"—"X" being the usual mathematical symbol for an unknown.

Excited by his chance discovery, Röntgen dropped his other research and concentrated on investigating the properties of the X-rays. In a few weeks of intense work, he discovered the follow-ing facts: (1) X-rays can cause various other chemicals besides barium platinocyanide to fluoresce. (2) X-rays can pass through many materials which are opaque to ordinary light. In par-ticular, Röntgen noticed that X-rays could pass right through his flesh, but were stopped by his bones. By placing his hand be-tween the cathode-ray tube and the fluorescent screen, Röntgen could see on the screen the shadow of the bones in his hand. (3) X-rays travel in straight lines; unlike electrically charged par-ticles, X-rays are not deflected by magnetic fields.

In December 1895, Röntgen wrote his first paper on X-rays. His report promptly aroused great interest and excitement. Within a few months, hundreds of scientists were investigating X-rays, and within a year roughly a thousand papers had been published on the topic! One of the scientists whose research was directly motivated by Röntgen's discovery was Antoine Henri Becquerel. Becquerel, although intending to investigate X-rays, instead chanced upon the even more important phenomenon of radioactivity.

In general, X-rays are generated whenever high-energy electrons strike an object. The X-rays themselves do not consist of electrons, but rather of electromagnetic waves. They are there-fore basically similar to visible radiation (that is, light waves), ex-cept that the wavelengths of X-rays are very much shorter.

The best known application of X-rays, of course, is their use in medical and dental diagnosis. Another application is radiotherapy, in which X-rays are used to destroy malignant tumors or

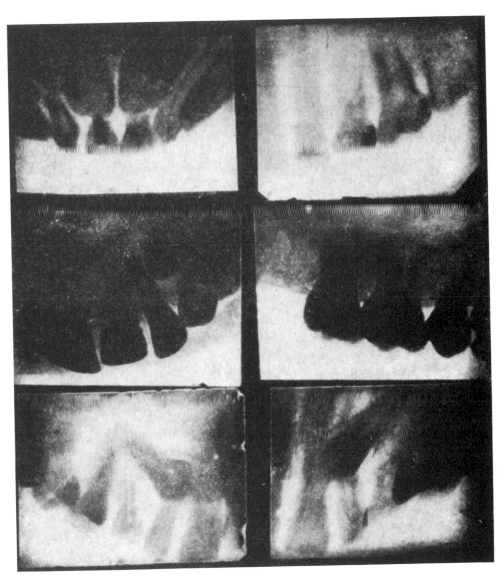

X-rays have facilitated great advances in dentistry.

to arrest their growth. X-rays also have many industrial applications. For example, they can be used to measure the thickness of certain materials or to detect hidden flaws. X- rays are also useful in many fields of scientific research, from biology to astronomy. In particular, X-rays have provided scientists with a great deal of information concerning atomic and molecular structure.

Röntgen deserves full credit for the discovery of X-rays. He worked alone, his discovery was unanticipated, and he followed it up superbly. Furthermore, his discovery provided an important stimulus to Becquerel and to other researchers.

Nevertheless, one should not overestimate Röntgen's importance. The applications of X-rays are certainly very useful; however, one cannot say that they have transformed our whole technology, as Faraday's discover of electromagnetic induction did. Nor can one say that the discovery of X-rays was of truly fundamental importance in scientific theory. Ultraviolet rays (whose wavelengths are shorter than those of visible light) had been known for almost a century. The existence of X-rays— which are similar to ultraviolet waves, except that their wavelengths are shorter still—therefore fits quite smoothly into the framework of classical physics. All in all, I think it quite reasonable to rank Röntgen significantly below Rutherford, whose discoveries were of more fundamental importance.

Röntgen had no children of his own; however, he and his wife adopted a daughter. In 1901, Röntgen was the recipient of the Nobel Prize in physics, the first one ever awarded. He died in 1923, in Munich, Germany.

72 JOHANN SEBASTIAN BACH

1685-1750

The great composer Johann Sebastian Bach was the first man to successfully combine the differing national styles of music which had existed in western Europe. By bringing together what was best in the Italian, French, and German musical traditions, he succeeded in enriching all of them. Not outstandingly famous during his own lifetime, Bach was half forgotten during the fifty years following his death. But his reputation has grown steadily during the last 150 years, and he is today generally acknowledged to be one of the two or three greatest composers of all time: in the opinion of some, the greatest of them all.

Bach was born in 1685, in the town of Eisenach, in Germany. It was his good fortune to be born into an environment where musical talent was admired and musical achievement encouraged. Indeed, the Bach family had been oustanding in the field of music for many years before Johann Sebastian was born. His father was a fine violinist, two of his great-uncles had been talented composers, and several of his cousins were highly respected musicians.

Bach's mother died when he was nine, and he was an orphan by the time he was ten. As a teenager, he received a scholarship to St. Michael's School in Lüneburg, partly because of his fine voice and partly on the basis of need. He graduated from St. Michael's in 1702, and the following year found a position as a violinist in a chamber orchestra. Over the next twenty years, he held a variety of positions. During his own lifetime, Bach was chiefly famous as a superb organ player, although he was a composer, teacher, and conductor as well. In 1723, when Bach was thirty-eight years old, he obtained the position of cantor of St. Thomas's Church in Leipzig. He held that position for the remaining twenty-seven years of his life. He died in 1750.

Although Bach was never without a good position and was always able to support his family, he was not nearly as famous during his own lifetime as Mozart and Beethoven (or even Franz Liszt or Frederic Chopin) became during their lifetimes. Not all of Bach's employers recognized his genius. In Leipzig, the council had wished to hire a "first rate musician"; it was only when they were unable to obtain the services of their first two choices that they reluctantly offered the position to Bach! (On the other hand, a few years earlier, when he had wished to leave his post as organist and concertmaster at the ducal court at Weimar for a new position, the duke was so reluctant to have him leave that he actually put Bach in prison. Bach spent over three weeks in jail before the duke finally relented.)

Bach married his second cousin when he was twenty-two years old. They had seven children together, but Bach's wife died when he was thirty-five years old. He remarried the following year, and his second wife not only helped raise the first seven children, but bore him an additional thirteen children. Only nine of Bach's children survived him, but four of those became well-known musicians in their own right. A talented family indeed!

Bach was a prolific composer. His works include approximately 300 cantatas; the set of 48 fugues and preludes that compose *The Well-Tempered Clavier*; at least 140 other preludes; more than 100 other harpsichord compositions; 23 concertos; 4 overtures; 33 sonatas; 5 masses; 3 oratorios; and a large variety of other pieces. All in all, Bach composed more than 800 serious pieces of music during his lifetime!

Bach was a Lutheran, and deeply religious. He wished his music to serve the church and the majority of his works are religious music. He did not attempt to invent new forms of music, but rather carried the existing forms to their highest peak.

During the half-century following his death, the music of Johann Sebastian Bach was largely ignored. (It is worth noting, though, that the greatest musicians of that era—Haydn, Mozart, and Beethoven *did* appreciate Bach's genius.) New musical styles were evolving, and the "old-fashioned" music of Bach went temporarily into eclipse. After 1800, however, there was a revival of interest in Bach's music, and since then his reputation and popularity have steadily climbed. Bach is more popular today, in this secular age, than he was during his own lifetime. It is indeed strange that a composer who was considered old-fashioned 200 years ago, both in style and in subject matter, should be widely admired today. What is the reason for his immense reputation?

In the first place, Bach is generally considered to be technically the best craftsman of all the major composers. He was acquainted with all the musical resources of his day, and could use each of them flawlessly. For example, no subsequent composer has ever rivaled Bach's artistic command of counterpoint (a technique in which two or more separate melodies are played at the same time). In addition, his works are admired for the logic and diversity of their orchestration, the cogency of their themes, and the expressiveness of their melodies.

To most serious students of music, the depth and complexity of structure of Bach's compositions give them a more lasting appeal than the more easily understood works of most other composers. Many people whose interest in music is more casual think of Bach as a rather difficult composer; however, it should be pointed out that his following is not confined to a small musical elite. His records probably sell better than those of any classical composer except Beethoven. (In the long run, of course, the works of Bach or Beethoven are listened to far more than the works of a "popular" composer who is all the rage for a while, but whose popularity proves transient.)

Where should Bach be ranked on this list? Plainly, he should be ranked below Beethoven: not only are Beethoven's works more popular, but he was also a daring innovator who did more to influence the course of musical history than Bach did. It likewise seems appropriate to rank Bach below Michelangelo, the leading figure in the visual arts, and far below Shakespeare, the greatest literary genius. But in view of the enduring popularity of Bach's music and the large influence it has had upon subsequent composers, it seems reasonable to rank him higher than any other artistic or literary figure.

A page from the score of the "Prelude and Fugue in B-Minor," written by J. S. Bach.

73

LAO TZU

fl. 4th *c.* B.C.

Of the many thousands of books which have been written in China, the one which has perhaps been the most frequently translated and read outside that country is a slender volume written over two thousand years ago and known as the *Lao Tzu,* or the *Tao Te Ching. The Tao Te Ching (Classic of the Way and its Power)* is the central text in which the philosophy of Taoism is expounded.

It is a subtle book, written in an extraordinary cryptic style and capable of many interpretations. The central idea concerns the *Tao,* which is usually translated "the Way" or "the Road." But the concept is somewhat obscure, since the *Tao Te Ching* itself begins by saying: "The *Tao* which can be told is not the eternal *Tao;* the name which can be named is not the eternal name." Nevertheless, we might say that *Tao* means roughly "Nature" or "the Natural Order."

Taoism takes the view that the individual should not struggle against the *Tao,* but should submit to it and work with it. Actively seeking to gain or exercise power is not so much immoral as it is foolish and futile. The *Tao* cannot be defeated; one should instead try to live in conformity with it. (A Taoist might point

out that water, which is infinitely soft, which flows without protest into the lowest places, and which responds to even the
weakest force without resistance, is nevertheless indestructible,
whereas the hardest rocks are worn away in time.)

For an individual human being, simplicity and naturalness
are usually advisable. Violence should be avoided, as should all
striving for money or prestige.One should not seek to reform the
world, but rather to respect it. For governments, also, a somewhat inactive policy is usually the wisest course. There are too
many statutes already. Passing more laws, or harshly enforcing
the old ones, usually makes matters worse. High taxes, ambitious
government programs, and making war are all contrary to the
spirit of the Taoist philosophy.

According to Chinese tradition, the author of the *Tao Te
Ching* was a man called Lao Tzu, who is said to have been an
older contemporary of Confucius. But Confucius lived in the
sixth century B.C., and both because of its style and its content,
few modern scholars believe that the *Tao Te Ching* was written
at such an early date. There is considerable dispute as to the
book's actual date of composition. (The *Tao Te Ching* itself
never mentions a specific person, place, date, or historical
event.) However, 320 B.C. is a good estimate—certainly within
eighty years of the true date, and probably much closer.

This problem has led to a great deal of dispute concerning
the dates—and even the existence—of Lao Tzu himself. Some
authorities believe the tradition that Lao Tzu lived in the sixth
century B.C, and have therefore concluded that he did not write
the *Tao Te Ching*. Other scholars have suggested that he is merely a legendary figure. My viewpoint, accepted only by a minority
of scholars, is that: (1) Lao Tzu was a real person, and the author
of the *Tao Te Ching*; (2) He lived in the *fourth* century B.C.; and
(3) The story that Lao Tzu was an older contemporary of Confucius is fictitious, and was fabricated by later Taoist philosophers in order to lend prestige to the man and his book.

It is worth noting that of the early Chinese writers neither
Confucius (551-479 B.C.), nor Mo Ti (fifth century B.C.), nor

Mencius (371-289 B.C.) makes any mention of either Lao Tzu or the *Tao Te Ching*; however, Chuang Tzu, an important Taoist philosopher who flourished about 300 B.C., mentions Lao Tzu repeatedly.

Since even the existence of Lao Tzu is in dispute, we should be skeptical of biographical details. But there are respectable sources for the following statements: Lao Tzu was born and lived in northern China. For part of his life he was an historian or

Taoist family sacrifices to the harvest moon.

curator of official archives, most probably at Loyang, the capital of the Chou dynasty monarchs. Lao Tzu was not his original name, but is rather an honorific title meaning roughly "old master." He was married and had a son named Tsung. Tsung later became a general in the state of Wei.

Although Taoism started as a basically secular philosophy, a religious movement eventually developed out of it. However, while Taoism as a philosophy continued to be based primarily on the ideas expressed in the *Tao Te Ching*, the Taoist religion soon became encrusted with an enormous number of superstitious beliefs and practices that have relatively little to do with the teachings of Lao Tzu.

Assuming that Lao Tzu actually was the author of the *Tao Te Ching*, his influence has been large indeed. The book is very short (less than six thousand characters in Chinese, and therefore small enough to fit on a single sheet of newspaper!), but it contains much food for thought. A whole series of Taoist philosophers have used the book as a starting point for their own ideas.

In the West, the *Tao Te Ching* has been far more popular than the writings of Confucius or of any Confucian philosopher. In fact, at least forty different English translations of the book have been published, a larger number than for any other book except the Bible.

In China itself, Confucianism has generally been the dominant philosophy, and where there is a clear conflict between the ideas of Lao Tzu and those of Confucius, most Chinese have followed the latter. Nevertheless, Lao Tzu has generally been highly respected by the Confucians. Furthermore, in many cases, Taoist ideas have simply been assimilated into Confucian philosophy, and have thereby influenced millions of persons who do not call themselves Taoists. Similarly, Taoism has had a marked influence on the Chinese development of Buddhist philosophy, and in particular on Zen Buddhism. Though few people today call themselves Taoists, there is no Chinese philosopher except Confucius who has had so widespread and enduring an impact on human thought as Lao Tzu.

74

VOLTAIRE

1694 - 1778

François Marie Arouet—better known by his pseudonym, Voltaire—was the leading figure of the French Enlightenment. A poet, playwright, essayist, novelist, short-story writer, historian, and philosopher, Voltaire was the apostle of freethinking liberalism.

Voltaire was born in 1694, in Paris. He was of middle class origin, and his father was a lawyer. In his youth, Voltaire attended the Jesuit college of Louis-le-Grand in Paris. Afterward, he studied law for a while, but soon dropped it. As a young man in Paris, he soon acquired the reputation of being a very witty fellow, full of clever jokes and satiric verses. Under the *ancien regime* in France, however, such cleverness could be dangerous, and as a result of some of his political verses, Voltaire was arrested and thrown into the Bastille. He spent almost a year in prison, where he occupied his time by writing an epic poem, the

Henriade, which later won considerable acclaim. In 1718, shortly after Voltaire was released from prison, his play *Oedipe* was
produced in Paris, where it was an enormous success. At twenty-
four, Voltaire was famous, and for his remaining sixty years, he
was a leading French literary figure.

Voltaire was clever with money as well as with words, and
he gradually became an independently wealthy man. In 1726,
however, he ran into some trouble. Voltaire had already
established himself as the wittiest and most brilliant conversa-
tionalist of his time (and perhaps of all time). He lacked,
however, the modesty which some French aristocrats felt was appropriate for a commoner. This led to a public dispute between
Voltaire and one such aristocrat, the Chevalier de Rohan, in
which Voltaire's wit got him the better of the verbal fighting.
Soon afterwards, however, the Chevalier had Voltaire beaten up
by a group of ruffians and, later on, thrown into the Bastille.
Voltaire was soon released from jail on the condition that he
leave France. He therefore went to England, where he stayed for
about two and a half years.

Voltaire's stay in England proved to be a major turning
point in his life. He learned to speak and read English, and
became familiar with the works of such famous Englishmen as
John Locke, Francis Bacon, Isaac Newton, and William Shakespeare. He also became personally acquainted with most of the
leading English thinkers of the day. Voltaire was impressed by
Shakespeare and by English science and empiricism; but what
most impressed him about the English was their political system.
English democracy and personal liberties presented a striking
contrast to the political conditions which Voltaire knew in
France. No English lord could issue a *lettre de cachet* and
thereby have Voltaire summarily thrown into jail; and if for any
reason Voltaire were to be detained improperly, a writ of habeas
corpus would soon get him released.

When Voltaire returned to France, he wrote his first major
philosophical work, the *Lettres philosophiques*, usually called
the *Letters on the English*. That book, which was published in

1734, marks the true beginning of the French Enlightenment. In the *Letters on the English*, Voltaire presented a generally favorable description of the British political system and of the ideas of John Locke and other English thinkers. Publication of the book aroused the anger of the French authorities, and Voltaire was again forced to leave Paris.

Voltaire spent most of the next fifteen years in Cirey, in eastern France, where he was the lover of Madame du Châtelet, the brilliant and educated wife of a marquis. In 1750, a year after her death, Voltaire went to Germany at the personal invitation of Frederick the Great of Prussia. Voltaire spent three years at Frederick's court in Potsdam. At first he got along well with the brilliant and intellectual Frederick, but eventually they quarreled, and in 1753, Voltaire left Germany.

After leaving Germany, Voltaire settled on an estate near Geneva, where he could be safe from both the French and Prussian kings. However, his liberal views made even Switzerland a bit dangerous for him. In 1758, therefore, he moved to a new estate in Ferney, near the French-Swiss border, where he would have two possible directions in which to flee in case of trouble with the authorities. He stayed there for twenty years, pouring out literary and philosophical works, corresponding with intellectual leaders throughout Europe, and entertaining visitors.

Through all these years, Voltaire's literary output continued undiminished. He was a fantastically prolific writer, perhaps the most voluminous author on this list. All told, his collected writings run to well over 30,000 pages. They include epic poems, lyric verse, personal letters, pamphlets, novels, short stories, plays, and serious books on history and philosophy.

Voltaire had always been a strong believer in religious toleration. However, when he was in his late sixties, a number of particularly horrifying instances of persecution of Protestants occurred in France. Aroused and outraged, Voltaire dedicated himself to an intellectual crusade against religious fanaticism. He wrote large numbers of political pamphlets opposing religious intolerance. Also, he took to ending all his personal letters with the words *Ecrasez l'infâme*, which means, "Stamp out the infamous thing." To Voltaire, "the infamous thing" was religious bigotry and fanaticism.

In 1778, when he was eighty-three years old, Voltaire returned to Paris, where he attended the premiere of his new play, *Irène*. Large crowds applauded him as the "grand old man" of the French Enlightenment. Hundreds of admirers, including Benjamin Franklin, visited him. But Voltaire's life was soon over. He died in Paris on May 30, 1778. Because of his outspoken anticlericalism, he could not receive a Christian funeral in Paris; but thirteen years later, victorious French revolutionaries had his remains dug up and reburied in the Panthéon in Paris.

Voltaire's writings are so voluminous that it would be very difficult to list even his major works in a short article. More important than the titles, though, are the basic ideas which he promoted throughout his career. One of his strongest beliefs was in the necessity for freedom of speech and of the press. A remark frequently attributed to him is: "I disapprove of what you say, but I will defend to the death your right to say it." Although Voltaire never actually made that explicit statement, it certainly reflects his attitude.

Another leading principle of Voltaire's was his belief in freedom of religion. Throughout his career, he steadfastly opposed religious intolerance and persecution. Although Voltaire believed in God, he firmly opposed most religious dogmas, and constantly presented the view that organized religion was basically a sham.

Quite naturally, Voltaire never believed that the titled aristocrats of France were wiser or better than he, and his audience learned that the so-called "divine right of kings" was a lot of nonsense. Although Voltaire himself was far from a modern-style democrat (he tended to prefer a strong but enlightened monarch), the main thrust of his ideas was plainly opposed to any form of hereditary rule. It is therefore not surprising that most of his followers came to favor democracy. His political and religious ideas were thus in the mainstream of the French Enlightenment, and they contributed substantially to the French Revolution of 1789.

Voltaire was not himself a scientist, but he was interested in science and was a firm supporter of the empirical outlook of Francis Bacon and John Locke. He was also a serious and capable historian. One of his most important works was his universal history, the *Essay on the Manners and Spirit of Nations*. This book differed from most previous histories in two main respects: first, Voltaire recognized that Europe was only a small part of the world, and he therefore devoted a considerable portion of his work to Asian history; second, Voltaire took the view that cultural history is, in general, far more important than political history. His book is therefore concerned more with social and economic conditions and the development of the arts, than with kings and the wars they fought.

Voltaire was not as original a philosopher as several others on this list. To a considerable extent, he took the ideas of other men, such as John Locke and Francis Bacon, restated them, and popularized them. However, it was through Voltaire's writings, more than anyone else's, that the ideas of democracy, religious toleration, and intellectual freedom were disseminated throughout France, and for that matter, throughout much of Europe. Though there were other important writers (Diderot, d'Alembert, Rousseau, Montesquieu, etc.) in the French Enlightenment, it is fair to say that Voltaire was the preeminent leader of that movement. In the first place, his pungent literary style, long career, and voluminous output assured him a far greater audience than any of the other writers. In the second place, his ideas were characteristic of the entire Enlightenment. And in the third place, Voltaire preceded all the other important figures in point of time. Montesquieu's great work, *The Spirit of the Laws*, did not appear until 1748; the first volume of the famed *Encyclopedie* came out in 1751; and Rousseau's first essay was written in 1750. By contrast, Voltaire's *Letters on the English* was published in 1734, and he had already been famous for sixteen years when that appeared.

Voltaire's writings, with the exception of the short novel *Candide*, are little read today. They were, however, very widely read during the eighteenth century, and Voltaire therefore played an important role in the changing climate of opinion that ultimately resulted in the French Revolution. Nor was his influence confined to France: Americans such as Thomas Jefferson, James Madison, and Benjamin Franklin were also acquainted with his works, and many of Voltaire's ideas have become part of the American political tradition.

Voltaire's funeral.

75 JOHANNES KEPLER

1571-1630

Johannes Kepler, the discoverer of the laws of planetary motion, was born in 1571, in the town of Weil der Stadt, Germany. That was just twenty-eight years after the publication of *De revolutionibus orbium coelestium*, the great book in which Copernicus set forth his theory that the planets revolved about the sun rather than the earth. Kepler studied at the University of Tübingen, obtaining a bachelor's degree in 1588 and a master's degree three years later. Most scientists of the day refused to accept the heliocentric theory of Copernicus; but while Kepler was at Tübingen he heard the heliocentric hypothesis intelligently expounded, and he soon came to believe in it.

After leaving Tübingen, Kepler was for several years a professor at the Academy in Graz. While there he wrote his first book on astronomy (1596). Although the theory which Kepler propounded in that book turned out to be completely incorrect, the book so clearly revealed Kepler's mathematical ability and originality of thought, that the great astronomer Tycho Brahe invited him to become his assistant at his observatory near Prague.

Kepler accepted the offer and joined Tycho in January 1600. Tycho died the following year; however, Kepler had made such a favorable impression in the intervening months that the Holy Roman Emperor, Rudolph II, promptly appointed him to succeed Tycho as Imperial Mathematician. Kepler was to hold that post for the rest of his life.

As the successor to Tycho Brahe, Kepler inherited the voluminous records of the careful observations of the planets that Tycho had made over many years. Since Tycho, who was the last great astronomer before the invention of the telescope, was also the most careful and accurate observer the world had yet seen, those records were invaluable. Kepler believed that a careful mathematical analysis of Tycho's records would enable him to determine conclusively which theory of planetary motion was correct: the heliocentric theory of Copernicus; the older, geocentric theory of Ptolemy; or perhaps a third theory propounded by Tycho himself. However, after years of painstaking numerical calculation, Kepler found to his dismay that Tycho's observations were not consistent with *any* of those theories!

Eventually, Kepler realized what the problem was: he, like Tycho Brahe and Copernicus, and like all the classical astronomers, had assumed that planetary orbits consisted of circles, or combinations of circles. In fact, however, planetary orbits are not circular, but rather *elliptical*.

Even after discovering the basic solution, Kepler still had to spend many months in complicated and tedious calculations to make sure that his theory satisfied Tycho's observations. His great book, *Astronomia nova*, published in 1609, presented his first two laws of planetary motion. The first law states that each planet moves around the sun in an elliptical orbit, with the sun at one focus. The second law states that a planet moves more quickly when it is closer to the sun; the speed of a planet varies in such a way that the line joining the planet and the sun sweeps out equal areas in equal lengths of time. Ten years later, Kepler published his third law: the more distant a planet is from the sun, the longer it takes to complete its revolution, with the square of the period of revolution being proportional to the cube of the distance from the sun.

Kepler's laws, by providing a basically complete and correct description of the motions of the planets around the sun, solved one of the basic problems of astronomy, one whose solution had eluded even such geniuses as Copernicus and Galileo. Of course, Kepler had not explained *why* the planets moved in the orbits they do; that problem was solved later in the century by Isaac Newton. But Kepler's laws were a vital prelude to Newton's grand synthesis. ("If I have seen further than other men," Newton once said, "it is because I stood on the shoulders of giants." Doubtless, Kepler was one of the giants to whom he was referring.)

Kepler's contribution to astronomy is almost comparable to that of Copernicus. Indeed, in some ways Kepler's achievement is even more impressive. He was more original, and the mathematical difficulties he faced were immense. Mathematical techniques were not as well developed in those times as they are today, and there were no calculating machines to ease Kepler's computational tasks.

In view of the importance of Kepler's achievements, it is surprising that his results were almost ignored at first, even by so great a scientist as Galileo. (Galileo's neglect of Kepler's laws is particularly surprising since the two men had corresponded with each other, and since Kepler's results would have helped Galileo to refute the Ptolemaic theory.) But if others were slow to appreciate the magnitude of his achievement, Kepler understood it himself. In a burst of exultation he wrote:

> *I give myself up to divine ecstasy...My book is written. It will be read either by my contemporaries or by posterity—I care not which. It may well wait a hundred years for a reader, as God has waited 6,000 years for someone to understand his work.*

Gradually though, over the course of a few decades, the significance of Kepler's laws became apparent to the scientific world. In fact, later in the century, a major argument in favor of Newton's theories was that Kepler's laws could be deduced from them. Conversely, given Newton's laws of motion, it is possible to rigorously deduce Newton's laws of gravitation from Kepler's laws. To do so, however, would require more advanced mathematical techniques than were available to Kepler. Even without such techniques, Kepler was perspicacious enough to suggest that planetary motions were controlled by forces emanating from the sun.

In addition to his laws of planetary motion, Kepler made various minor contributions to astronomy. He also made significant contributions to the theory of optics. His later years, unfortunately, were clouded by personal problems. Germany was descending into the chaos of the Thirty Years' War, and it was a rare individual that could escape serious difficulties.

One problem he had was in collecting his salary. The Holy Roman emperors had been slow payers even in comparatively good times. In the chaos of war, Kepler's salary fell far in arrears. Since Kepler had married twice and had twelve children, such financial difficulties were serious indeed. Another problem concerned his mother, who in 1620 was arrested as a witch. Kepler spent much time in an eventually successful attempt to have her released without being tortured.

Kepler died in 1630, in Regensburg, Bavaria. In the turmoil of the Thirty Years' War, his grave was soon destroyed. But his laws of planetary motion have proven a more enduring memorial than any made of stone.

76

ENRICO
FERMI

1901-1954

Enrico Fermi, the man who designed the first nuclear reactor, was born in 1901, in Rome, Italy. He was a remarkably brilliant student and received a Ph.D. in physics from the University of Pisa before he was twenty-one years old. By the time he was twenty-six, he was a full professor at the University of Rome. By then he had already published his first major paper, one which concerned an abstruse branch of physics called quantum statistics. In that paper, Fermi developed the statistical theory used to describe the behavior of large aggregations of particles of the type today referred to as *fermions*. Since electrons, protons, and neutrons—the three "building blocks" of which ordinary matter is composed—are all fermions, Fermi's theory is of considerable scientific importance. Fermi's equations have enabled us to gain a better understanding of the nucleus of the atoms, of the behavior of degenerate matter (such as occurs in the interior of certain types of stars), and of the properties and behavior of metals—a topic of obvious practical utility.

In 1933, Fermi formulated a theory of beta decay (a type of radioactivity) which included the first quantitative discussion of the neutrino and of weak interactions, both important topics in present-day physics. Research of that kind, though not readily comprehensible by laymen, established Fermi as one of the world's leading physicists. However, Fermi's most important accomplishments were yet to come.

In 1932, the British physicist James Chadwick had discovered a new subatomic particle, the neutron. Starting in 1934, Fermi proceeded to bombard most of the known chemical elements with neutrons. His experiments showed that many types of atoms were able to absorb neutrons, and that in many cases the atoms resulting from such a nuclear transformation were radioactive. One might have expected that it would be easier for a neutron to penetrate an atomic nucleus if the neutron were moving very rapidly. But Fermi's experiments showed that the reverse was true, and that if fast neutrons were first slowed down by making them pass through paraffin or water, they could then be more readily absorbed by atoms. This discovery of Fermi's has a very important application in the construction of nuclear reactors. The material which is used in reactors to slow down the neutrons is referred to as a *moderator*.

In 1938, Fermi's important research on the absorption of neutrons resulted in his being awarded a Nobel Prize in physics. Meanwhile, however, he was having trouble in Italy. In the first place, Fermi's wife was Jewish, and the Fascist government in Italy had promulgated a set of harshly anti-Semitic laws. In the second place, Fermi was strongly opposed to Fascism—a dangerous attitude under Mussolini's dictatorship. In December 1938, when he went to Stockholm to accept his Nobel Prize, Fermi did not return to Italy. Instead, he went to New York, where Columbia University, delighted to add one of the world's greatest scientists to its staff, had offered him a position. Fermi became a United States citizen in 1944.

In early 1939, it was reported by Lise Meitner, Otto Hahn, and Fritz Strassmann that the absorption of neutrons sometimes caused uranium atoms to fission. When that report came out, Fermi (like several other leading physicists) promptly realized that a fissioning uranium atom might release enough neutrons to start a chain reaction. Furthermore, Fermi (again like several others) soon foresaw the military potentialities of such a chain reaction. By March 1939, Fermi had contacted the United States navy and tried to interest them in the development of atomic weapons. However, it was not until several months later, after Albert Einstein had written a letter on the subject to President Roosevelt, that the United States government became interested in atomic energy.

Once the American government did become interested, the scientists' first task was to construct a prototype atomic pile in order to see whether a self-sustaining chain reaction was indeed feasible. Since Enrico Fermi was the world's leading authority on neutrons, and since he combined both experimental and theoretical talents, he was chosen to head the group attempting to construct the world's first nuclear reactor. He worked first at Columbia University and then at the University of Chicago. It was in Chicago, on December 2, 1942, that the nuclear reactor which had been designed and constructed under Fermi's supervision first went into successful operation. That was the true beginning of the atomic age, for that was the first time that mankind succeeded in setting off a nuclear chain reaction. Notice of the successful test was promptly sent back East with the cryptic but prophetic words, "The Italian navigator has entered the new world." Following this successful test, it was decided to go ahead at full speed with the Manhattan Project. Fermi continued to play an important role in that project as a leading scientific advisor.

After the war, Fermi became a professor at the University of Chicago. He died in 1954. Fermi was married and had two children. Chemical element number 100, fermium, is named in his honor.

Fermi is an important figure for several reasons. In the first place, he was indisputably one of the greatest scientists of the twentieth century, and one of the very few who was outstanding both as a theoretician and as an experimenter. Only a few of his most important scientific achievements have been described in this article, but Fermi actually wrote well over 250 scientific articles during his career.

In the second place, Fermi was a very important figure in the creation of the atomic bomb, though several other persons played equally important roles in that development.

Fermi's chief importance, however, derives from the leading role he played in the invention of the nuclear reactor. That Fermi deserves the principal credit for that invention is quite clear. He first made major contributions to the underlying theory, and then actually supervised the design and construction of the first reactor.

Since 1945, no atomic weapons have been used in warfare, but a large number of nuclear reactors have been built to generate energy for peaceful purposes. Reactors are likely to be an even more important source of energy in the future. Furthermore, some reactors are used to produce useful radioisotopes, with applications in medicine and in scientific research. Reactors are also—and more ominously—a source of plutonium, a substance which can be used to build atomic weapons. There are understandable fears that the nuclear reactor may pose great hazards to humanity, but nobody claims that it is an insignificant invention. For better or worse, Fermi's work is likely to have a large influence on the world in the years to come.

77

LEONHARD EULER

1707-1783

Leonhard Euler, the eighteenth-century Swiss mathematician and physicist, was one of the most brilliant and prolific scientists of all time. His work finds pervasive applications throughout physics and in many fields of engineering.

Euler's mathematical and scientific output was simply incredible. He wrote thirty-two full-length books, several of which comprise more than one volume, and hundreds upon hundreds of original articles on mathematics or science. All told, his collected scientific writings fill more than seventy volumes! Euler's genius enriched virtually every field of pure and applied mathematics, and his contributions to mathematical physics have an unending range of applications.

Euler was particularly adept at demonstrating how the general laws of mechanics, which had been formulated in the preceding century by Isaac Newton, could be applied to certain frequently-occurring types of physical situations. For example, by applying Newton's laws to the motion of fluids, Euler was able to develop the equations of hydrodynamics. Similarly, by a careful analysis of the possible motions of a rigid body, and by the application of Newton's principles, Euler was able to develop a set of equations that completely determines the motion of a rigid body. In practice, of course, material objects are not completely rigid. Euler, however, also made important contributions to the theory of elasticity, which describes how solid objects are deformed by the application of outside forces.

Euler also applied his talents to the mathematical analysis of astronomical problems, particularly the three-body problem which deals with the question of how the sun, earth, and moon move under their mutual gravitational attraction. That problem—a problem for the twenty-first century—is still not completely solved. Incidentally, Euler was the only prominent scientist of the eighteenth century who (correctly, as it turned out) supported the wave theory of light.

Euler's fertile mind often provided the starting point for mathematical discoveries that have made other men famous. For example, Joseph Louis Lagrange, the French mathematical physicist, developed a set of equations ("Lagrange's equations") which are of great theoretical importance and which can be used to solve a wide variety of problems in mechanics. The basic equation, however, was first discovered by Euler, and is usually referred to as the Euler-Lagrange equation. Another French mathematician, Jean Baptiste Fourier, is generally credited with the creation of the important mathematical technique known as Fourier analysis. Here, too, the basic equations were first discovered by Leonhard Euler, and are known as the Euler-Fourier formulas. They find wide application in many different fields of physics, including acoustics and electromagnetic theory.

In his mathematical work, Euler was particularly interested in the fields of calculus, differential equations, and infinite series. His contributions to those fields, although very important, are too technical to be described here. His contributions to the calculus of variations and to the theory of complex numbers are basic to all subsequent developments in those fields. Both topics have a wide range of applications in scientific work, in addition to their importance to pure mathematics.

Euler's formula, $e^{i\theta} = \cos\theta + i\sin\theta$, shows the relationship between trigonometric functions and imaginary numbers, and can be used to find the logarithms of negative numbers. It is one of the most widely used formulas in all of mathematics. Euler also wrote a textbook of analytic geometry, and made significant contributions to differential geometry and ordinary geometry.

Although Euler had a happy facility for mathematical discoveries that were capable of scientific application, he was almost equally adept in the field of pure mathematics. Unfortunately, his many contributions to the theory of numbers are too recondite to be described here. Euler was also an early worker in the field of topology, a branch of mathematics that has become very important in the twentieth century.

Last but not least, Euler made important contributions to our present system of mathematical notation. For example, he is responsible for the common use of the Greek letter π to represent the ratio of the circumference of a circle to its diameter. He also introduced many other convenient notations which are now commonly used in mathematical work.

Euler was born in 1707, in Basel, Switzerland. He was admitted to the University of Basel in 1720, when he was only thirteen years old. At first he studied theology, but he soon switched to mathematics. He received a master's degree from the University of Basel at seventeen, and when he was twenty accepted an invitation by Catherine I of Russia to join the Academy of Sciences at St. Petersburg. At age twenty-three he became professor of physics there, and at twenty-six he succeeded the famous mathematician Daniel Bernoulli in the Chair of Mathematics. Two years later he lost the sight of one eye; nevertheless, he continued to work with great intensity, turning out a long succession of brilliant articles.

In 1741, Frederick the Great of Prussia lured Euler away from Russia and induced him to join the Academy of Sciences in Berlin. He remained in Berlin for twenty-five years, returning to

Russia in 1766. Shortly afterward, he lost the sight of his other eye. Even this calamity, however, did not halt his research. Euler possessed a spectacular facility for mental arithmetic, and until the year he died (1783, in St. Petersburg, at the age of seventy-six), he continued to turn out first-rate papers in mathematics. Euler was married twice and had thirteen children, eight of whom died as infants.

All of Euler's discoveries would eventually have been made, even had he himself never lived. I think, though, that the proper criterion to apply in such a case is to ask the question: how different would science and the modern world be if the discoveries that he made had never been made at all? In the case of Leonhard Euler the answer seems fairly clear: modern science and technology would be greatly retarded, indeed almost unthinkable, without Euler's formulas, equations, and methods. A glance at the indexes of mathematics and physics textbooks shows references to: the Euler angles (rigid body motion); Euler's constant (infinite series); the Euler equations (hydrodynamics); Euler's equations of motion (dynamics of rigid bodies); Euler's formula (complex variables); the Euler numbers (infinite series); Euler's polygonal curves (differential equations); Euler's theorem on homogeneous functions (partial differential equations); Euler's transformation (infinite series); the Bernoulli-Euler law (theory of elasticity); the Euler-Fourier formulas (trigonometric series); the Euler-Lagrange equation (calculus of variations; mechanics); and the Euler-Maclaurin formula (numerical methods)—to mention only the most important examples.

In view of all this, the reader may wonder why Euler has not been ranked higher on this list. The principal reason is that although he was brilliantly successful in showing how Newton's laws could be applied, Euler never discovered any original principles of science himself. That is why such figures as Harvey, Röntgen, and Gregor Mendel, who each discovered basically new scientific phenomena or principles, have been ranked above him. Nevertheless, Euler's contributions to science, engineering, and mathematics were immense.

78

JEAN-JACQUES ROUSSEAU

1712-1778

The famous philosopher Jean-Jacques Rousseau was born in 1712, in Geneva, Switzerland. His mother died shortly after his birth, and when Rousseau was ten years old, his father was exiled and left Geneva, leaving Rousseau behind. Rousseau himself left Geneva in 1728, when he was sixteen years old. For many years Rousseau was an unknown, wandering from one place to another, and from one temporary position to another. He had several love affairs, including one with Thérèse Levasseur, by whom he had five illegitimate children. He placed all five children in a foundling home. (Eventually, when he was fifty-six years old, he married Thérèse.)

In 1750, at the age of thirty-eight, Rousseau leaped to sudden fame. The Academy of Dijon had offered a prize for the best essay on the subject of whether or not the arts and sciences were beneficial to human society and morals. Rousseau's essay, in which he concluded that the net result of the advancement of the sciences and arts was *not* beneficial to mankind, won first prize and promptly made him a famous man. Many other writings followed, including the *Discourse on the Origin of Inequality* (1755); *La Nouvelle Héloise* (1761); *Émile* (1762); *The Social Contract* (1762); and his *Confessions* (1770), and they all contributed to his prestige. In addition, Rousseau, who had always had a strong interest in music, wrote two operas, *Les muses galantes* and *Le devin du village*.

Although at first Rousseau was a friend of several of the liberal writers of the French Enlightenment, including Denis Diderot and Jean d'Alembert, his ideas soon began to diverge seriously from the others. By opposing Voltaire's plan for the formation of a theater in Geneva (Rousseau asserted that a theater was a school for immorality), Rousseau earned Voltaire's lasting enmity. Aside from that, Rousseau's general emotionalism contrasted sharply with the rationalism of Voltaire and the Encyclopedists. From 1762 on, Rousseau had serious trouble with the authorities because of his political writings. Some of his associates had become estranged from him, and about this time Rousseau started to become distinctly paranoid. Although a number of people befriended him, Rousseau, who was suspicious and hostile, quarreled with virtually all of them. For the last twenty years of his life, he was generally an embittered and miserably unhappy man. He died in 1778, in Ermenonville, France.

Rousseau's writings are said to have been a significant factor in the rise of socialism, nationalism, romanticism, totalitarianism, and anti-rationalism, as well as having paved the way for the French Revolution and contributed substantially to modern ideals of democracy and equality. He is credited with having had a major influence on educational theory. It has been contended that the theory that human beings are almost exclusively the product of their environment (and therefore completely malleable) is derived from his writings. And, of course, he is associated with the idea that modern technology and society are bad, and with originating the ideal of the "noble savage." If he were indeed responsible for all these concepts, he would be entitled to a much higher place on this list. It seems to me, however, that many of these claims are incorrect or badly exaggerated.

Consider, for example, the concept of the noble savage. In the first place, Rousseau never used that phrase, nor was he an admirer of the natives of the South Sea Islands, or of the American Indians. The idea of the noble savage had, moreover, been common long before Rousseau's time, and the well-known English poet John Dryden had used those exact words more than a century before Rousseau was born. Nor did Rousseau take the attitude that society was necessarily bad. Quite the contrary, he always insisted that society was necessary for man.

That Rousseau originated the idea of the "social contract" is completely false. The idea was discussed at length by John Locke, whose works were published before Rousseau was born. In fact, the famous English philosopher Thomas Hobbes had discussed the idea of the social contract even before Locke.

What about Rousseau's opposition to technology? It is quite obvious that the two centuries since Rousseau's death have seen unprecedented growth in technology. To the extent that Rousseau opposed technology, he was obviously completely ineffectual. Furthermore, the anti-technological bias existing today is derived not from Rousseau's writings, but is rather a response to the undesirable effects which the unrestrained applications of technology have produced during the last century.

Many other thinkers have suggested that environmental factors are of overwhelming importance in the formation of human character, and I think it unreasonable to credit Rousseau for this rather common idea. Similarly, nationalism was an important force long before the French philosopher lived, and he had little to do with its rise.

Did Rousseau's writings help pave the way for the French Revolution? To some extent they undoubtedly did, and probably

An etching of Rousseau by Naudet.

significantly more so than those of Diderot or d'Alembert. However, the influence of Voltaire, whose writings were earlier, more numerous, and more clearly written, was a good deal greater in this regard.

It is quite true that Rousseau was anti-rationalist by temperament, particularly in contrast with the other famous French writers of his day. But anti-rationalism was not new: our political and social beliefs are usually grounded in emotions and prejudices, although we frequently concoct seemingly rational arguments to justify them.

But if Rousseau's influence is not as great as some of his admirers (or opponents) have claimed, it is nevertheless very large. It is perfectly true that he was an important factor in the rise of Romanticism in literature, and his influence on educational theory and practice has proven even more important. Rousseau minimized the importance of book learning in a child's education, recommended that a child's emotions should be educated before his reason, and emphasized the importance of a child's learning through experience. (Incidentally, Rousseau was an early advocate of the advantages of breast feeding.) It may sound astonishing that a man who abandoned his own children should have had the audacity to lecture other people on how to raise theirs, but there is no question that Rousseau's ideas have profoundly influenced modern educational theory.

There are many interesting and original ideas in Rousseau's political writings. But dominating them all is a passionate desire for equality, and an equally passionate feeling that the existing structure of society is unbearably unjust. ("Man is born free; and everywhere he is in chains.") Rousseau may not himself have called for violence, but he surely inspired others to prefer violent revolution to gradual reform.

Rousseau's views on private property (as well as on many other points) frequently contradicted each other. He once described property as "the most sacred of all the rights of citizens." However, it seems safe to say that his attacks on private property had a greater effect on the attitudes of his readers than did his laudatory comments. Rousseau was one of the first modern writers of importance to seriously attack the institution of private property, and he can therefore be considered one of the forebears of modern socialism and Communism.

Lastly, one must not ignore Rousseau's constitutional theories. The central idea of *The Social Contract* is, in Rousseau's words, "the total alienation of each associate, and all his rights, to the whole community." Such a phrase leaves little room for civil liberties or for a bill of rights. Rousseau was himself a rebel against authority, but a major effect of his book has been to justify later totalitarian regimes.

Rousseau has been criticized as an extremely neurotic (not to say paranoid) personality, as a male chauvinist, and as a muddled thinker whose ideas are impractical. Such criticisms are largely justified. But far more important than his shortcomings are his flashes of insight and brilliant originality, which have continued to influence modern thought for over two centuries.

79
NICCOLÒ MACHIAVELLI

1 4 6 9 - 1 5 2 7

The Italian political philosopher Niccolò Machiavelli is notorious for his blunt advice that a ruler interested in maintaining and increasing his power should make use of deceitfulness, cunning, and lies, combined with a ruthless use of force.

Denounced by many as an unscrupulous scoundrel, praised by others as a hard-headed realist who dared to describe the world as it really is, Machiavelli is one of the few writers whose works have been closely studied by philosophers and politicans alike.

Machiavelli was born in 1469, in Florence, Italy. His father, a lawyer, was a member of a prominent family, but was not well off financially. Throughout Machiavelli's lifetime—the height of the Italian Renaissance—Italy was divided into many small principalities, in contrast to such relatively unified states as France, Spain, and England. It is therefore not surprising that in his day Italy was militarily weak, despite the brilliance of her culture.

During Machiavelli's youth, Florence was ruled by the famous Medici ruler, Lorenzo the Magnificent. But Lorenzo died in 1492, and a few years later, the Medici were driven from Florence. Florence became a republic, and in 1498, the twenty-nine-year-old Machiavelli obtained a high position in the Florentine civil service. For the next fourteen years, he served the Florentine Republic and engaged in various diplomatic missions in its behalf, traveling to France, to Germany, and within Italy.

In 1512, the Florentine Republic was overthrown, and the Medici returned to power. Machiavelli was dismissed from his office, and the following year, he was arrested on suspicion of being involved in a conspiracy against the new Medici rulers. He was tortured, but maintained his innocence and was released that same year. Afterward, he retired to a small estate at San Casciano, not far from Florence.

During the next fourteen years, he wrote several books, of which the two most famous are *The Prince* (written in 1513) and the *Discourses Upon the First Ten Books of Titus Livius*. Among his other works are *The Art of War*, a *History of Florence*, and *La Mandragola* (a fine play, still performed occasionally). However, his principal fame rests upon *The Prince*, perhaps the most brilliantly written and certainly the most easily readable of all philosophical treatises. Machiavelli was married and had six children. He died in 1527, at the age of fifty-eight.

The Prince may be considered a primer of practical advice for a head of state. The basic point of view of the book is that in order to succeed, a prince should ignore moral considerations entirely and depend upon strength and cunning. Machiavelli stresses heavily the importance—above all else—of a state being well-armed. He emphasizes that only armies conscripted from a state's own citizens are reliable; a state that depends on mercenary troops, or upon the troops of other states, is necessarily weak and endangered.

Machiavelli advises the prince to gain the support of the populace, since otherwise he will have no resource in adversity. Of course, Machiavelli understands that sometimes a new ruler, in order to secure his power, must do things that displease his subjects. He suggests, though, that, "...in taking a state the conqueror must arrange to commit all his cruelties at once, so as not to have to recur to them every day... Benefits should be granted little by little, so that they may be better enjoyed."

To be successful, a prince must surround himself with capable and loyal ministers; Machiavelli warns the prince to shun flatterers and offers advice on how to do so.

In Chapter 17 of *The Prince*, Machiavelli discusses whether it is better for a prince to be loved or feared:

> *The reply is that one ought to be both feared and loved, but...it is much safer to be feared than loved, if one of the two has to be wanting...for love is held by a chain of obligation which, men being selfish, is broken whenever it serves their purposes; but fear is maintained by a dread of punishment which never fails.*

Chapter 18 is entitled "In What Way Princes Must Keep Faith." Machiavelli states that "...a prudent ruler ought not to keep faith when by so doing it would be against his interest..." He adds, "Nor have legitimate grounds ever failed a prince who wished to show excuse for the non-fulfillment of his promise," for, "...men are so simple and so ready to obey present necessities, that one who deceives will always find those who allow themselves to be deceived." As a natural corollary of such views, Machiavelli advises his prince to be suspicious of the promises of others.

The Prince has often been called "a handbook for dictators." Machiavelli's career and his other writings indicate that in general he preferred republican government to dictatorship. But he was appalled by the political and military weakness of Italy, and he wished for a strong prince who would unite the country and drive out the various foreign invaders whose armies were injuring the land. It is interesting to note that although Machiavelli advocated that the prince adopt a cynical and ruthless practicality, he himself was idealistic and patriotic, and was not very adept at the deception that he recommended.

Few political philosophers have been so vehemently denounced as Machiavelli has been. For years, he was condemned as virtually the devil incarnate, and his name was employed as a synonym for duplicity and cunning. (Not infrequently, the most vehement denunciations came from those who practiced what Machiavelli preached—a hypocrisy of which Machiavelli might approve, in principle!)

Bust of Niccolò Machiavelli by an unknown Florentine sculptor.

Criticisms of Machiavelli on moral grounds do not, of course, indicate that he has been uninfluential. More pertinent in that respect is the objection that his ideas were not particularly original. There is some truth in such a claim. Machiavelli stated repeatedly that he was not suggesting a new policy, but rather was pointing out the techniques that many successful princes, from time immemorial, had already used successfully. In fact, Machiavelli constantly illustrates his suggestions by giving striking examples from ancient history, or from more recent Italian events. Cesare Borgia (whom Machiavelli praises in *The Prince*) did not learn his tactics from Machiavelli; quite the reverse, Machiavelli learned from him.

Although Benito Mussolini was one of the few political leaders ever to praise Machiavelli publicly, there is no doubt that a large number of prominent political figures have read *The Prince* with care. It was said of Napoleon that he slept with a copy of *The Prince* beneath his pillow, and similar remarks have been made concerning Hitler and Stalin. Still, it does not seem clear that Machiavellian tactics are more prevalent in modern politics than they were before publication of *The Prince*. That is the principal reason why Machiavelli has not been ranked higher in this book.

But if the extent of Machiavelli's effect on political practice is unclear, his influence on political theory is indisputable. Earlier writers, such as Plato and St. Augustine, had intertwined politics with ethics or theology. Machiavelli discussed history and politics in purely human terms, and simply ignored moral considerations. The central question, he implies, is not how people *should* behave, but how they actually *do* behave; not who *should* have power, but how men *actually* achieve power. That political theory is discussed today in a far more realistic manner than formerly is to no small extent due to Machiavelli's influence. He is rightly considered to be one of the principal founders of modern political thought.

80 THOMAS MALTHUS

1766 - 1834

In 1798, a previously obscure English parson, Thomas Robert Malthus, published a short but highly influential book entitled *An Essay on the Principle of Population as It Affects the Future Improvement of Society.*

Malthus's basic thesis was the idea that the growth of population tends to outrun the growth of food supply. In his original essay, Malthus presented this idea in fairly rigid form, claiming that population tended to increase geometrically (i.e., exponentially, such as the numbers in the series *1, 2, 4, 8, 16* . . .) whereas the food supply tended to increase only arithmetically (i.e., linearly, as the numbers in the series *1, 2, 3, 4, 5* . . .). In later editions of his book, Malthus restated his thesis in less rigid terms, saying only that population tended to increase indefinitely until it reached the limit of the food supply. From both forms of his thesis, Malthus drew the conclusion that the bulk of mankind was doomed to live in poverty and near-starvation. In the long run, no advances in technology could avert that result, for increases in the food supply are of necessity limited, while "the power of population is indefinitely greater than the power of the earth to produce subsistence for man."

But can not population growth be checked in some other way? Indeed it can be. War, pestilence, or other disasters frequently reduce the population. But these scourges provide only temporary relief from the threat of overpopulation, and at an obviously unpleasant cost. Malthus suggested that a preferable way of avoiding overpopulation would be "moral restraint"—by which he appears to have meant a combination of late marriage, premarital chastity, and voluntary restraints on the frequency of marital intercourse. Malthus, however, was realistic enough to realize that most people would not exercise such restraint. He concluded that, as a practical matter, overpopulation was virtually inevitable, and that poverty was therefore the almost inescapable fate of most human beings. A pessimistic conclusion indeed!

Although Malthus himself never advocated population control through the use of contraceptive devices, the suggestion of such a policy was a natural consequence of his basic ideas. The first person to publicly advocate the widespread use of contraceptive devices in order to prevent overpopulation was the influential British reformer, Francis Place (1771-1854). Place, who had read Malthus's essay and was strongly influenced by it, wrote a book in 1822, advocating contraception. He also disseminated birth control information among the working classes. In the United States, Dr. Charles Knowlton published a book on contraception in 1832. The first "Malthusian League" was formed in the 1860s, and the advocates of family planning have continued to gain adherents. Since Malthus himself disapproved, on moral grounds, of the use of contraceptives, the advocates of population control by means of contraception are usually referred to as neo-Malthusians.

Malthus's doctrine has also had an important effect on economic theory. Economists influenced by Malthus came to the conclusion that, under normal conditions, overpopulation would prevent wages from rising significantly above the subsistence level. The famous English economist David Ricardo (who was a personal friend of Malthus) stated: "The natural price of labor is that price which is necessary to enable the laborers, one with another, to subsist and to perpetuate the race, without either increase or diminution." This theory, generally referred to as the "iron law of wages," was accepted by Karl Marx, and became a critical element in his theory of surplus value.

Malthus's views also influenced the study of biology. Charles Darwin stated that he had read the *Essay on the Principle of Population*, and that this provided him with an important link in his theory of evolution by natural selection.

Malthus was born in 1766, near Dorking, in Surrey, England. He attended Jesus College of Cambridge University, where he was an excellent student. He graduated in 1788 and was ordained an Anglican clergyman in the same year. In 1791, he got a master's degree, and in 1793, he became a fellow of Jesus College.

The first version of his famous work was originally published anonymously, but it was widely read and soon brought Malthus fame. A longer version of his essay was published five years later, in 1803. The book was repeatedly revised and expanded, the sixth edition appearing in 1826.

Malthus married in 1804, at the age of thirty-eight. In 1805, he was appointed professor of history and political economy at the East India Company's College at Haileybury. He remained at that position for the rest of his life. Malthus wrote several other books on economics, the most important being the *Principles of Political Economy* (1820). That book influenced many later economists, particularly the important twentieth-century figure John Maynard Keynes. In his later years, Malthus received many honors. He died in 1834, at the age of sixty-eight, near Bath, England. Two of his three children survived him. There were no grandchildren.

Since the use of contraceptives did not spread widely until long after Malthus died, it is sometimes suggested that Malthus was not really influential. I think that this view is incorrect. In the first place, Malthus's ideas strongly influenced both Charles Darwin and Karl Marx, perhaps the two most influential thinkers of the nineteenth century. In the second place, although the policies of the neo-Malthusians were not immediately adopted by the majority of the population, their suggestions were not ignored, and their ideas never died out. The present-day birth control movement is a direct continuation of the movement started during Malthus's own lifetime.

Thomas Malthus was not the first person to call attention to the possibility that an otherwise well-governed country might suffer from overpopulation. That idea had been previously suggested by several other philosophers. Malthus himself pointed out that both Plato and Aristotle had discussed the topic. Indeed, he quotes Aristotle, who had written, in part, "...in the generality of states, if every person be left free to have as many children as he pleases, the necessary consequence must be poverty...."

But if Malthus's basic idea was not entirely original, one should not underestimate his importance. Plato and Aristotle had only mentioned the idea in passing, and their brief remarks on the topic had been largely ignored. It was Malthus who elaborated the idea and wrote extensively on the subject. More important, Malthus was the first person to stress the overwhelming importance of the problem of overpopulation, and to bring this problem to the attention of the intellectual world.

81 JOHN F. KENNEDY
1917-1963

John Fitzgerald Kennedy was born in 1917, in Brookline, Massachusetts. He was President of the United States from January 20, 1961, to November 22, 1963, when he was assassinated in Dallas, Texas. I shall omit most of the other biographical information concerning Kennedy, partly because such information is generally well known, but primarily because most of Kennedy's personal and political activities have little relevance to his presence on this list.

A thousand years from now, neither the Peace Corps, nor the Alliance for Progress, nor the Bay of Pigs is likely to be much remembered. Nor will it seem very important what Kennedy's policies were concerning taxes or civil rights legislation. John F. Kennedy has been placed on this list for one reason only: he was

the person who was primarily responsible for instituting the
Apollo Space Program. Providing that the human race has not
blown itself to smithereens in the intervening time, we can be
fairly sure that even 5,000 years from now, our trip to the moon
will still be regarded as a truly momentous event, one of the great
landmarks in human history.

I will discuss the importance of the moon program a little
further on. First, however, let me deal with the question of
whether John F. Kennedy is really the man who deserves the
most credit for that trip. Should we not instead credit Neil Armstrong or Edwin Aldrin, the first men who actually set foot on the
moon? If we were ranking people on the basis of enduring fame,
that might be the correct thing to do, for I rather suspect that
Neil Armstrong is more likely to be remembered 5,000 years from
now than John F. Kennedy. From the standpoint of influence,
however, Armstrong and Aldrin were completely unimportant.
If by some misfortune those two men had died two months prior
to the launching of Apollo 11, there were a dozen well-trained
and highly competent astronauts who could have taken their
places.

Should we then give the credit to Wernher von Braun, or to
some other scientist or engineer who made an important contribution to the science of space travel? There is no doubt that
Wernher von Braun did more than his share to advance space exploration (as did such important predecessors as Konstantin
Tsiolkovsky, Robert H. Goddard, and Hermann Oberth). Once,
however, the political decision had been made to proceed with
the Apollo project, no one scientist—nor any group of ten
scientists—was crucial to its success. The crucial breakthrough in
the trip to the moon was not a particular scientific advance, but
rather the political decision to go ahead and spend 24 billion
dollars on the project.

Well, what about the political decision then? Would not
that decision have been made sooner or later, even without John
F. Kennedy? I strongly suspect—although, of course, there is no
way of being absolutely certain—that eventually some govern-

ment would have decided to finance a manned voyage to the moon. Certainly, John F. Kennedy did not force through the Apollo program over the objections of the public.

On the other hand, neither was there any great public pressure in favor of such a grandiose project. If in 1959 or 1960, the United States Congress had passed legislation setting up the Apollo program and appropriating the funds for it, and if the bills had then been vetoed by President Eisenhower, *then* it

On July 20, 1969, the Apollo 11 astronauts left this footstep on the moon, fulfilling Kennedy's pledge of May 1961 to land a manned space-craft on the moon "before this decade is out."

might be said that Kennedy was merely going along with the tide of public opinion. The actual facts, however, are quite different: many Americans wanted some sort of space program, but there was no great public clamor for a really large program. Indeed, even after the success of Apollo 11, there was considerable public argument over whether the project had been worth the expense. Since 1969, of course, the NASA budget has fallen drastically.

It is plain therefore that it was John F. Kennedy's leadership which was actually responsible for getting the Apollo project started. It was he who in May 1961 committed the United States to landing a manned spacecraft on the moon, "before this decade is out." It was he who obtained the appropriations from Congress, and it was under him that the program was set up. One may be convinced that a moon program would have been established sooner or later anyway (which is not completely certain); nevertheless, Kennedy is the person who actually did it.

Some people, of course, still feel that the Apollo project was just a gigantic boondoggle and not really important. So far, there has been little move to make the anniversary of July 20, 1969 (the date of the actual landing on the moon), a national holiday. On the other hand, we might remember that although Columbus Day was not celebrated in the sixteenth century, it is celebrated today as the dawn of a new age.

Even if the Apollo project is never followed up, it will be forever remembered as one of the greatest achievements of the human race. I suspect, however, that the Apollo program eventually will be followed up, and that space travel will play a far greater role in the future than it has in the past. If so, our descendants will feel that the voyage of Apollo 11, like Columbus's voyage across the Atlantic, was the start of an entire new era in human history.

82 GREGORY PINCUS

1903-1967

Gregory Pincus was the American biologist who played the principal role in the development of the oral contraceptive pill. Although he was never particularly well known, he had far more actual influence on the world than many people who are world-famous.

The pill has a twofold importance. In a world that is increasingly concerned with the dangers of overpopulation, the significance of the pill as an agent for population control is obvious. Less direct perhaps, but equally revolutionary, is the effect the pill has had in changing sexual mores. It is widely recognized that over the last thirty years there has been a revolution in sexual attitudes in the United States. Doubtless, there are many other political, economic, and sociological factors that have influenced that revolution; but the largest single factor has clearly been the advent of the pill. Previously, the fear of unwanted pregnancy was a major factor in inhibiting many women from engaging in pre-marital, or even marital, sex. Suddenly, women have been presented with the opportunity to engage in sexual relations without fear of pregnancy, and the change in circumstances has frequently produced a change in both attitude and behavior.

It might be objected that the development of *Enovid* (the first birth control pill) was not really all that important, since safe and reasonably reliable contraceptive methods had been known previously. Such an argument ignores the distinction between a method of contraception that is technically effective and one that is psychologically acceptable. Before the development of the pill, the contraceptive most recommended by "experts" was the diaphragm. Diaphragms are indeed safe and reasonably reliable, but in practice the great majority of women were, and still are, reluctant to use them. It is noteworthy that when the pill was first being tested, many hundreds of women preferred to take a chance with an untried (and perhaps dangerous) method of birth control, rather than use the safe and time-tested diaphragm.

It might also be objected that the development of *Enovid* was not really such a great triumph, since there are some risks to health involved in its use, and since it may eventually be superseded—perhaps even in the near future—by newer and safer drugs or devices. But in the nature of things, future methods of contraception can represent only a comparatively slight improvement, since the pill is already widely accepted and is generally satisfactory. (It is worth noting that over the past thirty years—a period during which many millions of American women began using the pill regularly—life expectancy among American women has *increased* significantly. That fact alone should make it obvious that the pill is not a *major* health hazard.) History will, or at least should, consider the development of *Enovid* in the 1950s as the crucial breakthrough in birth control methods.

Many persons contributed to the development of the oral contraceptive pill. Indeed, the idea had been talked about for a long time; the trouble was that nobody knew just what chemicals should go inside such a pill. Curiously, the key discovery had been made as far back as 1937. In that year, A. W. Makepeace, G. L. Weinstein, and M. H. Friedman had demonstrated that injections of progesterone (one of the female sex hormones) would inhibit ovulation in laboratory animals. However— perhaps because hypodermic injections did not sound like an at- tractive method of birth control, or perhaps because progester- one was at that time an extremely expensive chemical—that discovery had not aroused the interest of birth control advocates.

The main development of the pill did not start until about 1950, when the American biologist Gregory Pincus began to work on the problem. Apparently it was Margaret Sanger, the long-time advocate of family planning, who persuaded him to work on the project. She could hardly have chosen a better man, for Pincus was an expert in steroid metabolism and in the physiology of reproduction in mammals, as well as being director of laboratories at the Worcester Foundation for Experimental Biology, in Shrewsbury, Massachusetts.

Apparently Pincus, with his superb combination of technical knowledge and scientific intuition, hit upon the general nature of the solution almost immediately. Soon he had Dr. Min-Chueh Chang, a researcher at the Worcester Foundation, testing pro- gesterone on laboratory animals, to see if it would suppress ovulation even when taken orally. Chang's experiments were successful. This was certainly a promising beginning, particular- ly in view of the fact that a few years earlier a chemist named Russell Marker had invented a way to synthesize progesterone cheaply.

Another important contributor was Dr. John Rock, a gyne- cologist who, at Pincus's suggestion, conducted tests which show- ed that progesterone, taken orally, would inhibit ovulation in human females. However, Rock's research also disclosed two serious difficulties with using progesterone as an oral contraceptive. In the first place, it only suppressed ovulation about 85 percent of the time. In the second place, unreasonably large doses were needed to accomplish even that.

But Pincus, who was convinced that he was on the right track, was not ready to give up. He realized that there might be another compound chemically similar to progesterone, but without its disadvantages. In September 1953, he asked various chemical companies to send him samples of any synthetic steroids they had manufactured that were chemically related to progesterone. Pincus tested the chemicals that he received, and one of them, norethynodrel (manufactured by G. D. Searle and Company), seemed particularly effective.

This was a lucky break for Pincus, since when he had begun his research, back in 1950, norethynodrel had not even existed! It had been synthesized in 1952 by Dr. Frank B. Colton, a biochemist working in the Searle laboratories, and was later patented in his name. However, neither Colton nor any of his supervisors at G. D. Searle had been deliberately trying to create an oral contraceptive—nor at the time did they realize they had created one.

Further tests performed by the research group that had been assembled by Pincus indicated that norethynodrel would be still more effective if supplemented by a small admixture of another chemical, mestranol. It was this combination of drugs which was eventually marketed by G. D. Searle and Company as *Enovid*.

By 1955, Pincus could see that the time was ripe for a large-scale field test of the pill. The tests were begun in April 1956, in a suburb of San Juan, Puerto Rico, under the supervision of Dr. Edris Rice-Wray. Within about nine months, her tests indicated how strikingly effective the oral contraceptive pill was. Nevertheless, testing was continued for three more years before the Food and Drug Administration approved the marketing of *Enovid* in May 1960.

From the foregoing, it is obvious that Gregory Pincus did not develop the contraceptive pill by himself. It was Frank Colton who actually created norethynodrel; clearly, Colton and the various chemists who paved the way for his achievement are entitled to a considerable part of the credit. Similarly, various other men who worked with the Pincus group, including John Rock, Min-Chueh Chang, and Dr. Celso-Ramon Garcia made important contributions. For that matter, Dr. Rice-Wray, Margaret Sanger, and various others whom I have not mentioned each played a role in the overall accomplishment. Nevertheless, there seems no doubt that Gregory Pincus was the principal figure and the driving force behind the entire project. He was the scientist who decided to devote his time and effort to an active search for an oral contraceptive; he was the one who had the scientific and organizational ability to carry the project through successfully; he thought of the basic idea, obtained financing for the research, and got other talented men to work on the project. He had the vision and determination to push the project through to successful completion, and he is the one who has received, and who deserves, the principal credit for the accomplishment.

Gregory Pincus was born in 1903, in Woodbine, New Jersey, the son of Russian-Jewish parents. He graduated from Cornell in 1924, and received a doctorate from Harvard in 1927. Afterward, he did research in several institutions, including Harvard and Cambridge, and was a professor at Clark for several years. In 1944, he helped found the Worcester Foundation for Experimental Biology, and for a long time afterwards was director of laboratories there. He was the author of over 250 scientific papers, as well as a book, *The Conquest of Fertility*, published in 1965.

During his lifetime, Pincus received many scientific honors; however, neither he nor any of the men involved in the development of the pill received a Nobel Prize. When Pincus died in Boston, in 1967, his death went almost unnoticed by the general public, and for that matter, by most scientists. Today, few encyclopedias even mention his name. Nevertheless, he was the principal architect of one of the most significant developments in human history.

83

MANI

216-276

The third-century prophet Mani was the founder of Manichaeism, a religion which, though extinct today, at its height had a very large number of followers. Originating in the Middle East, Manichaeism spread as far west as the Atlantic Ocean and as far east as the Pacific. It endured for well over a thousand years.

The religion that Mani created was an interesting synthesis of ideas from earlier religions. Mani recognized Zoroaster, Buddha, and Jesus as true prophets, but claimed to have received a later and more complete revelation than any of them.

Though Buddhist and Christian elements are present in Mani's religion, the doctrine that seems most striking (at least to Westerners) derives from Zoroastrian dualism. Mani taught that the world is not ruled by a single deity, but is rather the site of a continuous struggle between two forces. One of these is the evil principle, which Mani identified with darkness and matter; the other is the good principle, which he identified with light and spirit. Superficially this sounds somewhat like the Christian notions of God and the Devil; however, in Manichaeism the good and evil principles are considered to be basically equal in power. As a consequence of this belief, the philosophical paradox of the existence of evil, which has so troubled Christian and Jewish philosophers, presents no problem at all in Manichaean philosophy.

There is no space here to describe the details of Manichaean theology. However, it must be mentioned that as a consequence of their identification of man's soul with the good principle and his body with the evil principle, Manichaeans believed that all sexual relations—even for the purpose of procreation—should be avoided. There were also prohibitions against the eating of meat and the drinking of wine.

At first sight, it might seem impossible for such a doctrine to gain and retain a large following. However, the full set of prohibitions was not applicable to the ordinary member of the Manichaean Church, but only to a small number called "the Elect." Ordinary members, "the Hearers," were permitted to have wives (or mistresses), to raise families, to eat meat, to drink wine, and so on. There were various religious rites that the Hearers were bound to observe, and they were obliged to support the Elect, but the moral code imposed upon them was not unreasonably difficult. (There are, of course, other religions where celibacy is required of priests or monks, but not of the mass of followers.) The souls of the Elect went straight to paradise after death; for the Hearers the route to paradise was somewhat longer. However, some Manichaean sects, such as the Cathari, believed that Hearers could achieve paradise as readily as the Elect, and in addition, were accorded considerable license while alive.

Mani was born in 216, in Mesopotamia, which at that time was part of the Persian Empire under the Arsacid or Parthian dynasty. Mani himself was of Persian ancestry and was related to the Arsacid rulers. Most Persians subscribed to some form of Zoroastrianism, but Mani was brought up in a small religious sect that was strongly influenced by Christian doctrine. He had religious visions when he was twelve, and he began to preach his new religion when he was twenty-four. Not very successful at first in his native land, he traveled to northwest India, where he succeeded in converting a local ruler.

In 242, he returned to Persia, where he gained an audience with King Shapur I. Although Shapur did not become a convert, he was well impressed with Mani and permitted him to teach his new religion throughout the Persian Empire. (This later Persian Empire is sometimes called the Sassanid Empire, after a new dynasty established about 226.) For the next thirty years or so, under Shapur I and Hormizd I, Mani preached without hindrance and gained large numbers of followers. During this period, missions were also sent to foreign countries. However, Mani's success aroused the antagonism of the priests of the Zoroastrian religion, which became the state religion of Persia during the Sassanid dynasty. About 276, after a new king, Bahram I, ascended the throne, Mani was arrested and imprisoned. After a cruel twenty-six-day ordeal, he died.

During his lifetime, Mani wrote several books: one in Persian, the others in Syriac (a Semitic langauge closely related to the Aramaic of Jesus' time). These became the canonical books of the Manichaean religion. After the religion became extinct, the Manichaean scriptures were lost; however, some have been rediscovered during the twentieth century.

From the beginning, Manichaeism was a vigorously proselytizing religion. During the prophet's own lifetime his religion gained adherents from India to Europe. After he died, it continued to grow, eventually spreading as far west as Spain and as far east as China. In the West, it reached its height during the fourth century, at which time it was a serious rival to Christianity. (St. Augustine was an adherent of Manichaeism for nine years.) But after Christianity became the state religion of the Roman Empire, Manichaeism was severely persecuted, and by about 600, it was largely eliminated from the West.

It was still strong, however, in Mesopotamia and Iran. From there it spread into Central Asia, Turkestan, and western

China. In the late eighth century, it became the official religion of the Uighurs, who controlled a substantial region in western China and Mongolia. It also spread into China proper, all the way to the coast, and from there to the island of Taiwan. However, the advent of Islam in the seventh century ultimately resulted in the decline of Manichaeism. Starting in the eighth century, the Abbasid Caliphs in Baghdad severely persecuted Manichaeism, and after a while it died out in Mesopotamia and Iran. From the ninth century on, it declined in Central Asia as well, and the Mongol invasions of the thirteenth century practically finished it off. Nevertheless, Marco Polo encountered Manichaean communities in eastern China in about 1000.

Meanwhile, various sects deriving from Manichaeism arose in Europe. The Paulicians appeared in the Byzantine Empire starting in the seventh century. The Bogomils, who were strongest in the Balkans, appeared about the tenth century. But the most notable of these European offshoots were the Cathari (better known as the Albigensians, after the French town of Albi, which was one of their strongholds). In the twelfth century, the Cathari gained a wide following in Europe, particularly in southern France. The Albigensians, though their doctrines more closely resembled Manichaeism, considered themselves Christians; the orthodox Church authorities considered them to be heretics. Eventually, Pope Innocent III, the most powerful and least tolerant of medieval popes, called for a crusade against them. The crusade began in 1209; by 1244, after an appalling loss of life and the devastation of a large part of southern France, the Albigensians were thoroughly crushed. Nevertheless, Catharism did not become extinct in Italy until the fifteenth century.

Any religion has a large effect upon the lives of its sincere adherents. For this reason, the founder of even a minor religion is frequently a person of considerable influence. Manichaeism, although it is now extinct, was for a time a major religion, and Mani was therefore a very influential person. (An unfortunate, but not negligible consequence of Mani's teachings was that

A miniature, probably of the 8th or 9th century, depicting two rows of Manichaean priests in ritual costume.

other established religions launched numerous persecutions to crush Manichaeism.)

Mani's personal role in the creation of the new religion was overwhelming. He founded it, devised its theology, and prescribed its moral code. It is true that many of his ideas derived from earlier thinkers, but it was Mani who combined these separate strands of thought into a distinctive new system. He also made many converts to Manichaeism by his preaching, created its ecclesiastical organization, and wrote its holy scriptures. Rarely has an important mass movement been so strikingly the creation of a single founder. It is obvious that the religion he founded would never have come into existence without him, and in this respect, Mani, like many religious leaders, seems to be far more important than most scientists and inventors.

Mani, therefore, clearly belongs somewhere on this list: the question is where? Obviously, he should be ranked far below the founders of the three principal world religions (Christianity, Islam, and Buddhism), whose followers over the course of time have numbered in the billions. On the other hand, even though Zoroastrianism and Jainism still survive today while Manichaeism has disappeared, it appears that Manichaeism, which at its height had far more adherents than either of those two religions, had a larger overall impact on the world than they did. It is for that reason that Mani has been ranked higher than either Zoroaster or Mahavira.

84 LENIN

1870-1924

Vladimir Ilyich Ulyanov, best known today by his pseudonym, Lenin, was the political leader principally responsible for the establishment of Communism in Russia. An ardent disciple of Karl Marx, Lenin initiated policies that had only been hinted at by Marx himself. Because of the rapid spread of Lenin's variety of Communism into many areas of the world, he must be acknowledged as one of history's most influential men.

Lenin was born in 1870, in the town of Simbirsk (now called Ulyanovsk in his honor), in Russia. His father was a loyal government official, but his older brother, Alexander, was a young radical who was executed for having taken part in a plot to assassinate the Czar. By the age of twenty-three, Lenin had himself become a fervent Marxist. In December 1895, he was arrested by the Czarist government for his revolutionary activities and spent fourteen months in jail, after which he was exiled to Siberia.

In the course of his three years in Siberia (which do not appear to have been particularly unpleasant for him), he married a fellow revolutionary, and produced the book *The Development of Capitalism in Russia*. His term in Siberia ended in February 1900, and a few months later Lenin traveled to western Europe. He spent the next seventeen years there, working as a professional revolutionary. When the Russian Social-Democratic Workers Party, to which he belonged, split into two factions, Lenin became the leader of the larger faction, the Bolsheviks.

World War I presented Lenin with his great opportunity. The war was a military and economic disaster for Russia, and it greatly increased dissatisfaction with the entire Czarist system. The Czarist government was overthrown in March 1917, and for a while it seemed that Russia might be governed by a democratic regime. Upon learning of the czar's downfall, Lenin immediately returned to Russia. When he got there, he was perceptive enough to see that the democratic parties, though they had already established a provisional government, had no great power, and that there was an excellent opportunity for the well-disciplined Communist party to seize control, despite its small numbers. He therefore urged the Bolsheviks to work for the immediate overthrow of the provisional government and its replacement by a Communist one. An attempted uprising in July was unsuccessful, and Lenin had to go into hiding. A second attempt, in November 1917, succeeded, and Lenin became the new head of state.

As a government leader, Lenin was ruthless but highly pragmatic. At first, he pushed for an uncompromising and rapid transition to a completely socialistic economy. When this did not work out, he was flexible enough to reverse himself, and to institute a mixed capitalist-socialist economy, which continued in the Soviet Union for several years.

In May 1922, Lenin had a serious stroke, and between then

and his death in 1924, he was almost completely incapacitated. Following his death, his body was carefully enbalmed and preserved, and put on display in a mausoleum in Red Square in Moscow.

Lenin is primarily important as the man of action who led the Bolsheviks to power in Russia, and by so doing established the first Communist government anywhere in the world. He was the man who first took the theories of Karl Marx and translated them into actual political practice. The establishment of that first foothold was one of the turning points of modern history. From 1917 to 1979 there was a continual expansion of Communist power throughout the world, and for a while approximately one-third of the Earth's population lived under Communist rule.

Although primarily important as an active political leader, Lenin has also exerted considerable influence through his writings. Lenin's ideas were not really in contradiction to those of Marx, but they did represent a marked change in emphasis. Lenin was enormously interested in the tactics of revolution, and he considered himself an expert at them. He constantly stressed the need for violence: "Not a single problem of the class struggle has ever been solved in history except by violence," is a typical quotation. Marx makes only occasional reference to the dictatorship of the proletariat. Lenin was almost obsessed by the topic, e.g., "The dictatorship of the proletariat is nothing else than power based upon force and limited by nothing—by no law and by absolutely no rule."

How important are Lenin's purely political ideas? In the first edition of this book I wrote:

> The most distinctive feature of the Soviet government has not been its economic policies (there are socialist governments in various other countries), but rather its technique for retaining political power indefinitely. Since Lenin's day, not a single Communist government anywhere in the world, after once being firmly established, has been overthrown. By firmly controlling all institutions of power within the country—the press, the banks, the churches, the labor unions, etc.—Communist

governments seem to have eliminated the possibility of internal overthrow. There may be a weak point in their armor, but if so, no one has yet found it.

That paragraph might have sounded reasonable at the time I wrote it, in 1977; but the events of the past few years show that I was completely mistaken. Far from being invulnerable, Leninist regimes have been toppling right and left. Lenin hoped—and his opponents feared—that by combining prison camps and propaganda, he had devised a system of government that would endure for centuries. He was wrong, and his historical importance is therefore much less than I had feared.

However, even if Lenin's importance as a theorist has been overrated (his economic ideas, of course, are derived almost entirely from Karl Marx), he nevertheless has significance as a man of action—the practical political leader who seized power and used it to transform his country. But in judging his place in history, we must first compare the importance of his actions with those of his successor, Joseph Stalin.

Lenin, after all, ruled for only five years. During those five years he completely destroyed the power of the Russian aristocracy, and he *started* the country on the road to socialism. But it was Stalin, not Lenin, who forced most Soviet farmers into collectives; it was Stalin, not Lenin, who virtually eliminated private business enterprises within the Soviet Union; and it was under Stalin, not Lenin, that Soviet Communism was transformed into a global force, with activities vigorously challenging the West in virtually every country on Earth.

Lenin, during his few years in power, was responsible for several million deaths, and he did establish a set of prison camps as a means of crushing political opposition to the Communist program. However, it was under Stalin that that set of prison camps (the so-called "*Gulag Archipelago*") reached their full extent; and it was under Stalin that the great majority of the government purges and killings occurred.

Should we nevertheless say that, since Lenin preceded Stalin

МИ СТАЛИ ВОЛІ НА СТОРОЖІ

Woodcut of Lenin and Red Guards with the motto:
"We stand on guard for freedom."

and prepared the way for him, Lenin should be considered the more important of the two? A case which is perhaps closely corresponding is that involving King Philip II of Macedon and his son, Alexander the Great. Philip was a brilliant leader whose military and organizational skills certainly prepared the way for Alexander and gave him his opportunity. However, Alexander did so much with that opportunity—far more than anyone had anticipated, and probably far more than most other men would have done—that I consider it appropriate to assign the larger part of the responsibility for what occurred to Alexander. By similar reasoning, I conclude that Stalin was a more influential figure than Lenin.

But even if Lenin is not as important as Stalin (or as Marx, whose writings provided the theoretical basis and stimulus for the whole Communist movement), he is still a major figure. Not only did he pave the way for Stalin in the USSR; but in addition, his writings, his policies, and his example all had a profound influence on Communist movements in many other countries.

It is sometimes claimed that the extraordinary loss of life that occurred in the Soviet Union was not due to the Leninist system

418

itself, but was a result only of the extreme cruelty and ruthlessness of Stalin. This view seems incorrect to me. In the first place, millions of people in the USSR were killed during the period of Lenin's rule, before Stalin took power. Furthermore, there have been leaders in various other Communist states who have engaged in the utmost brutality and destructiveness. A prominent example is Pol Pot, who ruled Cambodia from 1975 to 1979. In that relatively brief period roughly two million Cambodians died—an even greater proportion of the population than were killed by Stalin during the twenty-five years he headed the Soviet Union. Even if the system which Lenin established does not *invariably* result in such massacres, it certainly seems to make it relatively easy for such excesses to occur. Lenin may have spent his entire life in an attempt to eliminate oppression, but the net result of his activities was the destruction of individual liberties throughout a sizable portion of the world.

Since it now appears that the Marxist/Leninist movement will *not* endure for many centuries (as I had feared when I wrote the first edition of this book), it no longer seems appropriate to include Lenin among the top twenty persons in this book. However, it still seems reasonable to rank him in the top 100. His transforming influence on Russia is sufficient to make him comparable in importance to Peter the Great; and if one also takes into account his impact on other countries, it seems clear that Lenin should be ranked even higher than Peter, although well below Stalin.

85

SUI WEN TI

5 4 1 - 6 0 4

The Chinese emperor Sui Wen Ti (original name: Yang Chien) succeeded in reunifying China after it had been badly divided for hundreds of years. The political unity that he established has persisted throughout most of the intervening centuries. As a result, China has usually been one of the most powerful countries in the world. Another important result of the political unity is that the population of China—which comprises roughly one- fifth of the total world population—has suffered far less frequently from the horrors of war than have the inhabitants of Europe, the Middle East, or most other parts of the world.

An earlier emperor, Shih Huang Ti, had unified China in the third century B.C. His dynasty, the Ch'in, was destroyed soon after his death; however, it was succeeded fairly promptly by the Han dynasty, which ruled all of China from 206 B.C. to 220 A.D. After the Han dynasty fell, China underwent a long period of internal disunity, roughly analogous to the Dark Ages in Europe, which followed the fall of the Roman Empire.

Yang Chien was born in 541 into one of the powerful families of northern China. He received his first military appointment when he was only fourteen years old. Yang Chien was very capable and rose rapidly in the service of his ruler, the emperor of the northern Chou dynasty. His assistance in helping that ruler gain control of most of northern China did not go unrewarded, and in 573, Yang Chien's daughter was married to the crown prince. Five years later the emperor died. The crown prince appears to have been mentally unbalanced, and a struggle for power soon ensued. Yang Chien was the ultimate winner of that struggle, and in 581, at the age of forty, he became recognized as the new emperor. He was not, however, content to be the emperor of northern China only. After making careful preparations, he invaded southern China in 588. The invasion was rapidly successful, and in 589, he became the ruler of all of China.

During his reign, Sui Wen Ti built a spacious new capital city for the reunited empire. He also started construction of the Grand Canal, which connects China's two greatest rivers: the Yangtze in central China and the Hwang Ho (or Yellow River) in the north. This canal, which was completed during his son's reign, helped to unify northern and southern China.

One of the emperor's most important reforms was the institution of the system of selecting government officials by means of civil service examinations. For many centuries, that system provided China with a highly capable corps of administrators by constantly bringing highly talented men—from all over the country and from all social classes—into government service. (The system had first been introduced during the Han dynasty, however, in the long interval following the fall of the Han, many government posts had become hereditary.)

Sui Wen Ti also enforced the so-called "rule of avoidance": the principle that provincial governors could not serve in the province in which they had been born. This was a precautionary measure, preventing favoritism and at the same time preventing any provincial governor from acquiring too strong a power base.

Though capable of bold action when that was necessary, Sui Wen Ti was generally a cautious man. He avoided extravagance, and he appears to have lightened the tax burden on his subjects. His foreign policy was, on the whole, successful.

Sui Wen Ti seems to have had far less self-confidence than

most rulers or conquerors of comparable success. Though a powerful and successful ruler of millions of people, he seems to have been unusually henpecked. His able wife, although domineering, was of great assistance to him, both in his rise to power and during his reign. Sui Wen Ti died in 604, at the age of sixty-three. It is widely suspected that he was the victim of foul play by his second son (the empress's favorite), who succeeded him.

The new emperor suffered reverses in foreign policy, and eventually revolts against his rule broke out in China. He was killed in 618, and with his death the Sui dynasty came to an end. It was not, however, the end of Chinese unity. The Sui was promptly followed by the T'ang dynasty, which lasted from 618 to 907. The T'ang emperors retained the general governmental structure of the Sui rulers, and under them, China remained united. (The T'ang dynasty is often considered to be China's most glorious period, partly because of its military strength, but even more because of the great flowering of art and literature that occurred then.)

Just how important a figure was Sui Wen Ti? To form a judgment on that question, one might try comparing him with the celebrated European monarch Charlemagne. There is a distinct parallel between the careers of the two men: roughly three centuries after the fall of Rome, Charlemagne succeeded in reuniting a large part of western Europe; similarly, about three and one-half centuries after the fall of the Han dynasty, Sui Wen Ti succeeded in reuniting China. Charlemagne, of course, is far more famous in the West; however, it appears that Sui Wen Ti was the more influential of the two rulers. In the first place, he succeeded in reuniting all of China, whereas many significant areas of western Europe (such as England, Spain, and southern Italy) were never conquered by Charlemagne. In the second place, the reunification accomplished by Sui Wen Ti endured, whereas Charlemagne's empire was soon divided and never regained its unity.

In the third place, the cultural achievements of the T'ang

dynasty resulted, at least in part, from the economic prosperity which followed the political unification of China. By contrast, the short-lived Carolingian Renaissance ended with the death of Charlemagne and the dissolution of his empire. Finally, Sui's institution of the civil service examinations had profound long-term effects. For all these reasons—even taking into account that on the whole Europe has played a more important role in world history than China has—Sui Wen Ti had more effect on history than Charlemagne did. Indeed, few monarchs, either in China or in Europe, have had as enduring an impact as did Sui Wen Ti.

86
VASCO
DA GAMA
c. 1460-1524

Vasco da Gama was the Portuguese explorer who discovered the direct sea route from Europe to India by sailing around Africa.

The Portuguese had been searching for such a route since the days of Prince Henry the Navigator (1394-1460). In 1488, a Portuguese expedition headed by Bartolomeu Dias had reached and rounded the Cape of Good Hope at the southern tip of Africa and returned to Portugal. With this achievement, the Portuguese king understood that the long quest to find a sea route to the Indies was now near success. However, there were various delays, and it was not until 1497 that the expedition to the Indies actually set forth. To head the expedition, the king selected Vasco da Gama, a minor aristocrat who had been born in about 1460, in Sines, Portugal.

Da Gama set out on July 8, 1497, with four ships under his command and a total crew of 170 men, including interpreters who could speak Arabic. The expedition first proceeded to the Cape Verde Islands. Then, rather than following the coastline of Africa as Dias had done, da Gama sailed almost due south, far out into the Atlantic Ocean. He proceeded south for a long way, and then turned east to reach the Cape of Good Hope. It was a well-chosen route, faster than following the coast down, but it required much more daring and navigational skill. Because of the route he had chosen, da Gama's ships were out of sight of land for an astonishing ninety-three days—more than two and one-half times as long as Columbus's ships had been!

424

Da Gama rounded the Cape of Good Hope on November 22, and then sailed up the east coast of Africa. On the way north, he stopped at a few cities under Moslem control, including Mombasa and Malindi in present-day Kenya. In Malindi, he picked up an Indian pilot who guided him on a twenty-three-day run across the Arabian Sea to India. On May 20, 1498, about ten months after his departure from Portugal, da Gama arrived at Calicut, the most important trade center of southern India. The Hindu ruler of Calicut, the Zamorin, at first welcomed da Gama. However, the Zamorin was soon disappointed by the cheap goods that da Gama offered him as gifts. Combined with the hostility of the Moslem merchants who had previously dominated the trade routes of the Indian Ocean, this prevented da Gama from concluding a trade treaty with the Zamorin. Still, when he left Calicut in August, da Gama had a fine cargo of spices on board to show to his sovereign, as well as a number of Indians.

The trip back home proved more difficult than the voyage out. It took about three months to get across the Arabian Sea, and many of the crew died of scurvy. Ultimately, only two ships got back safely: the first reached Portugal on July 10, 1499; da Gama's own ship arrived two months later. Only fifty-five members of the crew—less than one third of those who started out—had survived the round-trip voyage. Nevertheless, when da Gama returned to Lisbon, on September 9, 1499, both he and the king correctly understood that his two-year voyage had been a tremendous success.

Six months later, the Portuguese king dispatched a follow-up expedition under the command of Pedro Alvares Cabral. Cabral duly reached India, discovering Brazil en route (though some historians believe that other Portuguese explorers may have discovered it much earlier), and returned to Portugal with a large quantity of spices. But some of Cabral's men had been killed in Calicut, so in 1502, Vasco da Gama was sent back there on a punitive mission, heading a fleet of twenty ships.

Da Gama's behavior on this expedition was utterly ruthless.

Off the Indian Coast, he seized a passing Arab ship, and after removing its cargo but not its passengers, burnt the ship at sea. All of those on board—several hundred people, including many women and children—perished. When he arrived at Calicut, da Gama imperiously demanded that the Zamorin banish all Moslems from the port. When the Zamorin hesitated, da Gama seized, killed, and dismembered thirty-eight Hindu fishermen, and then bombarded the port. Enraged but helpless, the Zamorin granted da Gama's demands. On his way back home, da Gama established some Portuguese colonies in East Africa.

For those deeds, he was richly rewarded by the King of Portugal, who awarded him titles and granted him estates, pensions, and other financial rewards. Da Gama did not return to India until 1524, when a new Portuguese king appointed him viceroy. A few months after his arrival in India, he fell ill, and he died there in December 1524. He was eventually reburied near Lisbon. Da Gama was married and had seven children.

The basic significance of Vasco da Gama's voyage is that he opened a direct sea route from Europe to India and the Far East, the effect of which was felt by many countries.

In the short run, the greatest impact was upon Portugal. Through control of the new trade route to the East, this formerly poor country on the outskirts of the civilized world soon became one of the richest countries in Europe. The Portuguese rapidly built up a substantial colonial empire around the Indian Ocean. They had outposts in India, in Indonesia, on Madagascar, on the east coast of Africa, and elsewhere. This, of course, was in addition to their holdings in Brazil and to their colonial empire in west Africa, which they had begun to develop even before da Gama's voyages. The Portuguese succeeded in retaining several of these colonies until the last half of the twentieth century.

Vasco da Gama's opening of a new trade route to India was a severe setback to the Moslem traders that had formerly controlled the trade routes of the Indian Ocean. Those traders were soon thoroughly defeated and displaced by the Portuguese. Furthermore, the overland trade routes from India into Europe fell into disuse, because the Portuguese sea route around Africa was cheaper. This was injurious both to the Ottoman Turks and to the Italian trading cities (such as Venice) that had formerly controlled the eastern trade. For the rest of Europe, however, this meant that goods from the Far East were a good deal cheaper than they had been previously.

Ultimately, however, the greatest impact of Vasco da Gama's voyage was not upon Europe or the Middle East, but rather upon India and Southeast Asia. Before 1498, India had been isolated from Europe. Indeed, through most of history India had been a fairly self-contained unit, with the only important foreign influences coming from the northwest. Da Gama's voyage, however, brought India into direct contact with European

Vasco da Gama's ship rounds the Cape of Good Hope.

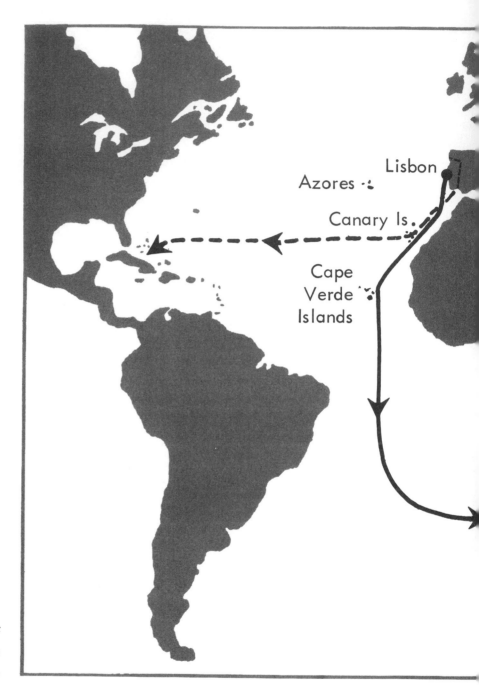

Lisbon

Azores

Canary Is.

Cape
Verde
Islands

The voyages of
Vasco da Gama
and Columbus.

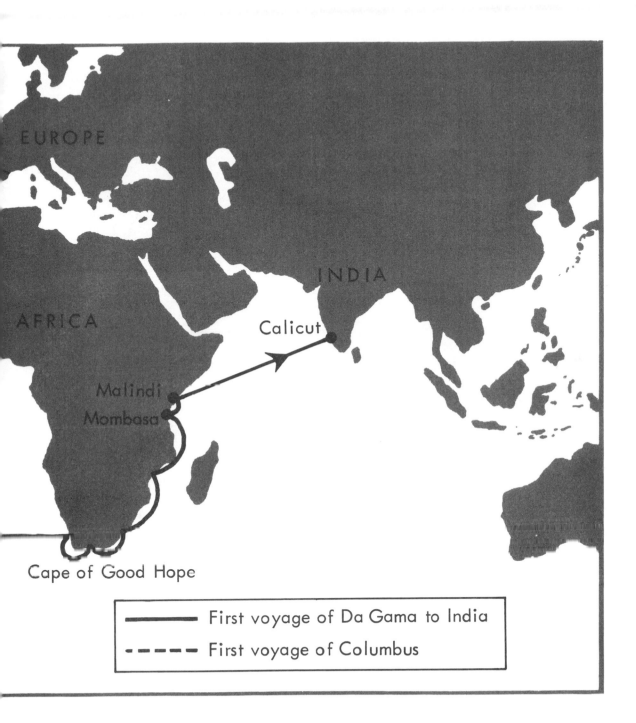

EUROPE

AFRICA

INDIA

Calicut

Malindi
Mombasa

Cape of Good Hope

| | First voyage of Da Gama to India |
| ----- | First voyage of Columbus |

429

civilization via the sea routes. The influence and power of the
Europeans grew steadily stronger in India, until by the last half
of the nineteenth century, the entire subcontinent was subject to
the British crown. (It might be remarked that this was the only
time in history that all of India was united under a single ruler.)
As for Indonesia, it fell first under European influence, and then
under complete European control. Only in the mid-twentieth
century did these areas regain autonomy.

The obvious person with whom to compare Vasco da Gama
is Christopher Columbus. In some ways, the comparison favors
da Gama. His voyage, for example, was a far more impressive
achievement. It was very much longer than Columbus's in both
distance and duration—more than three times as long, in fact! It
required far better nagivation. (Columbus, no matter how far off
course he went, could hardly have missed the New World,
whereas da Gama could easily have missed the Cape of Good
Hope and gotten lost in the Indian Ocean.) Furthermore, unlike
Columbus, da Gama succeeded in reaching his original destina-
tion.

It might be argued, of course, that Vasco da Gama did not
discover a new world, but merely made contact between the
Europeans and a region already populated. The same, however,
is true of Columbus.

Columbus's voyages ultimately had a tremendous impact
upon the civilizations pre-existing in the western hemisphere; da
Gama's voyage ultimately resulted in a transformation of the
civilizations of India and Indonesia. In judging the relative importance of Columbus and da Gama, it should be remembered
that, although North and South America are each enormously
larger in area than India, India has a larger population than all
the countries in the Western Hemisphere combined!

Nevertheless, it seems plain that Columbus was vastly more
influential than Vasco da Gama. In the first place, the voyage
around Africa to India was *not* prompted by any suggestion of
Vasco da Gama's. The Portuguese king had decided to send such
an expedition long before he chose Vasco da Gama to head it.

Columbus's expedition, however, had been instigated by Columbus himself, and it was his persuasiveness that induced Queen Isabella to finance it. Had it not been for Columbus, the New World (though it surely would have been discovered eventually) might have been discovered substantially later, and by a different European country. On the other hand, had Vasco da Gama not lived, the Portuguese king would simply have selected another man to head the expedition. Even if that man was incompetent and failed, the Portuguese would surely not have abandoned their long effort to find a direct route to India when it seemed so near success. Moreover, given the existing set of Portuguese bases along the west coast of Africa, there was little chance that another European nation would have been able to reach India first.

In the second place, European influence on India and the Far East was not nearly as overwhelming as European influence on the Western Hemisphere. The civilization of India was eventually vastly modified by its contact with the West. However, within a few decades of Columbus's voyage the major civilizations of the New World were virtually destroyed. Nor is there any parallel in India to the creation of the United States of America in the Western Hemisphere.

Just as one cannot credit (or blame) Christopher Columbus for all the events that have since occurred in the Western Hemisphere, so one cannot credit da Gama with all the results of direct European contact with the East. Vasco da Gama forms but one link in a long chain that includes: Henry the Navigator; a whole set of Portuguese captains who explored the west coast of Africa; Bartolomeu Dias; da Gama himself; his immediate successors (such as Francisco de Almeida and Alfonso de Albuquerque); and many other men. I feel that Vasco da Gama was easily the most important single link in that chain; however, he does not stand out nearly as much as does Columbus in the corresponding chain of persons involved in the Europeanization of the Western Hemisphere, and it is principally for that reason that he has been ranked so far below Columbus.

87 CYRUS THE GREAT

c. 5 9 0 B.C.- 5 2 9 B.C.

Cyrus the Great was the founder of the Persian Empire. Starting as a subordinate ruler in southwest Iran, he overthrew—by a remarkable series of victories—three great empires (those of the Medes, Lydians, and Babylonians), and united most of the ancient Middle East into a single state stretching from India to the Mediterranean Sea.

Cyrus (Kurush in the original Persian) was born about 590 B.C., in the province of Persis (now Fars), in southwest Iran. The area was at that time a province in the empire of the Medes. Cyrus was descended from a line of local chiefs who were vassals of the king of the Medes.

Later tradition created an interesting legend concerning

432

Cyrus, somewhat reminiscent of the Greek legend of King Oedipus. According to this legend, Cyrus was the grandson of Astyages, king of the Medes. Before Cyrus's birth, Astyages had a dream that his grandson would someday overthrow him. The king ordered that the infant be killed promptly after his birth. However, the official entrusted with the job of killing the infant had no heart for such a bloody deed, and instead handed him over to a shepherd and his wife with instructions that they put the child to death. But they, too, were unwilling to kill the boy, and instead reared him as their own. Ultimately, when the child grew up, he indeed caused the king's downfall.

This story (the details may be found in Herodotus) seems obviously fictitious, and virtually nothing is known of Cyrus's early years. We do know that some time about 558 B.C., Cyrus succeeded his father, Cambyses I, as king of the Persians, which made him a vassal of the Median king. About 553 B.C, however, Cyrus rebelled against his overlord, and after a war lasting for three years, succeeded in overthrowing him.

The Medes and the Persians were very closely related, both in origins and in language. Since Cyrus retained most of the laws of the Medes and much of their administrative procedure as well, his victory over the Medes was more like a change of dynasty than a foreign conquest.

Cyrus, though, soon showed that he desired foreign conquest also. His first target was the Lydian Empire in Asia Minor, ruled by King Croesus, a man of legendary wealth. Cyrus's iron proved more than a match for Croesus's gold, and by 546 B.C., Cyrus had conquered the Lydian Empire and made Croesus his prisoner.

Cyrus then turned his attention to the east, and in a series of campaigns, subdued all of eastern Iran and incorporated it into his empire. By 540 B.C., the Persian Empire extended as far east as the Indus river in India and the Jaxartes (modern-day Syr Darya) in Central Asia.

With his rear protected, Cyrus could now concentrate on the richest prize of all, the wealthy Babylonian Empire, centered

THRACE

BLACK SEA

LYDIAN
EMPIRE

CILICIA

•Sardis

Athens

MEDITERRANEAN   SEA   Damascus•

Jerusalem

•Memphis

EGYPT

RED

•Thebes

Nile R.

	Lydian Empire	(about 560 B.C.)
	Empire of the Medes	"
	Babylonian Empire	"

Cyrus the Great and
the Persian Empire.

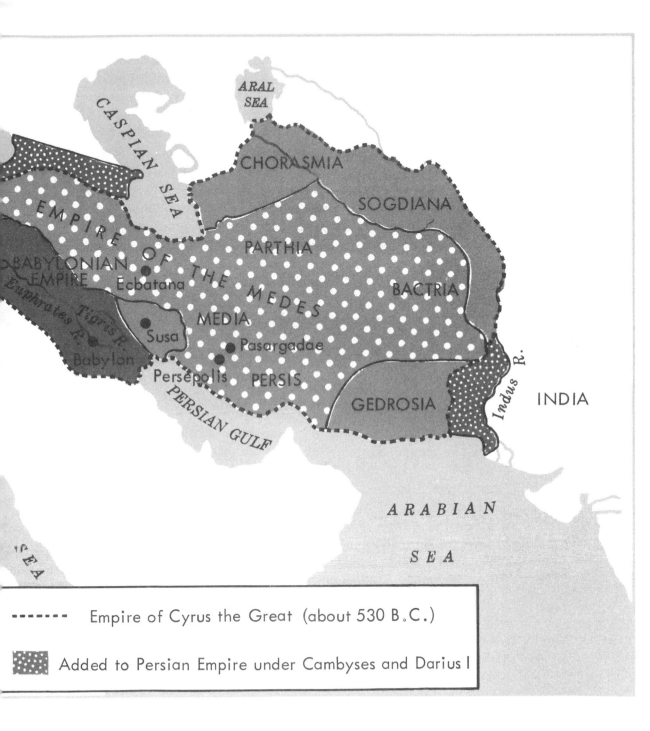

ARAL SEA

CASPIAN SEA

CHORASMIA

SOGDIANA

EMPIRE

OF THE MEDES

PARTHIA

BACTRIA

BABYLONIAN
EMPIRE

Ecbatana

Euphrates R.

Tigris R.

Susa

Babylon

MEDIA

Pasargadae

Persepolis

PERSIS

Indus R.

INDIA

GEDROSIA

PERSIAN GULF

SEA

ARABIAN

SEA

- - - - - - -   Empire of Cyrus the Great (about 530 B.C.)

Added to Persian Empire under Cambyses and Darius I

in Mesopotamia but ruling the entire Fertile Crescent of the ancient Middle East. Unlike Cyrus, the Babylonian ruler Nabonidus was not popular with his subjects. When Cyrus's armies advanced, the Babylonian troops had no taste for the pointless struggle, and in 539 B.C., Babylon surrendered to Cyrus without a fight. As the Babylonian Empire had included Syria and Palestine, those regions, too, were added to the domains under Cyrus's control.

Cyrus spent the next few years consolidating his rule and reorganizing the enormous empire that he had won. Then he led an army to the northeast to conquer the Massagetae, who were nomadic tribes living in Central Asia, east of the Caspian Sea. The Persians were victorious in an early skirmish. But in a second battle, fought in 529 B.C., they were defeated, and Cyrus—ruler of the greatest empire the world had yet seen—was slain.

Cyrus was succeeded by his son, Cambyses II. Cambyses defeated the Massagetae in a return engagement, recovered his father's body, and buried it at Pasargadae, the old Persian capital. Cambyses then went on to conquer Egypt, thus uniting the entire ancient Middle East into a single empire.

Cyrus was clearly a leader of immense military ability. But that was only one facet of the man. More distinctive, perhaps, was the benign character of his rule. He was exceptionally tolerant of local religions and local customs, and he was disinclined to the extreme brutality and cruelty which characterized so many other conquerors. The Babylonians, for instance, and even more notably the Assyrians, had massacred many thousands and had exiled whole peoples whose rebellion they feared. For example, when the Babylonians had conquered Judea in 586 B.C., they had deported much of the population to Babylon. But fifty years later, after Cyrus had conquered Babylonia, he gave the Jews permission to return to their homeland. Were it not for Cyrus, therefore, it seems at least possible that the Jewish people would have died out as a separate group in the fifth century B.C. Cyrus's decision in this matter may have had political motivations; nevertheless, there seems little doubt that he was a remarkably humane ruler for his time. Even the Greeks, who for a long period considered the Persian Empire to be the chief threat to their own independence, never ceased to regard Cyrus as a thoroughly admirable ruler.

So well had Cyrus done his work, that even after his death the Persian Empire continued to expand. It endured, in fact, for about two hundred years, until its conquest by Alexander the Great. For most of those two centuries, the lands ruled by Persia enjoyed internal peace and prosperity.

Alexander's conquest did not mark the permanent end of the Persian Empire. After Alexander's death, one of his generals, Seleucus I Nicator, gained control of Syria, Mesopotamia, and Iran, thereby establishing the Seleucid Empire. However, foreign control over Iran did not last very long. In the middle of the third century B.C., there was a rebellion against Seleucid rule, led by Arsaces I, who claimed to be descended from the Achaemenids (the dynasty of Cyrus). The kingdom founded by Arsaces— known as the Parthian Empire—eventually gained control over Iran and Mesopotamia. In 224 A.D., the Arsacid rulers were replaced by a new Persian dynasty, the Sassanids, who likewise claimed descent from the Achaemenids, and whose empire endured for over four centuries.

The career of Cyrus the Great represents one of the major turning points in world history. Civilization had first arisen in Sumeria, somewhat before 3000 B.C. For over twenty-five centuries, the Sumerians and the various Semitic peoples who succeeded them (such as the Akkadians, the Babylonians, and the Assyrians) had been at the very center of civilization. For all that time, Mesopotamia had been the richest and most culturally advanced region of the world (with the exception of Egypt, which was roughly on the same level). But Cyrus's career—which, incidentally, marks roughly the mid-point of recorded history— brought that chapter of world history to an end. From then on, neither Mesopotamia nor Egypt was the center of the civilized world, either politically or culturally.

Furthermore, the Semitic peoples—who made up the bulk of the population of the Fertile Crescent—were not to regain their independence for many centuries to come. After the Persians (an Indo-European people), were to come the Macedonians and the Greeks, followed by a long succession of Parthian, Roman, and Sassanid rulers, all of whom were Indo-Europeans. It was not until the Moslem conquests of the seventh century—almost twelve centuries after Cyrus the Great—that the Fertile Crescent was again controlled by Semitic peoples.

Cyrus is significant not merely because he won a lot of battles and conquered a lot of territory. Of greater importance is the fact that the empire he established permanently altered the political structure of the ancient world.

The Persian Empire, despite its considerable territorial extent and duration, did not have nearly as great an impact on history as did such longer-lived empires as the Roman, British, or Chinese empires. But in estimating Cyrus's influence, one should keep in mind that what he accomplished would probably never have occurred without him. In 620 B.C. (a generation before Cyrus was born), no one would have suspected that within a century the entire ancient world would be under the rule of a previously obscure tribe from southwest Iran. Even in retrospect, it does not appear that the rise of the Persian Empire was one of those historical events which, because of preexisting social or economic factors, was bound to happen sooner or later. Thus, Cyrus was one of those rare men who have actually altered the course of history.

The tomb of Cyrus the Great at Pasargadae.

88

PETER

THE

GREAT

1672-1725

Peter the Great is generally acknowledged to be the most out-standing of the Russian czars. The policy of westernization that he instituted was a major factor in the transformation of Russia into a great power.

Peter was born in 1672, in Moscow, the only son of Czar Alexis and his second wife, Natalia Narishkina. Peter was not yet four years old when his father died. Since Alexis also had had thirteen children by his first wife, it is hardly suprising that there was a lengthy and sometimes violent struggle over the succession to the throne. On one occasion, the young Peter even had to flee for his life. For several years, Peter's half-sister Sophia served as regent, and it was not until 1689, when she was removed from that office, that Peter's position became reasonably secure.

Russia in 1689 was a backward region, centuries behind western Europe in almost every way. Towns were fewer than in the West. The institution of serfdom was flourishing—indeed, the number of serfs was increasing, and their legal rights declin-ing. Russia had missed both the Renaissance and the Reforma-tion. The clergy was ignorant; literature was almost nonexistent; mathematics and science were ignored or despised. In contrast with western Europe, where Newton had recently written his

Principia, and where literature and philosophy were flourishing, Russia was almost medieval.

In 1697-98, Peter made a lengthy trip to western Europe, a trip which was to set the tone for the succeeding years of his reign. Peter took about 250 people along with him on this "grand embassy." By using a pseudonym (Pyotr Mikhaylov), Peter was able to see many things which he could not have observed otherwise. In the course of this trip, Peter worked for a period as a ship's carpenter with the Dutch East India Company in Holland. He also worked in the Royal Navy's dockyard in England, and he studied gunnery in Prussia. He visited factories, schools, museums, and arsenals, and even attended a session of Parliament in England. In short, he learned as much as he could about Western culture, science, industry, and administrative techniques.

In 1698, Peter returned to Russia and embarked on a far-ranging series of reforms designed to modernize and westernize the Russian state. In order to encourage the introduction of Western technology and techniques, Peter brought many Western technicians into Russia. He also sent many young Russians to study in western Europe. Throughout his reign, Peter encouraged the development of industry and commerce. Under his rule, towns grew in size and the bourgeoisie increased in numbers and in influence.

During Peter's reign, the first good-sized Russian navy was built. Furthermore, the army was remodeled on the Western style, the troops were provided with uniforms and modern firearms, and Western style military drilling was instituted. Peter also instituted many changes in the Russian civil administration, including the sensible reform of promoting civil servants on the basis of their performance in office, rather than their hereditary rank.

In social matters, also, Peter encouraged westernization. He decreed that all beards must be cut off (though he later modified the decree), and men at court were ordered to dress in the Western style and were encouraged to take up smoking and the drinking of coffee. Although at the time many of his proposals met with strenuous opposition, the long-term effect of these policies was that much of the Russian aristocracy eventually developed Western manners and culture.

Not surprisingly, Peter considered the Russian Orthodox Church to be a backward and reactionary force. Peter succeeded in partly reorganizing the Orthodox Church and in gaining considerable control over it. Peter instituted secular schools in Russia and encouraged the development of science. He also introduced the Julian calendar and modernized the Russian alphabet. During his reign, the first newspaper was established in Russia.

In addition to all these domestic reforms, Peter engaged in a foreign policy that had important consequences for the future. Under him, Russia was involved in wars both with Turkey in the south and with Sweden in the north. Against Turkey he initially had some success, conquering the port of Azov in 1696, and thereby providing Russia with some access to the Black Sea. Later in his reign, however, the Turks got the better of the fighting, and in 1711 he was forced to cede Azov back to Turkey.

In the war against Sweden, the sequence of events was almost exactly reversed, with the Russians defeated at the beginning and victorious at the end. In 1700, Russia joined with Denmark and Saxony in a war against Sweden, which at that time was a major military power. (Poland, too, later declared war on Sweden.) At the battle of Narva, in 1700, the Russian forces were badly defeated. Following this battle, the Swedish king turned his attention to his other enemies. Meanwhile, Peter rebuilt the Russian army. Eventually, the battle between Sweden and Russia was resumed, and at Poltava, in the year 1709, the Swedish army was decisively defeated.

The Russian territorial gains from the war included (roughly) Estonia and Latvia, plus a substantial area near Finland. Although the area conquered was not extremely large, it was important because it gave Russia an outlet on the Baltic Sea, and therefore a "window to Europe." On the banks of the Neva River, on some of the land conquered from Sweden, Peter founded a new city, St. Petersburg (today known as Leningrad).

In 1712, he moved his capital there from Moscow. Thereafter, St. Petersburg became the major point of contact between Russia and western Europe.

Peter's various domestic policies and foreign wars were, of course, very costly, and inevitably led to the imposition of additional taxes. Both the high taxes and the reforms themselves angered many Russians, and there were several revolts, all of which Peter crushed ruthlessly. Though he had many opponents in his own day, today both Russian and Western historians agree that Peter was the greatest of the Russian czars.

In his person, Peter made an imposing appearance. He was tall (at least 6' 6"), strong, good-looking, and energetic. He was full of lusty and boisterous high spirits, and was mirthful, although his humor was often rather crude. He sometimes drank heavily, and he had a violent streak in him. In addition to his political and military skills, Peter had studied carpentry, printing, navigation, and shipbuilding. An unusual monarch!

Peter was married twice. He married his first wife, Eudoxia, when he was seventeen. They lived together for only a week, and when he was twenty-six, he had her sent to a convent. In

*At the Battle of Poltava, the Russian forces under
Peter the Great decisively defeated the Swedish.*

1712, he divorced her and married another woman. His second wife, Catherine, was a Lithuanian girl of humble birth. Peter had a son, Alexis, by his first wife; however, Peter and his son were on bad terms. In 1718, Alexis was arrested on charges of conspiracy against Peter. He was arrested, tortured, and died in jail. Peter himself died in St. Petersburg in early 1725, at the age of fifty-two. He was succeeded by his widow, Catherine (not to be confused with Catherine the Great).

Peter the Great is on this list because of the important role he played in the westernization and modernization of Russia. However, since the rulers of many other countries have pursued similar policies, one might reasonably ask why Peter has been included on this list and most of the others omitted.

It is true enough that *today*, in the twentieth century, most heads of state see the importance to their nations of adopting Western methods, particularly in science and technology. In 1700, however, the desirability of westernization was not obvious to most persons outside of Europe. What makes Peter so significant is that he was two centuries ahead of his time in realizing the importance of westernization, and in modernizing his country. Because of Peter's foresight, Russia, which at his accession had been a very backward country, was able to pull well ahead of most countries in the world. (However, because of the very rapid progress that western Europe made during the eighteenth and nineteenth centuries, Russia was unable to draw abreast of western Europe.)

The contrast with Turkey, the other important state on the eastern frontiers of Europe, is particularly striking. Turkey and Russia were both semi-European countries. During the two centuries immediately preceding Peter's reign, Turkey was more advanced than Russia militarily, economically, and culturally. (For that matter, Turkey had been more advanced than Russia throughout most of history.) But there was no Turkish sultan around 1700 who realized the importance of rapid westernization and who pushed his country in that direction. Therefore, while Russia, from Peter's time on, made rapid strides, Turkey made only slow progress. It was not until the twentieth century that Kemal Ataturk led Turkey in a program of rapid modernization. By that time, Russia was more advanced industrially and educationally than Turkey.

Today, of course, we take Russian predominance over Turkey for granted. Suppose, however, that instead of Peter the Great in Russia there had been, at that time, a great reforming sultan in Turkey. Then Turkey might well be a major power today, and probably would control the region which instead became Soviet Central Asia. (The residents of that region are Moslems, and are far more closely related to the Turks than they are to the Russians.)

Peter the Great was not a ruler who simply floated with the current, but was rather a man who was ahead of his time. His foresight quite possibly changed history and diverted it into a path it might not otherwise have followed. For these reasons, it seems plain to me that Peter is entitled to a place on this list.

In deciding where to rank Peter, I have been somewhat influenced by the comparison between him and Queen Elizabeth I of England. Elizabeth is much more *famous*, particularly in the West. However, I think I would find it difficult to persuade even the most fair-minded Russian that Elizabeth was more *influential* than Peter the Great. Peter was far more innovative, far more original. Whereas Elizabeth mainly represented a consensus of her people's desires, Peter pulled the Russians in a direction in which they had never previously contemplated going. The difference between the rankings of the two would be even larger were it not for the fact that through most of the intervening centuries, England has played a far more significant role in the world than Russia has.

89

MAO ZEDONG

1893–1976

Mao Zedong led the Communist party to power in China, and for the next twenty-seven years presided over a remarkable and far-reaching transformation of that vast nation.

Mao was born in 1893, in the village of Shaoshan, in Hunan province, the son of a well-off peasant. In 1911, when Mao was an eighteen-year-old student, a rebellion broke out against the decaying Ch'ing dynasty, which had ruled China since the seventeenth century. Within a few months the imperial government was overthrown, and China was declared a republic. Unfortunately, the leaders of the revolution were unable to establish a stable, unified government in China; and the revolution inaugurated a long period of instability and civil war—one which lasted, in fact, until 1949.

As a young man, Mao became steadily more leftist in his political ideas, and by 1920 he was a confirmed Marxist. In 1921, he was one of the twelve original founders of the Communist party of China. However, his climb to the top of the party leadership was rather slow, and it was not until 1935 that he became the leader of the party.

Meanwhile, the Communist party of China was engaged in a long, slow, and quite unsteady path to power. The party suffered major setbacks in 1927 and in 1934, but managed to survive them. After 1935, under Mao's leadership, the party's strength steadily increased. By 1947, it was ready for all-out war against the Nationalist government headed by Chiang Kai-shek. In 1949, their forces were victorious, and the Communists gained complete control of the Chinese mainland.

The China that Mao, as head of the party, now came to govern had been torn by war for the better part of thirty-eight years. China was a poverty-stricken, underdeveloped country, whose teeming, tradition-bound millions were mainly illiterate peasants. Mao himself was fifty-six years old, and it appeared that the bulk of his career was behind him.

In fact, however, the period of Mao's greatest influence was just beginning; and by the time of his death, in 1976, Mao's policies had transformed China. One aspect of that transformation was a general modernization of the country. In particular, there was a rapid industrialization, combined with great improvements in public health and education. These changes, though obviously very important, are of a sort that occurred in quite a few other countries during the same period, and they alone would not be sufficient to justify Mao's place on this list.

A second accomplishment of Mao's government was the transformation of China's economic system from capitalism to socialism. Just a few years after Mao died, however, his successor (Deng Xiaoping) started to reintroduce various aspects of a free-market economy into China. We cannot yet be sure just how far this process will go; but it now seems likely that within five or ten years China will abandon socialism and will become a capitalist nation again. The economic policies of Mao therefore seem far less important than they once did.

Mao had originally believed that the industrial workers of the cities would provide the strongest base of support for the Communist party, an idea which was in accordance with Marx's own thinking. However, about 1925, Mao came to the conclusion that, at least in China, the party's main support would come from the peasantry. He acted accordingly, and, during the long power struggle with the Nationalists, Mao's power base was always in the countryside. This idea was carried over during his years as head of state. For example, whereas Stalin, in Russia, usually stressed industrial development, Mao generally paid more attention to agricultural and rural development. Nevertheless, China's industrial production increased markedly under Mao's leadership.

Politically, of course, Mao installed a thoroughly totalitarian system. At least 20 million of his countrymen—quite possibly 30 million or more—met their deaths at the hands of Mao's regime, making his reign perhaps the bloodiest in all human history. (Only Hitler, Stalin, and Genghis Khan can challenge Mao for this dubious "honor.") There was some liberalization after Mao died; but attempts to convert China into a democracy have been firmly repressed by Deng Xiaoping, sometimes—as in the June 1989 massacre in Tiananmen Square in Beijing—quite savagely.

Of course, it was not Mao Zedong alone who determined the policies of the Communist government. He never exercised the sort of one-man control that Stalin did in the Soviet Union. Nevertheless, it is clear that Mao was by far the most important figure in the Chinese government from 1949 until his death in 1976.

One project for which he seems to bear chief responsibility was the "Great Leap Forward" of the late 1950s. Many observers think that that project, which included an emphasis on small scale, labor-intensive production methods, which could be carried out on the rural communes, was a failure. (In any event, it was eventually abandoned.) Another project which Mao supported, over the opposition of various other Chinese leaders, was the "Great Proletarian Cultural Revolution" of the late 1960s. This was a major upheaval—in some senses almost a civil war between Mao and his supporters on the one hand, and the entrenched Communist party bureaucracy on the other.

It is interesting to note that Mao was already in his mid-sixties

Chinese citizens celebrate the 18th anniversary of Mao's takeover of the mainland.

when the "Great Leap Forward" began, was well past seventy when the Cultural Revolution was instituted, and was almost eighty when, in a dramatic change of policy, he commenced a rapprochement with the United States.

It is always difficult to assess the long-term influence of a recent political figure. In the first edition of this book I gave Mao a very high ranking because I thought that the Communist system which he had established in China was likely to endure for a long time. That no longer seems probable. China appears to be abandoning socialism; and the dictatorial political system which Mao bequeathed China, though still in place, no longer seems secure.

While Mao was alive, it appeared that he might turn out to be as important a figure as Shih Huang Ti. Both were Chinese, and both were architects of revolutionary changes in their country. However, the influence of Shih Huang Ti on China endured for some twenty-two centuries, while the influence of Mao seems to be fading rapidly.

448

It seems more appropriate to compare Mao with Lenin, who also lived in the twentieth century. Just as Mao was the leader who established Marxism in China, so Lenin was the one who established it in Russia. At first sight, Mao seems the more important of the two: After all, China has more than three times the population of the Soviet Union. But Lenin preceded Mao, set an example for Mao, and influenced Mao's thinking. Furthermore, by establishing the world's first Communist state, Lenin had an enormous *worldwide* influence, far more influence outside his own country than Mao did. Taking that into consideration, it seems that Mao should be ranked somewhat below Lenin.

Chairman Mao participates in Chinese scholastic celebrations.

90

FRANCIS BACON

1561-1626

Though for years he was a leading English politician, and though he devoted the majority of his time and energy to furthering his political career, Francis Bacon has been included in this book solely because of his philosophical writings. In those writings, he was the herald of the new age of science: the first great philosopher to realize that science and technology could transform the world, and an effective advocate of scientific investigation.

Bacon was born in London, in 1561, the younger son of a high government official under Queen Elizabeth. When he was twelve years old, he entered Trinity College in Cambridge; however, after three years he left without receiving a degree. Starting at sixteen, he served for a while on the staff of the British ambassador in Paris. But when Bacon was only eighteen, his father died suddenly, leaving him with rather little money. He therefore studied law, and at age twenty-one he was admitted to the bar.

450

His political career started soon after that. When he was twenty-three, he was elected to the House of Commons. However, although he had highly-placed relatives and friends, and despite his obvious brilliance, Queen Elizabeth steadily refused to appoint him to any major or lucrative position. One reason for this was his courageous opposition in Parliament to a certain tax bill which the queen strongly supported. Since Bacon lived extravagantly and was constantly in debt (once he was actually arrested for debt), he could ill afford such independent behavior.

Bacon became a friend and advisor of the Earl of Essex, a popular and politically ambitious young aristocrat. In turn, Essex became a friend and generous benefactor of Bacon. However, when Essex's overweening ambition led him to plan a coup against Queen Elizabeth, Bacon warned him that he would put loyalty to his Queen first. Essex tried his coup anyway; it failed, and Bacon played an active role in the earl's prosecution for treason. Essex was beheaded, and the entire affair left many persons with adverse feelings toward Bacon.

Queen Elizabeth died in 1603, and Bacon became an adviser to her successor, King James I. Although James did not always take his advice, he did appreciate Bacon, and during James's reign, Bacon advanced steadily in the government. In 1607, Bacon became solicitor general; in 1613, he became attorney general; and in 1618, he was appointed Lord Chancellor of England, a position roughly equivalent in importance to that of the Chief Justice of the Supreme Court in the United States. That same year, he was appointed a baron; and, in 1621, he was appointed a viscount.

But then disaster struck. As a judge, Bacon had accepted "gifts" from litigants before him. Though that was a rather common practice, it was plainly illegal. His political opponents in Parliament eagerly seized upon the opportunity to remove him from power. Bacon confessed and was sentenced to imprisonment in the Tower of London and a large fine. Also, he was permanently barred from public office. The king soon released

Bacon from jail and remitted his fine, but Bacon's political career was ended.

Now, one can recall quite a few instances of high-ranking politicians who have been caught taking bribes, or otherwise violating the public trust. Frequently, when such persons are caught, they whine and defend themselves by asserting that everybody else is cheating also. If taken seriously, this defense would seem to mean that no crooked politician should be punished unless every other crooked politician is punished first. Bacon's comment on his conviction was somewhat different: "I was the justest judge that was in England these 50 years; but it was the justest censure in Parliament that was these 200 years."

Such an active and crowded political career would not seem to leave much time for anything else. Still, Bacon's lasting fame, and his place on this list, are due to his philosophical writings rather than to his political activities. His first important work was his *Essays*, which first appeared in 1597 and were gradually enlarged. The *Essays*, which are written in a pithy and brilliant style, contain a wealth of penetrating observations, not merely on political matters but on many personal matters as well. Some characteristic remarks are:

> *Young men are fitter to invent than to judge, fitter for execution than for counsel, and fitter for new projects than for settled business; ...Men of age object too much, consult too long, adventure too little.... Certainly it is good to compound employments of both, ...because the virtues of either age may correct the defects of both....*
>
> OF YOUTH AND AGE

> *He that hath wife and children hath given hostages to fortune...*
>
> OF MARRIAGE AND SINGLE LIFE

(Bacon himself was married, but had no children.)

But Bacon's most important writings concern the philosophy of science. He had planned a great work, the *Instauratio Magna* (or *Great Renewal*), in six parts. The first part was intended to review the present state of our knowledge; the second part was to describe a new method of scientific inquiry; a third was to include a collection of empirical data; a fourth was to contain illustrations of his new scientific method at work; the fifth was to present some provisional conclusions; and the last part was to be a synthesis of the knowledge gained from his new method. Not surprisingly, this grandiose scheme—perhaps the most ambitious undertaking since Aristotle—was never completed. However, *The Advancement of Learning* (1605) and the *Novum organum* (1620) can be considered the first two parts of his great work.

The *Novum organum* (or *New Instrument*) is perhaps Bacon's most important book. The book is basically a plea for the adoption of the empirical method of inquiry. The practice of relying entirely upon the deductive logic of Aristotle was stultifying, and a new method of inquiry, the inductive method, was required. Knowledge is not something we start with and deduce conclusions from; rather it is something we arrive at. To understand the world, one must first *observe* it. First collect the facts, Bacon said, then draw conclusions from these facts by means of inductive reasoning. Although scientists have not followed Bacon's inductive method in every detail, the general idea he expressed—the crucial importance of observation and experimentation—form the heart of the method used by scientists ever since.

Bacon's last book was *The New Atlantis*, an account of a utopian commonwealth situated on a fictional island in the Pacific. Although the setting is reminiscent of Sir Thomas More's *Utopia*, the whole point of Bacon's book is different. In Bacon's book, the prosperity and welfare of his ideal commonwealth depend upon and result directly from a concentration on scientific research. By implication, of course, Bacon was telling his readers that intelligent application of scientific research could make the people of Europe as prosperous and happy as those living on his mythical island.

One might fairly say that Francis Bacon was the first truly modern philosopher. His overall outlook was secular, rather than religious (though he firmly believed in God). He was rational rather than superstitious; an empiricist rather than a logic-chopping scholastic. In politics, he was a realist rather than a theoretician. And along with his classical learning and great literary skill, he was sympathetically attuned toward science and technology.

Though a loyal Englishman, Bacon had a vision which went far beyond his own country. He distinguishes three kinds of ambition:

> *The first is of those who desire to extend their own power in their native country; which kind is vulgar and degenerate. The second is of those who labor to extend the power of their country and its dominion among men; this certainly has more dignity, though not less covetousness. But if a man endeavor to establish and extend the power and dominion of the human race itself over the universe, his ambition...is without doubt both a more wholesome thing and a nobler than the other two.*

Though Bacon was the apostle of science, he was not a scientist himself, nor did he keep abreast of the advances being made by his contemporaries. He ignored Napier (who had recently invented logarithms) and Kepler, and even his fellow Englishman, William Harvey. Bacon correctly suggested that heat was a form of motion—an important scientific idea; but in astronomy, he refused to accept the ideas of Copernicus. It should be remembered, though, that Bacon was not attempting to present a complete and correct set of scientific laws. Instead, he was trying to present a survey of what needed to be learned. His scientific guesses were only intended to serve as a starting point for further discussion, not as the final answer.

Francis Bacon was not the first person to recognize the usefulness of inductive reasoning; nor was he the first to understand the possible benefits which science could bring to society. But no man before him had publicized those ideas so widely and so enthusiastically. Furthermore, partly because Bacon was such a good writer, and partly because of his fame as a leading politician, Bacon's attitudes toward science actually had a great deal of influence. When the Royal Society of London was founded, in 1662, to promote scientific knowledge, the founders named Bacon as their inspiration. And, when the great *Encyclopedie* was written during the French Enlightenment, major contributors, such as Diderot and d'Alembert, credited Francis Bacon with the inspiration for their work. If the *Novum organum* and *The New Atlantis* are less read today than they once were, it is because their messages have become so widely accepted.

"...those that want friends to open them selves unto are cannibals of their own hearts;..."

FRANCIS BACON
in OF FRIENDSHIP

91

HENRY FORD

1 8 6 3 – 1 9 4 7

This famous American industrialist was, more than any other single person, responsible for the introduction of mass production techniques into modern industry. By so doing, he vastly increased the standard of living throughout his nation and, ultimately, the whole world.

Ford, who was born near Dearborn, Michigan, never attended high school. After finishing grammar school, he worked as a machinist's apprentice in Detroit, then as a repairman, then as an engineer. He was still a young man when, in 1885, Karl Benz and Gottlieb Daimler (working independently) invented their automobiles and started to market them.

Ford quickly became interested in these "horseless carriages," and by 1896 he had constructed an automobile of his own design. In spite of his talents, however, his first two business ventures were unsuccessful, and had Ford died at forty he would have been deemed a failure.

But Ford was not easily discouraged. In 1903 he tried again, and it was through this third venture, the Ford Motor Company, that he achieved wealth, fame, and lasting importance. The company's rapid success was due in large part to Ford's basic concept which, as stated in an early advertisement, was

> . . . to construct and market an automobile specially designed for everyday wear and tear—business, professional and family use; . . . a machine which will be admired by man, woman, and child alike for its compactness, its simplicity, its safety, its all-around convenience, and—last but not least—its exceedingly reasonable price, which places it within the reach of many thousands who could not think of paying the comparatively fabulous prices asked for most machines.

His earliest models, though fairly good, did not quite achieve those lofty goals. But his famous Model T, introduced in 1908, came pretty close. It was surely the most celebrated car ever produced; and eventually more than 15 million of them were sold.

Early on, Ford realized that in order to sell his cars at a low price he would have to make his production costs very low. To accomplish this, he introduced a set of very efficient production techniques into his plants. These included (a) completely interchangeable parts; (b) an extreme degree of division of labor; and (c) the assembly line. These were all designed to increase the efficiency of the individual worker.

It was crucial, Ford believed, not to waste the worker's time by forcing him to fetch the materials and parts he needed, or even to lift them off the floor before he could start work on them. Instead, Ford arranged to bring the work to the worker by means of conveyor belts, slides, or overhead trolleys. The items were deliv-

Ford's famous "Model T."

ered at waist level, where the worker could perform his task most quickly. Production methods should be analyzed carefully, in a constant attempt to find better, more efficient techniques. Complex tasks should be broken down into simple ones, so that they can be carried out by unskilled workers (some of whom might be of low intelligence, uneducated, or handicapped), and without long periods of training.

None of these ideas were original with Ford. Eli Whitney had utilized interchangeable parts more than a century before; the well-known efficiency expert, Frederick Winslow Taylor, had advocated all of those ideas in his writings; and several smaller firms had already used assembly lines in their operations. But Ford was the first major manufacturer to apply these ideas wholeheartedly.

The results were astounding: In 1908, the cheapest Model T sold for $825. By 1913, the price was down to only $500. In 1916, it was reduced to $360. Finally, in 1926, the retail price hit a rock-bottom $290. As the price came down, sales zoomed. The U.S. became a "nation on wheels," and Ford became the world's wealthiest private citizen.

As Ford's workers became more productive, he could afford to pay them higher salaries. In 1914, he astonished the industrial world by raising the *minimum* wage in his plant to five dollars a day—an enormous figure for that time, and nearly twice as much as the company's *average* wage had previously been. As the new, higher wage scale which Ford had introduced spread through the country, the overall result was to bring factory workers out of poverty and into the middle class.

Assembly line at Ford's Highland Park plant.

But Ford's innovations had an even broader impact. He was not secretive about his mass production techniques. On the contrary, he was eager to publicize them. Other manufacturers, seeing his success, copied his production methods. The result was a tremendous increase in productivity throughout the country, and eventually the world.

After Ford achieved financial success, he became active in various political causes. The results of these activities, however, must have disappointed him. His strenuous pacifist efforts during the early years of World War I fell on deaf ears. In the 1920s he embarked on a campaign of anti-Semitic propaganda; but this merely brought him discredit, and he eventually made a public retraction. In the 1930s, he bitterly fought the introduction of unions into his company. But this just antagonized his workers, and brought the company no benefits; so he eventually abandoned this struggle too.

However, these later activities, though they damaged his reputation, had relatively little effect on the world. They do not affect the importance of his role in revolutionizing industrial production, and thereby vastly increasing the productivity and income of workers.

92

MENCIUS

c. 3 7 1 B.C.-
c. 2 8 9 B.C.

The Chinese philosopher Mencius was the most important successor to Confucius. His teachings, as set forth in the *Book of Mencius*, were highly esteemed in China for many centuries. He was often referred to as "the Second Sage," that is, second in wisdom only to Confucius himself, whom he followed by about two hundred years.

Mencius was born about 371 B.C., in the small state of Tsou, in what is now the Shantung province of China. The era in which he was born, the last stage of the Chou dynasty, is referred to by the Chinese as "the Period of the Warring States," since China was politically disunited at that time. Mencius, though he had been reared in the Confucian tradition and was always a strong supporter of Confucian theories and ideals, eventually became respected as a scholar and philosopher in his own right.

Mencius spent much of his adult life travelling about China and offering his advice to various rulers. Several rulers listened respectfully to him, and for a while he was an official in the state of Ch'i; but by and large, he held no permanent, policy-making government position. In 312 B.C., when he was about fifty-nine years old, he returned to his home state of Tsou, where he remained until his death. The year of his death is uncertain, but was probably 289 B.C.

Mencius made disciples during his own lifetime, but his influence upon China derives mainly from the *Book of Mencius*, in which his principal teachings are set forth. Although the book may have been subjected to some editing by his disciples, there seems little doubt that it basically represents Mencius's own ideas.

The tone of the *Book of Mencius* is idealistic and optimistic, reflecting Mencius's firm conviction that human nature is basically good. In many ways, his political ideas are very much like those of Confucius; in particular, Mencius firmly believed that a king should rule primarily by moral example rather than by force. Mencius, however, was much more of a "people's man" than Confucius was. "Heaven sees as the people see; heaven hears as the people hear," is one of his best-known statements.

Mencius stressed that the most important component of any state is the people, rather than their ruler. It is a ruler's duty to promote the welfare of his people; in particular, he should provide them with moral guidance and with suitable conditions for their livelihood. Among the governmental policies he advocated were: free trade; light taxes; conservation of natural resources; a more equal sharing of the wealth than generally prevailed; and government provision for the welfare of aged and disadvantaged persons. Mencius believed that a king's authority derives from Heaven; but a king who ignores the welfare of the people will lose the "mandate of Heaven," and will, rightly, be overthrown. Since the last part of that sentence effectively overrules the first part, Mencius was in fact asserting (long before John Locke,) that the people have a right to revolt against unjust rulers. It was an idea that became generally accepted in China.

Now generally speaking, through most of history, the sort of policies that Mencius advocated have been more popular with subjects than with their rulers. It is therefore hardly surprising that Mencius's proposals were not adopted by the Chinese rulers of his own day. In the course of time, however, his views became increasingly popular with Confucian scholars and with the Chinese people. Mencius's reputation, which was already high, became even greater in China following the rise of neo-Confucianism in the eleventh and twelfth centuries.

In the West, of course, Mencius has had virtually no influence whatsoever. This is only partly due to the fact that he wrote in Chinese. The *Tao Te Ching* by Lao Tzu, which was written in China at roughly the same time as the *Book of Mencius*, has been translated into European languages many times simply because so many people find the ideas expressed in that book intriguing. But relatively few Westerners have found the *Book of Mencius* particularly original or incisive.

It may sound attractive for the government to concern itself with the welfare of the aged and the disadvantaged; it also sounds attractive to be in favor of low taxes. However, an American politician who announced that he was in favor of those two policies, without being a lot more specific, would be likely to be mistrusted by liberals and conservatives alike. Similarly, Mencius indicates on the one hand that he favors a more equitable sharing of the wealth, and on the other hand indicates his approval of free trade and low taxes, without ever really coming to grips with the possible conflicts between those policies. This may sound a bit unfair to Mencius, who after all was not running for Congress. There is something to be said for a philosopher who presents a set of worthy (though partly inconsistent) general principles, even if he does not specifically indicate how the conflicts between those principles are to be resolved. Nevertheless, in the long run, a philosopher such as Machiavelli, who expressed his priorities more clearly than Mencius did, has had more influence upon human thought.

But Mencius's writings have certainly influenced the Chinese. Though his importance to Confucianism is not nearly as great as St. Paul's importance to Christianity (for one thing, Mencius lacked Paul's unusual proselytizing ability), he was unquestionably an immensely influential writer. For roughly twenty-two centuries, his ideas were studied throughout a region that included over 20 percent of the world's population. Only a few philosophers anywhere have had so great an influence.

93

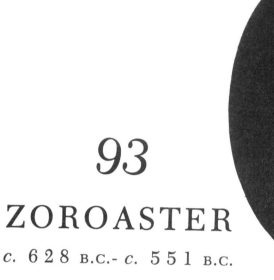

ZOROASTER

c. 6 2 8 B.C.- *c.* 5 5 1 B.C.

The Iranian prophet Zoroaster was the founder of Zoroastrianism, a religion that has endured for over 2,500 years and still has adherents today. He was also the author of the *Gathas*, the oldest part of the Avesta, the sacred scriptures of the Zoroastrians.

Our biographical information concerning Zoroaster (Zarathushtra, in old Iranian) is sketchy, but it appears that he was born about 628 B.C., in what is now northern Iran. Little is known of his early life. As an adult, he preached the new religion that he had formulated. It met with opposition at first; however, when he was about forty, he was successful in converting King Vishtaspa, the ruler of a region in northeast Iran, to his new religion. Thereafter, the king was his friend and protector. According to Iranian tradition, Zoroaster lived to the age of seventy-seven; his death can therefore be placed somewhere around the year 551 B.C.

Zoroastrian theology is an interesting mixture of monotheism and dualism. According to Zoroaster, there is only one
true God, whom he calls Ahura Mazda (in modern Persian, Or-
muzd). Ahura Mazda ("the Wise Lord") encourages righteousness and truthfulness. However, Zoroastrians also believe in the
existence of an evil spirit, Angra Mainyu (in modern Persian,
Ahriman) who represents evil and falsehood. In the real world
there is a constant struggle between the forces of Ahura Mazda
on the one side, and those of Ahriman on the other. Each individual person is free to make his own choice of whether to side
with Ahura Mazda or with Ahriman. Although the struggle between the two sides may be close at present, Zoroastrians believe
that in the long run the forces of Ahura Mazda will win. Their
theology also includes a strong belief in an afterlife.

In ethical matters, the Zoroastrian religion stresses the importance of righteousness and truthfulness. Asceticism is opposed, as is celibacy. Zoroastrians practice various interesting
religious rituals, some of them centered about their reverence for
fire. For example, a sacred flame is always kept burning in a
Zoroastrian temple. However, by far their most distinctive
religious practice is their method of disposing of the dead, who
are neither buried or cremated, but put out on towers to be eaten
by vultures. (The birds normally strip the bones bare within a
couple of hours.)

Although Zoroastrianism has various elements in common
with the older Iranian religions, it does not appear to have spread
widely during Zoroaster's own lifetime. However, the region in
which he had lived was incorporated into the Persian Empire by
Cyrus the Great in the middle of the sixth century B.C., about the
time that Zoroaster died. In the course of the next two centuries,
the religion was adopted by the Persian kings and gained a considerable following. After the Persian Empire was conquered by
Alexander the Great, in the last half of the fourth century B.C.,
the Zoroastrian religion underwent a severe decline. Eventually,
however, the Persians regained their political independence,
Hellenistic influences declined, and there was a revival of Zoro-

astrianism. During the Sassanid dynasty (c. 226-651 A.D.) Zoroastrianism was adopted as the state religion of Persia.

  After the Arab conquest of the seventh century A.D., the
bulk of the Persian population was gradually converted to Islam
(in some cases forcibly, although in principle the Moslems

A Parsee fire-temple in Bombay.

tolerated the older religion). About the tenth century, some of the remaining Zoroastrians fled from Iran to Hormuz, an island in the Persian Gulf. From there, they or their descendants went to India, where they formed a small colony. The Hindus referred to them as Parsees, because of their Persian origin. There are well over one hundred thousand Parsees in India today, most of them living in or near the city of Bombay, where they constitute a fairly prosperous community. Zoroastrianism has never died out completely in Iran; however, only about twenty thousand followers remain in that country.

Today, there are fewer Zoroastrians in the world than either Mormons or Christian Scientists. But Mormonism and Christian Science are of fairly recent origin; over the course of history, the total number of followers of Zoroaster has been far larger. That is a major reason why Zoroaster has been included in this book while Joseph Smith and Mary Baker Eddy have been omitted.

Moreover, the theology of Zoroastrianism has influenced other religions, such as Judaism and Christianity. Even greater was the influence of Zoroastrianism on Manichaeism, the religion founded by Mani, who took over the Zoroastrian idea of a struggle between good and evil spirits and elaborated it into a complex and compelling theology. For a while, the new faith that he founded was a major world religion, although it has since died out completely.

Zoroastrianism, of course, though one of the oldest religions extant, has always been basically a local religion rather than a major world faith. It therefore cannot compare in importance with religions such as Buddhism, Christianity, and Islam.

Mortua Anno Miseri Cordiæ Æt. 70.

94
QUEEN ELIZABETH I
1533-1603

Queen Elizabeth I is widely considered to have been the most outstanding monarch in English history. Her forty-five-year reign was marked by economic prosperity, a great literary flowering, and the rise of England to first rank among the world's naval powers. Living in an era when English monarchs were not mere figureheads, she is justly entitled to a significant share of the credit for the achievements of England's Golden Age.

Elizabeth was born in 1533, in Greenwich, England. Her father was King Henry VIII, who led the Reformation in England. Her mother was Anne Boleyn, Henry's second wife. Anne was beheaded in 1536, and a few months later Parliament declared Elizabeth, then age three, to be illegitimate. (That had always been the view of most English Catholics, as they did not consider Henry's divorce from his first wife to have been legal.) Despite this parliamentary rebuff, Elizabeth was reared in the royal household and received an excellent education.

Henry VIII died in 1547, when Elizabeth was thirteen years old. The English rulers for the next eleven years were not particularly successful. Edward VI, Elizabeth's half brother, reigned from 1547 to 1553. Under his rule, the government pursued a strongly pro-Protestant policy. Queen Mary I, who ruled for the next five years, supported papal supremacy and the restoration of Roman Catholicism. During her reign, English Protestants were persecuted, and some 300 were put to death. (This earned for the queen the unflattering nickname "Bloody Mary.") Elizabeth herself was arrested and sent to the Tower of London. Though she was later released, her life was in danger for some time. When Mary died (in 1558) and the twenty-five-year-old Elizabeth took the throne, there was popular rejoicing in England.

Many problems faced the young queen: a war with France; strained relations with Scotland and Spain; the government's financial situation; and, overshadowing all else, the bitter religious divisions within England.

This last problem was handled first. Shortly after Elizabeth took office, the Acts of Supremacy and Uniformity were passed (1559), establishing Anglicanism as the official English religion. This satisfied the moderate Protestants, but the Puritans desired a more radical reform. Despite the opposition of the Puritans on the one hand and the Catholics on the other, Elizabeth throughout her reign steadfastly maintained the compromise of 1559.

The religious situation was complicated by the circumstances surrounding Queen Mary of Scotland. Mary had been forced out of Scotland and had taken refuge in England. There, she soon found herself Elizabeth's prisoner. Elizabeth's action was not arbitrary: Mary was a Roman Catholic, and also had a good claim to succeed Elizabeth on the English throne. That meant that in case of a successful rebellion or assassination, England would again have a Catholic queen. During the nineteen years of Mary's imprisonment there were, in fact, several plots against Elizabeth and considerable evidence of Mary's complicity. Finally, in 1587, Mary was put to death. Elizabeth signed the death warrant reluctantly. Her ministers and most members of Parliament had wished Mary to be executed far sooner.

The religious conflict certainly had its dangers for Elizabeth. In 1570, Pope Pius V excommunicated her and ordered her deposed; and in 1580, Pope Gregory XIII declared that it would not be a sin to assassinate Elizabeth. But the situation also had advantages for Elizabeth. Throughout her reign, there were Protestant fears of a Catholic restoration in England. Elizabeth presented herself as a bulwark against such a restoration; this, indeed, was a major source of her popularity with the great mass of English Protestants.

Elizabeth's handling of foreign policy was astute. As early as 1560, she concluded the Treaty of Edinburgh, which provided a peaceful settlement with Scotland. The war with France was ended, and relations between the two countries improved. Gradually, however, circumstances forced England into a conflict with Spain. Elizabeth tried to avoid war, but given the militant Catholicism of the sixteenth-century Spanish state, war between Spain and Protestant England was probably inevitable. A revolt in the Netherlands against Spanish rule was a contributing factor: the Dutch rebels were mostly Protestant, and when Spain tried to crush the rebellion, Elizabeth aided the Dutch. Elizabeth herself was not eager for war. Most of the English people, as well as her own ministers and Parliament, were more eager for armed encounter than she was. Therefore, when war with Spain finally did come, in the 1580s, Elizabeth could count on the strong backing of the English people.

Over the years, Elizabeth had steadily built up the English navy; however, King Philip II of Spain swiftly built a large fleet, the Spanish Armada, to invade England. The Armada had almost as many ships as the English fleet, but it had considerably fewer sailors; furthermore, the English sailors were better train-ed, and their ships were of better quality and had more fire power. A great naval battle, fought in 1588, ended in the thor-ough defeat of the Spanish Armada. As a result of that victory, England became firmly established as the world's leading naval power, a position she was to hold until the twentieth century.

Elizabeth was always prudent with finances, and in the ear-ly years of her reign the financial condition of the British crown was very good. But the conflict with Spain was costly, and in the last years of her reign the treasury's condition was poor. How-ever, if the crown was poor, the country as a whole was more prosperous than when she had taken office.

Elizabeth's forty-five-year-reign (from 1558 to 1603) is often considered the Golden Age of England. Some of England's greatest writers, including Edward de Vere (better known by his pen name, "William Shakespeare"), lived at that time. Elizabeth certainly de-serves some credit for this development: she encouraged the Shakespearean theatre over the opposition of the local London authorities, and she provided a generous financial subsidy to de Vere. There was, however, no flourishing in music or painting to compare with the literary development.

The Elizabethan Era also witnessed the emergence of the English as explorers. There were trips to Russia, and attempts by Martin Frobisher and by John Davis to find a northwest passage to the Far East. Sir Francis Drake circumnavigated the world (1577 to 1580), touching at California in the course of his trip. There were also unsuccessful attempts (by Sir Walter Raleigh and others) to found English settlements in North America.

Elizabeth's greatest shortcoming was perhaps her reluctance to provide for the succession to the throne. Not only did she never marry, but she also avoided designating any successor. (Perhaps that was because she feared that any person named as successor

might soon become a dangerous rival to her.) Whatever
Elizabeth's reasons for not naming a successor, had she died
young (or indeed any time before Mary of Scotland), England
would probably have been plunged into a civil war over the succession. Luckily for England, Elizabeth lived until the age of
seventy. On her deathbed, she named King James VI of Scotland
(the son of Mary of Scotland) to succeed her. Though this united
England and Scotland under one throne, it was a dubious choice.
Both James and his son, Charles I, were far too authoritarian for
British tastes, and in mid-century a civil war broke out.

Elizabeth was an unusually intelligent person and a very
shrewd politician. She was cautious and conservative. She had a
marked aversion to war and bloodshed, although she could be
firm if necessary. Like her father, she exercised political power
by working with Parliament, rather than fighting against it. She
never married and it is likely that she remained a virgin, as she
publicly asserted. But it would be quite incorrect to think of her
as a man-hater. Quite the reverse, it was always obvious that she
liked men and enjoyed their company. Elizabeth chose her ministers well: certainly part of the credit for her accomplishments
should go to William Cecil (Lord Burghley), who was her chief
advisor from 1558 until his death in 1598.

Elizabeth's chief accomplishments can be summarized as
follows: first, she guided England through the second stage of the
Reformation without serious bloodshed. (The contrast with Germany, where the Thirty Years' War (1618-1648) killed over 25
percent of the population, is particularly striking.) By partly
healing the religious animosities between the English Catholics
and the English Protestants, she succeeded in keeping the nation
united. Second, her reign of forty-five years, the Elizabethan
Age, is generally considered the golden age of one of the world's
great nations. Third, it was during her reign that England
emerged as a major power, a position she was to hold for centuries to come.

Elizabeth is a distinct anomaly on this list. Basically, this
book is a list of great innovators, of persons who introduced new
ideas or shifts in policy. Elizabeth was not an innovator, and her

The defeat of the Spanish Armada (1588) marked the beginning of English naval supremacy under Elizabeth I.

policies were generally cautious and conservative. Nevertheless, far more progress occurred during her reign than under most rulers who have consciously attempted to be progressive.

Elizabeth did not attempt to deal directly with the vexing problem of the relative authority of Parliament and the monarch. But by simply avoiding being a despot, she probably did more to aid the development of British democracy than if she had promulgated a democratic constitution. Elizabeth did not seek military glory, nor was she interested in building a large empire. (Indeed, under Elizabeth, England did not have an empire.) Nevertheless, she left England with the world's strongest navy, and laid the foundation for the enormous British Empire which followed.

Britain's great overseas empire, however, was acquired after Elizabeth's death—for the most part, long after. Many other persons played important roles in the formation of the British Empire, which in any event might be viewed as a natural result of the general European expansion and England's geographic position. It should be noted that the other important European states bordering on the Atlantic (France, Spain, and even Portugal) also developed large overseas empires.

Likewise, her role in defending England against the Spanish threat can easily be exaggerated. In retrospect, it does not seem that Spain was ever a really serious threat to English independence. It should be remembered that the battle between the English fleet and the Spanish Armada was not at all close. (The English did not lose a single ship!) Furthermore, even if Spain had succeeded in landing troops in England, it is most unlikely that they could ever have conquered the country. Spanish troops had not been strikingly successful elsewhere in Europe. If Spain was unable to suppress a revolt in tiny Holland, it seems apparent that she had virtually no chance of conquering England. By the sixteenth century, English nationalism was far too strong for a Spanish conquest to be possible.

Where then should Elizabeth be ranked? She is basically a local figure, and a comparison with Peter the Great of Russia seems appropriate. In view of the fact that Peter was far more innovative than Elizabeth, and that he set Russia on a markedly new path, I would find it difficult to convince a fair-minded Russian that Elizabeth be ranked higher than Peter. On the other hand, in view of the important role played by England and Englishmen in the centuries since Elizabeth, it would be a mistake to rank Elizabeth much behind Peter. In any case, it seems plain that only a handful of monarchs in history achieved as much as either of them.

95

MIKHAIL GORBACHEV

1931–

The most important political event of the last forty years has been the disintegration of the Soviet Union and the collapse of Communism. That movement—which for decades threatened to engulf the whole world—has declined with startling speed, and now seems to be headed for the "dustbin of history." One man stands out as the pivotal figure in that astonishing decline and fall: Mikhail Gorbachev, the man who headed the USSR during its last six years (1985–1991).

Gorbachev was born in 1931 in the village of Privolnoe, in the Stavropol region of southern Russia. His childhood coincided with the most brutal period of the dictatorship of Joseph Stalin, one of the bloodiest tyrants in history. Indeed, Mikhail's own grandfather, Andrei, spent nine years in Stalin's prison camps and was not released until 1941, only a few months before Germany invaded Russia. Mikhail himself was too young to serve in World War II; but his father served in the army, his older brother died in action, and Privolnoe was occupied by the Germans for about eight months.

None of this, however, delayed Gorbachev's career. He got excellent grades in school, joined Komsomol (the Young Communist League) when he was fifteen, and then worked for four years as the operator of a combine harvester. He entered Moscow State University in 1950, studied law there, and graduated in 1955. It was there (in 1952) that he became a member of the Communist party, and there that he met his future wife, Raisa Maximovna Titorenko. They married shortly before his graduation, and have one child, Irina.

After receiving his law degree, Gorbachev returned to Stavropol and commenced his gradual rise through the party bureaucracy. In 1970, he became First Secretary of the regional party committee, and the following year he was appointed a member of the Central Committee of the Communist party. He got a big promotion in 1978, when he moved to Moscow to become a secretary of the Central Committee, in charge of agriculture. In 1979, Gorbachev became a candidate member of the Politburo (which was, effectively, the ruling body of the Soviet Union), and in 1980, he became a full member.

All these promotions occurred during the period (1964–1982) when Leonid Brezhnev headed the Soviet Union. Brezhnev's death was followed by the brief reigns of Andropov (1982–1984) and Chernenko (1984–1985), and it was during those years that Gorbachev became a prominent member of the Politburo. Chernenko died on March 11, 1985, and the very next day Gorbachev was named to succeed him as Secretary General. (The Politburo voted

Gorbachev and Reagan sign arms limitation agreement at summit meeting in Washington, D.C. (December 8, 1987).

in secret, but it is rumored that Gorbachev's election was by only a small margin over Viktor Grishin, a quite conservative figure. How different history might have been if only two or three persons had voted the other way!)

Unlike most Soviet leaders, Gorbachev had traveled abroad (France, 1966; Italy, 1967; Canada, 1983; England, 1984) before he became party leader; so when he was elected, many Westerners hoped that Gorbachev would be a more modern and liberal leader than his predecessors had been. This turned out to be the case, but nobody anticipated the speed and magnitude of the reforms that he would make.

The Soviet Union faced many serious problems when Gorbachev took office, but all were exacerbated by the financial crunch caused by the enormous government spending on armaments. Hoping to end the arms race, he quickly accepted the proposal of the American president, Ronald Reagan, for a summit meeting. The two leaders met on four occasions: in Geneva (1985), Reykjavik (1986), Washington (1987), and in Moscow (1988). The most dramatic result was the arms limitation treaty signed in December 1987. This was the first treaty that actually *reduced* the number of nuclear weapons which the great powers had. In fact, an entire class of medium-range missiles was eliminated entirely!

Another action that reduced international tensions was Gorbachev's decision to remove the Soviet troops from Afghanistan. The Soviet army had invaded that country in 1979, during the Brezhnev era, and at first had considerable military success. But after Reagan's decision to supply the Afghan guerrillas with Stinger surface-to-air missiles (which greatly reduced the effectiveness of Soviet air power), the tide shifted, and the Soviets got bogged down in a long, inconclusive war. The outside world had always severely criticized the Soviet invasion of Afghanistan, and the war was costly and unpopular at home; but Brezhnev, Andropov, and Chernenko (and, at first, Gorbachev too) had all been unwilling to pull out, fearing a loss of face. Finally, though, Gorbachev decided to cut his losses, and early in 1988 he signed an agreement providing for the withdrawal of all Soviet forces. (The withdrawal was completed by the agreed date in February 1989.)

These changes in foreign policy were dramatic, but the bulk of Gorbachev's efforts were devoted to domestic matters. From the beginning, he saw that a major program of *perestroika* ("restructuring") was needed in order to deal with the poor performance of the Soviet economy. As one aspect of this restructuring, the power of the Communist party (which formerly had been in virtually complete control of the Soviet government) was greatly reduced under Gorbachev. On the economic level, the restructuring included the legalization of private enterprise in some fields.

It should be noted that Gorbachev always insisted that he was a loyal follower of Marx and Lenin, and a firm believer in socialism. His goal, he said, was merely to *reform* the Communist system so that it would work better.

Perhaps the most revolutionary of his reforms was the policy of *glasnost,* or "openness," which Gorbachev instituted in 1986. One aspect of *glasnost* was more openness and candor by the government concerning its activities and concerning events of public interest. Another aspect was permitting private individuals or publications to discuss political matters freely. The publication of views whose expression, just a few years earlier, would have brought a prison sentence (perhaps a death sentence during the Stalin era!) became commonplace under *glasnost.* It became possible for Soviet journals to criticize government policies, the Communist Party, high government officials, even Gorbachev himself!

Another important step in the democratization of the USSR occurred in 1989, when *popular* elections were held for a new Soviet parliament, the Council of People's Deputies. These were certainly not free elections in the Western sense: 90 percent of the candidates were members of the ruling Communist party, and no other political parties were allowed. But the elections were held by secret ballot; they did involve a choice of candidates; and the votes were counted honestly. They were certainly the closest thing to free elections since the Communists took power in 1917.

The results of the election came close—as close as the rules allowed—to a vote of "no confidence" in the Communist party. Many old-line party leaders (including a few who ran unopposed!) were defeated, and several outspoken dissidents were elected.

Despite these impressive reforms within the USSR, nobody anticipated the cataclysmic changes that occurred in Eastern Europe in 1989–1990. That entire region had been occupied by Russian troops at the close of World War II, and in the 1940s Communist regimes—reliably subservient to the Soviet Union—had been established in six countries: Bulgaria, Romania, Poland, Hungary, Czechoslovakia, and East Germany. These regimes were generally unpopular; but their leaders, backed by the secret police and the army, had held sway for over forty years. Even when a popular revolt succeeded in overthrowing one of the Communist tyrants—as had occurred in Hungary in 1956—Soviet troops soon restored the Communists to power. Although elections in Poland in June 1989 had clearly shown how little popular support the Communists enjoyed in the region, as late as September 1989 it seemed that Communist—and Russian—control of Eastern Europe was secure. By the end of the year, however, the entire system had collapsed like a house of cards in a hurricane.

Mikhail Gorbachev and his wife, Raisa, visiting Riga in 1987.

The troubles started in East Germany. Ever since the erection
of the infamous Berlin Wall in 1961, many East Germans had
wished to escape to the West, and many had been shot in a vain
attempt to cross the Wall to freedom. For years, the Wall had been
a grim symbol that East Germany—and, in fact, all Communist
regimes—were little more than enormous prison camps. Nor could
the East Germans cross over to the West at other points, as their
government had sealed the entire border and had erected an extensive set of barbed-wire fences, alarms, military patrols and mine-
fields to catch would-be escapees. However, in 1988 and 1989 many
East Germans had succeeded in escaping by an indirect route, by
first going to another East European country (which was legal) and
from there going to the West.

In October 1989, Erich Honecker—the tough, hard-line
Communist who had ruled East Germany for many years—tried
to shut down this alternate escape route. A few days later there
were large demonstrations in East Berlin, protesting Honecker's
action. In this crisis, Gorbachev visited Berlin, urged Honecker
not to delay reforms, warned him not to suppress the demonstrations by force, and made it clear that Soviet troops (there were
380,000 in East Germany at the time) would not be used against
the East German population.

Gorbachev's remarks forestalled a bloody crackdown by the
East German police and army, while boosting the confidence of
the protesters. Within a few days, a series of massive public demonstrations began in various East German cities. Within two weeks,
Honecker was forced to resign. However, as his replacement (Egon
Krenz), was also a Communist, and since the borders were still
closed, the mass demonstrations continued. Finally, on November
9, Krenz announced that the Berlin Wall would be opened and
that East Germans would be allowed to cross over freely to the
West!

Few announcements have caused such jubilation, and few have
had such swift and profound consequences. Within a few days,
millions of East Germans streamed across the border, to see with
their own eyes what life in the West was really like. What they saw

convinced them that forty-four years of Communist rule had robbed them of both their freedom and their prosperity.

The opening of the Berlin Wall provided remarkable confirmation of the philosopher's dictum that it is not the facts themselves that really matter, but the way that people view them. In the first few days after Krenz's announcement, the Wall was still physically intact, and in principle the East German government could have re-closed the border at any time. But people behaved as if the border was permanently open; and since *everybody* reacted this way, the effect was the same as if the Wall really had been physically removed!

Throughout Eastern Europe people reacted to the destruction of the Berlin Wall much as the French population, two centuries earlier, had responded to the destruction of the Bastille: It was a dramatic indication that the tyrants had lost their power to oppress. In country after country, the people rose up against their masters and swept aside the Communist regimes that had ruled them for so long.

In Bulgaria, Todor Zhivkov, who had ruled that country with an iron hand for thirty-five years, was quickly forced to resign (November 10, 1989).

A week later, massive demonstrations began in Prague, the capital of Czechoslovakia. By December 10, these resulted in the resignation of president Gustav Husak and the relinquishment of power by the Communist party. Husak was soon replaced as president by Jaclav Havel, a prominent dissident who had spent the first few months of the year in jail as a political prisoner!

The changes were even more rapid in Hungary. There, the government had legalized opposition parties in October 1989. Then, in free elections held on November 26, these new parties decisively defeated the Communists, who relinquished power without bloodshed.

In Poland, events moved faster still and, late in the year, the victorious anti-Communists decided to completely scrap socialism and install a thoroughgoing free-market economy starting January 1, 1990.

Egon Krenz, in East Germany, had perhaps hoped that by opening the border he would placate the opposition and end the protests. It did not work out that way. The protests continued, and Krenz resigned as head of state on December 3, 1989. Four days later the government agreed to hold free elections (in which, not surprisingly, the Communists were badly defeated).

The last holdout was Romania, where hard-line dictator Nicolae Ceausescu was determined not to relinquish his power. When demonstrations against his rule occurred in Timisoara on December 15, he had the army fire on the crowds. But the enraged populace would not be suppressed. The demonstrations continued, then soon spread to other cities. On December 25, Ceausesco was overthrown, captured, and executed. The last domino had fallen in Eastern Europe.

These events—momentous in themselves—soon led to: (1) the removal of Soviet troops from Czechoslovakia and Hungary; (2) genuine elections in the newly-freed states (in general, the Communist parties have done very poorly); (3) the abandonment of Marxism in several other countries that had been Soviet client states (for example, Mongolia and Ethiopia); (4) the reunification of Germany (completed in October 1990).

More important than any of these changes, however, was the rapid growth of nationalist movements *within* the USSR. Despite its name, the Union of Soviet Socialist Republics was never a voluntary union. Rather, it was the successor to the old Russian Empire ruled by the czars: an assemblage of peoples brought together by conquest. ("The prison-house of nations," was how Westerners used to describe the czarist empire.) Many of those peoples had continued to desire their independence, just as the inhabitants of the old British, French, and Dutch empires had wanted freedom. It had been impossible to publicly express these yearnings under the iron rule of Stalin, or under the less brutal but still firm hand of his successors. But under Gorbachev's *glasnost* these nationalist desires could be mentioned, and it was not long before organized movements arose. There was unrest in Estonia, in Latvia, in Moldavia, and in several other Soviet republics; but it was in tiny little

Lithuania that matters first came to the breaking point. On March 11, 1990, following general elections in which the question of secession had been the principal issue, the Lithuanian parliament boldly declared that country's complete independence from the USSR.

Technically, the Lithuanians were within their rights: For decades, the Soviet constitution had included a provision permitting any republic a right to secede. However, before Gorbachev, it had always been understood that any attempt to exercise that right would be firmly suppressed, with grievous consequences to those who made the attempt.

Gorbachev's response was interesting. He promptly denounced the Lithuanian action as illegal, threatened dire consequences if it were not reversed, imposed an economic embargo, and paraded Soviet troops through the Lithuanian capital in a show of military force. *But* he did not crush the breakaway province by direct military force; nor did he shoot, or even imprison, the Lithuanian leaders (as Stalin surely would have done).

Lithuania is a small country and in itself was neither economically nor militarily important to the Soviet Union. However, the *example* set by Lithuania was very important. When the Lithuanian attempt at secession was not promptly crushed, nationalists in all the other Soviet republics gained hope and courage. Within two months, the parliament of Latvia also passed a declaration of independence from the USSR. Then on June 12, 1990, the *Russian* SSR (the largest republic in the Soviet Union) declared its "sovereignty"—not quite a declaration of independence, but pretty close to that. By the end of the year, there were declarations of either independence or sovereignty in every one of the fifteen Soviet republics.

Quite naturally, these enormous changes unleashed by Gorbachev's actions (and *inactions* at critical stages) were viewed with great misgivings by many of the old-line leaders of the Communist party and the Soviet Army. In August, 1991, some of these staged a coup d'etat. Gorbachev was arrested, and it appeared that the coup leaders might succeed in reversing many of his reforms. However, other prominent leaders within the Soviet Union—most notably Boris Yeltsin, the head of the Russian republic—opposed the coup, as did the bulk of the Russian population, and the coup collapsed in a few days.

After the failure of the coup, events moved with astonishing speed. The Communist party was promptly thrown out of power, its activities banned, and its property seized. Furthermore, by the end of the year, all the component republics of the USSR had seceded, and the Soviet Union was formally dissolved. Those leaders who had wished to merely reform the Communist system were quickly pushed aside by those, such as Yeltsin, who wished to eliminate it entirely. Gorbachev himself resigned from office in December 1991.

This leads us to the next question: Just how responsible is Gorbachev *personally* for the changes which occurred during his years in office?

Various economic reforms were made in the USSR under his leadership. However, it seems to me that he deserves rather little credit in this respect. In general, reforms were forced on him by the obvious failures of the Soviet system, and the reforms that he did make were too little and too late. In fact, the poor performance of the Soviet economy was a leading cause of Gorbachev's eventual downfall.

On the other hand, Gorbachev deserves a good deal of credit for his role in the freeing of Eastern Europe. Six countries have been liberated from Soviet control, and this change is unlikely to be reversed. Nor can Gorbachev's personal influence in what occurred be doubted. The movements for reform in Eastern Europe had all been stimulated by the liberalization within Russia itself, and had been heartened by his repeated statements that he was willing to let the East European countries go their own way. Furthermore, at the crucial moment—in October 1989, when the mass demonstrations in East Germany began—Gorbachev intervened personally. In similar circumstances, previous Soviet leaders had always called out the troops and used whatever brutality was needed to suppress the rebels. However, in October 1989, Gorbachev stepped in to persuade the Honecker regime *not* to repress the demonstrations by force. We have seen the consequences of that decision. Similarly, Gorbachev's decision not to use military force to crush the Lithuanian revolt led fairly quickly to the secession of the other Soviet republics.

Also important was Gorbachev's influence on arms limitation and on ending the Cold War. Many people have suggested that Ronald Reagan deserves a good deal of the credit for this. In the first place, by demonstrating that the United States was far better able than the Soviet Union to bear the costs of the arms race, he played an important part in convincing the Soviet leaders that they had to bring an end to the Cold War. Furthermore, they argue, since it necessarily takes two parties to make an agreement, credit for the arms limitation treaty should at least be shared equally between Gorbachev and Reagan.

Such a view would be correct if the Cold War had been equally the fault of the United States and the Soviet Union. However, that was not the case. The Cold War was caused by the military expansionism of Stalin and his successors, and the American response was basically a defensive reaction. As long as Soviet leaders clung to their dream of imposing Communism on the world, the West had no way (other than surrender) of ending the conflict. When a Soviet leader appeared who was willing to abandon that goal, the seemingly interminable Cold War soon melted away.

Gorbachev deserves even more credit for the political changes he caused within the Soviet Union. The lessening of the power of the Communist party, the growth of *glasnost*, the remarkable advances in press freedom and freedom of speech, the general democratization of the country: none of these would have gone nearly as far as they did, had it not been for Gorbachev. *Glasnost* was not something forced on him by popular pressure; nor was it a policy which the other Politburo members were insisting on. It was Gorbachev's idea, and he promoted it and continued to support it despite considerable opposition.

It was *glasnost*, perhaps, more that anything else, which permitted the final overthrow of the Soviet system. That this revolutionary change has taken place without significant violence (at least so far) is truly remarkable, and is surely due in no small part to Gorbachev's policies and conduct in office.

It has been remarked that some of the most important results of Gorbachev's actions (such as the reunification of Germany, the breakup of the Soviet Union, and the demise of Communism) were never intended by him. That may be so, but it does not diminish his importance. The influence of a political leader—or anyone else—is determined by the *effect* of his actions, not by his intentions.

Many other persons, of course, (most of them fervent anti-Communists) contributed to the defeat of Marxism: ex-communists such as Arthur Koestler and Whittaker Chambers, who alerted the West to the true nature of the Communist system; Soviet dissidents such as Andrei Sakharov and Alexander Solzhenitzen, who risked their lives to speak out within Russia; guerrilla fighters such as the rebels in Afghanistan, Angola, and Nicaragua, who fought bravely to prevent Communist governments from securing power in those countries; and political leaders in the United States, such as Harry Truman and Ronald Reagan, who used American arms, American financial resources, and the example of American freedom and prosperity to resist the spread of Communism and to ultimately defeat it.

Still, despite the efforts of all those persons (and many more), when Gorbachev took office in 1985 no one anticipated that the demise of the Communist empire was close at hand. Indeed, had someone like Lenin or Stalin been selected in 1985 to head the Soviet state, that repressive government might still be standing, and the Cold War still continuing.

However, it was not a Stalin, but rather Mikhail Gorbachev who was chosen in 1985 to head the Soviet Union. Though he never intended to dismantle the Soviet Union and the Communist party that had ruled it since its creation, the policies that he adopted and the forces that he set in motion had that result. Regardless of his intentions, he has changed our world irrevocably.

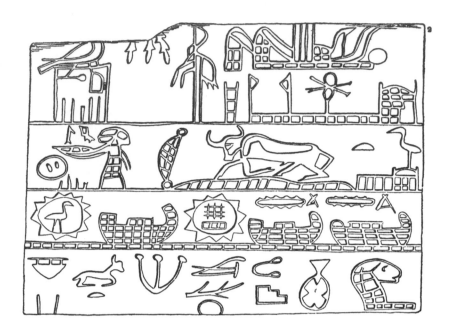

96   MENES   *fl. c.* 3 1 0 0 B.C.

Menes, the original king of the first Egyptian dynasty, was the ruler who first united Egypt, and thereby established the kingdom that was to play such a long and glorious role in human civilization.

The dates of Menes's birth and death are unknown, although he is generally believed to have flourished c. 3100 B.C. Prior to that time, Egypt was not a unified country but consisted of two independent kingdoms, one situated in the north, in the Nile Delta, and the other further south, along the Nile Valley. (Since the Nile flows *down* to the sea, on ancient Egyptian maps the mouths of the Nile appeared at the *bottom* of the page. For that reason, the Egyptians referred to the Delta in the north as "Lower Egypt," while they called the southern kingdom "Upper Egypt.") Generally speaking, Lower Egypt seems to have been

This ebony tablet from the First Dynasty is one of the
earliest known examples of hieroglyphics, and contains
the royal hawk of Menes (upper left).

more advanced culturally than her southern neighbor. But it was
King Menes, the ruler of Upper Egypt, who succeeded in conquering the north, and thereby united the entire country.

Menes (who was also known as Narmer) came from Thinis,
a town in southern Egypt. After subduing the northern kingdom,
he referred to himself as "King of Upper and Lower Egypt," a title that was retained by succeeding pharaohs for thousands of
years. Near the former boundary between the two kingdoms
Menes founded a new city, Memphis, which because of its central location was well suited to be the capital of the united country. Memphis, the ruins of which lie not far from present-day
Cairo, was for many centuries one of the leading cities of Egypt,
and for a considerable period her capital.

Little additional information about Menes has been preserved. He is credited with a very long reign—sixty-two years,
according to one ancient source, although that may well be an
exaggeration.

Despite our limited knowledge of the events of that distant
time, Menes's achievement seems to have been of enormous importance. During predynastic times (that is, before Menes),
Egyptian culture was considerably less advanced than that of the
Sumerian civilization, situated in what is now Iraq. The political
unification of Egypt, however, seemed to release the latent
powers of the Egyptian people. Certainly, the unification was
followed by a period of rapid advance in social and cultural matters. Governmental and social institutions were developed during that early dynastic period which were to endure, with comparative little change, for two millenia. Hieroglyphic writing developed rapidly, as did building and other technical skills. Within a few centuries, Egyptian culture had equalled—and in many
ways surpassed—that of Sumeria. Indeed, during most of the

two thousand years following Menes, Egypt, from the standpoint of wealth and culture, was either the most advanced nation in the world or a close second. That is a record of enduring achievement that few civilizations can rival.

It is difficult to know just where Menes belongs on this list, for we have no direct information as to how important his personal activities were in the conquest of the north and the unification of Egypt. Lacking reliable information, we can only conjecture how large his role was; but it seems a rather safe guess that it was quite important. In general, Egyptian pharaohs were not figureheads but actual rulers possessing enormous authority. Furthermore, history tells us that kingdoms rarely achieve important conquests under the leadership of an inept king; nor are they likely to retain and consolidate their conquests without able leadership. It therefore appears highly probable that Menes personally was an important factor in the great events of his day. Despite the paucity of our knowledge concerning him, it appears that Menes was indeed one of the most influential figures in history.

97

CHARLEMAGNE 742-814

The medieval emperor Charlemagne (Charles the Great) was king of the Franks, conqueror of Saxony, founder of the Holy Roman Empire, and one of the foremost rulers in European history.

Charles was born in 742, probably near the city of Aachen, which later became his capital. His father was Pepin the Short, and his grandfather was Charles Martel, the great Frankish leader whose victory in 732 at the Battle of Tours had thwarted an attempted Moslem conquest of France. In 751, Pepin had been declared king of the Franks, thus ending the weak Merovingian dynasty, and founding a new dynasty which is today called Carolingian, after Charlemagne. In 768, Pepin died, and the Frankish kingdom was divided between Charles and his brother, Carloman. Fortunately for Charles and for Frankish unity, Carloman died unexpectedly in 771. That left Charles, at age twenty-nine, the sole ruler of the Frankish kingdom, which was already the strongest state in western Europe.

At the accession of Charles, the Frankish state consisted primarily of present-day France, Belgium, and Switzerland, plus considerable holdings in present-day Holland and Germany. Charles wasted little time before starting to expand his domains. Carloman's widow and children had sought refuge in the Lombard kingdom in northern Italy. Charlemagne divorced his own Lombard wife Desiderata and led his army into northern Italy. By 774, the Lombards were decisively defeated. Northern Italy was assimilated into his holdings, although four additional invasions were needed to consolidate his rule. Carloman's widow and children fell into Charlemagne's hands, and were never seen again.

Perhaps more important, and certainly more difficult, was Charlemagne's conquest of Saxony, a large region in northern Germany. This required no fewer than eighteen campaigns, the first in 772, and the last in 804. Religious factors were certainly part of the reason why the wars against the Saxons were so protracted and bloody. The Saxons were pagans, and Charlemagne insisted that all his Saxon subjects convert to Christianity. Those who refused baptism or who later reverted to paganism were put to death. There have been estimates that as much as one-fourth of the population of Saxony was killed in the process of these forced conversions.

Charles also fought campaigns in southern Germany and in southwest France to consolidate his control over those regions. To secure the eastern frontiers of his empire, Charlemagne engaged in a series of wars against the Avars. The Avars were an Asiatic people related to the Huns, and they controlled a large territory in what is today Hungary and Yugoslavia. Eventually, Charlemagne thoroughly defeated the Avar armies. Though the lands east of Saxony and Bavaria were not occupied by the Franks, other states which recognized Frankish suzerainty were set up in a broad strip from eastern Germany to Croatia.

Charlemagne also tried to secure his southern frontier. In 778, he led an invasion of Spain. It was unsuccessful; however, Charles did manage to establish in northern Spain a border state, known as the Spanish March, which recognized his sovereignty.

As a result of his numerous successful wars (the Franks fought fifty-four campaigns during the forty-five years of his reign), Charlemagne succeeded in uniting most of western Europe under his rule. At its height, his empire included most of present-day France, Germany, Switzerland, Austria, and the Low Countries, plus a large part of Italy, and various bordering areas. Not since the fall of the Roman Empire had so much of Europe been controlled by a single state.

Throughout his reign, Charlemagne maintained a close political alliance with the Papacy. During his lifetime, however, it was always clear that Charlemagne, rather than the Pope, was the dominant partner.

The high point, or at least the most famous event, of Charlemagne's reign occurred in Rome, on Christmas Day in the year 800. On that day, Pope Leo III placed a crown on Charles's head and proclaimed him the emperor of the Romans. In principal, this meant that the Western Roman Empire, which had been destroyed more than three centuries earlier, was being restored, and that Charlemagne was now the rightful successor to Augustus Caesar.

Actually, of course, it was ridiculous to maintain that Charlemagne's empire was a restoration of imperial Rome. In the first place, the territory ruled by the two empires was quite different. Charlemagne's empire, large as it was, included only about half of the territory of the Western Roman Empire. The region common to both empires included Belgium, France, Switzerland, and northern Italy. But England, Spain, southern Italy, and northern Africa, which had all formed part of the Roman Empire, were outside of Charlemagne's control; whereas Germany, which formed an important portion of his dominion, had never been under Roman rule. In the second place, Charlemagne was not Roman in any sense whatever: not by birth, not by outlook, not by culture. The Franks were a Teutonic tribe, and Charlemagne's native tongue was an old Germanic dialect, though he also learned to speak Latin. Charles lived most of his life in northern Europe, particularly in Germany, and made only four visits to Italy. The capital of his empire was not Rome but Aachen, in present-day Germany, not far from the Dutch and Belgian borders.

Charlemagne's usual political astuteness failed him badly when it came to the question of the succession to his throne. Although he had spent most of his life fighting wars to unify a

Charlemagne's Empire.

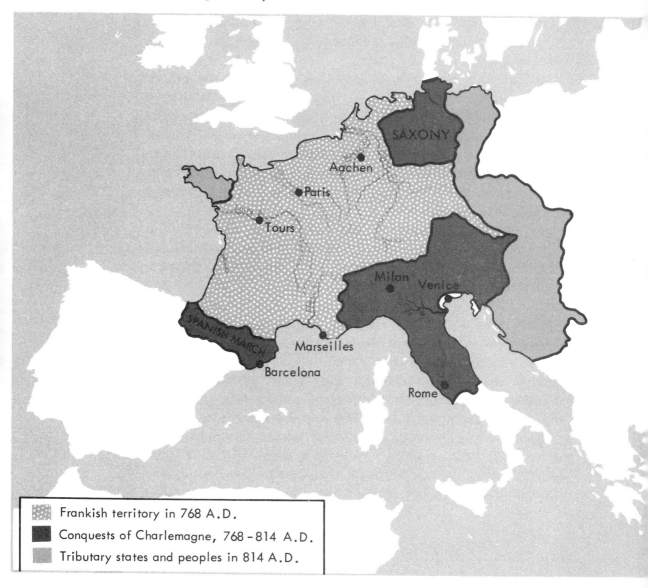

Frankish territory in 768 A.D.

Conquests of Charlemagne, 768–814 A.D.

Tributary states and peoples in 814 A.D.

large portion of western Europe, he could think of no cleverer plan than that of dividing the Empire between his three sons when he died. Such a procedure is usually an infallible prescription for engendering warfare. As it turned out, however, his two eldest sons died shortly before Charlemagne himself. As a result, his third son, Louis the Pious, was able to inherit Charlemagne's empire intact when Charlemagne died in Aachen, in 814. However, Louis showed no better judgment than his father had when it came to the succession: he, too, wished to divide the empire among his sons. After some fighting, Louis's sons finally signed the Treaty of Verdun (in 843), by which the Frankish empire was divided into three portions. The first portion comprised most of present-day France; the second included a large portion of Germany; and the third included both northern Italy and a wide strip straddling the French-German border.

Now, there are some persons who estimate Charlemagne's influence more highly than I do. It has been said that he restored the Roman Empire; that he reunited western Europe; that he brought Saxony into western Europe; that he set the pattern for most of the succeeding history of western Europe; that he safeguarded western Europe from external threats; that he established the rough boundaries of France, Germany, and Italy; that he spread Christianity; and that his coronation by the Pope set the stage for the centuries-long struggle between the State and the Church in Europe. To my mind, such claims are greatly exaggerated. In the first place, the so-called Holy Roman Empire was not really a restoration of the Roman Empire at all, but rather a continuation of the Frankish kingdom that Charlemagne had inherited.

The unification of western Europe would have been highly significant if Charlemagne had indeed succeeded in accomplishing it. However, Charlemagne's empire fell apart within thirty years after his death, and was never subsequently reunited.

The present borders of France, Germany, and Italy have virtually nothing to do with either Charlemagne or Louis the Pious. The northern boundary of Italy largely follows the geographical boundary of the Alps. The Franco-German border roughly follows a linguistic boundary, which in turn roughly follows the northern boundary of the old Roman Empire.

To give Charlemagne any substantial credit for the spread of Christianity seems quite unjustified to me. Christianity had been spreading northwards through Europe for centuries before Charlemagne's reign, and continued to do so for centuries thereafter. Quite apart from the point that Charlemagne's forced conversion of the Saxons was morally dreadful, it was also totally unnecessary. The Anglo-Saxons in England were converted to Christianity without being massacred, and in succeeding centuries, the various Scandinavian peoples were also converted by persuasion rather than by force.

What about the notion that Charlemagne's military victories succeeded in safeguarding western Europe from external attack? Not so. During the entire ninth century, the northern and western coasts of Europe were subjected to a devastating series of attacks by the Vikings, or Norsemen. At the same time, Magyar horsemen invaded Europe from the East, and Moslem raiders harassed the continent in the south. It was one of the least secure periods in Europe's history.

The struggle for dominance between civil authorities and the Church was a persisting feature of European history, even in regions that were not part of the Carolingian Empire. Such a struggle, indeed, was inherent in the aspirations of the medieval Church, and would have occurred (though perhaps in slightly different form) without Charlemagne. His coronation in Rome was an interesting incident, but hardly a crucial causative factor in the overall struggle.

I think that it would be difficult to convince an educated Chinese or Indian that Charlemagne should be considered nearly as important as such men as Shih Huang Ti, Genghis Khan, or Asoka. Indeed, if Charlemagne is compared with Sui Wen Ti, it seems fairly clear that the Chinese emperor was the more important of the two. The unification of China engineered by Sui Wen Ti has had a lasting effect, whereas Charlemagne's unification of western Europe hardly endured for a generation.

Although Charlemagne's importance has been somewhat overrated by Europeans, his short-term influence was certainly large. He destroyed the Lombard and Avar states and conquered Saxony. Large numbers of people died in his wars. On the positive side, there was a brief cultural renaissance during his reign (which, however, ended quickly after his death).

There were also various long-term consequences of his career. For centuries after Charlemagne, German emperors engaged in an ultimately futile struggle to control Italy. Without Charlemagne's example, it is quite possible that they would have paid less attention to Italy and devoted more effort to expanding to the north or east. It is also true that the Holy Roman Empire, which Charlemagne started, managed to endure until the early nineteenth century. (For much of that time, however, the actual power of the Holy Roman Emperor was slight, and effective power in Germany was divided among innumerable small states.)

But Charlemagne's most important achievement was probably his subjugation of Saxony, which brought that important region into the mainstream of European civilization. That was an accomplishment similar to Julius Caesar's conquest of Gaul, though not quite as important, since Saxony is a substantially smaller region.

The Treaty of Verdun set the borders of present-day France and Germany.

98

HOMER

fl. 8th *c.* B.C.?

For many centuries, there have been disputes concerning the authorship of the Homeric poems. When, where, and how were the *Iliad* and the *Odyssey* composed? To what extent were they based on previous compositions? Were the *Iliad* and the *Odyssey* composed by the same person? Indeed, was either one composed by a single author? Perhaps there was no such individual as Homer, and the two poems developed by a process of slow accretion, or were assembled by editors from a group of poems of varying authorship. Scholars who have spent many years studying these questions do not agree with each other; how then can a person who is not a classical scholar know what the true answers are? Of course, I do not *know* the answers; nevertheless, in order to decide where (if anywhere) Homer belongs on this list, I have made the following assumptions:

The first assumption is that there was indeed a single principal author of the *Iliad*. (It is simply too good to have been written by a committee!) In the centuries preceding Homer, many shorter poems on the same subject matter had been composed by other Greek poets, and Homer drew heavily on their work. But Homer did far more than merely assemble the *Iliad* from pre-existing shorter poems. He selected, arranged, reworded, and added—all the while infusing the final result with his own unique artistic genius. Homer, the man who created this masterpiece, most probably lived in the eighth century B.C., although many other dates, mostly earlier, have been suggested. I have also assumed that the same man was the principal author of the *Odyssey*. Although the argument (based in part on difference in style) that the two poems were composed by different authors has some force, on the whole the similarities between the two poems far outweigh their differences.

From the foregoing, it is obvious that very little is known about Homer himself; indeed, there is no certain biographical data concerning him. There is a very strong and ancient tradition, dating back to early Greek times, that Homer was blind. However, the striking visual imagery in the two poems suggests that if Homer was indeed a blind man, he was certainly not blind from birth. The language used in the poems strongly suggests that Homer came from Ionia, the region on the eastern side of the Aegean Sea.

Although it seems difficult to believe that such lengthy and carefully constructed poems could have been composed without any writing, most scholars seem to agree that they were at least primarily, and perhaps completely, oral compositions. It is not certain when the poems were first reduced to writing. Considering their length (in combination almost 28,000 verses), it seems rather unlikely that they could have been transmitted with reasonable accuracy unless they were written down not very long after their original composition. In any event, by the sixth century B.C., the two poems were already considered to be great classics, and the biographical information concerning Homer was already lost. Thereafter, the Greeks always considered the *Odyssey* and the *Iliad* to be the nation's supreme literary masterpieces. Amazingly, through all the intervening centuries and all the changes of literary style that have occurred, Homer's reputation has never diminished.

In view of Homer's great fame and reputation, it is with

some trepidation that I have accorded him so low a ranking on this list. I have done so in part for the same reason I have assigned most other literary and artistic figures relatively low places. In the case of Homer, the discrepancy between reputation and influence seems to be particularly large. Though his works are frequently studied in school, in today's world relatively few people read Homer after they have left high school or college. The contrast with Shakespeare, whose plays and poems *are* read, and whose plays are frequently produced and well attended, is quite striking.

Nor is Homer widely quoted. Although Homeric quotations are to be found in Bartlett's, few are used in everyday conversation. Here again, there is a marked contrast with Shakespeare, and also with such authors as Benjamin Franklin and Omar Khayyam. A widely repeated phrase such as, "a penny saved is a penny earned," may actually influence personal behavior and even political attitudes and decisions. There are no comparable lines in Homer that are widely quoted today.

Why, then has Homer been included on this list at all? There are two reasons. The first reason is that the number of people—added up over the centuries—who have personally heard or read Homer's poems is extremely large. In the ancient world, Homer's poems were much more popular than they are now. In Greece, his works were familiar to the general population, and for a long time influenced religious and ethical attitudes. The *Odyssey* and the *Iliad* were well-known, not merely by literary intellectuals, but by military and political leaders as well. Many ancient Roman leaders quoted Homer, and Alexander the Great carried a copy of the *Iliad* with him in his campaigns. Even today, Homer is the favorite author of some people, and most of us have read his works (at least in part) in school.

Even more important, perhaps, has been Homer's influence on literature. All the classical Greek poets and playwrights were deeply influenced by Homer. Such figures as Sophocles, Euripides, and Aristotle—to name just a few—were steeped in the Homeric tradition, and all had derived their notions of literary excellence from him.

Homer's influence on ancient Roman authors was almost as great. All accepted his poetry as the standard of excellence. When Virgil—often considered the greatest of Roman authors—wrote his masterpiece, the *Aeneid*, he deliberately patterned it after the *Iliad* and the *Odyssey*.

Even in modern times, virtually every writer of note has been affected either by Homer himself or by writers, such as Sophocles or Virgil, who were themselves powerfully influenced by Homer. No other author in history has had nearly such a widespread and long-continued influence.

That last point is perhaps the crucial one. Over the course of the last one hundred years, it is quite possible that Tolstoy has been more widely read and more influential than Homer. But Tolstoy had no influence whatsoever during the preceding twenty-six centuries, whereas Homer's influence has continued for 2,700 years or more. That is an awfully long time, and one not apt to be matched by many other literary figures, or, indeed, by figures in any field of human endeavor.

An illustration by John Flaxman from Homer's Iliad, *depicting the funeral of the great warrior Hector.*

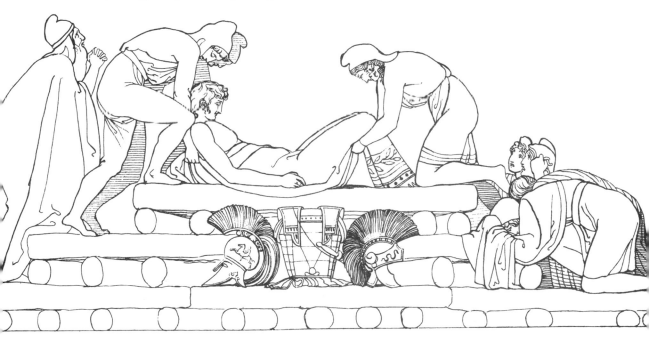

99

JUSTINIAN I   483-565

The Emperor Justinian is renowned for the great codification of Roman law that was carried out during his reign. The Code of Justinian preserved the product of Rome's creative genius in jurisprudence, and it later formed the basis for the development of the law in many European countries. Probably no other code of laws has had so enduring an impact on the world.

Justinian was born about 483, in Tauresium, in present-day Yugoslavia. He was the nephew of Justin I, a nearly illiterate Thracian peasant who had worked his way up through the army to become the ruler of the Eastern Roman Empire. Justinian, although likewise of peasant origin, received a good education and, with his uncle's help, advanced rapidly. In 527, Justin, who was childless, made Justinian co-emperor with him. Later that year Justin died, and from then until his own death in 565, Justinian was sole emperor.

In 476, just seven years before Justinian's birth, the Western Roman Empire had finally succumbed to the onslaught of the barbarian Germanic tribes, and only the Eastern Roman Empire, with its capital in Constantinople, remained intact. Justinian was determined to reconquer the lost lands of the West and to restore the Roman Empire, and the better part of his energy while emperor was devoted to this end. In this project he was partly successful, since he did manage to recapture Italy, North Africa, and part of Spain from the barbarians.

However, Justinian's place on this list depends not so much on his military feats as upon his role in the codification of Roman law. As early as 528, the year after he took office, Justinian set up a commission to produce a code of imperial laws. Their work was first published in 529, then revised, and enacted into statute in 534. At the same time, all prior edicts and statutes not included in the code were repealed. This *Codex* became the first portion of the *Corpus Juris Civilis*. The second portion, called the *Pandects*, or the *Digest*, was a summary of the views of prominent Roman legal writers. That, too, was authoritative. The third part, the *Institutes*, was basically a text or handbook for law students. Finally, those laws passed by Justinian after the adoption of the *Codex* were brought together into the *Novellae*, which was published after Justinian's death.

Of course Justinian himself, busy as he was with his various wars and administrative duties, could not personally draft the *Corpus Juris Civilis*. The codification which Justinian ordered was actually carried out by a group of legal scholars under the supervision of the great lawyer and legal expert Tribonian.

Justinian, an exceedingly energetic man, also devoted a good deal of effort to administrative reforms, including a partly successful campaign against governmental corruption. He stimulated trade and industry, and engaged in a large public building program. Under him, many fortresses, monasteries, and churches (including the famous Hagia Sophia in Constantinople) were built or reconstructed. This building program and his wars resulted in a large increase in taxes, and considerable discontent.

A Byzantine mosaic at the Church of San Vitale at Ravenna depicts the Emperor Justinian.

In 532, there was a rebellion (the Nika riots) which nearly cost him his throne. After he suppressed that rebellion Justinian's throne was generally secure. Still, at his death in 565, there was considerable popular rejoicing.

Justinian was greatly aided by his very able wife, Theodora, and a few words about her seem appropriate. Theodora was born about 500. In her youth, she was an actress and courtesan, and gave birth to an illegimate child. She was in her twenties when she met Justinian and became his mistress. They were married in 525, just two years before he assumed the imperial throne. Justinian recognized his wife's outstanding capabilities, and she became his principal advisor and was entrusted with various diplomatic duties. She had a considerable influence upon his legislation, including some laws passed to improve the rights and status of women. Her death in 548 (of cancer) was a grave loss to Justinian, although the remaining seventeen years of his reign were reasonably successful. Theodora, who was beautiful as well as brilliant, was the subject of many works of art.

Justinian's placement on this list is primarily due to the importance of the *Corpus Juris Civilis*, which constituted an authoritative restatement of Roman law. As such, it was important in the Byzantine Empire for centuries. In the West, it was largely forgotten for about five hundred years. About 1100, however, the study of Roman law was revived, particularly in the Italian universities. During the late Middle Ages, the *Corpus Juris Civilis* became the principal basis of the developing legal systems of Continental Europe. Countries where this occurred are said to have civil-law systems, as opposed to the common-law systems that generally prevail in English-speaking countries. The *Corpus Juris Civilis* was not adopted *in toto* anywhere. However, parts of it were incorporated into the civil law, and throughout much of Europe, it became the basis for legal study, training, and discourse. Since many non-European countries eventually adopted parts of the civil law, the influence of the *Corpus Juris Civilis* has been remarkably wide.

Despite this, it would be a mistake to overestimate the importance of the Justinian Code. There were other important influences on the development of civil law besides the *Corpus Juris Civilis*. For example, the laws concerning contracts derived more from the practice of merchants and the decisions of merchants' courts than from Roman law. Germanic law and Church law also influenced the civil law. In the modern era, of course, European laws and legal systems have all been extensively revised. Today, the substantive law in most civil law countries bears relatively little resemblance to the Code of Justinian.

100

MAHAVIRA *c.* 599 B.C.- *c.* 527 B.C.

Mahavira (which means "great hero") is the name by which the Jains usually refer to Vardhamana, the leading figure in the development of their religion.

Vardhamana was born in 599 B.C., in northeast India, the same general area in which Gautama Buddha was born, though a generation earlier. Indeed, the similarity of the life stories of the two men is truly amazing. Vardhamana was the younger son of a chief, and like Gautama was reared in considerable luxury. At the age of thirty, he abandoned his wealth, his family (he had a wife and daughter), and his comfortable surroundings, and decided to seek spiritual truth and fulfillment.

Vardhamana became a monk in the small and very ascetic Parsvanatha order. For twelve years he engaged in deep meditation and reflection, all the while enduring the extremes of asceticism and poverty. He fasted frequently, and he retained no personal property of any sort, not even a small cup or dish with which to drink water or collect alms. Although at first he retained one garment, after a while he discarded even that and walked

506

about completely naked. He would allow insects to crawl over his bare skin and would not brush them off, even when they bit him. Even in India, where itinerant holy men are more common than they are in the West, Mahavira's appearance and behavior frequently aroused taunts, insults, and blows, all of which he endured without reprisal.

When he was forty-two, Mahavira decided that he had finally attained spiritual enlightenment. He spent the remaining thirty years of his life preaching and teaching the spiritual insights that he had gained. When he died, in 527 B.C., he had many disciples.

In some ways Mahavira's doctrines are very similar to those of Buddhism and Hinduism. Jains believe that when a human being's body dies, his soul does not die with it but is reincarnated in some other being (not necessarily human). This doctrine of transmigration of souls is one of the foundations of Jainist thought. Jains also believe in *karma*, the doctrine that the ethical consequences of an act affect one's lot in a future existence. To remove the accumulated load of guilt from one's soul, and thereby to purify it, is a primary goal of the Jainist religion. In part, Mahavira taught, this can be achieved by the denial of sensual pleasures. Jainist monks, in particular, are supposed to practice a rigorous asceticism. It is noteworthy that deliberately starving oneself to death is considered praiseworthy!

A very important aspect of Jainism is the great stress it lays on the doctrine of *ahisma*, or nonviolence. Jains emphasize that *ahisma* includes nonviolent behavior to animals as well as to human beings. As one consequence of this belief, Jains are vegetarians. However, devout Jains carry the principle of *ahisma* to far greater extremes than that: a devout Jain, quite literally, will not kill a fly; nor will he eat in the dark, as he might accidentally swallow an insect, and thereby cause its death. Indeed, a sufficiently devout and well-to-do Jain will hire someone to sweep the street in front of him as he walks, so that he does not accidentally step on and kill an insect or worm!

From such beliefs, it logically follows that a religious Jain cannot in good conscience plow a field. In fact, the Jains actually do not engage in agriculture. For that matter, many other occupations involving manual labor are forbidden by their religion. Jainism provides a stiking example of how religious doctrines can drastically affect the entire manner of living of a whole community. Although they dwell in a land that is overwhelmingly agricultural, the majority of Jains have been engaged in trade or finance for centuries. Jainist religious attitudes have also led them to prize industriousness. Consequently, it is not suprising that the Jains are a prosperous group, and that their participation in Indian intellectual and artistic activities has been high in proportion to their numbers.

Originally, Jainism had no caste system. However, through constant interaction with Hinduism, a caste system has developed within Jainism—though one far less extreme than that of the Hindus. Similarly, although Mahavira himself never spoke of a God or gods, through contact with Hinduism some worship of deities has arisen. Since there are no writings by Mahavira, some absorption of doctrines from Hinduism was probably inevitable. There has, however, been considerable influence in the other direction as well. Jainist moral objections to animal sacrifice and to the eating of meat appear to have markedly affected Hindu practice. Furthermore, the Jainist doctrine of nonviolence has been a continuing influence upon Indian thought, even down to modern times, For example, Gandhi was strongly influenced by the teachings of the Jainist philosopher Shrimad Rajachandra (1867-1900), whom he considered to be one of his gurus, or spiritual teachers.

The Jains have never been a very numerous sect, and today there are only about 3,500,000 of them in all of India. That may not sound like a very large fraction of the world's population; however, added up over a period of 2,500 years it comes to quite a large number of persons. In judging Mahavira's importance, one should take into account that Jainism, perhaps even more than most other religions, has had a large and continuous effect upon the lives of its adherents.

HONORABLE MENTIONS
AND INTERESTING MISSES

While this book was being written, many friends and associates of the author suggested the names of various historical figures who they felt might reasonably be included in the main section of the book.

Quite a few of those suggestions were adopted; others, for one reason or another, were rejected. Below are the names of a hundred interesting figures who, the author finally concluded, do *not* belong among the 100 most influential persons in history—although, undoubtedly, strong arguments can be made on behalf of a considerable number of these persons.

On the succeeding pages are brief articles about ten of those figures, indicating the author's reasons for omitting them from the top hundred. It should not be assumed that the author thinks that those ten (in some order) would be numbers 101-110 if the main list were extended, or that the persons named below would be numbers 101-200.

Abraham
Aesop
Howard H. Aiken
Susan B. Anthony
St. Thomas Aquinas
Archimedes
Aristarchus of Samos
Richard Arkwright
Neil Armstrong
Charles Babbage
Antoine Henri Becquerel
Jeremy Bentham
Otto von Bismark
Niels Bohr

Louis de Broglie
Nicolas Sadi Carnot
Cheops (Khufu)
Winston Churchill
Karl von Clausewitz
Rudolf Clausius
Marie Curie
Gottlieb Daimler
Dante Alighieri
King David
Democritus
Mary Baker Eddy
Robert C. W. Ettinger
George Fox

Benjamin Franklin
Frederick the Great
Betty Friedan
Galen
Mohandas K. Gandhi
Karl Friedrich Gauss
Hammurabi
Georg Wilhelm Friedrich
    Hegel
Henry VIII
Henry the Navigator
Theodor Herzl
Hippocrates
Thomas Hobbes
James Hutton
Ikhnaton
Isaiah
Joan of Arc
Immanuel Kant
Kemal Ataturk
John Maynard Keynes
Har Gobind Khorana
Martin Luther King, Jr.
Alfred C. Kinsey
Gustav Robert Kirchhoff
Kublai Khan
Gottfried Wilhelm von
    Leibniz
Etienne Lenoir
Leonardo da Vinci
Abraham Lincoln
Liu Pang (Han Kao Tsu)
Louis XIV
James Madison
Ferdinand Magellan
The Virgin Mary
Meijo Tenno
    (Emperor Mutsuhito)

Dmitri Mendeleev
Montesquieu
Maria Montessori
Samuel Morse
Wolfgang Amadeus Mozart
Muawiya I
Gerard K. O'Neill
Blaise Pascal
Ivan Pavlov
Pablo Picasso
Marco Polo
Ptolemy (Claudius
    Ptolemaeus)
Pythagoras
Ronald Reagan
Rembrandt
Franklin Delano Roosevelt
Sankara
Erwin Schrodinger
William B. Shockley
Joseph Smith
Socrates
Sophocles
Sun Yat-sen
William Henry Fox Talbot
Tamurlane
Edward Teller
Henry David Thoreau
Charles H. Townes
Harry S. Truman
Alessandro Volta
Selman A. Waksman
James D. Watson &
    Francis Crick
Robert A. Watson-Watt
Mary Wollstonecraft
Frank Lloyd Wright
Boris Yeltsin
Vladimir Zworykin

ST. THOMAS AQUINAS

c. 1225-1274

The Italian philosopher Thomas Aquinas is famous for his theological writings, and particularly for his *Summa Theologica*, which is perhaps the most authoritative statement of Catholic theological doctrines ever produced.

It is safe to say that no one has ever worked out a complete system of philosophy in such detail and with such careful consideration as Aquinas did. The reader, even if he disagrees with Aquinas's assumptions or conclusions, can hardly fail to be impressed by the overpowering intellect of the man. However, a considerable part of Aquinas's writings concern abstract and metaphysical questions that most persons do not find of great practical importance. He discussed ethical questions also; however, his writings, though they systematized earlier Catholic beliefs, did not represent a great change in ethical ideas or in political outlook. Nor does it seem likely that many persons have been converted to Catholicism or Christianity by reading Aquinas's works. Therefore, no matter how clever or correct Aquinas's speculations may have been, I doubt that they have had much influence upon human behavior or upon the course of history. It is for that reason that he has been omitted from the main list in this book.

ARCHIMEDES

287 B.C.- 212 B.C.

Archimedes is generally acknowledged to be one of the most brilliant mathematicians and scientists of the ancient world. He is sometimes credited with having discovered both the principle of the lever and the concept of specific gravity.

In fact, however, the lever had been known and used for many centuries before Archimedes. He seems to have been the first to explicitly state the formula describing the effect of the lever, but Egyptian engineers had made frequent and capable use of levers long before Archimedes.

The concept of the density (weight per unit volume) of an object, as opposed to the total weight of the object, had likewise been known before Archimedes. In the famous story of Archimedes and the crown (the story that ends with him jumping out of his bath and running through the streets shouting "Eureka"), what Archimedes had discovered was not a new concept, but rather an ingenious application of a known concept to a specific problem.

As a mathematician, Archimedes was undoubtedly outstanding. In fact, he came quite close to formulating integral calculus—more than eighteen centuries before Isaac Newton succeeded in doing so. Unfortunately, a convenient system of mathematical notation was lacking in Archimedes' day. Equally unfortunately, none of his immediate successors was a truly first-rate mathematician. As a result, Archimedes' brilliant mathematical insights turned out to have far less effect than they might have had. It therefore appears that although Archimedes' talents were indeed remarkable, his actual influence was not great enough to warrant including him among the first hundred names in this book.

CHARLES BABBAGE

1 7 9 2 - 1 8 7 1

The English inventor Charles Babbage worked out the principles behind the general-purpose digital computer a full century before the development of the large modern electronic calculating machines. A machine he designed, which he called the "analytical engine," was capable in principle of doing everything that modern calculators can do (though not nearly as quickly, since the analytical engine was not designed to operate electrically). Unfortunately, because nineteenth-century technology was not sufficiently advanced, Babbage was not able to complete the construction of the analytical engine, despite the expenditure of a large amount of time and money. After his death, his extremely ingenious ideas were nearly forgotten.

In 1937, however, Babbage's writings came to the attention of Howard H. Aiken, a graduate student at Harvard University. Aiken, who had himself been trying to design a computing machine, was greatly stimulated by Babbage's ideas. With the collaboration of IBM, Aiken was able to construct the *Mark I*, the first large general-purpose computer. In 1946, two years after the *Mark I* went into operation, another group of engineers and inventors completed the *ENIAC*, the first *electronic* calculating machine. Since then, advances in computer technology have been extremely rapid.

Since calculating machines have had such a great impact on the world already, and are likely to prove even more important in the future, I was tempted to include Charles Babbage in the main section of this book. After careful consideration, however, I concluded that Babbage's contribution to the development of computers was not significantly greater than that of Aiken, or than that of John Mauchly and J. P. Eckert (who were the leading figures in the design of the *ENIAC*). For that matter, at least three of Babbage's predecessors—Blaise Pascal, Gottfried Leibniz, and Joseph Marie Jacquard—made contributions that seem to have been comparable in importance to Babbage's. Pascal, a French scientist, mathematician, and philosopher, invented a mechanical adding machine back in 1642. In 1671, Gottfried Wilhelm von Leibniz, philosopher and mathematician, devised a machine that could add, subtract, multiply, and divide. Leibniz was also the first to point out the importance of the binary system, a system of notation that is extensively employed in modern computing machines. Jacquard was a Frenchman who, in the early nineteenth century, invented a device that employed punched cards to control the operation of a loom. The Jacquard loom, which was very successful commercially, had a significant influence on Babbage's thinking. It may also have influenced Herman Hollerith, an American who, in the late nineteenth century, adapted punched cards for use in Census Bureau tabulations.

The principal credit for the development of the modern computer must, therefore, be divided among several men. Though each of the men mentioned here made a significant contribution, no one of them stands out clearly above the others. Neither Babbage, therefore, nor any of the others, seems quite worthy of inclusion in the main section of this book.

CHEOPS

fl. 2 6 th *c.* B.C.

The Egyptian king Khufu (Cheops is the Greek form of his name) is best remembered for his construction of the Great Pyramid at Giza, which was apparently built to be his tomb. His exact dates of birth and death are unknown, but it is believed that he flourished during the twenty-sixth century B.C. We know that his capital was at Memphis, in Egypt, and that he had a long reign, but little else is known of his life.

It seems safe to say that the Great Pyramid is both the most celebrated and the most remarkable structure ever built by human beings. Even in ancient times it was regarded as one of the Seven Wonders of the World. Although the other six structures have long since fallen into ruin, the Great Pyramid remains, a striking memorial to the king who built it.

The perfection of its construction, as well as its sheer size, are awe-inspiring. Although the top thirty feet of the Great Pyramid have been destroyed, it still stands 450 feet high—about the height of a thirty-five-story building! Roughly 2,300,000 blocks of stone, averaging about two and one-half tons apiece, were used in its construction. Because the Great Pyramid contains a set of internal chambers and passages, the stones used in building it had to be of varying sizes, adding to the complexity of the construction task.

Just how the ancient Egyptians, working some forty-six centuries ago, without any modern equipment or machinery, were able to construct this vast monument is unclear. Certainly, it required careful planning and superb administrative ability to successfully marshal the resources of the country for this gigantic task. If we accept the common estimate that it took twenty years to build the Great Pyramid, then we find that an average of more than 300 stone blocks were put in place each day. Clearly, in order to quarry that number of blocks, to transport them to the site of the pyramid, to cut them to the exact shape desired, and to accurately place them was an enormous task. A whole fleet of boats must have been needed to transport the blocks, and a well-planned supply system was needed to feed the army of workers engaged in the project.

The Great Pyramid has already endured for over 4,500 years, and will probably still be standing long after every building constructed by modern engineers has crumbled to dust. It is virtually indestructible; not even a direct hit by an atomic bomb would obliterate it! Of course, it is slowly being worn away. However, at the present rate of erosion it will probably last for over a million years.

It therefore seems plain that Cheops, a man who has truly left his mark on the world, has achieved an enduring fame, perhaps more so than any other person who has yet lived. (Will men like Napoleon or Alexander the Great be remembered at all, even ten thousand years from now?) But fame is very different from influence, and while Cheops probably had a great effect upon the lives of his contemporary Egyptians, he does not appear to have had much influence either upon foreign nations or succeeding ages.

MARIE CURIE

1 8 6 7 - 1 9 3 4

Marie Curie (original name: Maria Sklodowska) is much more famous than many of the scientists whom I have included in the first hundred persons on my list. It seems to me, however, that her great fame is based not so much upon the importance of the scientific work she did as upon the fact that a woman did it. Her career demonstrated, in the clearest possible fashion, that a female was capable of high-quality scientific research. For this reason she has become very celebrated, so much so that many persons have the impression that she was the person who discovered radioactivity. In fact, however, radioactivity was discovered by Antoine Henri Becquerel. There is no question whatsoever of Becquerel's priority, for it was not until after Marie Curie had read an account of Becquerel's discovery that she (and her husband, Pierre, who was an equally talented scientist) commenced their investigations of the subject.

Marie Curie's most celebrated actual accomplishment was the discovery and isolation of the chemical element radium. Prior to that, she had discovered another radioactive element, which she named "polonium" after her native land, Poland. These are admirable achievements, but are not of major importance in scientific theory.

In 1903, Marie Curie, Pierre Curie, and Antoine Henri Becquerel were jointly awarded the Nobel Prize in physics. In 1911, Marie Curie was awarded another Nobel Prize, this one in chemistry, making her the first person to win two Nobel Prizes.

It is interesting to note that Marie Curie had young children at the time that her most important scientific research was accomplished. Her eldest daughter, Irene, also became a highly successful scientist. Irene married another talented scientist, Jean Frédéric Joliot, and the two of them, working together, discovered *artificial* radioactivity. For this discovery (which might be considered a "descendant" of the discovery of natural radioactivity!) the Joliot-Curies shared a Nobel Prize in 1935. Marie Curie's second daughter, Ève, became a noted musician and author. Quite a family!

Madame Curie died in 1934 of leukemia, quite probably caused by repeated exposure to radioactive materials.

BENJAMIN FRANKLIN

1 7 0 6 - 1 7 9 0

I think it fair to say that Benjamin Franklin was the most versatile genius in all of history, with notable accomplishments in an even wider range of fields than the renowned Leonardo da Vinci. It is astonishing, but true, that Franklin had highly successful careers in at least four quite separate areas of human endeavor: business, science, literature, and politics.

Franklin's business career was a classic rags-to-riches story. His family in Boston had not been well-to-do, and as a young man in Philadelphia, he was virtually penniless. By his early forties, however, Franklin had become a prosperous man through his printing shop, his newspaper, and his other business activities. Meanwhile, in his spare time, he studied science and taught himself four foreign languages!

As a scientist, Franklin is best known for the basic research he performed concerning electricity and lighting. However, he also devised several highly useful inventions, including the Franklin stove, bifocal lenses, and the lightning rod. The latter two inventions are widely used even today.

Franklin's first literary efforts were as a successful journalist. Soon he was publishing *Poor Richard's Almanac*, in which he demonstrated his unusual talent for turning a clever phrase. (Few writers have left behind so many well-remembered sayings.) In later years, he composed his autobiography, one of the most famous ever written, and one still widely read and enjoyed.

In politics, Franklin was successful as an administrator (he was a postmaster general for the colonies, and under him the postal service showed a profit!); as a legislator (he was re-elected repeatedly to the Pennsylvania legislature); and as a diplomat (he was a very popular and successful ambassador to France during a crucial period in American history). In addition, he was one of the signers of the American Declaration of Independence, and later served as a member of the Constitutional Convention.

Overlapping all these fields, to some extent, was Franklin's fifth "career" as a public-spirited promoter and organizer. For example, he was one of the founders of the first hospital in Philadelphia. He helped to organize the first fire company in the colonies, and he pushed successfully for the formation of a municipal police department. He organized a circulating library (the colonies' first) and a scientific society (still another first!).

Like all of us, Franklin had troubles and grievous disappointments. Nevertheless, his life stands out as a remarkable example—perhaps the most striking in history—of one well-spent. Blessed with good health for most of his eighty-four years, Franklin had a long, exciting, useful, varied, and generally happy sojourn on earth.

In view of the foregoing, it was very tempting to include Franklin in the main section of this book. However, no one of his contributions seems nearly important enough for him to be considered one of the hundred most influential persons in history; nor in my opinion, do all of his achievements combined.

MOHANDAS GANDHI

1869-1948

Mohandas K. Gandhi was the outstanding leader of the movement for an independent India, and for that reason alone several people have suggested that he be included in the main section of this book. It should be remembered, though, that Indian independence from England was bound to come sooner or later; in fact, given the strength of the historical forces tending toward decolonization, we can today see that Indian independence would surely have been achieved within a few years of 1947 even had Gandhi never lived.

It is true that Gandhi's technique of nonviolent civil disobedience was ultimately successful in persuading the British to leave India. It has been suggested, however, that India might have gained independence sooner if the Indians had adopted more forceful methods instead. Since it is hard to decide whether on the whole Gandhi speeded up or delayed Indian independence, we might reasonably conclude that the net effect of his actions was (at least in that respect) rather small. It might also be pointed out that Gandhi was *not* the founder of the movement for Indian independence (the Indian National Congress had been founded as early as 1885), nor was he the main political leader at the time independence was finally achieved.

Still, it might be maintained that Gandhi's principal importance lies in his advocacy of nonviolence. (His ideas, of course, were not entirely original: Gandhi specifically said that they were derived in part from his readings of Thoreau, Tolstoy, and the New Testament, as well as from various Hindu writings.) There is little doubt that Gandhi's policies, if universally adopted, would transform the world. Unfortunately, they have not been generally accepted, even in India.

It is true that in 1954-55 his techniques were used in an attempt to persuade the Portuguese to relinquish control of Goa. However, the campaign did not succeed in its goal, and a few years later, the Indian government launched an armed invasion. In addition, in the last forty years, India has fought three wars with Pakistan and a border war with China. Other countries have been equally reluctant to adopt Gandhi's techniques. In the roughly eighty years since he introduced those techniques, the world has seen the two bloodiest wars in all history.

Must we therefore conclude that as a philosopher Gandhi was basically a failure? At the present time, it certainly seems that way; however, it is worth remembering that forty years after Jesus died an intelligent, well-informed Roman would doubtless have concluded that Jesus of Nazareth was a "failure"—if, indeed, he had heard of Jesus at all! Nor could anyone in 450 B.C. have predicted how influential Confucius would turn out to be. Still, judging from what has occurred so far, Gandhi seems entitled only to an honorable mention in this book.

ABRAHAM LINCOLN

1809-1865

Abraham Lincoln, the sixteenth president of the United States, is one of the most famous and most admirable political leaders that this country—or any country—has ever produced. Why, then, has he not been included on my list? Was not the freeing of some 3,500,000 slaves a major accomplishment?

Indeed it was. However, in retrospect we can see that the forces—

throughout the world—working toward the abolition of slavery were irresistable. Many countries had abolished slavery even before Lincoln took office, and within sixty-five years of his death, most other countries did so. The most that Lincoln can be credited with accomplishing is having hastened the process in one country.

Still, it might be asserted that Lincoln's chief accomplishment was in holding the United States together in the face of the secession of the southern states, and for that alone he deserves a place on this list.

But it was the election of Lincoln that touched off the secession of the southern states. Nor is it clear that the North would have failed to win the Civil War if someone other than Lincoln had been President. After all, the North started the war with a great advantage in population, and an even greater one in industrial production.

Even if the North had not prosecuted the Civil War to a successful conclusion, the overall course of history might not have been greatly altered. The bonds of language, religion, culture, and trade between the North and the South were very great, and it seems probable that they would eventually have reunited. If the period of disunity had lasted for twenty years—or even for fifty years—it would still be a minor incident in world history. (It should also be remembered that, even without the South, the United States would now be the fourth most populous nation on earth and the leading industrial power.)

Does this mean that Lincoln was an unimportant figure? Not at all! His career profoundly influenced several million people for a generation. However, that still does not make him as important as a man such as Mahavira, whose influence has continued for many centuries.

FERDINAND MAGELLAN

c. 1 4 8 0 - 1 5 2 1

The Portuguese explorer Ferdinand Magellan is celebrated as the leader of the first expedition to circumnavigate the earth.

His expedition was perhaps the most outstanding voyage of exploration in all human history. The complete trip took just under three years. Of the five small, clumsy, leaky vessels with which Magellan started out, only one returned to Europe safely; and of the 265 men who started the voyage, only eighteen came back alive! Magellan himself was one of those who died during the voyage (although not until after he had led the expedition over the most difficult part of the trip). But in the end, the expedition was successful, and it proved beyond any dispute that the earth was round.

It is quite plain that the success of the expedition was principally due to Magellan's leadership and to his iron determination. Much of the crew wished to turn back after a few months; indeed, Magellan had to suppress a mutiny in order to continue onward. His combination of skill and perseverance entitle him to be considered the greatest of all navigators and explorers.

The actual influence of his achievement, however, was comparatively small. Educated Europeans already knew quite well that the earth was round. Nor did the route Magellan traveled become an important trade route. Unlike the voyage of Vasco da Gama, Magellan's trip did not have a major influence on either Europe or the East. Therefore, although his feat has rightly brought him undying fame, it does not make him one of the hundred most influential persons in history.

LEONARDO DA VINCI

1 4 5 2 - 1 5 1 9

Leonardo da Vinci was born in 1452 near Florence, Italy, and died in 1519. The intervening centuries have not tarnished his reputation as perhaps the most brilliant universal genius that ever lived. If this were a list of *outstanding* persons, Leonardo would definitely be included among the first fifty names. However, his talent and reputation seem greatly in excess of his actual influence upon history.

In his notebooks, Leonardo left behind sketches of many modern inventions, such as airplanes and submarines. While these notebooks attest to his brilliance and originality, they had virtually no influence upon the development of science. In the first place, Leonardo did not actually build models of those inventions. In the second place, although the ideas were very clever, it does not appear that the inventions would actually have worked. It is one thing to think of the *idea* of a submarine or airplane; it is another and very much harder thing to work out a precise, detailed, practical design and to construct a model which actually works. The great inventors are not those men who had brilliant ideas but failed to follow up on them; rather, they are those persons—like Thomas Edison, James Watt, or the Wright brothers— who had the mechanical aptitude and the patience to work out the details and to overcome the difficulties so as to construct something which was actually functional. Leonardo did not do that.

Furthermore, even had his sketches included every detail necessary to make his inventions work, it still would have made little difference, for the inventions were buried in his notebooks, and these were not published until centuries after his death. By the time the notebooks (whose text, incidentally, is in mirror writing) were published, the ideas behind his inventions had already been independently discovered by others. We conclude that as a scientist and inventor, Leonardo was without significant influence.

His eligibility for this list, therefore, depends primarily upon his artistic achievements. Leonardo was a first-rate artist, though no more outstanding than such men as Rembrandt, Raphael, Van Gogh, or El Greco. With regard to his effect on later artistic developments, he was far less influential than either Picasso or Michelangelo.

Leonardo had a regrettable habit of starting ambitious projects and never completing them. As a result, his output of completed paintings was very much smaller than that of the other men just mentioned. By frequently shifting to a new project before completing an old one, Leonardo succeeded in frittering away a considerable portion of his extraordinary talents. Although it may seem odd to refer to the man who painted the Mona Lisa as an underachiever, that seems to be the conclusion of most persons who have carefully studied his career.

It is possible that Leonardo da Vinci was the most talented person who ever lived, but his enduring accomplishments were comparatively few. Although a renowned architect, he does not seem to have ever designed a building that was actually constructed. Nor does a single sculpture made by him survive today. All that remains of his prodigious talents are a considerable number of drawings, a few magnificent paintings (fewer than twenty survive), and a set of notebooks which make twentieth-century readers marvel at his genius, but which had little if any influence upon science or invention. Talented as he was, Leonardo was not one of the hundred most influential persons who have ever lived.

Leonardo da Vinci (self-portrait).

SOME FINAL COMMENTS

Since the men and women in this book have had such a tremendous effect on the world we live in, it might be interesting to examine some characteristics of the group as a whole.

The first thing that we notice is that a large majority of them come from Europe. (A statistical breakdown of their places of origin can be found in Table A.) From that table, it appears that the British have made a greater contribution to human civilization than have the people of any other region or nation. It is interesting to note that, of the eighteen British on this list, no fewer than five came from Scotland. (All five, in fact, are in the top half of this list.) Since the Scots constitute only about one-eighth of one percent of the world's population, this represents a truly astonishing concentration of talent and achievement.

As can be seen from Table B, the persons on this list are not distributed uniformly throughout recorded history. On the contrary, an unusually large number of them flourished during the sixth to third centuries B.C. After that, there was a long period of quiescence. However, starting in the fifteenth century, conditions were again ripe for progress—or at least for change—and succeeding centuries have supplied an increasing number of names to this list. (It is still too early, of course, to tell whether our own century will ultimately make as many outstanding contributions as the nineteenth century did.)

History books often devote most of their space to a discussion of political events. In my opinion, however, scientific advances have done far more to shape the world we live in, and it is therefore no accident that there are more scientists and inventors on this list than there are political or military leaders. Table C shows how many people in this book were involved in each of the major categories of human endeavor.

Since quite a few of the religious leaders have been ranked near the top of my list, Table C (which merely considers the *number* of persons in each category and ignores their positions on the list) somewhat underrates the importance of religion in human affairs. Conversely, Table C somewhat overestimates the importance of political events, since the majority of the political figures in this book are on the lower half of the list.

It is interesting to note that at least nineteen of the people on this list never married. (Since data is not available on everybody, the actual figure may be slightly higher.) That is a surprisingly high figure for a group whose members seem to have been, for the most part, more prosperous and healthy than the general population.

Even of those who married, not all had offspring. At least twenty-six persons on this list appear to have had no children. In addition, there are several persons who had children, but whose line is known to have died out within a generation or two. Though information is not available in every instance—and though the possibility of illegitimate offspring can never be excluded—it appears likely that only about half the people in this book have any living descendants.

All of the people on this list, of course, were highly intelligent, and the majority of them were well educated. Only seven of them were illiterate, most of those achieving their fame as military leaders.

Finally, we might mention the curious fact that at least ten of the persons on this list suffered from gout, a figure enormously out of proportion to the incidence of the disease in the general population. The high frequency of gout among great men has aroused the interest of medical researchers.

APPENDIX

TABLE A

The People in This Book:
Where Did They Come From?

REGION	NUMBER OF PERSONS ON MAIN LIST	
Great Britain	18	
Germany & Austria	15	
France	9	
Italy	8	TOTAL EUROPE
Greece	5	69
Spain	3	
Russia	4	
Other Europe	7	
United States	8	
South America	1	
New Zealand	1	
Africa	3	
China	7	
India	3	TOTAL ASIA
Mongolia	1	18
Western Asia	7	
TOTAL	100	

NOTE: Euclid, Homer, Aristotle, and Alexander the Great have all been included in the total for Greece. Stalin has been included in the total for Russia. Alexander Graham Bell has been included in the total for Great Britain, where he was born and raised, rather than in the total for the United States.

TABLE B

The People in this Book: When Did They Flourish?

PERIOD	NUMBER OF PERSONS ON MAIN LIST
Before 600 B.C.	3
600 B.C.-201 B.C.	13
200 B.C.-1400 A.D.	16
15th century	4
16th century	9
17th century	9
18th century	12
19th century	18
20th century	16
TOTAL	100

NOTE: Jefferson has been counted as an eighteenth-century figure; Planck as a nineteenth-century figure; Marconi and Freud as twentieth-century figures.

TABLE C

The People in this Book: What Did They Do?

FIELD OF ENDEAVOR	NUMBER OF PERSONS ON MAIN LIST
Scientists & Inventors	36
Political & Military Leaders	31
Secular Philosophers	14
Religious Leaders	11
Artistic & Literary Figures	5
Explorers	2
Industrialists	1
TOTAL	100

NOTE: Pizarro and Cortés have been counted as military leaders rather than as explorers. Freud has been counted as a scientist rather than as a philosopher. Confucius, Lao Tzu, Descartes, and Aristotle have been counted as secular philosophers.

PICTURE ACKNOWLEDGMENTS

American Telephone and Telegraph, 224

American Fabrics and Fashions Magazine, 29

Arthur Goodfriend, *What Can a Man Believe*, Farrar, Straus & Young, 1952, 363, 401

British Broadcasting Corporation, 276

Culver Pictures, 286

Ford Motor Company, 450, 459, 558

French Embassy Press and Information Service, 253

George Eastman House, 243

Philipp Giegel, 35

John Hancock Insurance Company, 198

Information Service of India, 506

John F. Kennedy Archive, 399

Metropolitan Museum of Art, Fletcher Fund, 1925, 504

National Library of Medicine, 195

Novosti Press Agency, 455, 475, 480

Philadelphia Museum of Art. Given by the Samuel H. Kress Foundation, 107, 110

Potter and Brumfield Division of American Machine Foundry, Inc., 121

Rand Corporation, 248

The Royal Institution, 118

Smithsonian Institution, 301

Wide World, 52, 59, 205, 225, 236, 291, 377, 403

Every effort has been made to locate the copyright owners of all the pictures listed above. If due acknowledgment has not been made, we sincerely regret the omission and request forgiveness.

INDEX

Page numbers in italics refer to illustrations.

More History Books From Carol Publishing